AlabamaNorth

The Working Class in American History

Editorial Advisors
David Brody
Alice Kessler-Harris
David Montgomery
Sean Wilentz

A list of books in the series appears at the end of this book.

(Courtesy of the Western Reserve Historical Society, Cleveland)

AlabamaNorth

African-American Migrants, Community, and Working-Class Activism in Cleveland, 1915–45

Kimberley L. Phillips

UNIVERSITY OF ILLINOIS PRESS

URBANA AND CHICAGO

Go down Moses way down in Egypt Land
Tell old Pharoah
Tell old Pharoah
Let my, let my, let my people go

—Birmingham Jubilee Quartet,
   "Way Down in Eygptland," 1930

Lord how far am I from Canaan
[Well, well] Angels singing and doorbells ringing in glory
Lord how far am I from Canaan?

—Soul Stirrers, "How Far Am I from Canaan," 1952

CONTENTS

Acknowledgments • xiii

Introduction: "Militancy and Courage" in AlabamaNorth: African-American Migrants and the Crossroads of Southern Black Culture • 1

1. "Pins" North: The Routes of African-American Migration to Cleveland • 15

2. Encountering Work: African-American Workers' Experiences in the Cleveland Labor Market, 1915–29 • 57

3. "Join a Union": African-American Workers and Organized Labor, 1915–30 • 98

4. A New World in the City: Making Homes in Cleveland • 127

5. "AlabamaNorth": A Community of Southerners • 161

6. "The Future Is Yours": Store Boycott Campaigns and Black Workers' Militancy • 190

7. "The Plight of Negro Workers": Federal Initiatives and African-American Working-Class Militancy during World War II • 226

Conclusion: We Will Make a Way Somehow: The Legacy of a Southern Past in a Northern City • 253

Notes • 261
Index • 327

Illustrations follow page 126

ACKNOWLEDGMENTS

FROM MY PERSPECTIVE, this study of black migrants in Cleveland seemed to take an awfully long time to finish. Other historians have reminded me—some with great bemusement—that first book projects often begin to germinate in the early years of graduate school and do not appear to end until decades later. My son, Peter, has a different perspective. Now nine years old, he cannot remember a year without first the dissertation and then the book claiming much of my time at home. Taking more than a decade to grow a books means that I probably have forgotten how many people I have inconvenienced, imposed upon, or just plain harassed during the process. I learned early, however, that while I might take responsibility for the book's final shape, I hardly crafted it alone.

During the various stages of this project's metamorphosis from a seminar paper into a book, I have had the good fortune of receiving invaluable guidance and support. I could not have started the process without the help of David Montgomery, who handed me a slim maroon book that recounted the history of the Future Outlook League (and I thank the *Plain Dealer* columnist Richard Perry for giving it to Montgomery). Through writing a short seminar paper for David, I became intrigued by this working-class organization, whose actions and leaders dominated the front pages of Cleveland's black newspapers for nearly two decades. As I began to expand the study, Nancy Cott joined David Montgomery in enthusiastically endorsing the project as a dissertation. Her extraordinary editorial skill and sharp attention to detail guided me through the difficult process of crafting a coherent analysis out of disparate sources. David Montgomery's probing questions are legendary, and I received quite a few. As any one of the women and men who have had the good fortune to be Nancy's and David's students will attest, they are not only generous but also model scholars and teachers.

During my years in graduate school at Yale University and continuing through my various teaching appointments at Macalester College, Case Western Reserve University, and the College of William and Mary, a stalwart group of friends and colleagues have listened, read, and commented on my ideas, conference papers, and book chapters. I especially thank Mia Bay, Adam Green, Cindy Hahamavitch, A. Yvette Huginnie, Cathy Kelly, Sarah Lipton, Scott Nelson, Peter Rachleff, Jonathan Sadowsky, Karen Sawislak, and Carol Sheriff. Dana Frank, Joseph Reidy, Eileen Boris, Earl Lewis, Thomas Sugrue, Rick Halpern, Dan Letwin, Kenneth Kusmer, and Kenneth Clarke have provided keen insight and helpful advice at various stages of turning the dissertation into a manuscript. Chapters four and five received close attention from Peter Stearns, Jim Barrett, Julia Greene, and Bruce Laurie. David Katzman, Eric Arnesen, and Jennifer Luff read the manuscript several times, providing critical insight as I struggled through the various reconceptualizations of arguments and ideas. Eric generously sent newspaper clippings that he found while doing his own work. During the many years I have lived in Cleveland, John Grabowksi, Adrienne Lash Jones, and Samuel W. Black have graciously offered guidance. Samuel Black provided unlimited access to unprocessed manuscripts and photographs in the African-American manuscripts collection at the Western Reserve Historical Society. Longtime labor activist Jean Tussey introduced me to the rich (and at the time largely uncollected) resources for the study of labor history in Cleveland. She has been an untiring critic of labor history that remains confined to academic audiences. I will spend the next several years thanking Patricia Miles Ashford, who taught me how to think about oral interviews as collaborative efforts and not just historical evidence. Along the way, we crafted a scholarly camaraderie and a friendship that has been very important to me.

I was significantly helped in the writing and editing stages of the manuscript. Research grants from Case Western Reserve University and the College of William and Mary provided research assistants. With indefatigable energy and ingenuity, Jeff Yost, Steve Colman, Devorah Lissek, Ericka Thomas, and Monica Cunningham patiently tracked down articles, books, and newspapers. Richard Wentworth and Emily Rogers provided critical guidance in navigating the manuscript through the University of Illinois Press.

I have benefited from black Cleveland's long tradition of having keen observers who either wrote down what they experienced or carefully committed their lives to memory. Some of the published memoirs and autobiographies are well known; I hope this study makes the others more visible. I am particularly grateful to the women and men who consented to interviews with either me or others. Judge Jean Murrell Capers, Linton Freeman, Ruth Freeman, Josephus Hicks, Natalie Middleton, and Arthur Turner were especially generous in allowing me to interview them. Barbara Smith, a writer who grew up in Cleveland, suggested how I might end the book, and I thank her for it.

My parents, Don and Myrtle Phillips, have been prouder parents than parents should feel compelled to be. They once drove through a snowstorm to hear me give a talk about migration to Cleveland. They have reminded me that while history must be accurate it must also be compelling to read. My father has frequently provided sharp insight into what I have tried to recount; he has always had an unerring editorial eye, and I thank him for offering trenchant critiques with such polite prefaces as "May I make a suggestion?" My mother has kept alive her own family's experience of migrating from Louisiana to California and she undoubtedly planted the interest in me; she equally deserves the credit for giving me the love for teaching. More recently, my parents have enthusiastically stepped in to help keep my household running smoothly while I wrote in peace. Since they have lived with the study (and certainly financed part of it when I was in graduate school), they are most likely relieved that it is finally finished.

This book's genesis and completion has coincided with the creation of my own family, and I hope that each has been enriched by the presence of the other. Not a one in our house can remember when diapers, toys, and notecards have not littered the tables and floors. My husband would be the first to say that I often held a child and wrote a paragraph at the same time— but he has certainly done more than his share of household tasks. Mark has been an enthusiastic supporter of this project, insisting that I spend Saturdays in my office, where I could write without interruptions from kids. He may not have typed the book, but he made sure that I had the computer I wanted. When I discovered that gardening relieved my stress and renewed my creativity, he did not balk at the addition of trowels and seed packets to our domestic chaos. I thank him for understanding that this book would not always encroach on our lives. Our children, Peter and Nina, deserve the most thanks, however. They have every right to be aggrieved by my preoccupation with this book, but instead they have been amazingly kind. I have dedicated this book to them as both a gesture of loving thanks and a sign of my great awe. Each in his or her own way has expressed pride in "mommy's long book on the computer." Often I felt no such pleasure as I sometimes chose to write instead of mother them. That they could be patient comes from their grace, and it is their grace that has always sustained me.

"Militancy and Courage" in AlabamaNorth: African-American Migrants and the Crossroads of Southern Black Culture

HE STANDS ON A GRANITE PEDESTAL, THE sinewy veins of his back carefully delineated in various shades of dark brown. Clad only in dungarees and steel-toed work boots, his body strikes an agile pose. His bent legs and arms suggest movement and energy, his body ready to gesture and dance. His outstretched left arm beckons while the right points toward a long bridge backdropped by the skyscrapers of a city. These moving arms guide a stream of black women and men dressed in traveling clothes. Their shawled and covered heads, bent bodies, and anxious faces announce fatigue. The pedestal, which dominates the center of the painting, has been inscribed with these words:

MILITANCY
COURAGE
EQUAL ECONOMIC OPPORTUNITY

To the lower right of the pedestal, two men clothed like the guide chisel more words into its side. At the top of the painting, seemingly suspended in air, a banner reads THE FUTURE OUTLOOK LEAGUE. Though clearly an homage to the organization, besides a visible date, little else is known about the picture.

While little is known about the artist who rendered this large and vibrant painting, the image is nonetheless multisensorial with an iconography deeply enmeshed in African-American vernacular of the midtwentieth century.[1] The sure gestures of the guide and the steady movement of the travelers form a rich tapestry of sacred and secular images. Underneath a noisy bridge, guide and travelers—a train of underground people—meet. Like Moses, the guide delivers the oppressed from Egypt and Pharaoh (the mountains in the background are shaped like pyramids) and leads them into New Jerusalem;[2] as they cross over into Canaan, he offers a new set of commandments and the promise of a rejuvenated spirit.[3] Will they wade into the water? Equally vivid secular images dominate. The half-clothed men, like the folk hero John Henry, present a pronounced masculinity in the shape of a sensualized body. The pedestal, then, is not simply a platform for a dancing guide; rather, he stands on the foundation of a new gender identity renegotiated by and for the black working class. The suffering that the travelers encountered in the twentieth-century Jim Crow South becomes disrupted as new tools are offered to the migrants. Wage work in the postwar factories and service trades might offer adequate compensation for their labor. More than anything, the guide conveys a "psychic stance" that black migrants might acquire, transforming their haggard bodies into militant, courageous bodies.[4]

The movement from South to North, from uncompensated labor to self-determination, demonstrates the synthesis of southern and northern black experiences that converged in Cleveland, Ohio, during the first half of the twentieth century. The painting conveys the popular midcentury belief that the North, not the South, offered the greater possibilities for blacks to determine their economic and social freedom. At the same time, such self-determination would rest on the sacred and secular vernacular culture that had been forged out of southern black experiences. This picture invites multiple readings, suggesting that it is not simply an allegory of African Americans' migration out of the South; rather, it is a confluence of various symbols and material conditions of black expressivity crafted out of southern folk culture and the collective and historical experiences of migration. The painting calls to viewers who respond with a knowing eye: they, too, may have heard kin's migration narratives filled with struggle and hope; they may have heard or written blues lyrics and gospel hymns about traveling; they may have stood behind the plow, wielded the hammer, or held the mop. Although the painting's meanings would have resonated most for those who had witnessed the Future Outlook League's successes between 1935 and 1952, to those who saw it then and those who have seen it since, it calls to a collective memory recognizable to black audiences who have stood at similar junctures.[5]

While the painting reveals much about black southern working class self-representations, it equally obscures the gender, social, and class relations of the period. Although critical components of black militancy during these years, black women have been nearly painted out of the picture. From the time of the Future Outlook League's inception in 1935, women had been critical organizers and participants in its boycotts. By the late 1940s, women made up the majority of the membership. The emphasis on the heroics of black men in this painting, then, denies black women's role as the vanguard of community-based militancy.

This study simultaneously explores and recovers black migrant life celebrated in this painting. As one of the primary destinations for tens of thousands of migrants from the Deep South between 1915 and 1945, Cleveland provides ample opportunity to understand how southern black workers associated their experiences in the South with community building and working-class activism in the North. Migrants' moves north established complex networks of kin and friends and infused the city with a highly visible southern African-American culture. Intending to find better work and provide for families, they sought to reweave community by connecting traditions from the Deep South with the promises of the urban North. Rebuffed in neighborhoods, limited in job opportunities, and increasingly confined to segregated institutions, African Americans drew on a variety of cultural and organizational experiences and beliefs created in the South while also turning to new forms of individual and collective activism in workplaces and the city.

Although no longer active, the Future Outlook League (FOL) has remained vivid in the memory of many black Clevelanders. The organization's founder and only president, Alabama migrant John O. Holly, still elicits great respect. In 1935, the FOL began as Cleveland's version of the "Don't Buy Where You Can't Work Campaign" sweeping through numerous black communities. The league staged aggressive boycotts against store owners in the Central Area of the city who depended on African Americans as customers, but refused to hire them as workers.[6] While the boycotts yielded impressive results, they were typically combative and occasionally violent. The noisy pickets generated sharp critiques from traditional black and labor leaders until the early 1940s. Black workers, still facing discrimination from the American Federation of Labor and the newly formed Congress of Industrial Organizations, launched a union in 1938. That same year, the FOL claimed 10,000 members, began a weekly newspaper, and opened branches in other cities in the state.[7] Despite the erosion of some barriers to industrial employment and union membership during World War II, the FOL maintained its working-class support until the late 1950s. Along the way, it revitalized the moribund local branch of the National Association for the Advancement of Colored People (NAACP) and launched African Americans into politics and union leadership.[8]

The league's emergence as an organization of militant workers departed from organizers' desire to help African-American men open stores of their own. Holly initially sought white-collar employment where he and others would learn how to "become future merchants."[9] This goal and its ideological underpinnings quickly evaporated as the FOL's activism attracted the attention of radical black organizers in the Unemployed Councils, socialists, and unemployed women, men, and southern migrants interested in wage work, not business ownership. Through the FOL, thousands of blacks obtained work in service and transportation occupations; many of these jobs were those that white workers affiliated with AFL locals had prevented blacks from entering through their exclusionary policies and force.[10] By 1938, many of the street battles pitted unemployed African Americans against organized white workers. These struggles, along with growing demands from league members, pushed the FOL to pursue the protection of black workers along the lines of a union.

Few who had met him would confuse Holly with the guide in the painting, yet it conveys his charisma and energy. A small man with a rapid-fire Alabama dialect, Holly had a demeanor that departed from the city's northern-born black politicians of the early twentieth century.[11] Decried as uneducated, crass, and loud, Holly's style, rooted in a southern black vernacular, incited great criticism from black elites. His cadence—the way he talked and walked, his combative approach toward finding work for blacks—meant that he was reviled by those blacks wedded to a process of quiet back-room negotiations. While other black leaders in the city viewed Holly with great suspicion, working-class blacks in Cleveland revered him as "a hero." Meeting him in 1948, the politician Carl Stokes recalled Holly as a "greasy haired, short, very black, homely" talker from Alabama who practiced confrontation politics decades before it became commonplace in the 1960s.[12]

Ironically, the very disdain and criticism that Holly and the FOL elicited from longtime black leaders translated into a working-class autonomy largely absent in black boycott efforts in other northern cities. Arguments over tactics and style had undermined the efficacy of many of these efforts or led to the demise of others.[13] In sharp contrast, the weekly meetings of the FOL had a highly participatory and inclusive character that enabled black women and men to not only share their experiences about work and unemployment but also openly critique the ideology and strategy of black middle-class leaders. During these conversations they advanced a community ethos about the need to organize as workers around interests that differed from those of employers, regardless of race.

Protest by unemployed African Americans had erupted throughout the 1920s and the first half of the 1930s, but always these attempts had been reined in by sharp critiques from employers and black elites. During these years, blacks' frustration over their widespread exclusion from wage employment mounted. Motivated by both the inactivity of traditional black leaders and their particular experiences wrought by the depression, black Clevelanders joined other unemployed people in street protests organized by the Unemployed Councils. By 1935, the appearance of banners proclaiming "Fools Trade Where They Cannot Work" became a magnet for unemployed women and men who had attempted to protest at the start of the depression but had been denounced by black leaders. By 1937, militant protest had become so frequent that African-American workers had appropriated the streets as their own. On this new stage, the black unemployed demanded work by waging economic war on recalcitrant employers. At the same time, they openly critiqued a middle-class leadership that had demanded the black poor's silence. Indeed, whether leading a picket, ensuring support for a boycott, or finding jobs, FOL members witnessed an immediate and heady support for their actions.[14]

The ascendancy of a militant working-class organization of migrants from the Deep South and the dominance of unemployed migrants and women within the organization marked a dramatic shift in black Cleveland's regional, cultural, and organizational identity. Though working-class migrants had been in the majority since 1915, a small northern-born elite continued to dominate the community through the middle of the following decade, expressing a consciousness that distinguished themselves along color, class, and regional lines.[15] Acknowledging blacks' exclusion from skilled and semi-skilled work, many of the old elite nonetheless pinned these inequalities and the marked increase in segregation that took place in the 1920s on the large population of migrants from the Deep South. Often describing Cleveland as the "Negro's Paradise" before the war, many longtime residents noted the erosion of congenial social relations between blacks and whites. African-American professionals, too, hoped that middle-class social welfare efforts, northern education, and an emphasis on acculturation would relieve the constrictions of segregation.[16]

While the northern-born elite publicly and privately differentiated itself from the new arrivals, African-American migrants from the Deep South created a rich associational life that ranged from religious institutions to workplace associations. As thousands of men and women arrived after 1915 from the industrial cities of Birmingham and Bessemer and the small towns and rural areas of Alabama, they slowly renamed the city "AlabamaNorth." Though conditions while they aggressively battled employers' racist hiring practices. Most important, the FOL organized in the service sector, which had yet to receive attention from either the AFL or the CIO.

In the context of these dynamics, the FOL provided black women with an unprecedented opportunity to find nondomestic employment, leadership roles, and union protection. Moreover, while the AFL and the CIO sought to organize black men already employed in auto, steel, and the construction trades, as a group, African-American women were the least likely to find wage work outside private service. The CIO's call for shop floor organization had little meaning for women not allowed through the door of most industrial workplaces unless—as Natalie Middleton discovered in the 1930s—they held "a mop or a broom." In the last two years of the 1930s, black women became the most energetic champions of the FOL, pinning their hopes on a community-based labor association rather than on unions still unsure about racial equality, unwilling to tackle the racist hiring policies of employers, and uncommitted to the organization of black women. While historians continue to debate whether the CIO and the AFL unions were racially egalitarian, the weekly records of the FOL demonstrate that African-American workers questioned both and instead affirmed their own agency and autonomy.[40] They did not readily accept union policies that tepidly called for racial egalitarianism; nor did they simply wait for unions to organize them.[41]

During World War II, the FOL's activism expanded beyond black neighborhoods and into the city's courts. Beginning in 1943, the FOL undertook a highly choreographed court battle on behalf of black women excluded from industrial employment, highlighting the ineffectiveness of the World War II presidential executive order that had established the Committee on Fair Employment Practices. This community-based struggle during the war was linked to a national campaign waged by A. Philip Randolph against blacks' exclusion from industrial employment. Such ties raise important questions about the ways that local community-based black protest may have been influenced by external struggles and, in turn, how local struggles may have influenced national efforts.

Though largely defunct by the late 1950s, the Future Outlook League has continued to remain an important memory in black Cleveland. By the time Carl Stokes ran for mayor in 1967, he understood the need to respect if not adopt the style of Deep South migrants and the community-based tactics of the FOL. Stokes's recognition, however, came from having driven John O. Holly around Ohio after he left the FOL to organize black voters for the Democratic party.[42] Today, most leaders in Cleveland claim some association with Holly and the FOL; others claim direct descendance as children of FOL members. Even those who sharply criticized Holly or remained aloof from the FOL's efforts tend to offer approval decades later, conceding that Holly "was a man ahead of his times."[43] Whether it was used as a calling card or as part of an individual's, or an organization's, genealogy, African Americans in Cleveland have claimed the FOL as an inheritance from their migrant past.

While I have relied on traditional evidence found in institutional records, census data, government reports, and the like in this study, I draw equally on written and oral testimony from African-American migrants and their organizations. Within its weekly newspaper and in the recorded minutes of its weekly meetings, FOL members left an important glimpse into what was on many African-American workers' minds during these years. Other sources, in particular music and oral narratives as well as reports and newspapers from working-class organizations, provide an unusual opportunity to reconstruct what has eluded other historians of African Americans in Cleveland. This study sustains the voices of the African-American working class. Part of this effort has been aided by methods from oral history, ethnomusicology, cultural theory, anthropology, and gender history that have sharpened scholars' understanding of African Americans' expressive culture. These interdisciplinary methodologies offer new entrances into old, seemingly fully constructed and analyzed, historical moments while also providing a more complex understanding of African-American community formation in the urban North.

Though I sought out specific individuals, I also spoke with anyone who was willing to participate.[44] When individuals expressed reluctance, I simply did not interview them or I waited until the individual felt comfortable. Once it became known that I was conducting interviews, some individuals approached me because they felt they had something to offer or because other interviewers had overlooked them. This pattern was particularly true for women in the Future Outlook League who felt they had been ignored in earlier studies. In the midst of many of the interviews, women and men strove to help me understand what they meant; some of the men and women I interviewed carefully explained their motivations or an event "to set the record straight" because he or she did not want the past "gotten wrong." In such moments the implication was always clear: recounting the community's past was a joint effort, and responsibility for veracity was to be shared equally. In several instances, some asked me to turn my tape recorder off so that they could explain privately, clearly, and carefully just what they meant. I was often handed private papers or pointed to other records so that I "could check" their claims; several interviewees suggested others who held quite different or contradictory recollections from their own. That they urged me to interview, and not ignore, these individuals suggests they not only considered that they might be useful to me but also that they understood these views to be as equally valid as their own. Without using the language that historians claim as their task, these women and men urged me to collect a range of different views and then sift through and verify them. In many ways, this study—grounded in the collective voices of black people who migrated and settled in Cleveland—could not have been accomplished without their help.

As I completed this study, the Western Reserve Historical Society shifted its attention from displaying the collections of plates and dresses of the elite in the city toward mounting public exhibits to reflect the diverse ethnic and racial groups of its people. Part of this endeavor has included a renewed effort to collect artifacts and interviews of African Americans. In 1996 I participated in this transformation, serving as curator of an exhibit on African-American religious experiences in the city.[45] Dozens of men and women freely donated their time, artifacts, and memories to this exhibit, making much easier my task of crafting a visual and written narrative that adequately captured their deep river of faith and their long struggle to make worship reflect their past as southern migrants. As one of the city's most popular gospel choirs, the Prayer Warriors—founded and directed by Herb Thomas—led hundreds of us into the exhibit on its opening night, we were all aware of the collective creativity it takes to raise a hymn. The sensibility that undergirded the exhibit has equally influenced this study: I said then, and I say now, look what we made together.

ONE

"Pins" North: The Routes of African-American Migration to Cleveland

I pick up my life . . .
Gone up North
Gone out West,
Gone!

—Langston Hughes,
"One-Way Ticket"

AFTER A DECADE AND A HALF of moving between temporary jobs in Alabama, South Carolina, and New York City, Josephus Hicks left the South permanently in the mid-1930s and migrated to Cleveland. Raised in the steel camps of Bessemer, Alabama, by a father who had labored as a minister and as a steelworker and a mother who had worked sometimes simultaneously as a teacher and a domestic, Hicks had learned early that for African Americans in the South steady work was hard to find and keep. After completing high school, Hicks joined male friends who alternated jobs as agricultural laborers along the Atlantic states and service workers in New York City. Though Hicks eventually completed four years of school at South Carolina State and later taught courses there, he frequently did not receive a salary from the cash-strapped college. He returned to agricultural and occasional summer service work. Because of the Great Depression, Hicks "didn't see any differences [in] the money you could earn in New York City and the money that you could earn in South Carolina." Hicks felt other "pins" pushing him north besides differences in wages. Like so many black men and women of his generation, Hicks found living in the South oppressive and he wanted the "expansiveness of the city, the advantages of the libraries, the movies, and the social activities." He most desired to leave behind the "managing of Negroes" and the "routines of subordination" dictated by legal restrictions in the South. Although Josephus Hicks's migration to Cleveland was distinctly shaped by his experiences with work and life in a segregated South, by the time he decided to move he followed a pattern of family migration out of Alabama and into the city. Nearly a decade earlier, Hicks's mother and sister left the South to join his mother's sister and husband. As early as 1915, all had heard from a network of kin and friends that Cleveland provided more favorable economic and social opportunities than Alabama did.[1]

The complicated and protracted migration of Josephus Hicks—shaped by his constant search for work, the desire to leave behind the stultifying parameters of segregation, and his efforts to maintain ties with kin and friends—typified the experiences of many African-American men and women leaving the Deep South for Midwestern cities like Cleveland. The more than a million and a half African Americans who left the South permanently for cities in the urban North, Midwest, and West between 1915 and 1945 did so within a larger pattern of migration that had begun in the midst of the Civil War and continued until the last third of the twentieth century.[2] As Peter Gottlieb noted, this migration had its origins in "the overarching transformation of African-American life which began after Emancipation."[3] Blacks' moves into nonagricultural wage work in southern towns and cities, which provided important urban and industrial experiences that would benefit them in their later moves north, were coupled to economic changes in the rural south.[4] This model offers a more nuanced take on the older model of blacks pushed out of the South because of the lack of rural opportunities and pulled north because of industrial work. Despite its advancement, Joe William Trotter Jr. has suggested that the proletarian model, "like the earlier models, gives inadequate attention to the roots of black migration in the southern black experience, including the role of black kin and friendship networks."[5] How did migration north flow out of such networks, experiences, and values in African-American culture, such as self-reliance, independence from oppression, and taking care of kin?

Greater attention to the narratives of men and women like Josephus Hicks provides important insight into the subtle and important links African Americans made between their departure from agricultural life and labor, their experiences with wage labor in the South, and the values of kin and community in the process of moving north. In this chapter I examine how African-American men and women interpreted, decided, and managed moves between rural and urban living in the South prior to their move north. Beginning in their households, rural blacks sought to temper the vagaries of farm life through reciprocal labor, and these arrangements carried over into familial decisions about wage labor in towns and cities of the South. I will examine the household and communal strategies African Americans utilized during their movements to the urban North as well. Such a focus illustrates the range of strategies individuals and families crafted to negotiate the intricate and complex routes from rural to first southern and then northern urban locations and work. Attention to these experiences allows us to see more than strategies, however. African Americans' accounts of their departures from the South foreground the centrality of familial ties over time and distance in their often circular moves in the South, their decisions to go north, and their choice of destinations. Communal, familial, and individual values, then, provided equally critical roles in blacks' decisions to move as did the lure of industrial labor.

African-American migration in and out of the South arose from shifts that began after the Civil War as thousands of freed people searched for more favorable economic and social conditions away from white supervision. While few blacks left rural areas of the South, many moved short distances within states to search for land or the best sharecropping arrangements. Through the end of the century, white southerners passed legislation to inhibit black geographic mobility and ensure the availability of a concentrated and low-wage labor population. By the start of the next century the pace of migration rose as the demand for labor in southern industries grew and acreage devoted to agriculture declined. Increasing numbers of men found work in the New South industries of coal, steel, timber, and railroads. Higher-paying industrial and service work brought African Americans into cities and towns, and the black urban populations of the Deep South cities of Birmingham, Montgomery, Mobile, Atlanta, and Savannah grew considerably. Black women in particular found better work and social opportunities in cities and towns. The desire for better education and safety and greater access to black institutions equally influenced African Americans' move to cities and towns.[6]

While not the first nor the last mass departure from the South, African Americans' mass movement between 1915 and 1930 appeared particularly dramatic for several reasons. First, though the migration originated in individual and communal circumstances, African Americans' departure signaled a collective disavowal of racial and economic oppression.[7] Second, while over one million blacks left the South between 1910 and 1930, half of these migrated between 1916 and 1918. Finally, a majority of these migrants settled in a handful of mid-Atlantic and Midwestern cities. Cleveland, Chicago, Detroit, New York City, and Pittsburgh received more than half of the total number of black migrants.[8] From 1920 to 1930, over a quarter million blacks left rural areas of the South for its cities, with many continuing north. Over the next decade until after World War II, tens of thousands of blacks traveled north. In each of these stages of migration, kin and friend networks provided critical information, support, and resources. Even as migration out of rural areas and out of the South altogether gradually subsided from the dramatic high in 1916–18, these networks sustained concentrated streams of migrants northward.[10]

While blacks' history of movement predated the 1915 mass migration, the rapid advance and acceleration of capitalist social relations that demanded their subordination distinctly shaped how they moved in the South. As numerous historians have demonstrated, agrarian capitalism prevailed after 1870, but freed people did not necessarily acquire greater labor power.[9] Indeed, the spread of the cotton economy led to new coercive measures to control how, when, and where blacks worked. Geographic mobility may have been a hallmark of freedom for former slaves, but white planters (and far too often northern whites as well) perceived black mobility as a crime and not as the right of free labor. It is important, then, to think of the struggle to control the availability of black labor, the effort to limit if not prohibit black landownership, and the effort to determine how blacks worked (not for themselves but for whites) as distinct but related processes.

Blacks did not view the triumph of white supremacy and whites' control over market relations in the South as inevitable. Rather, between 1870 and 1940, black and white southerners engaged in a struggle over those market relations. Blacks' movement in the South was not simply an attempt to be independent from white control; it was also an attempt to find the best opportunity to participate and shape the southern economy and exercise their rights as free workers. If whites sought to determine how fixed or mobile black workers would be, most often choosing the former over the latter, black workers in turn hoped to tip the balance of power in their own favor. Agrarian capitalism may have reduced many blacks to the status of peasants, but southern whites' efforts to include them as low-wage workers in New South industries paradoxically provided a means for greater black autonomy. White landowners and industrialists may have used coercion to control black labor and reduce their competition over it, but I will demonstrate how black workers hoped that movement back and forth between farm and nonagricultural labor would give them some better work options. While the white Alabamian and industrialist James Bowron noted that many white employers in the South perceived black migration as "the darky's joyride," he conceded others had begrudgingly recognized that blacks had left the South because they had been economically exploited and physically endangered.[10]

For a half century after Emancipation African Americans pursued a variety of routes in their quest to build an independent economic life. In the wake of the demise of slavery, owning land of their own and growing crops of their choice stood at the center of this independence.[11] For African Americans, having land represented autonomy from white control and their rightful inheritance from ancestors who had tilled southern soil while held in bondage. The majority of former slaves preferred to plant crops for subsistence, not profit. Even when forced into contracts, freed people nonetheless pursued ways to advance themselves. If former slaves could not immediately own land, acquiring tools and mules or bargaining for better contracts might lead to that end. Whenever possible, black workers took advantage of the scarcity of labor in areas where planters sought to cultivate cotton. Though most planters initially preferred gang and wage labor, black resistance forced many white landowners to reconsider the terms of their economic relationship with black workers. From African Americans' perspective, sharecropping seemed the best route toward landownership and autonomy. Backed by legislation, planters determined that they could wield greater labor discipline as landlords over tenant households based on kin relationships. It seems, then, that planters and black male heads of households may have had a loosely shared notion of patriarchy under which women's and children's labor could be controlled. As Leslie Schwalm noted, the intent of Reconstruction policy was to "reinforce the power and privilege of masculinity."[12]

As African Americans continued to claim individual and collective autonomy, many planters looked to the old order for cues to manage their former slaves. Even as Reconstruction governments established mechanisms for both blacks and whites to acquire land and protect their rights as tenants, planters refused to concede. More often than not, planters reacted to blacks' pursuit of the vote and economic autonomy with physical force; by the 1870s these efforts frequently took the form of organized terror. Riots instigated by conservative Democrats became a common feature at Republican political rallies.[13] As Democrats claimed victory and mounted an aggressive campaign to subvert black political and economic autonomy, black people increasingly saw their economic mobility foreclosed by the state. White elites, backed by a coalition of white planters and industrialists, proclaimed a "New South" based on an agrarian capitalism committed to the production of cotton and the development of an industrial and urban region. Robin D. G. Kelley has reminded us, however, that "the feudal values of the Old South echoed faintly in the background." Planters and their urban industrial counterparts generally agreed that the economic solvency of the South would rest on the exploitation of labor, particularly that of African Americans.[14]

African Americans did not readily acquiesce to either the new political or the economic order. Black Republican strongholds remained in a number of areas of the South as late as the turn of the century, but in Georgia and Alabama the loss of the party's power was much swifter. Though the majority of black men found it difficult to vote by the 1880s, they nonetheless insisted on maintaining ties to the land in the hope of being future owners of the soil. Their various strategies to become independent landowners ranged from aggressive attempts to maintain an independent political voice in highly organized Republican clubs and Union Leagues to forming militia companies such as the Lincoln Guards in Macon, Georgia, to refusing to vote as whites demanded in Alabama, no matter the personal cost. On farms, black workers strove to buy and rent land, while others sought the best terms under sharecropping. When such strategies failed, blacks moved from one area of the state to another, particularly into the Black Belt counties of southern Alabama. This movement appears to have been precipitated by the desire to affirm their freedom and later to ensure their safety and pursue the building of black institutions.[15]

While blacks fought back individually and collectively, white Democrats solidified their control over the South's political and economic future, determining that blacks had to be removed from the electoral process altogether. Backed by sympathetic state legislatures and courts, planters began wrestling political control away from blacks first through extralegal violence and then through disfranchisement.[16] In addition, landowners' coercion—frequently manifested in violence—did much to close off economic and social mobility for blacks. Through legal and violent extralegal efforts, white planters hoped to end any economic partnership with blacks that may have been established during Reconstruction and intended to ensure blacks' subservience in market and labor relations. By the close of the 1880s, blacks in the Deep South felt the absence of black state legislators resulted in a variety of laws that diminished and outright inhibited any form of blacks' subsistence on the land. Numerous laws put in place between 1880 and the first decades of the next century established the parameters of rural economic behavior, defining much of black autonomy as criminal. Planters acted to ban fishing and hunting and prohibit nighttime trading. Other legislation attempted to halt blacks' independent participation in rural economies by preventing black sharecroppers from pricing and selling their cotton. This new legislation focused primarily on limiting black workers' claims to ownership of the land and its products. In Georgia, new legislation defined sharecropping as wage labor, not a form of tenure, and black farm workers could no longer participate in decisions about crops or the use of land.[17]

As a result, in the Black Belt of Alabama, the pace of African-American land acquisition slowed. Instead, the majority continued to work as either sharecroppers or agricultural laborers. Renting land and sharecropping might have provided black farmers some mobility, but the furnishing system—in which planters and merchants advanced supplies and fertilizers based on the future crop—limited their move into property ownership. Many found themselves subjected to all sorts of chicanery to ensnare them into hard labor and endless debt. Those farmers who challenged the system or questioned the debt found local and state officials ready supporters of planters even as blacks' rights were violated. By the last decade of the nineteenth century, planters in Alabama had effectively reduced blacks to an agricultural proletariat. These declines contrasted with the increase in black landownership elsewhere. The number of blacks who owned farms in Georgia increased by 48 percent between 1900 and 1920.[18]

Whether coerced or spurred by their desire to acquire more credit, blacks grew more cotton at a time when other countries were beginning or increased their cotton production. Between the 1890s and the 1920s, local newspapers expounded and planters preached that not much else was worth producing for profit, though cotton prices decreased each year. While the introduction of new fertilizers in the late nineteenth century enabled farmers to increase their cotton output, the greater yield lowered prices. James Little learned early that "Cotton, old King Cotton, was the white folks crop in Alabama." White landowners' economic and political control of sharecropping meant that he and other black farmers grew cotton and little else.[19]

Besides control over the choice of crops, planters meant to limit and control black labor mobility, and the law became a powerful means to thwart black independence. From the last two decades of the nineteenth century into the first three decades of the next, white landowners successfully enacted legislation to compel blacks to labor and limit their mobility. In 1903, first Georgia and then Alabama—with six other southern states following in as many years—made it a crime for blacks to break contracts by not paying back advances or refusing to work for repayment for food and seed. Those who did were subjected to harsh fines and imprisonment. Enticement laws prevented employers and their agents from "persuading any tenant, servant, or laborer to violate a labor contract." Though vagrancy was not often monitored before 1900, states passed laws against it. The enforcement of these laws became more commonplace during the first decade of the twentieth century; scattered evidence suggests that some local areas resorted to vagrancy roundups during acute labor shortages. As legal challenges to these statutes took place, states responded by passing harsher laws that prevented labor agents and other employers from enticing black workers away from one job for another; other laws attempted to prevent blacks from breaking contracts and becoming vagrants. William Cohen has linked the passing of such legislation with the triumph of white hegemony based on legal segregation. The control of black labor became "part of a broader attempt to reestablish white dominance in all areas of southern life."[20]

The punishment for blacks who broke contracts or attempted to leave farms was imprisonment and fines, which funneled a significant number into the convict-lease system or peonage. In a study of the impact of these laws in Georgia, Joseph Reidy concluded that the "criminal codes worked hand in glove with the convict-lease system" and "quickly evolved into a weapon for terrorizing the black labor force." Pete Daniel found that by 1900, as much as one-third of all sharecroppers in Alabama, Mississippi, and Georgia were being held against their will. The patchwork of laws, along with threats and intimidation, became powerful weapons preventing the physical mobility of African Americans and insuring their indebtedness in a cotton economy.[21]

Yet even as planters sought at various times to keep black workers immobile, African Americans nonetheless claimed or took their freedom whenever possible. Indeed, in the midst of these repressive laws and tactics many blacks did move, though most often only short distances and without much change in their status. Ties to family and kin networks, along with knowledge about the area and future employers, tended to work against long-distance moves. Even so, a move of a mile or two could make a significant difference, particularly since moves that black workers claimed as their own often emerged out of the desire to choose living and working arrangements that would provide the most autonomy. Nate Shaw, for example, made several moves until he settled on land owned by a man he described as only "a little better man" than the previous men for whom he had worked. Each time he moved, he hoped that he would have more autonomy to decide what he might grow or which fertilizer to use. Most often, he chafed under the daily indignities he suffered, as others controlled how he worked. The reasons that compelled blacks to move, rather than the disincentives to stay, garnered much derision from white observers, who labeled the frequency of these moves as "shiftlessness," a term, Jacqueline Jones has suggested, that was "all-purpose" and "used to refer to indolence and moral laxity" as much as it defined a particular departure.[22]

White landowners' desire to maximize their profits and maintain a stable labor population introduced a contradictory but complementary pattern of prohibiting black mobility and removing them from the land altogether. Planters, not the state, dictated either the enforcement or the relaxation of state legislation. What constituted a reliable worker and contract favorable to a planter depended on a range of shifting goals. First, planters had an interest in adjusting the size of their labor force whenever they saw fit, thus the purging of black farm workers became a seasonal event. While some plant-ers and sharecroppers may have ended their relationships more or less am-icably, scores were forced to leave through coercive and often violent means. Second, many planters sought to retain the most productive black sharecrop-pers through laws, intimidation, or violence. Conversely, few planters want-ed to retain either combative or unproductive workers, even if they had debts. Black farmers have described a range of white landowners' practices to per-mit or inhibit blacks' economic independence and mobility. Nate Shaw made it clear that where he moved was not often his "free choice because I wasn't allowed." When he did not "make his crop" or "fell out" with the landown-er, he moved.[23]

Nevertheless, for Nate Shaw and other African-American farmers, the means to "get ahead" economically rested on their ability to minimize their costs, maximize their labor, and retain the option to leave for better work conditions. Unable to invest in machines or purchase the latest fertilizers, black landowners, tenants, and sharecroppers found that experts exhorted them to become self-sufficient, work hard, and stay in one place. While black workers aspired to the first and certainly adhered to the second, they reject-ed the third. "Black resourcefulness and black departures," Sydney Nathans reminds us, gave notice to white landowners that black folk intended to be independent. Given the enormous effort to impede their movement, Afri-can Americans' migration out of Georgia and Alabama was slight between 1890 and 1910 and their rates of movement within geographic regions re-mained lower than that of white sharecroppers and renters. But for African Americans the value of independence through mobility remained vivid, and when the circumstances arose, they moved.[24]

African-American rural farm households in the Deep South lived and arranged work during the last decade of the nineteenth century and first decades of the twentieth century in keeping with their geographic location, form of tenancy, and type of crop production. In the Black Belt counties of Alabama and Georgia, fewer blacks owned land than they did in other areas of the coastal South, and they overwhelmingly produced cotton as sharecrop-pers. The demands of cotton crops meant that blacks labored intensively from the preparation of the fields in early spring to the harvest of the cotton in the fall. Black men, older boys, and some women plowed the fields, with few people able to prepare more than four acres a day. Once the cotton began to grow, it had to be chopped to remove weeds and separate the plants. The chopping and hoeing continued until midsummer. The laborious work of picking the cotton began in early September and continued through Octo-ber. Sara Brooks, an Alabamian who migrated to Cleveland in the late 1930s, recalled this process as "the tiredest thing! You had to stoop down all the time, you gotta pull the sack. That stoopin with the sack hung on your back, draggin up and down the row! Oh, that was the most tiresome thing I ever seen!"[25]

In addition to the seemingly endless tasks and responsibilities associated with plowing, planting, and harvesting, black men also maintained the animals, farm equipment, and tools. Sara Brooks recounted the sight and sound of her father sharpening his plow each spring: "In the country, the wide open country it was quiet you know, and you could hear so far! We could hear other peoples when they'd be sharpenin their plows, too, like we say, 'Mr. Harrison sharpenin his plows this mornin,' or Mr. Jackson or Mr. Strong." In addition to the farm work her father regularly performed, this highly competent man repaired his tools; maintained his home, barn, and fences; caned chairs; and constructed baskets. During the hunting season black men shot squirrels and rabbits and they fished in the summer.[26]

Older sons labored alongside their fathers and adult male kin while learning to understand the soil, how to handle mules and horses, and how to grow cotton, corn, and wheat. Nate Shaw noted the importance of this training: "There's a heap to a wheat crop; you got to know how to raise wheat and take care of it." Though Shaw had significant disagreements with his father, he learned much about farming from him. Before they married, young black men were frequently hired out to other farmers or they worked for kin to learn about crops and earn wages to purchase their own equipment and seed. More often than not, white landowners appropriated this labor. But sons resented fathers who practiced harsh control of family labor. Nate Shaw chafed against the demands of his father, who insisted on dictating how Shaw would work. Equally problematic, Shaw criticized his father for taking the wages he earned, not because he felt entitled to them but because he perceived his father as lazy. As an adult working for himself, Shaw resisted handing the fruit of his labor over to white landowners who did not work alongside him. Years later, Shaw demanded that his own children work for him; because he worked hard, too, he did not perceive himself as behaving like either his father or white planters.[27]

African-American women performed arduous and varied labor as they moved back and forth between the household, care of children, and the fields. Women grew a variety of vegetables and fruits in kitchen gardens made up of large plots surrounding their houses. Gardens provided the mainstay of many families' diets; thus women had to plan crops that would extend into the end of the year. If a sharecrop family managed to stay in place after accounts were settled in the fall and if they managed to grow winter vegetables such as potatoes and sweet potatoes, then they had more to eat. Along with gardens, many women raised chickens, cows, and hogs to supplement diets with eggs, milk, butter, and meat. Some women managed to squeeze out extra crops of vegetables and fruits and produced enough butter and collected sufficient eggs to share, barter, or sell them. How and where black women bartered or sold their produce cannot be readily recovered from their narratives or the records of store merchants; nonetheless, the more a woman's garden and animals yielded the less the family depended on merchants and landowners, which thereby increased self-sufficiency.[28]

Women had extensive and demanding household and child care duties, which they perceived as necessary to the productivity and self-sufficiency of their farms. Everyday household tasks such as washing clothes, for example, became a major endeavor, especially if a well was not accessible; women could spend hours bending over streams or hauling water. Knowledge of making soap out of ashes or constructing wash buckets out of oak instead of pine— which had a toxin that ruined clothes—was essential. Until the first decade of the twentieth century, rural black women continued to have more children than their urban counterparts and white southern women. In a world where the infant mortality rate was high, the health and well-being of children required knowledge of medicinal herbs. Equally important, many women sought to avoid frequent pregnancies. Sara Brooks's mother died from a self-induced abortion, and Brooks would later attempt to terminate an unplanned pregnancy through the aid of a midwife.[29]

However pressing reproductive labor may have been, few black women could give either their children or their household work full attention. Newly married women frequently hired out their labor, either to family or to white landowners. Women with older children, particularly sons, may have had more opportunity to focus on household work. Often out of necessity—when their husbands worked outside jobs for wages, when they did not have older children who could work, when they did not have resources to hire their own workers—women had to labor in their own fields. Even when children could help, some women continued to grow cotton for cash. In sharecropping, married and older single women tended to work in fields full-time, fitting in household work and care of children when time and task allowed. In short, along with household labor and child care, women helped farm. How one Georgia farm woman organized her productive and reproductive labor provides insight: the woman and her daughters took turns cooking; she sewed all the family's work clothes as well as leisure clothing for the women, cared for the poultry and garden, prepared all the dairy and poultry products to be marketed, and preserved and canned fruits.[30]

In whatever capacity African-American women worked, their labor was

the crops and you weren't at school, you were either chopping cotton, hoeing cotton, replanting corn or hoeing around the corn." Unlike sons, daughters had the added pressure to work in households alongside their mothers cooking, washing, and caring for younger children. In addition to helping with the cooking, the daughters did all of the family washing and cleaned the house; in families with small children, older girls cared for them as well. While young boys helped in gardens or watched younger siblings, older sons ceased to do so. Sarah Rice expressed her perception that daughters bore a disproportionate share of the work: "I always thought the girls had the worst time, because we had to do most of the work."[39]

Hard work and the careful attention to how each family member labored meant that some black farm families pieced together a living. Though the Alabamian James Little was an able sharecropper, the labor of eight children and his wife provided him with additional time to raise enough vegetables, cows, and pigs for his family to eat and sell. Though cotton prices continued to decline, black farm families attempted to grow and yield more; others included corn and wheat as both cash crops and feed. The extra income earned from selling butter and chickens or hiring out to another farmer enabled some black farmers to purchase fertilizers, mules, and cows. The wages women earned from their extra produce could purchase better clothing for church, such as hats, collars, and shoes. Sara Brooks described how the intense labor of all her family members enabled her father to add on to their home, paint it, and then furnish it. Sarah Rice recalled that her family had a table and enough chairs for everyone; they owned china and glasses, all earned from her mother's peddling of eggs and chickens. She noted that for the first time she became aware that her family was better off than the majority of farm families in her rural Black Belt community.[40] This expansion of the household economy complicates historians' explanations of an emerging black peasantry.

The Rices and other black sharecropping families who worked hard and practiced thrift frequently found themselves in debt or without food. Rain and drought, the power of landowners to sever contracts or claim mysterious debts, illness, or death wreaked havoc on farm production and household economies. One long year Sarah Rice's father worked as a minister and as a sharecropper, which limited the time he could devote to growing his own cotton. The landowner considered him a half-hand farmer and figured his wages accordingly. Rice recalled that "because we were thirteen miles out in the country, there was nobody we could work for. We didn't have anything to carry to town to peddle—chickens, or eggs or vegetables—we just couldn't buy anything to eat." The lack of cash and enormous debt made work all the more tedious; the absence of a plow meant hard labor with the hoe. In lieu of an expensive mule, sometimes older children pulled the plow.[41]

While black farm families ascribed to regular, hard labor, they nonetheless made distinctions between the labor they performed for themselves and the coerced labor they performed for whites. Under sharecropping, landowners claimed rights to whatever was produced, even the cotton seeds. Black sharecropping families struggled to acquire the materials and the time to plow, plant, and cultivate for themselves, but only after the other field work was done. In his narrative Nate Shaw sought to represent himself as a competent and fair man. He resented any encroachment on the time he spent laboring in the fields. Once when his father interrupted his work, Shaw cut the visit short and returned to the plow. Though his actions sprang from a long feud with his father, whom he described as lazy, Shaw was equally aware of who owned half of the crop he produced: "I was dutiful to my labor, I had to put it out. I didn't want to come up behind with nothin in *my* field if I could help it." Shaw felt that the more he labored and produced, the more he could claim as his own. James Little expressed similar tensions about working for shares. Little had a long relationship with the white man who owned the land, but he was nonetheless aware that the man made the decisions about what he could grow.[42]

African Americans' belief that they would gain autonomy and economic mobility through sharecropping faltered as white landowners retained control over what black farmers produced and how they labored. Carl Kelsey noted in his turn-of-the-century study that in central Alabama "the size of [the black farmer's] family is known and the riders see to it that he keeps all the working hands in the field. If the riders have any trouble with a Negro they are apt to take it out in physical punishment, to 'wear him out,' as the phrase goes." As more and more black men and women became casual farm laborers after 1900 in Alabama and Georgia, they encountered some of the most brutal conditions in the South. Moreover, planters demanded that entire families labor from "sun to sun," leaving many with little time or energy to cultivate enough food to survive. Charles S. Johnson interviewed men and women who described their condition in the fields as "half-starved" and exhausted from working for wages that they rarely "saw on time."[43]

Despite the growing disadvantages of sharecropping, African Americans persisted in their attempts to make a living from the land by including wage work off of farms as part of their family economy. A wide variety of evidence confirms that while white landowners sometimes went to great lengths to limit black mobility, more and more black workers experienced greater mobility in rural areas after 1900. These countervailing patterns can be explained by the expansion of industries in both the rural and urban South after 1880. As cotton prices continued to fall after 1890, landowners turned from producing cotton and rice to growing trees for the lumber and turpentine industries, which reduced the demand for black agricultural workers. How black sharecroppers and agricultural workers labored thus began to change at the close of the nineteenth century, providing or forcing greater mobility upon many. While black landownership expanded, generally the average acreage of black farms remained confined to small holdings of the least desirable land. More telling, between 1890 and 1920, tens of thousands of African Americans no longer labored exclusively on farms and took up permanent and part-time work in rural industries, towns, and cities.[44]

As increasing numbers of landowners ceased to bind blacks to full-year contracts, black men's and women's participation in wage labor away from farms became common. During the winter months when men and women had little if any field work, many sought a variety of short-term wage labor. Men laid tracks, hauled lumber, dredged streams, and built bridges and roads. As late as the 1920s, black men did much of the skilled work of rebuilding the barns and homes of landowners; others repaired farm machinery. In nearby towns, black men sorted, lifted, and hauled goods at stores. Daughters in sharecropping households had traditionally worked for others during the harvest, but increasing numbers of black women, particularly older ones and young women without children, sought nonagricultural labor. Unlike men, however, women had fewer options and typically labored in domestic service, worked in laundries, or assisted midwives. By their early teens, many black girls began working for whites in nearby towns.[45]

While the back-and-forth movement between agricultural labor and wage work in towns and cities schooled many young men and women in the art of cobbling together a livelihood through migration, many African Americans intended neither long nor permanent stays. Rather, young black men and women sought wage work away from farms with the intention of acquiring and saving money for future economic independence as well as attaining some "experience in the world." Robert F., for example, departed from the Mississippi Delta in the winter to New Orleans; he returned to his parents' farm in the spring to plant crops. He repeated this route for several years because his earnings supplemented his family's low agricultural income. He intended to purchase his own farm someday. Married men, like Nate Shaw, left their wives to care for farms while they earned money for seed, fertilizers, and farm animals.[46]

Young black women and men left rural homes for familiar places or went to areas where other family or friends lived and worked. When Besphene W.

left her family farm in Alabama for Jackson, Florida, to work in the tobacco factory, for example, she lived with relatives; in the spring she returned to Alabama to labor in the fields. Similarly, young men chose areas where family members had migrated; lumber camps, railroads, and fertilizer yards typically had clusters of kin and friends. Compared with the low wages they earned in agricultural labor, blacks found those off farms to be much higher. Nate Shaw earned $3.00 a load for hauling lumber. Black men who cleared land for the railroads in 1910 earned between $1.50 and $3.00 for a workday. By 1916, porters and hod carriers received $.80 to $1.25 per day. In contrast, farm hands received $.50 to $.75 a day.[47] Thanks in part to this wage work, black landownership began increasing after 1900, peaking by 1910. In addition, black tenants came to depend less on advances and more on the wages of family.

While nonagricultural wage labor became more desirable and in many cases the only option, black women and men made their choices in the complicated framework of kin needs and farm responsibilities. Parents and wives encouraged single and married black men to enter the extractive industries precisely because the work was temporary. Such work could be structured around the needs of agricultural labor. Nate Shaw hauled lumber after he got his "crop planted and laid by." Because so many black men fit nonfarm wage work into the "off times and rainy days," Steven A. Reich has suggested that employers like lumber operators did not "reduce [black workers] to dependent wage laborers." Wage work provided necessary cash for many, but did not pull black men permanently into camps as long as other family members continued to maintain crops. While track building for the railroad, black men typically boarded with other black farm families during the week and then went home on Saturday afternoons. Proximity to kin and the desire to farm drew black men home on a regular basis; these ties disrupted the work rhythms that railroad and lumber operators attempted to impose.[48]

In these nonagricultural jobs, African Americans typically labored in segregated gangs or sections, under terms that they found distasteful. On the docks of Mobile, Alabama, or while clearing and grading land for the construction of a railroad line in central Alabama, black men worked under white supervision that was often violent and abusive. As Edwin L. Brown noted, for black men, gang work "reinforced centuries of exploitation and continued the antebellum tradition of separation into 'black' and 'white' jobs." In his study of dock work along the Gulf Coast, Eric Arnesen documented the labor of African Americans in Mobile as they loaded lumber under "harsh working conditions and lower wages." Similarly, work in the log mills was done in gangs under grueling conditions. One Alabama woman described her husband's white boss as "mean to work for."[49] Though Gus Joiner carried two-hundred-pound cross ties in a camp in Milwaukee in the 1920s, he worked alongside black men who had done similar work in Alabama and Georgia a decade earlier. "These were big men," he recalled, but "a lot of their shoulders were raw from carrying those slabs."[50]

Both the dangerous work conditions and the seasonal nature of rural industrial work sustained black workers' reluctance to leave farms and family permanently. Robert C. stuffed drilled holes with dynamite for a fertilizer company in Georgia. Because the dust was toxic, he wore rags tied around his mouth and nose, but it did not prevent him from regularly coughing up blood. It was not uncommon for men to be injured in lumber mills or on the railroads. Women, too, faced new dangers: no longer under the protective watch of family, young women became vulnerable to sexual exploitation; many faced daily insults from white men.[51] Paradoxically, the temporary nature of rural industries periodically forced African Americans back to farms or other rural labor. The turpentine industry appeared and disappeared in the pine forests of Georgia and Alabama. In 1900, black men could readily find work nearly year round; ten years later, work was scarcer, hitting its peak in May and once again in September. Some men found its shortened cycle appealing; generally, however, the work attracted some of the most transient of men since distance and isolation made it less attractive to those with strong ties to farms. Carter G. Woodson concluded that much of the rural industrial work in the Deep South was temporary in nature, fitting the needs of both the "farmer and the promoter of industry." Rural workers may readily have helped compress cotton after they picked it, with the land and the machinery owned by the farmer. When African Americans found industrial jobs after the completion of agricultural work in the fall, employers tended to lower wages since they faced no competition from farmers or other industries.[52]

Because of the highly segregated labor market in the Deep South, employers maintained poor work conditions. The railroad unions attempted to eliminate, often successfully, black workers from full-time, better-paid, and skilled positions through strikes and acts of terror. The quickening pace of segregation strengthened white workers' ability to use intimidation and threats and expect black subservience as a benefit of their positions as skilled workers. "Even where unions were weak or nonexistent," Eric Arnesen has argued, "managers kept the top positions an all-white preserve." By the early 1920s, black workers found little beyond temporary section maintenance and construction work on most lines. At the close of the decade, black men held the majority of 829,372 track jobs in the South, but most of this work was casual and unskilled. On the docks of Mobile, white union workers dominated the higher-paid loading of timber onto ships.[53] The temporary nature of this work meant that blacks often lived in makeshift camps known more for their unsanitary living conditions than for their advantages over rural living. Most important, many of these camps rarely allowed for the maintenance of family or the creation of enduring community institutions, two goals that had long animated black culture and shaped black values. Black men from Alabama traveled a great distance, joining black Texans and Louisianians in the piney woods where work could be had all year round. But these were temporary camps, and Alabama workers rarely brought their families. The lack of family, the short time needed to fell trees, and the poor conditions of work and camps tended to pull men away from these jobs on a regular basis. Alabama workers shared with black men from nearby rural communities the desire to be with family. Men from local farms returned home frequently, sometimes for long periods of time to work or participate in celebrations and holidays. Alabamians, frustrated by the lack of contact with their families, left for good since these rough, makeshift camps did not encourage family settlement or sustain community organizations. Churches atrophied and other institutions either never developed or withered away. As a result, lumber operators found it nearly impossible to sustain a stable labor supply and instead watched blacks, along with Mexican and European immigrants, "filter through" their camps. Even when mill operators constructed low-cost single-family dwellings or provided small plots of land for gardens, the drive to minimize costs and boost profits meant these efforts were rarely sustained.[54]

In addition to their high labor turnover, black workers regularly vocalized their resistance to the harsh conditions of New South industrial labor. The work songs that emerged out of the social relations of work suggest both the pervasive abuse of white bosses and the range of resistances that black men mounted. These songs, many folklorists have argued, reveal a work culture rooted in post-Emancipation black rural values that espoused a strong desire for personal dignity and freedom from coerced supervision. As Zora Neale Hurston collected African-American folktales in Florida and Georgia in the 1930s, she recognized how black sawmill workers' joking and storytelling gave them some reprieve from the "sun and sawdust, sweat and sand." Songs forged while lining and maintaining railroad tracks, for instance, relieved some of the burden of backbreaking work. Black railroad callers throughout the South exhorted the gangs of ten to twelve men to strain at the rail and line it together. By the 1930s "John Henry"—"the king of railroad track-laying songs"—mixed pride of skill with masculine bravado. But it also set an alternate pace of work than that of white bosses hollering "work, work, work." Songs like "Mule on De Mount," another popular work song with wide distribution and many sons away from the coke ovens and coal mines, but many families strove to steer them into other work. Gus Joiner would have labored in the ovens, but his mother typically had ten boarders who paid eight dollars a week. Grant Joiner had the coal company deduct the boarders' fees from their salaries. "So he got a pay check from the coal company just the same as though he was working for the coal company." With the money earned by his wife, Grant Joiner opened up a grocery store; he bought a wagon and a mule and hauled vegetables brought up from North Carolina to sell in the coal camps. Gus Joiner recalled that "six days a week during the summer months he had a different route each day. He'd load that wagon up with chickens, eggs, to-matoes, you name it." These jobs enabled the Joiners to keep their son out of the mines and in school. Icabod Flewellen's father successfully kept him out of the mines and pushed him to finish school. Like Grant Joiner, Flewel-len's father pursued labor outside of the mines by recruiting other black workers to labor in them.[61]

Gus Joiner did eventually work in the mines, first alongside his father and then with other black men. As a child, Joiner "enjoyed hearing those old coal miners swapping experiences, talking about when you know the top is work-ing." When he was forced into the mines for lack of work in the North dur-ing the late 1920s, he knew from listening to the men that he faced danger as dust sifted through the top board in an area he was told to clean up alone. Knowing that his white boss had violated safety rules established for the mines, Joiner informed him that the area was not safe. The supervisor soon retract-ed his curses when he saw rocks pouring into the car. When asked how he knew "the top was working," Joiner responded that he "just knew." Later, he realized that if he had not listened to black miners as a child he "would have been dead, would have been buried." Joiner learned to listen and "witness" from other black men, even when it meant that he had to challenge whites.[62]

Unlike the lumber, turpentine, and coal camps of Alabama, the coal camps of the upper South were more favorable to the settlement of black households. While the long-term or permanent moves away from rural communities were often precipitated by the unavailability of economic options, families tend-ed to move together or in a chain. As blacks moved to coal camps, many fam-ilies recreated households and communities in new settings. Thornton D. simultaneously lost his parents to death and the family farm to debt in Boli-gee, Alabama. He made his way to Kentucky to work in the coal mines; with-in a year his younger siblings and other extended kin joined him. Some black farm families in Cleveland, Mississippi, found it impossible to maintain their self-sufficiency. At the urging of several young men, a significant portion of the community left for the coalfields of Kentucky; eventually, several families migrated together to Cleveland.[63] Such networks meant that employers had to do very little recruiting, an important consideration in the South, where enticement laws could be enforced.

Whether working in coal mines, lumber, and steel or on the docks and railroads, African-American workers witnessed or participated in bitter workplace struggles that involved unions. Though black workers could be found in a variety of segregated or biracial unions, most unions in the South were "white men's unions." Given that much of the work blacks found was temporary and seasonal, many black workers confronted organized white workers, who had actively helped to ensure that such work would be temporary and poorly paid. Such practices, however, could be dangerous to unions, since employers appeared to have been no more loyal to white workers than to blacks. In many instances, employers turned to black workers not out of any desire to hire them but out of a desire to break unions. The railroad unions and the International Longshoremen's Association took different approaches to the high presence of black labor, but they shared highly racist practices even as biracial union activity arose. As numerous studies have suggested, organized white workers' decisions to exclude black workers—or include them in highly segregated ways—was practiced racism and intimately linked with their class identities.[64]

Although work in the coal mines presented different opportunities for black workers to participate in unions, they most often came in the framework of discrimination. By the late 1920s, thousands of black men belonged to the United Mine Workers (UMW). Many had participated in some of the most protracted strikes in the Alabama and West Virginia coalfields, joining with whites to garner important concessions from employers. Joe William Trotter Jr. notes that in "the Paint Creek–Cabin Creek coal strike of 1912–13, white mountaineers, immigrants, and blacks won an important victory, including recognition of their union." In the end, however, white workers insisted on and won the right to limit blacks' and immigrant workers' access to better jobs and benefits. Without a doubt, these union efforts took place in the Jim Crow South and rarely challenged its practices or ideologies. In the World War I era African Americans formed a critical mass in the West Virginia coal mines and they remained vital to union struggles. As employers mounted a violent and repressive campaign to break the UMW, black, white, and immigrant workers developed "mutual loyalties" alongside the tradition of discrimination within the UMW.[65] That so many black workers remarked on it suggests how unusual this new solidarity had been. However limited in practice, the UMW represented an ideal for behavior between black and white workers that could potentially challenge discrimination. Black men understood the contradictions in the union, but in spite of the restrictions, many black miners crafted a complicated race and class consciousness that simultaneously bound them to and made them critics of the UMW and their black communities.

Just how many black workers who eventually migrated north entered southern industries as strikebreakers will remain unknown, but from 1890 to the 1930s, organized white workers linked blacks and scabs. Knowingly or not, many black workers did act as strikebreakers; the same was true for other groups of workers. Certainly a strike by union workers may have immediately signaled to some blacks that their access to higher-paying industrial work would be unimpeded. But numerous examples also suggested to them that work as a strikebreaker could be temporary at best and dangerous at worst. Moreover, those blacks who responded to employers' calls confronted black unionists. But the specific link between scabs and blacks permeated white workers' discourse and the depiction underscored their racism.

Scattered evidence suggests that some workers did migrate with the hope of joining unions. This goal was not confined to men, since some black women were eligible to join railroad unions. Other migrants belonged to unions in the South and intended to do so in the North. Even as many workers perceived unions as exclusionary, blacks who belonged were equally tolerated and revered by other blacks and others in the working class. Black miners and bricklayers, for example, were often leaders in working-class churches and clubs; some owned homes, sent children to school, and had wives who did not work in white women's kitchens. The sons and daughters of these workers watched their parents and other adults in their communities exude dignity, autonomy, and courage. These organized workers and their children carried their experiences north, and many became critical organizers in the biracial struggles that black and white workers mounted in the industrial settings of Cleveland between 1915 and the 1930s.

Most black workers who migrated north neither participated in unions nor acted as strikebreakers. Instead, the daily struggles that African-American workers waged in and out of southern workplaces left an indelible legacy for their experiences in wage work in the North. Footdragging and quitting were variously individual or collective acts, but African-American cultural values sanctioned such efforts. Abusive employers and poor work conditions demanded immediate responses, and African-American workers drew upon a wealth of collective experience to react. However racist organized white workers may have been—and historians are still engaged in a struggle to determine to what extent—when given a choice, black workers chose unions that practiced racial egalitarianism, affirmed their dignity, and provided them with autonomy.[66]

In the context of the Jim Crow South, mobility remained African Americans' most important response to discrimination. Unmarried young men and women in particular pursued wage labor away from farms. The way in which these young men and women labored, therefore, differed from how their parents did. First, young black men and women began moving into the growing towns and cities in greater numbers. Second, it was not uncommon for young men to migrate to other states to perform agricultural labor for long periods of time. Others went to New York City and Long Island to work as bell captains, bellhops, and waiters during the summer months.[67]

Several historians have persuasively argued that these moves provided training for the longer migration north, creating a growing population of blacks who were predisposed to move to the North. Equally important, migration within a limited geographic area provided them with important skills that would enable them to more easily negotiate their departure for northern cities. But reliance on wage labor in an urban environment led to diminished ties to the rural South for some and frayed patience with rural life for others. Certainly many young blacks found life in rural areas especially trying after time in a town or city. Others, such as Sara Brooks, remembered a youth that had included repetitive and relentless labor that yielded only subsistence returns. Many found the ongoing poverty and the declining profitability of growing cotton a disincentive to establishing a life in rural areas. Consequently, many blacks completely severed ties to sharecropping. In addition to the external pressures, bad weather, debt, and segregation further impeded the possibilities of landownership and profitable crop maintenance. As young men and women matured, many no longer expected to make a living solely from farming. Black landownership in the Deep South peaked in 1910, though many still clung to the land as tenants until 1930. Despite the shift in the expectations about agricultural work, young black men and women retained the strong cultural ideas of self-sufficiency. As children, they had been taught how to work hard and strive for self-improvement. When opportunities appeared to be closed in rural areas, it became necessary to work and live elsewhere.[68]

By 1910, the expanding black population in cities and industries of the New South, whether out of desire or need, attested to their diminished ties to the land as their primary livelihoods. Census data show that between 1900 and 1920, 1.5 million blacks left rural areas for the cities of the South, North, and West; by 1920, one-third of the black population—some 3.5 million—

lived and worked in cities. As a group, blacks who labored in agriculture became the minority among all black wage earners in the second decade of the twentieth century.[69]

The emergence of industrial cities such as Birmingham provided black men with virtually unlimited access to unskilled jobs. Employment in the steel mills, however, was often circumscribed. Employers overwhelmingly consigned black men to the dirtiest, heaviest, and most dangerous labor— "nigger work." Such hard, hot, and rough jobs were viewed as too demeaning for native-born white workers. In Birmingham steel mills, employers regularly hired black men for the most arduous part of casting work, labor now done by machines in northern mills. Despite the circumscribed nature of the work, by 1910 blacks held 90 percent of the unskilled jobs in the Birmingham steel district, making the city and the surrounding areas one of the largest black urban communities in the New South.[70]

While industrial segregation limited black workers' job opportunities, Henry McKiven has noted that the system was "not so unyielding that black workers could not achieve some control over their working lives." By the turn of the century, the jobs black men held were primarily unskilled and segregated, but they dominated certain jobs, which ironically gave them "some degree of leverage in some sectors of the labor market." Employers, unable either to penetrate other labor markets or lure southern and Eastern European immigrants into unskilled and dangerous steel jobs, had to provide black workers with higher wages during periods of restricted labor markets.[71]

In contrast, African-American women's wage opportunities in the New South industries were severely limited. Though segregation laws in some areas precluded black women's access to jobs as machine tenders, some employers nonetheless found loopholes and used blacks in a variety of menial capacities. Outside of the rougher labor in the tobacco mills and box, rag, paint, and varnish factories, black women remained confined to private household labor. More typically, black women continued to labor in domestic service as cooks, nurses, and household servants; others combined day labor as domestic workers and agricultural workers on the outskirts of cities and towns. White employers often demanded constant service and subservience from black household workers, while subjecting these women to sexual harassment, nonpayment of wages, and other forms of abuse. In many instances, however, black women resented the constant demands on their time and the assaults to their personal dignity. Though certainly shaped by racist attitudes and stereotypes, employers' loud and public complaints about the inadequacies of their servants document black women's private and public displays of resistance. Willie Ruff overheard his mother describe to her friends how she regularly wore the clothes of the white woman for whom she did laundry. Black women especially balked at the pretensions of employers whose economic situations were only slightly better than their own.[72]

The majority of black women wage earners recognized the constriction of their wage opportunities because of their particular location in a segregated labor market. Sara Brooks, for example, noted that the "coloreds" had "the heaviest and hardest job all the time." Segregation had limited the time she had spent in school, and as an adult she found her options narrowed because of her inability to read. "When I went to Mobile, to me it seemed that we wasn't gonna get nowhere nohow past the farm and past workin' for the white peoples because the colored women could mostly do fieldwork or babysit or cook and clean house in the South. That's where I was, see, and I didn't see that there was somethin better ahead until I got away from it." In Mobile, Brooks joined her sister and other black women in her neighborhood in doing daywork. During the fall they pieced together daywork, picking cotton, and laundry. The remainder of the year Brooks supplemented her meager earnings with yard work, picking pecans, and child care.[73]

But as Gavin Wright has concluded, the *overall* wage rates of southern industrial workers were low, and with little upward movement in wages or occupational mobility, black workers remained economically vulnerable, especially during downturns in the regional economy. By 1913, a depression and increased competition for unskilled urban employment and rural industrial work forced many blacks out of agricultural work—sharecropping and wage—and into an urban labor market where steady work was scarce.[74]

As in rural areas, black urban workers often created a variety of arrangements to establish households, offset low wages, and care for children. In cities, women's and men's combined labor made it possible to have some household solvency. Men and women understood their economic ties to one another and the necessity of each other's wages; consequently, the precariousness of their livelihoods bred an economic interdependence amongst men and women, though not necessarily an equality. When one or the other lost work they and their families often immediately felt the consequences. Belle Jones's parents, both born in slavery, finally settled in Mobile after 1910. They cobbled together income from his work at a cotton press and her occasional work as a seamstress. When work was scarce, they fed themselves with food from their garden and milk from their cow. Many women added the care of boarders; domestic workers were allowed to take leftover food from employers.[75]

But continued ties to kin networks in rural areas and the uneven access to wage opportunities in towns and cities mitigated against many blacks making a permanent transition to urban residency and labor. More distinctly, close proximity to kin networks provided financial aid and emotional support. Sara Brooks's older brother encouraged her to leave an abusive husband and a precarious financial situation and join him in a large town. Because he found greater wage-earning opportunities, he frequently provided his sister with a place to live and contacts with potential employers. Yet her brother possessed neither the economic means nor the household space to accommodate Sara's two children. Instead, three of her four children remained on the farm with her parents. Once her brother left for Cleveland, Sara's financial resources rapidly deteriorated. She later moved to Mobile to live with another brother and sister-in-law, but they, too, migrated north. Alone with a small child, Brooks moved frequently from room to room.[76]

More than anything, black workers in cities had to accommodate the frequent physical moves of households and the departure of men and older children looking for work. During World War I, cities became launching sites for migration north, particularly for black men. Unable or unwilling to move wives and children north, black men relied on their families to maintain households in their absence. After the war when northern employment was less available, such patterns continued when black men moved to nearby towns and cities in the South.

Older black women became the anchor for families maintaining kinship networks in cities. They established primary residences and took care of grandchildren while parents took advantage of distant labor opportunities. Older women's care of children was especially critical for single mothers because it allowed them access to their children but offered mobility. They supplemented diets and maintained rural traditions by planting gardens with familiar vegetables such as pole beans and greens. They provided an opportunity for young children to receive uninterrupted educations while teaching them the values of hard work and reciprocity. These urban arrangements were variations of patterns found in rural areas. Elizabeth Rauel Bethel found similar household patterns in South Carolina, suggesting the elasticity of black kinship systems, rather than indications of black family disorganization.[77]

As the black population in the Deep South cities of Birmingham, Montgomery, Mobile, and Atlanta significantly expanded, so too did black middle-class and working-class institutions and social life. In every southern city a vast array of black fraternal, benevolent, social, and church-based activities sprang up in the wake of in-migration. Often black men dominated, and middle-class men and women had more influence than other groups, though some secular and religious organizations were marked by a more democratic and inclusive manner. Some rural blacks who migrated to southern cities between 1905 and 1915 experienced a loss in status due to lowered incomes and the competition from better-educated, longtime urban residents.[78] None-theless, city life afforded these new residents an opportunity to carve out their own social spaces. Honky-tonks and house parties, like their rural anteced-ent, the jook joint, provided dancing, gambling, and drinking for black men and women. Robin D. G. Kelley has contended that these places and events became a "partial refuge from the humiliations and indignities of racism, class pretensions, and wage work." The communally created blues music, with its roots in the rural work songs, helped build "an alternative culture that placed more emphasis on collectivist, mutuality, and fellowship."[79]

The growth of black urban populations significantly increased the num-ber of leisure activities available, but many African-American workers found that low wages and Jim Crow significantly circumscribed their access to and participation in commercial leisure. Black men and women shared the sense of an expanding web of segregation in towns and cities that restricted their access to parks, theaters, and other public spaces and amusements. Josephus Hicks complained that he could not go to the public libraries, and he hated the segregated theaters.[80]

Black women's much lower wages meant that as a group they had less income for leisure. For single women, especially, their more vulnerable eco-nomic status increased their dependency on men to participate in public entertainment, such as money and transportation out of small towns for nearby dances and music. Sara Brooks and her friends rarely had the extra money to spend time dancing or listening to music in the honky-tonk in a larger town near Bainbridge, Alabama. After some months engaging in sex-ual relations with one man who had a car and thus could take her to social events, Brooks had an unplanned pregnancy. Though Brooks's women friends "were hipped to what they were doin'," she concluded that she "didn't know nothin'" about "how to avoid havin babies." Church leaders and other wom-en publicly condemned these leisure activities.[81]

Within this context of diminishing rural and urban wage opportunities after 1913, a confluence of events helped facilitate African Americans' depar-ture from the Deep South. First, the late 1890s infestation of the boll weevil in southeastern Texas slowly spread eastward. By 1916, the insect had moved through the crops of the Deep South, wrecking havoc in Alabama and Geor-gia. Despite the use of chemical and home remedies, such as a mixture of sulfur and molasses, the larvae continued to ruin crops and spread to Ala-bama. Many black farmers discovered the power "of the ashy-colored ras-cal." Nate Shaw noted that he, like many other black and white farmers, "was scared of him to an extent. I soon learnt he'd destroy a cotton crop. Yes, all God's dangers aint a white man. When the boll weevil starts in your cotton and go to depositin his eggs . . . that's when he'll kill you." By 1913, nearly twenty counties had been infested in southeastern Georgia.[82]

Other factors equally contributed to blacks collectively leaving the land for the urban South and North. Observers noted the widespread infestation of the boll weevil, but argued that the decline in acreage was precipitated by the prolonged bad weather in Alabama and Georgia. Investigators observing the migration after 1915 noted the "push" of farm disasters and the "pull" of jobs in the North with higher wages. In his 1920 study, Emmett J. Scott concluded that the move north was primarily a response to the lure of industries. He noted the expansiveness of the migration and observed that the movement of blacks and the boll weevil were not necessarily in synch: "The general direction of the spread of the movement was east to west. While efforts were being made to check the exodus from Florida, the good citizens of Texas are first beginning to note a stir of unrest in their sections. On the other hand, the march of the boll weevil, that stripped the cotton fields of the South, was from west to east." He acknowledged that in addition to weather and the boll weevil, other reasons lay behind the mass migration.[83] A decade of infestation had caused many black and white rural workers to turn to the cities for employment, but the intensification of the infestation between 1910 and 1915 precipitated a stampede on an already precarious urban labor market. The rise in the urban black unemployment rate from 13 percent in 1910 to 20 percent in 1920 and competition from whites signaled the displacement of black workers from many jobs in the urban South.[84]

Despite the devastation of farms from the boll weevil and African Americans' displacement from wage work in towns and cities, observers urged caution in simple conclusions about the causes behind the mass migration. Emmett J. Scott puzzled that the "most striking feature of the northern migration was its individualism." Investigators in Cleveland found that a majority of the recent arrivals in the city had worked and lived in southern cities and industries before their migration. Even as local newspapers announced the steady departures of African Americans, editors marveled at the variety of reasons blacks left the South. One letter to the editor of a black newspaper cautioned that the cause of the mass exodus was "complex and many-angled, not simple and categorical."[85]

Other contemporary observers attempted to discern what roles, if any, segregation and violence against African Americans played in the impetus for the departure, especially since many young men and women expressed a clear desire to escape the racial proscriptions that had limited their economic, social, and cultural opportunities. In letters sent to the *Chicago Defender,* the hope for better treatment was as important as higher wages. Continued racial violence and the threat of it were particularly evident in many areas where black migrants lived. In Georgia, for example, the number of lynchings rose between 1910 and 1919 and may have served as an important added incentive for black migration. Such an impetus to migrate is illustrated by the experience of Jeff W., who had initially rejected the decision to leave Ansley, Alabama, for Cleveland in the belief he should follow his male relatives into the ministry. He quickly changed his decision to migrate, however, after a cousin disappeared as a result of Ku Klux Klan violence.[86]

Though historians of southern racial violence express caution in the correlation between the rise in violence and black out-migration, other evidence suggests that the heightened awareness of violence against blacks and the attention given to such violence in the black press did play a significant role in blacks' decision to leave the South. The most well-known contemporary insight into the repressive and violent conditions blacks faced can be found in the letters sent in response to a story invented by the *Chicago Defender* in an attempt to increase its circulation. Letters poured in from all parts of the South demanding information about the supposed claim that on May 15, 1917, there would be a "great northern drive." These letters poignantly detailed low wages and underemployment, along with violent treatment, threats, and intimidation. One young man requested information about employment any place where he could be assured of "some protection as a good citizen under the Stars and Stripes."[87]

Black migrants did express the desire to distance themselves physically from the stultifying restrictions of segregation. Parents taught children to observe, although not necessarily believe or accept, the boundaries dictated by violence and segregation. Many blacks felt fear at one time or another when confronted with the violent and repressive system meant to keep them "in their place." Sara Brooks recalled never questioning a sign outside of an all-white town that read "Niggers Read and Run." As a child, Brooks's parents admonished her to avoid the town. Though some contemporary observers noted that blacks had historically been subjected to intimidation, violence, and racial ostracism, broader social changes in the second decade made acceptance of such abuse no longer possible. In private and public ways, blacks expressed disdain for segregation and questioned its validity. Those blacks who openly resisted whites were called "colored crazy."[88] In many ways, blacks' departure from the South was a response to and a defiance of the varied and coerced effort to keep them bound to segregation and violence.

These twin ideas—the search for more remunerative labor and the desire to escape the repressive controls based on race and class conflict—coincided with the demand for labor in northern industries. The start of

World War I precipitated the loss of immigrant labor in the North, and employers began to actively recruit black workers from the South. Beginning in 1916 railroad employers transported thousands of black men out of southern yards and moved them into the yards of Cleveland. They made appeals in southern black newspapers and used networks of kin and friends to sustain their recruitment throughout the war. James Robinson, an observer of the movement in Ohio as well as an interviewer of many black migrants, commented: "In this great folk wandering, Cincinnati serves as a junction where migrants from different points in the South are distributed to other points in the North rather than as a terminus. It is apparently too near the south which they are fleeing and does not offer the attractive wages afforded by Cleveland, Chicago and Pittsburgh."[89] As Robinson observed, many blacks wanted higher wages in a city as far removed from the traditions of the South as possible.

Black newspapers and journals published in northern cities devoted significant portions of their pages to articles on the better life and higher wages black migrants would find in the wartime North. Sarah Rice recalled that "there were no radios or newspapers, so when anybody had a magazine or a newspaper, they'd gather round to talk about the news." The *Chicago Defender* was the most eagerly awaited and widely read of these newspapers. Between 1915 and 1917, its editors give prominence to reports of lynchings, segregation, and the lack of black political rights. Its relentless and sharp critique of the South coexisted with accounts of blacks' ability to earn higher wages, vote, and send their children to school in the North. The national edition carried reports from other cities with growing black populations, providing additional evidence that higher wages extended beyond Chicago. Emmett Scott noted that the *Chicago Defender* brought "the North to them." W. E. B. Du Bois regularly described migration as an act of self-help in *Crisis*. Family and friends sent similar clippings from the *Cleveland Gazette*, equally known for its biting critiques of segregation in the South. "We were told," Bertha Cowan recalled, "that a better world awaited us."[90]

Sarah Rice witnessed the departure of blacks in the wake of the boll weevil infestation in central Alabama: "In the train station it was just like an exodus of black people traveling, going north to better their lives. . . . It was pathetic, like you see these people in these countries now, escaping for their lives with the bundles and stuff like that, because they didn't have suitcases. They just had sacks to put their clothes in, headrags on and everything, going north." Her account duplicates earlier observations of blacks fleeing the Natchez area for the Delta in 1908. In both instances, black workers and their families fled not only the boll weevil but also efforts to prevent them from departing. By 1913, similar efforts were made to prevent black migration out of Alabama and Georgia.[91]

The image of blacks fleeing for the North, however, overlooks the range of choices that they might make about their destination. Black workers and their families had been on the move in high numbers since the end of the nineteenth century, so it is tempting to see the World War I migration north as an extension of this pattern. But by 1910 black workers had a variety of opportunities in rural and urban industries of the South. While the black men, women, and children leaving the South between 1910 and 1920 numbered over half a million, the overwhelming majority of blacks remained in the South. Nate Shaw eloquently described the kind of choices he and other African Americans were making as the war started, the boll weevil made its way east, and industrial jobs in the South and the North became available:

> A heap of families, while I was livin on the Tucker place . . . was leavin goin north. Some of my neighbors even picked up and left. The boll weevil was sendin a lot of em out, no doubt. I knowed several men went north, some with their families and some without; they sent for their families when they got to where they was goin. More went besides what I knowed of, from all parts of this southern country. They was dissatisfied with the way of life here in the south—and when I was livin on the Pollard place it come pretty wide open to me and touched the hem of my garment. But my family was prosperin right here, I didn't pay no attention to leavin.

As Shaw suggests, the sense of deprivation in the South coincided with the availability of better-paying work and living opportunities in the North. Shaw did not leave, however, because he "was a farmin man" and he knew "more about this country than [he] knowed about the northern states."[92]

In many ways, the arrival of the boll weevil and the wartime need for labor were climaxes to a series of events that enabled blacks to consider the North as a place to work and live. As Neil Fligstein has commented, an individual's circumstances greatly influenced the act. When Nate Shaw worked acres for a man named Turner, he had attained some self-sufficiency. Naomi Morgan's family, who lived not far from Shaw, made a quite different choice. Her parents farmed in the shadow of Booker T. Washington's great experiment and considered themselves "better off farmers" than most. Despite their relative economic stability, the infestation of the boll weevil destroyed their crops, so they migrated to Birmingham. Morgan's father found work in a steel mill, which regularly hired blacks; soon after, he heard about higher-paying work in Cleveland. Though he migrated alone, he sent for his family within several months.[93]

The differing choices that Nate Shaw and Naomi Morgan's father made suggest that the decision to move had to rest on information about opportunities elsewhere. While a significant number of African Americans left rural areas for the North, their departures were usually precipitated by information about work or the departure of family members or friends. Sallie Hopson's family left rural Georgia only after her father had found a job working for the railroad. She recalled that "mostly the people coming north at the time would leave about eleven o'clock [at night]. Many had been share-croppers and wanted out of that life. Mother, sister, and I were some of the many. We rode that Central Georgia to Cincinnati." Hopson's family members changed trains and continued their journey to Cleveland.[94]

Whether black men and women left the South during the large migration of the 1910s or later in the 1920s, the decision to leave required plans and support from kin and the community. Leaving the South and settling in Cleveland became a family decision, requiring emotional and material support, even when only an individual made the move. Contemporary observers conceded that most migrants came under their own initiative, which indicated a sense of self-determination in their moves. Contemporary studies and personal accounts suggest the necessity to plan the departure as well as seek aid and cooperation from family and friends. Geneva Robinson represents this aspect of migration: she left Hodges, South Carolina, in 1921, accompanied by her grandmother. The women's trip had been arranged by other family members in response to a cousin in Cleveland who needed to work and requested household help and child care.[95]

For the majority of migrants, obtaining a ticket proved difficult since their low wages made the cost of a train ticket prohibitive. During the war, train fares increased slightly, making the cost of departure even greater. For blacks in rural areas buying tickets and boarding trains could also be dangerous or difficult. Sarah Rice recalled that catching a train in the rural South took courage and patience. At times, people spent days and nights in train stations, waiting for connections. Even with family in the North after 1920, the cost of travel remained a significant hurdle. When Allan Cole arrived in Cleveland after the war, he found only irregular work, and for months he was unable to respond to the pleas of his wife still living in the South. Eventually the two managed to purchase her ticket and pay off debts, but only after several years of separation. Because so many blacks left furniture and other personal property behind with family and friends, many later migrants purchased tickets by selling these items.[96]

Contemporary newspapers and informants claimed that thousands of black men were "lured away" by labor agents, but more often than not such rumors were unfounded. Some Cleveland employers did recruit, but they primarily confined their search for labor to particular areas and targeted specific populations, typically male ones. Labor agents from the Cleveland steel mills actively sought black workers in Alabama in the fall of 1916 but engaged in little recruitment through the remainder of the war. In at least one instance, steel owners simply shifted workers from a southern plant to a northern one. Feeling the loss of immigrant laborers, the New York Central Railroad, for example, sent agents to recruit southern black railroad workers. Promising higher wages and free housing, recruiters persuaded thousands of men to depart for Cleveland. Some of these men intended only temporary stints in the mills and yards of Cleveland, while many others decided to settle permanently and later brought their families.[97]

Investigators charged that these agents and recruiters often made false claims. Misrepresentation of wages and work conditions was widespread, and agents' promises that family members could eventually accompany the men were often simply lures. Black migrants to Cleveland reported in 1919 that they had been charged three dollars each for their transportation, of which one dollar went to a labor agent for the Lake Shore Railroad. After arrival, they discovered much of their first several months' salary paid for the tickets. In addition, many blacks were bilked out of their few dollars by men posing as agents. Some complained of threats and intimidation from whites. After 1917, employers ceased to recruit overtly and instead relied on information networks established by men already working in plants and on railroads.[98]

Black men who traveled alone had some greater flexibility in how and when they migrated. Some young men simply hopped freight trains. Gus Joiner recalled both the spontaneity and the danger of leaving the South through this method. At the age of seventeen, Joiner wanted to avoid the coke ovens and decided instead to see "the big city lights" of Chicago. Without informing his parents, Joiner "hopped this freight train one day" and headed north. With only a quarter in his pocket, Joiner was delayed by having to scavenge for food in Ohio and thirty days of hard labor in Indiana after police discovered him on the freight car. After several years of labor in the Chicago stock yards and a short stint in the coal mines of West Virginia, Joiner eventually migrated to Cleveland.[99] Joiner's decision to leave may have been spontaneous, but his circuitous route suggests that spontaneity could have dangerous consequences.

For many blacks, earlier moves to southern cities and border states made migration safer and less expensive. Because their families had accompanied

the South was more than sentimental or cultural. They had left part of themselves behind." Some women did abandon their children and simply disappeared, only to be found later traveling from one northern city to another.[104]

Despite the potential danger, some single women without children "roamed
and rambled" like men as they looked for employment. Age, better education,
and the lack of children, along with changing ideas about female self-sufficiency,
aided some young black women's mobility. Carrie Davenport, who had earned
wages from the age of six, joined a traveling Negro vaudeville show at the age
of seventeen. As a member of a female chorus, Davenport frequently performed
at midnight shows and then boarded a train the following morning. People
tended to see her choice of occupation as that of a "whore," but she continued to travel until she settled in 1922. Oral histories suggest that young wom-
en independently sought to take advantage of the higher-paying jobs in the
North, even if it meant continuation in domestic service. Thus, more typical
examples can be seen in the actions of Bertha Cowan, who left Lynchburg,
Virginia, with a friend; the two intended to "see the world." The young wom-
en heard about jobs in Cleveland, and they set about finding money and making plans to migrate. Once she arrived, Cowan then encouraged her family to
come when labor demands of the war increased employment opportunities.[105]

The decision to depart and the location for settlement was also determined by the availability of employment opportunities. Several studies have
illustrated the relationship between patterns of migration to northern cities
and the availability of employment opportunities. The steel and automotive
factories of Pittsburgh and Detroit lured more men. Cleveland, like Chicago, New York, and Philadelphia, provided favorable employment to both men
and women. Between 1915 and 1921, Cleveland became a major destination
for black migrants because of the simultaneous decline in foreign immigration and the expansion of manufacturing taking place before and during
World War I. Hundreds of letters poured into the Cleveland City-State Employment Bureau with requests for information about jobs and wages.[106]

Whatever the impetus to leave and means of travel, many African Americans linked geographic movement with their historic search for freedom.
This sense of mobility was typically expressed in religious terms. One man
recalled that the move to the North was like "moving to heaven. We wore new
clothes, carried our food in shoe boxes." Investigators picked up this sensibility in their descriptions of the migration as "an exodus." Using more secular, but nonetheless dramatic imagery, participants like Sally Hopson saw
themselves as part of a "great folk wandering." Langston Hughes, a migrant
from another Midwest city, described the influx of blacks into Cleveland
during 1917 as a "great dark tide from the South." Observers in Cleveland

attested to the waves of migrants flooding into the city. The *Cleveland Advocate* declared the movement to be "a REGULAR EXODUS. It is without head, tail, or leadership."[107]

The large out-migration of the war years became readily apparent, and state officials in the Deep South moved to prohibit blacks' departure. States quickly passed legislation to prevent labor agents from operating altogether or they passed high licensing fees and fines. In Alabama, nearly seventy-five thousand blacks (8.3 percent of the population) migrated north between the spring of 1916 and the beginning of 1917. State legislators passed a law requiring labor agents to obtain an expensive license. Those agents caught without a license faced a five-hundred-dollar fine and one year's hard labor. The City Commission in Montgomery, Alabama, passed an ordinance prohibiting any effort to "lure away" laborers to work elsewhere. Another ordinance made it illegal to publish, distribute, or post any information that might "entice" workers to leave the area or the state for jobs elsewhere. Planters resorted to threats, intimidation, and arrests of blacks on petty charges.[108]

These efforts, along with the cessation of World War I and continued race riots in many northern cities, did little, however, to halt black migration out of the South or instigate a mass return migration. Certainly the number of blacks leaving the South did diminish after 1920, but evidence suggests that this occurred in the early part of the decade. After the war, and especially after 1920, employers in Cleveland and in other northern cities circulated reports that they could no longer find work for incoming migrants. Nonetheless, agencies working with black workers and residents in the city noted that the number of migrants who arrived daily remained high. How many were migrants from other northern cities cannot be determined; a significant portion of blacks registering for work at the Cleveland Urban League noted that they had recently arrived in the North from Alabama and Georgia, two states with large out-migration between 1920 and 1930.[109]

Who migrated and why they left the South and came to Cleveland after 1920 did noticeably change, however. Increasingly, children made the journey by themselves. Some parents used the presence of extended kin and older sons and daughters to allow younger children to attend school. At the age of fourteen, Linton Freeman, along with his twin brother, left a farm in Georgia and arrived in Cleveland to attend school. Two older sisters worked as live-in domestics, paid for an apartment, and took care of their younger siblings on their days off. Here is a clear example of the ways that black women forged familial "links in a migration chain." Other parents desired to protect their children from segregation; in one instance, a woman packed her household belongings and bought tickets for her many children, all out of fear that her teenage sons would one day vocally reject the limitations of segregation.[110] In these instances, it is clear that women's familial responsibilities shaped decisions to migrate.

In general, migrants made their way to Cleveland through the direct and indirect aid and information provided by the already departed. As one investigator discovered, the most successful labor agent was the U.S. mail. "The Negro's success in the North has been far more effective in carrying off labor than agents could possibly have been." A letter in a mailbox with news of success had the capability of bringing "a new group to the promised land." The letters and stories of success provided a powerful testimony to hesitant would-be migrants. In addition, visits from those living in the North provided critical incentives. Within Brooks's family, no one had gone north until the late 1930s. "Well I hadn't heard anything about the North because I never known nobody to come no further than Birmingham, Alabama." Her brother left Alabama and soon urged Sara to come to Cleveland as well; visits from friends wearing new clothes reinforced her brother's efforts. Such information, spread through the everyday interactions of African Americans, ensured that while an individual may have been unfamiliar with the city, the community was not.[111]

In the decade after World War I, migration out of rural areas and into midwestern and northeastern cities transformed rural communities. Charles S. Johnson detailed the transformation in black households in Macon County, Alabama, as the remaining family members cared for children and aged relatives left behind. For some families, rumors of the whereabouts of kin and photographs "remained as almost mocking mementoes of a separation as complete as death." For many families, migration north provided an important option, particularly when compared with the declining farm and wage opportunities in the South. Henry Owens, the father of the Olympic gold medalist Jesse Owens, farmed in Oakville, a small cotton town just eight miles from Decatur, Alabama. Each year, whatever Henry Owens bought at the landowner's store totaled more than the price of the thousands of pounds of cotton he grew. Unable to read and afraid to demand an accounting, Henry Owens bitterly accepted each year's conclusion. Whether or not unusual frugality of the family and a higher yield of cotton turned the tide cannot be determined, but in 1921, Owens made more than he spent. Perhaps the landowner decided it was time to be rid of an overly productive sharecropper who was becoming impatient with the oppressive tactics, but he demanded renegotiation of the fifty-fifty contract to a sixty-forty contract that would be retroactive. The landowner threatened Owens, remarking that he needed to make an example of him for the other sharecroppers. Already past forty and fearful for his family, Owens handed over most of the family's personal property, including five mules, to the landowner and migrated to Cleveland.[112]

The sense of closing opportunities in rural life was sharp by the time Charles S. Johnson investigated black farm life in Macon County, Alabama, in the early 1930s. Black farmers who had managed to eke out a living at the turn of the century or who bought their own land had little to offer their children and grandchildren thirty years later. One farmer admitted that he had a few good years growing cotton between 1915 and 1927, but "if it wasn't for the boll weevil, it was the draught, and if wasn't the draught, it was the flood." More than anything, the lack of mechanization, the low price of cotton, and competition from other cotton-producing areas made his efforts yield increasingly little in return. In the end, one farmer concluded that he found it difficult "to figure out how to keep what I had" and pass it on to his children.[113]

The children of this and other black farmers found little incentive to farm, and the patterns of supplementing farming with earning wages in rural and urban industries no longer provided much help. Sara Brooks and her older brother, like many of their peers, left rural farms for nearby towns in the 1920s to earn a living for themselves and to supplement their parents' farms. The resources of rural and town households remained tightly interconnected, but each could be devastated by the loss of a crop or the loss of wages. Because of irregular incomes, many young men and women found it nearly impossible to set up households in towns while they worked in sawmills or in white households as domestic workers. Instead, they lived in abandoned shacks and traveled the distance each day to earn wages. Charles Johnson discovered that the demands of this pattern of wage earning fell heavily on women who remained behind in rural areas; more than 70 percent of these women combined all of the demands of housekeeping with farming. At the same time, men like Hosea Hudson grieved for his wife and young son as he moved from city to city in search of work.[114]

By the late 1920s, family stories typically included numerous accounts of migration to nearby or northern cities. Willie Ruff recalled hearing stories about family and friends who moved north. Though Ruff grew up in Sheffield, Alabama, during the Great Depression, he provides insight into how rural African Americans might have heard about work opportunities in the North after 1913. As numerous town ordinances were passed between 1916 and 1918 prohibiting the distribution of literature and newspapers with information about work in the North, the private and hidden world of black life became more important for blacks in search of information about migration. Ruff recalled that the newspapers read aloud in barbershops by black men and on the front porches by black families described "colored peoples lives," not the "doings" of white folks. Most important, black newspapers schooled would-be migrants in what they might expect in northern cities.[115]

African Americans who departed the Deep South for Cleveland between 1915 and the 1930s variously viewed their decision as a choice or as a necessity. For many black men and women, the possibility of more remunerative labor in the North provided a powerful incentive to leave farms and towns, families and friends. Many like Josephus Hicks and Sara Brooks made the decision to move north based on the presence of family and friends in the city. Whatever the reason behind individual and familial migration, African Americans left the South with the hope and the intent to make something better for themselves. These expectations combined with a host of experiences and values rooted in a segregated South and southern black culture provided a rich reservoir for migrants to draw upon once they arrived in Cleveland.

TWO

Encountering Work: African-American Workers' Experiences in the Cleveland Labor Market, 1915–29

> *The mills—*
> *Grinding new steel,*
> *Old men.*
>
> —Langston Hughes,
> *The Big Sea*

AFRICAN AMERICANS CAME TO Cleveland for a variety of reasons, but the majority of the tens of thousands of men and women arriving between the start of World War I and the Great Depression hoped to find more remunerative work. Newspaper advertisements in Birmingham and Atlanta, as well as those in the *Pittsburgh Courier* and the *Chicago Defender,* heralded plenty of jobs in steel, railroads, and services. Letters and visits from family and friends, along with rumors, lent credence to the reports of higher wages and better work conditions in the North.[1] By late 1917 wartime labor shortages and expansion of production pulled black men into industrial work at a rapid pace. The 1920 census documented that the percentage of men employed in domestic service dropped by more than half from 29.6 to 12.2; male employment in manufacturing increased dramatically from 29.8 to 63.2 percent. Though left with far fewer options, African-American women gained access to some industrial, clerical, and other nondomestic employment. Even those women who continued to labor in households found their wages were double those they had earned in the South.[2]

Yet in the World War I and postwar economy, African Americans encountered uneven access to unskilled industrial and service labor. On the one hand, a Cleveland manufacturer voiced the growing consensus among many of the city's large employers in 1917 when he declared that "colored labor is the only available class of labor at this time, and the manufacturers have made up their mind to employ them permanently."[3] Edgar E. Adams, owner of Cleveland tor of the economy. After 1910, automobile and auto parts manufacturing and garment making significantly expanded, as did the production of paints, varnishes, and chemicals. Wartime needs fueled the growth of these industries, and after 1919 the transportation, construction, and service sectors became large employers as well. By the start of the Great Depression, Cleveland was the fifth largest industrial city in the United States.[11]

The development and expansion of the city's industries between 1880 and 1910 depended heavily on the labor of an ethnically diverse population of immigrants, native-born whites from rural areas, and rarely on the small but growing population of African Americans. Between 1870 and 1910, the city's population grew from 92,000 to more than 560,000 as waves of immigrants arrived first from northern and then eastern Europe. Though the foreign-born constituted 30 percent of the population by 1910, they comprised over 70 percent of the industrial wage labor force, with increasing numbers laboring in unskilled positions. Cleveland's manufacturing capacity expanded and business owners attempted to compete nationally by consolidating production, cutting labor costs, and introducing new technology. The implementation of scientific management principles encroached upon skilled workers' control of the work processes; such changes established simple, repetitive tasks for the unskilled. These shifts in work processes led to the decline in industrial employment generally. In addition, the industrial labor force shifted from the domination of skilled laborers to that of semiskilled and unskilled workers. During the depressions of 1907–8 and 1913–15, this latter group experienced low wages, long periods of seasonal unemployment, and loss of jobs due to new technology.[12]

The population of African Americans was small, numbering less than 8,500 on the eve of the migration, but until the last decade of the nineteenth century, the percentage of men working in the skilled trades had been proportionate to their numbers. Kenneth Kusmer has charted their overall decline in skilled work between 1870 and 1910. Uneven and complex, African Americans' loss of skilled jobs occurred amidst the growth of unskilled work generally and the hiring of immigrant workers to fill these jobs. Equally important, the sharp color line in the American Federation of Labor excluded black workers from, or marginalized them in, the skilled trades of building and industry. But black men's entrance into the expanding unskilled jobs in manufacturing did not increase between 1890 and 1910. Employers had little need to use black workers when a steady supply of immigrants waited to fill the plethora of unskilled positions. These restrictive industrial hiring policies against blacks meant that by 1910 only several hundred men worked in mills and foundries as common laborers. A handful found employment in carpentry and masonry, but because of their exclusion from most of the building trade unions, skilled black workers typically were hired only in unskilled positions on city and road projects. The majority of black male wage earners labored as servants, barbers, and porters, though not in the more prestigious hotels and restaurants.[13]

African-American men found that steady, higher-paying work required unusual sacrifices. Elmer Thompson's father began laying asphalt in Cincinnati for a Cleveland-based company. Thompson worked year round for the company as a fireman, but was moved from city to city. By 1910, the company came to Cleveland, where Thompson decided to settle his family permanently. The company did not hire many black men, but those that did have jobs performed the most dangerous, difficult work. His son, Elmer, recalled: "[It] was extremely hot work and kind of dangerous too because you mixed the asphalt in those metal box cars (like tank cars). You mix it in there and every now and then the fumes would knock someone out and if you fall in that you're just through. They'd snatch your body out but the heat and the fumes were too much for you—you couldn't take it." The frequent departures from his family led Thompson to quit, and he returned to lower-paying work as a stable hand.[14]

As a group, black women had the least access to Cleveland industries, with the majority laboring in the lowest-paying occupations of domestic service. Between 1870 and 1910, black women steadily increased their participation in laundry work and household service. In contrast, increasing numbers of young white women entered clerical, retail, and industrial positions.[15] In a 1908 investigation of conditions in women's industrial labor, the Consumers' League of Cleveland discovered that only very young black women found employment in paper box-making factories. This work, notorious for its noxious fumes and low wages, relied upon temporary workers. "The fact that the trade offers little inducement in wages and makes no demand of highly skilled work while it has many processes of extreme simplicity, brings it the youngest workers." Unable to sit, box makers operated dangerous machines, earning between nine and fifteen cents for one hundred "well-constructed boxes." Because the work was of a "sticky, fussy, nature," most of the young women found it difficult to make more than one thousand boxes a day.[16]

By the eve of World War I, work was scarce for everyone in Cleveland. Shut out of industrial employment, blacks had held onto service work but even these jobs became hard to find. Interviews with longtime black male residents in 1914 revealed that many had been displaced in service work by immigrants. Though black men had dominated the service trades as bootblacks, barbers, and waiters, they increasingly found it difficult to remain in or enter into these trades. These men noted that employers, not unions, erected barriers to work and job mobility. By January 1914, ten thousand workers registered at the State-City Labor Exchange. Even during the summer months, when workers found their greatest opportunities for wage work, a hastily conducted survey of the various social agencies uncovered at least sixty-one thousand workers looking for work with few employers responding.[17]

Many Cleveland employers considered hiring African-American workers only when the more restricted labor market pushed them to do so. In the early months of 1915, the shifts of immigrant workers and native-born white women into wartime jobs meant that many companies continued to bar blacks from employment. Beginning in 1916 local observers noted that steel and railroad employers had started to hire hundreds of black men in heavy, unskilled positions. By the fall of 1916, however, employers had little demand for black common laborers, a pattern that continued into the winter of 1917. But by the spring, labor shortages of unskilled workers in the railroad yards, steel mills, and foundries forced many employers to reassess restrictive labor policies. Reports from the State-City Employment Service noted that after months of few requests for black workers, employers now competed for them. Well into the summer months, the large employers in particular "continually called" for workers, and some sought out and readily accepted black workers. Thousands of black men found employment in railroad yards, the blast furnaces, rolling mills, foundries, cast and wrought iron pipe factories, and malleable iron works. Others found jobs in the bolt, nut, washer, and rivet works. Both the Baltimore and Ohio and the New York Central Railroads hired black men to work on the tracks and to load and unload freight. Other employers, such as Swift and Company, hired black men for common labor and rough work in meatpacking.[18]

The shifts in hiring polices appear to have been precipitated as much by the expanded use of black workers as it was by the labor shortages in 1917. Railroads and steel mills moved thousands of black men into the city, often for temporary work in the spring and summer. In many instances, employers not only moved black men off of their own lines in the South but also recruited on others. Steel companies turned to the South for black workers, some for the first time; others drew workers out of affiliated mills, moving many hundreds of men at once. Word of recruitment and employment of such large numbers of black men drew thousands of migrants from the South and other nearby cities in the Midwest.[19]

In addition to this direct recruitment, African-American men had numerous opportunities to hear about northern jobs in southern workplaces, particularly the shops in Birmingham foundries and the railroad camps of

Kentucky and Tennessee. Investigators noted that "many migrants came of their own accord." Men heard about jobs from male friends and relatives and rumors of work in southern black barbershops, churches, and streets. Letters from northern relatives provided important details about wages, hours, and conditions. By the time many migrants arrived in the city, they had learned which plants and supervisors would or would not hire them. By 1917, many employers insisted that black migrants first register and be screened at the Negro Welfare Association and the State-City Employment Service, both privately operated agencies funded by large employers.[20]

African-American women learned about job opportunities through northern newspapers and heard about work from letters and visits from relatives. Women who worked cleaning railroads in the South heard about similar jobs in Cleveland. The majority of black women did not work in the large industrial settings in the South, however, and they relied more on personal connections and community networks for information than men did. Bertha Cowan heard about Cleveland at a funeral when Wills' Funeral Home in the city sent an embalmed body to Lynchburg. In addition, Cowan and an older woman heard that plenty of higher-paying domestic work was available for black women. Once in the city, however, these two women, like other black women arriving in Cleveland, hoped to find more options in employment. Most of these women were directed to the State-City Employment Service, where agents noted that the number of women in general and black women in particular who sought industrial work had increased, with few finding nondomestic work. Bureau workers who did place women in factory jobs noted that employers "had a great amount of prejudice in respect to engaging colored [sic] help."[21]

Despite the active recruitment by some employers, black workers found limited or circumscribed access to industrial opportunities. Employers hired black men either in small numbers or as the majority of the unskilled laborers in the large, open-shop corporations of the steel industry that lost immigrant laborers. Equally important, the decision to hire African Americans often coincided with a company policy adopted in other cities. National Malleable Steel Castings Company, for example, employed blacks in all nine of its foundries and steel mills.[22] Prior to the war the National Carbon Company did not employ blacks, but wartime labor shortages necessitated the recruitment of several hundred black men from plants in Birmingham and Troy, Alabama. Similar labor shortages compelled managers at the American Ball Bearing Company to hire black men as laborers in the yard, but they did not place them elsewhere in the plant.[23] The Grasselli Chemical Company, which produced explosives, did not hire blacks in Cleveland although it did at its East Chicago plant. The decision for Cleveland, however, was based on the plant's location in the midst of immigrant neighborhoods on the west side. White Motors refused to hire African Americans, but outside of Detroit, few black men found jobs in automobile factories anyway.[24]

Until World War I, northern railroad managers typically did not hire African-American men except as baggage and freight handlers. Regional hiring patterns of the Illinois Central differed markedly: on some of the southern lines black men predominated as firemen and brakemen, but in the North they could not hold any job with the railroad. By the late nineteenth century, the railroad brotherhoods in the North effectively kept black workers confined to yard work, and in cities like Cleveland the large immigrant population made a challenge to such barriers improbable. After 1915, however, these hiring patterns shifted dramatically as thousands of native-born white and immigrant men abandoned jobs in the yard for jobs paying higher wages elsewhere. Unable to hire enough new workers, labor recruiters working for the New York Central headed to the southern lines of the Illinois Central looking for black men to maintain locomotives and repair the tracks. By May 1917, New York Central Railroad reportedly brought five to ten thousand black men from the South to work in Collinwood and Linndale as yard laborers and station helpers. Investigators found that the Baltimore and Ohio Railroad had recruited thousands of men from the South as well. John Malone worked as a fireknocker for Illinois Central out of Louisville, a job he retained after the railroad recruited him to work in Cleveland. His son, Eddie Malone, joined him in the Collinwood yard of the New York Central as a mechanic's helper making the large grease cakes used to pack the axles and cylinders of the locomotives. Some of these men had held jobs as firemen and brakemen in the South, but in the North they quickly learned that a rigid color line barred them from their professions.[25]

In many instances, employers structured how they hired black workers by screening them before placing them in jobs. Though steel and railroad employers relied on labor recruiters, they also turned to the State-City Employment Service—first organized to manage casual workers—and the newly established Negro Welfare Association (which later became the Cleveland Urban League) to locate black workers. These structured hiring policies prohibited African-American workers' ability to apply directly to companies. Gone were the huge crowds of men looking for work. Instead, black, native-born white, and immigrant workers entered rooms segregated by skill and occupation. After separating workers into groups, the State-City Employment Service then directed workers to unskilled, temporary work or responded to employers' requests for black or white workers. Workers first visited company personnel managers, who implemented a variety of scientific management principles that had replaced the informal hiring practices of supervisors. Personnel managers continued to rely on racial stereotypes, however, to guide job placement.[26]

Despite the diminished power of supervisors in some plants, others continued to control the composition of the work force. Many smaller employers placed ads in newspapers requesting "good colored men" for specific jobs and then used supervisors to organize labor gangs by previous experience, age, sex, and marital status. All workers had to withstand the traditional "shakedown" foremen used to determine the "fitness" of a worker. Investigators from the Division of Negro Economics found widespread job selling by foremen, assistant foremen, "straw bosses," and "go-betweens" in Cleveland. A common practice amongst immigrant workers before 1900, this "pernicious system" of petty graft once again appeared with the influx of black workers. Hoping for more job mobility, some blacks reportedly paid fifteen to twenty-five dollars for low-wage jobs.[27]

Though Cleveland employers were hiring African Americans in greater numbers, most clung to older stereotypes about the "fitness" of blacks for industrial work. In many instances blacks' relegation to unskilled and common laborer positions reflected their replacement of immigrant laborers, who had been frequently confined to heavy, often temporary work with little job mobility. Employers had readily ascribed to the large groups of southern and eastern European workers an array of characteristics that made them unfit for anything but common labor. Often these characteristics included shiftlessness and viciousness, but few described them as infantile. In contrast, Cleveland employers typically described blacks as too childlike to do much more than common labor. One Cleveland employer expressed a popular belief that while black men were quite "happy and friendly," they tended "to overlook minor details which [were] essential for quality and production." Personnel managers regularly posited that because of sloppy and irregular work habits, black workers needed more supervision than other groups of workers, thereby making it impossible to hire them in more skilled positions. Employers variously claimed black workers were suitable for particular kinds of work or were not suitable for industrial work at all. One observer noted the irony of these claims, remarking: "The picture of the Negro as lazy and generally unsuited for strenuous occupations is thus to be set against the fact that he is often given the hottest and heaviest work."[28]

Despite the need for skilled and semiskilled workers, race continued to play an important role in limiting black men's access to higher-paying positions. In the steel industry, the largest single employer of black men, few found positions in the standard crafts. An assistant superintendent of a steel plant confirmed this exclusion: "We have Negroes in practically all departments, but we do not have them working in the standard crafts, such as patternmakers, diemakers, and machinists." By 1918, the Negro Welfare Association acknowledged that "numbers of black men" could not "find work in line with their training and experience." In the blast furnaces, for example, the overwhelming majority of blacks remained concentrated in the lowest skilled positions or worked as casual laborers. In the rolling mills, employers acknowledged that "there is an unwritten law that rollers' jobs belong to whites, and usually native born whites." Few employers reportedly inquired whether black workers had the experience for more skilled positions.[29]

As steel and railroad employers competed with one another for male labor, black men's wages, in general, increased to match those of white men in similar industries. Both contemporary and recent studies have found that with few exceptions black men did not receive lower wages solely based on race. In northern plants where blacks held the same jobs as whites, they received the same wages. Where differentials did occur, job classification, rather than race, dictated the lower wages that black men received. According to Peter Gottlieb, black men's lower wages in Pittsburgh were directly associated with their assignment to the lowest job categories and their weak seniority position. In Cleveland, the differences in black men's hours and wages from those of white men in similar industries reflected not only their low-level occupations but also their status as a majority of the work force in some plants and shops. Sterling D. Spero and Abram L. Harris observed that when blacks formed a large portion of the personnel of a plant "the general wage scale is frequently lower than where [they are] but a small minority." A 1918 study revealed little discrimination amongst black and white men working in the same industries, however, with each receiving an average pay of about twenty dollars per week.[30]

But scattered evidence of wage discrimination did exist. In one instance, "a well-known employer in Cleveland has made it a practice to employ a high percentage of Negroes. The wages he pays are notoriously low." Reports of discrimination in wages came almost daily in the city's black newspapers. Privy to the conversations of Cleveland employers while cutting their hair, George Myers claimed that members of the Cleveland Chamber of Commerce did not advocate equal wages for blacks. Other companies paid black men for piecework, though white workers received weekly wages. Standard Welding Company, for example, confined blacks to the heating room and the blocking and pickling departments, where wage rates were the lowest even though white workers performed similar tasks in other departments. Other companies hired black men to work on the night shifts, where they typically received lower wages for the least desirable and most dangerous jobs. In general, such occupational and workplace segregation resulted in wages on average as much as 10 to 12 cents less per hour than whites earned in the same jobs.[31]

With the greater number of African-American workers, segregated shops grew more common, which many employers viewed as necessary and desirable. To support their first view, they claimed that this system allowed for better supervision of black workers; to support their second, they claimed that white and immigrant workers would not tolerate mixed shops. Behind these two justifications, however, lurked employers' desire to use segregation and a heterogeneous work force to their advantage. The relegation of black workers to separate shops and yards created an illusion that the jobs they performed differed essentially from those of whites, both native-born and immigrant. By artificially creating differences through job classifications and assignments, employers maintained racial divisions and were able to replace whole groups of workers from one race with a group from another when labor was abundant or when attempts at workplace organization occurred.[32]

Employers may also have hired black workers to prevent white workers from either organizing or going out on strike, but more often employers claimed that white union workers would not allow blacks to be hired. Otis Steel, for example, defied the union, and by 1918 its shops were riven with work stoppages and walkouts. For months the company attempted to use black workers to break the strike, but to no avail. Only the cessation of the war and the defeat of the Steel Strike of 1919 ended white workers' walkout. By 1920, however, black workers were regularly hired by the company and armed guards maintained watch. In the fall of 1918, officials from the Urban League appealed to the Cleveland Railway Company to hire black men as conductors; the company refused on the grounds that the union would not allow it. This decision, however, had more to do with the company officials' policies about race then it did with the desire to respect organized white men: just months after the league's request, the company hired white women over the union's objections.[33]

When faced with limited job mobility, black men used the one recourse available to them—they quit, and did so at a rapid pace whenever better jobs or higher wages could be found. Despite the higher wages in steel and foundry work, blacks' turnover rate was high relative to their rates of employment. Employers in the foundries and mills complained that as a group, blacks made up 60 to 75 percent of the turnover, though they held no more than 10 percent of the positions; there was a similarly high turnover rate in the railroad shops, where a significant proportion of blacks held jobs. In sharp contrast, black semiskilled workers and those in the higher-paying machine shops had much lower turnover rates of no more than 25 percent.[34]

Employers read this pattern of behavior in a different way, justifying their hiring and placement policies on the basis of so-called racial deficiencies. Many cited the instability of black laborers as the most significant factor in preventing "respectable" ones from advancing. John T. Clark noted that the "general impression is that the young Negro from the South is a 'floater,' always ready to 'jack' his job in order to move to some other city." Others, such as National Malleable, linked the high labor turnover of blacks during the war to docility rather than any desire for higher wages. "The Negro is easily discouraged," claimed J. O. Houze, "and if he feels that he is not getting a square deal, the probabilities are that he will quit rather than protest." Some black investigators concurred with industrialists in their assessment of black workers. Emmett Scott, for instance, declared that while blacks were "loyal, willing and cheerful" workers, they also suffered from "shiftless ways." But he attributed the high turnover just as much to employers' practices of importing young, unmarried men from the South with "few responsibilities who register by their actions instability, irregularity, and general shiftlessness."[35]

While blacks occupied the lowest wage and job categories, they actually did not account for a major proportion of the labor turnover overall. Rather, the transience of unskilled and common labor remained widespread in Cleveland throughout the war. For instance, a foundry reported that out of 2,273 men who left, "two in every three had been there for less than thirty days and that fully ninety percent had worked there less than four months." As Emmett Scott suggested, "the instability of negroes is not so much a group characteristic as an expression of present tendencies in labor generally." Even Scott acknowledged that legitimate reasons for blacks to leave one job for another did arise. He conceded that "dissatisfaction with the treatment of petty white bosses, the necessity for ready money for the care of their families, the distance of the plants from the district in which Negro workmen live, and the unpleasant indoor work in certain factories" all contributed to the desire to leave one employer for another.[36]

Because of the conditions generally, some contemporary observers rejected racialized explanations for the high turnover of African-American workers. Employers acknowledged that blacks showed no greater tendency than other groups to leave one job for another. Out of seventy-five plants where blacks constituted 32.5 percent of the total employees, they accounted for less than 37 percent of the turnover. Investigators conceded that perhaps the higher turnover rates of blacks in some industries and occupations could be easily explained: in the face of limited choices, black workers accepted the only work, regardless of how temporary or disagreeable, employers hired them to do. When African-American men found more favorable labor and wage conditions they abandoned one job for another.[37]

Black workers responded to dangerous work conditions in similar ways. In 1917, approximately one of every eight steelworkers in the United States had an injury on the job. Yard laborers and night workers—positions that black men held in disproportionate numbers—had some of the highest injury rates. Such wartime work conditions had been highlighted earlier in hearings before Congress on labor conditions in the mills and foundries. Falling objects from overhead cranes, "explosions of hot metals, the overturning of molds or ladles of hot metal" made daily work dangerous. Steel work was hot, and in Cleveland it contrasted with the bitter cold of the winters. The photographer Margaret Bourke-White observed the Otis Steel Company in the 1920s, concluding that she knew "of no colder place than a steel mill in winter between 'heats' and no hotter place than a mill during a pour." The heat from the blast furnaces left scars and burned clothes; heart rates increased. In his autobiography, Langston Hughes described the physical and psychological impacts of these work conditions on his stepfather, who worked in a steel mill in Cleveland during the war years, earning "lots of money. But it was hard work, and he never looked the same afterwards." Despite high wages, the incessant noise, extreme heat, and long hours drove Hughes's stepfather, like many other black workers, out of the mills for less remunerative and more irregular employment.[38]

The inability to curtail the turnover of black workers any more than they could control white workers demanded the ongoing attention of employers. Some abandoned their belief in the free market, suggesting that the "cessation of advertising for help in the daily newspaper" or the publication of wage rates could stem the turnover. Railroad employers reportedly paid a five-dollar monthly bonus to workers who would stay for the summer months. These tactics suggest that while employers claimed to disdain young and unmarried black men, these very characteristics made them attractive as common laborers, particularly in the foundries. At National Malleable, for instance, young black men from the South made up a significant proportion of the laborers in the scrap yards and as the "shake-out men." Other employers sought to dictate the pool of workers from which they hired. By late 1917, some employers showed a preference for married and middle-aged men. Newspaper advertisements for jobs shifted from being solely race specific to include age as well. The National Carbon Company went a step beyond and filled jobs by race, age, and marital status.[39]

Industrialists turned to the Negro Welfare Association to help "adjust" and "stabilize" black labor groups to meet their demands. Some of the largest open-shop employers in the city served on the league's board of trustees; others regularly came to the league and requested "stable men." William Conners, the executive secretary, hired black social workers to "make Negro labor more stable, more responsive to productive demands, and more contented." These workers sought to steer blacks away from "unscrupulous agitators who may try to use them for dangerous purposes." They regularly went to shops and plants to admonish black workers to stay on their jobs. League officials passed out cards warning black workers to avoid watching the clock, arriving late, or loafing on the job. Blacks sympathetic to employers reproached black workers who changed jobs in search of "a perfect job. Well to be frank, we don't think there's any 'sich aminal.' It's up to us to make good now. Stay on the job! Don't be a grasshopper!"[40]

Black migrants entered Cleveland's industrial environment with diverging levels of skill and experience with industrial labor. Many had work experiences as common laborers in the South that had been highly segregated around race and gender.[41] Fewer, however, had acquired skills that qualified them for positions paying high wages. While most blacks had little access to skilled positions in Cleveland, the abundance of unskilled jobs enabled them to search for the best wage opportunities and work conditions. Their decision to leave one job for another was as much a response to deplorable work conditions as it was a display of self-determination, which increasingly took on a collective character. The Negro Welfare League found that black men left jobs for both higher wages and less segregated shops, suggesting that the high turnover had militant overtones. In at least one instance, such activism prompted the league to persuade one employer to cease "the practice of segregation of colored employees in the cafeteria" because it seriously affected "the morale of the men and [caused] them to leave their jobs." These quotidian responses to workplace conditions provided a training ground for blacks' future strike participation that would later enable them to join with immigrants in the 1919 steel strike.[42]

African-American workers in Cleveland openly resisted employers between 1917 and 1918, most often around the lack of mobility and the desire for greater dignity. Like other workers during these years, blacks readily protested low wages, limited job mobility, and long hours through work stoppages and slowdowns. In addition, black workers demanded, in highly collective ways, an end to segregated shops and the expulsion of abusive and racist supervisors. Though local black newspapers had chided black workers for leaving one job for another, open resistance against inequities based on color received support. The *Cleveland Advocate* gleefully reported in 1918 that black men had "laid down their tools and refused to work with or under a white foreman who continually showed hatred and prejudice toward his co-workers." A month later, the same newspaper reported that in another plant black workers objected to similar treatment from a white supervisor. Instead of a work stoppage, however, they demanded a black supervisor. When the company agreed to hire two, the workers then stipulated that they be chosen from the shop floor. In a west side plant, thirty-five black workers went out on strike when the company failed to give them more pay for work on Sundays.[43] These protests were not always successful, however. At the American Ball Bearing Company, laborers in the yard protested job restrictions and demanded access to work as cleaners and machinist's helpers. This protest elicited only promises from the company.[44]

Just as black men searched for remunerative labor, black women expected to earn money, but they found much narrower employment opportunities than those available to black men and other groups of women. Necessity, therefore, dictated that black women take advantage of the higher wartime wages in the jobs they already occupied and seek new job opportunities when available. Most defense industries wanted men or "specifically trained women." A study conducted by the Ohio Branch of the Council of National Defense reported that less than one-fifth of all women workers in Cleveland—4,192 women—moved into traditionally male employment. Cleveland industrialists explained their reluctance to replace men with women because, they claimed, such a move would "upset labor conditions." Instead, the council recommended encouraging and training women in their typical positions: as nurses, office workers, and volunteers. Even when women did move into traditionally male jobs, they did not receive equivalent wages. Instead the council found that "manufacturers are to a certain extent exploiting women with increased entrance into industry."[45]

Generally, few of Cleveland's war industries replaced male with female workers. If white women found few opportunities, black women found even less. From 601 responses to a questionnaire sent to industries throughout Ohio, investigators found that of 29,668 women that were employed, only 528 were black. The council discovered that in Cleveland "none of the firms indicated that they could use colored women to fill their present need for workers." The council only reluctantly proposed that a separate office of the Cleveland Free Labor Exchange devote its resources to finding employment for black women. But the general availability of white women workers deterred employers' hiring of black women for defense jobs. In late 1917, the number of white women looking for work increased markedly because of seasonal unemployment in textiles and Detroit industries, leading to an influx of 2,000 workers seeking jobs. In addition, shipping problems in fuel and sugar led to layoffs of women in the food industry.[46]

Even when faced with severe labor shortages in defense work, industrial employers did not readily employ black women. In the woolen industry, for example, manufacturers found it difficult to hire people to make military blankets, the least desirable work because of the low piece rates, but they refused to hire black women. Some employers did hire them in nondefense work as rag sorters and ribbon makers, the most poorly paid work in the garment trades. Some black women found work as pressers since employers felt the job was particularly suited to black women because "the Negro can stand heat better than a white girl." This was a reversal of the prewar occupational structure. Prior to the war, pressing had been dominated by men; as it became more mechanized, some occupations became unskilled and lower paid. By the end of the war, the Negro Welfare League had found employment for only several hundred black women in box and bag factories, packinghouses, and carbon works.[47]

Black women found the most opportunities for higher wages working for the railroads as common laborers. Before the war, white women, and only occasionally black women, had held some jobs cleaning offices, working in cafeterias, cleaning coaches, and mending upholstery. When better-paying industrial jobs lured men away from the big yards, railroad managers considered using convicts from the penitentiary to do heavy work. Instead of convicts, however, the railroad hired hundreds of women as laborers in the roundhouses, scrap yards, and docks for the New York Central, Baltimore and Ohio, and Pennsylvania Railroads. By the summer of 1918, numbers of black women had jobs as truckers, shearers, and yard workers sorting and hauling scrap and freight. Some of these women had worked for railroads in the South and had migrated in search of higher wages; many others came to the yards after months working in domestic service. Though the women frequently faced cold winds off of the lake in yards deemed unsanitary and uninviting, they found the wages high enough to continue working. Some women who had previous experiences in the railroads before the war found that their wages nearly doubled between early 1917 and late 1918; moreover, they found the work steadier than either common labor in factories or daywork in households. Married women with children noted that the early hours allowed them time to care for households and children.[48]

The heavy work and unsanitary yards led both the Labor Committee on Women for the Ohio Branch of the National Council on Defense and the

Women's Service Section to investigate local conditions. Unlike factory laborers, women railroad workers had no protection from laws that restricted the weight of packages. Those working in mail and freight handling typically lifted heavy furniture and boxes. Women noted that men often helped with the heaviest loads or the women worked in teams. Nonetheless, investigators from the Women's Service Section recommended that the railroad cease hiring women for common labor in the yards. By the fall of 1919 Cleveland women lost these better-paying jobs, and black women were the first to be fired and the last to be hired.[49]

Baltimore and Ohio officials admitted that black women performed more strenuous work than was popularly consider appropriate for women at the time, but they claimed the women had agreed to accept these conditions. One company personnel manager baldly stated that "the women who will offer themselves are likely to be married women who may already have suffered injury through incompetent or no medical attention at childbirth." In this instance, the sexual division of labor appeared more breachable because many employers viewed black women's physical capabilities as falling outside traditional norms for women. At a time when employers restricted white women from many jobs that required heavy labor, they nonetheless hired black women, believing that they were sturdier or already injured and, therefore, could withstand the physical demands. New York Central Railroad supervisors, in particular, perceived black and immigrant women as better suited to hard work than American-born white women. More to the point, employers claimed black women could work more like men because their lives differed inherently from those of white women.[50]

Despite the often strenuous labor and unpleasant work conditions, black women continued to seek out these jobs because they earned higher wages than they might have in domestic service. Even when black women found work with lower wages, the high turnover of workers generally meant that many black women hoped to move into jobs with better wages. Robert Lee Nickerson, a young black woman who left cleaning floors in a hospital to work in the railroad yard as a cleaner, soon moved into the scrap yard. When a male shearer became injured, Nickerson took over the shearing machine used to cut metal scraps into pieces that made them more manageable for women to carry. After weeks of handling the machine, Nickerson claimed the job as her own and then filed a report seeking the higher wage earned by the other male shearers. Though the yard foreman had not recommended that Nickerson receive the higher wage, he conceded that she "could tell the different classes of material and could direct the others what to do."[51] Nickerson's assertiveness may have been unusual, but her actions nonetheless suggest the kind of calculations that many black women made about how they would work.

Such calculus was most apparent in the job decisions made by black women who cleaned Pullman coaches. Before the war, the Pullman Company had hired immigrant women to clean inside its coaches in the New York Central Yards. The demand for workers generally, and for male workers in particular, nearly doubled the wages of women coach cleaners from seventeen cents per hour to thirty-three cents per hour. The smaller pool of male workers forced the Pullman Company to hire black women and some white women to clean the exterior of the cars, at which they earned less money than men but more money than inside cleaners, which offset their laboring in the year-round sharp winds that blew off Lake Erie. Since wartime legislation stipulated that women were not allowed to climb ladders and pull down the windows to clean, however, railroad supervisors did not intend to hire more women.[52]

Black women who cleaned inside the coaches managed a modicum of control over how they labored. By mid-1919 Katey Hogan, a black migrant from Georgia, had become a forewoman and directed gangs of black coach cleaners, all of whom had earned reputations as the most efficient workers. Working in teams of two, these women cleaned thirty to forty cars a day, sometimes more. Hogan assigned the jobs, with no one woman performing more work than another. Rather than demand that the women reclean, she followed behind the teams, mending curtains and cleaning spots they missed. Her teams' successes allowed Hogan to control the pace of their work and make recommendations about the hiring of black women. Though she informed the supervisor "not to send her 'any of these yellow ones to works for her, theys thinks they are white and don't knows how to work,'" her command spoke more about white women, who were perceived as less efficient and thorough in their cleaning. In the end, the foreman may have relied on stereotypes as much as Hogan's advice, but he decided that black women, and not whites, were preferable as workers. As Pullman coach cleaners during the war, black women had higher wages and limited access to a union, two features that other black women cleaning offices and yards could not claim.[53]

Yet black women railroad workers experienced and battled daily indignities in the yards. Women who cleaned the yards and offices had onerous hours and schedules, requiring many to arrive before dawn. Coach cleaners faced potential injuries, since railroad supervisors no longer allowed blue flags outside the cars when the cleaners were inside; without the flags, incoming cars frequently bumped the cars parked on the tracks. When black and white men and white women were more readily available for work, particularly during the winter months, railroad employers either did not hire black women or reassigned them to other lower-wage work. As the war waned, railroad employers ceased to hire them at all. Many black and white women performed similar work, but different job classifications meant that black women were assigned separate, unsanitary toilets and soiled, drafty lunchrooms. Even when black women had access to better facilities, they used separate basins and sat at separate tables from white women.[54]

Black women regularly resisted these indignities, often in collective and covert ways. Railroad women sought higher wages and steadier work, but they did not necessarily accept that either the work itself or their race and gender prevented them from maintaining their dignity. As Eric Arneson has noted, white men controlled gradations of work through their powerful railroad brotherhoods and considered themselves part of the American "labor aristocracy."[55] This point was not lost on many black women who cleaned up the much better restrooms and lunchrooms used by white men. Black women resisted the exclusionary practices of white employers and white railroad workers. Robert Lee Nickerson's repeated and successful appeal to increase her wage arose out of the desire to have her skill acknowledged. One black woman was so insistent that she be treated like a "lady" that both black and white workers and their supervisor made sure she never lifted or carried heavy objects. Well aware of the company policy requiring all workers to use the public restrooms assigned to their specific job classifications, Katey Hogan apparently did not ask her coach cleaners to comply. Instead of using their unsanitary and drafty outhouses, the women used the toilets in the coaches, soiling the tracks below. Much to the frustration of railroad supervisors who sought to stop the practice, the black male track cleaners sympathized with the women and cleaned the tracks rather than report the violation of company policy.[56]

African-American women found most of their new employment opportunities following the mechanization of black women's traditional field: laundries. Although married women and single heads of households continued to take in laundry in their homes, increasing numbers of black women found positions in mechanized steam laundries. This access denoted an important shift in hiring policies, since industrial laundry work had been virtually closed to black women prior to 1915. In the course of a day, laundry workers were often moved from sorting and marking to machines, which may have accounted for the earlier lack of black women workers. A report completed for the Division of Negro Economics revealed the predominance of black women in laundry work by the end of the war. According to the report, "power laundry work has furnished the opportunity for many Negro girls and women to earn a livelihood. In considerable numbers they have [moved] into the factory. This permits escape from the more undesirable conditions of the household laundry service." By the end of the decade, mechanized laundries became the largest single employer of women, and as in Chicago, black women accounted for at least half of the female industrial laundry laborers.[57]

Black women found steadier employment and higher wages in mechanized laundries than they had in home laundry work, though the hours were longer, the work was more strenuous, and the wages did not necessarily provide greater economic stability. With the proliferation of larger mechanized laundries, employers found it difficult to find white women willing to accept the unpleasant work and increasingly lower wages of the less-mechanized operations. As a result, black women generally worked in the least mechanized positions and laundries, where they found "little objection to them or color discrimination against them." In these older places the machinery was constructed with little "consideration for the operator." Even in the most mechanized laundries, women often labored in poorly ventilated rooms since employers claimed open windows blew soot on the clean laundry. African-American women in the sorting and marking rooms worked in the most "unpleasant and unhygienic" conditions; pressers had to continually hop from "one [foot] to the other." Those women who worked as manglers stood at steaming machines in a hot, low-ceilinged room. Despite the high wages, many black women found the work to be heavy and disagreeable. Marie Crawford, for example, worked for one dollar a day at Independent Laundry until the detergent made her too sick to continue.[58]

Between 1915 and 1920, three-quarters of African-American female wage earners continued to labor in household service, though even in this occupation women found that the war increased their wages, particularly in the summer months. Staff members in the Women's Division of the Cleveland State-City Employment Service lamented in 1915 that they had difficulty finding enough "general housework girls due to reduced immigration." Yet many employers only reluctantly hired black women. Instead, the black women were directed toward daywork, the lowest-paying and least desirable positions. With so few jobs beyond household positions available, black women moved to make the most of daywork. By 1917, women like Bertha Cowan and Margorie Glass readily found jobs as domestic workers with white families. In a report for the Urban League in April 1919, however, the executive secretary noted that many employers had hired black women for the first time.[59]

Once she arrived in Cleveland, Bertha Cowan immediately found help from other blacks, who told her where to work; men working for hotels passed on inquiries for domestic workers made by whites. With this information,

Cowan carefully chose where she intended to work. Other women made similar choices, though they were always aware of their more limited options for employment. Newspaper ads in wake of the migration frequently stipulated that only "intelligent colored girls from the South" should apply. Whenever possible, black women sought higher-paying nondomestic work, even when the work was common labor. With the shortage of black men and white women for service work generally, black women worked as cleaners for hotels, offices, and stores, abandoning lower-paying household work. For some black women, the shift into previously male- and white-female-dominated service employment provided more than higher salaries. As Mary Louise Williams discovered, obtaining "a man's job" as a steward in a hotel gave her "the joy of a position and salary instead of a job and wages." Williams did not have this position for long: "Peace was declared and with it came the return of the former assistant steward."[60]

Like other workers, African-American women responded to low wages, limited job opportunities, and undesirable conditions by quitting when better work became available. Aware that many of the jobs involved domestic work with lower wages than those of men and white women, African-American women had little incentive to heed employers' or personnel managers' commands to "stay on the job." Migrant women, no less than migrant men, sought "good wages," and quitting, not loyalty, remained the best route to job mobility. Despite the sharp rebukes of other workers, employers nonetheless perceived such moves as particular to black women, characterizing the "tendency to quit" as an indication of their irregular habits and irresponsible characters. J. O. Houze noted that the personnel managers at National Malleable found that the few black women the company hired to clean were impossible to manage because they tended to stay home or find work elsewhere whenever they desired. In response to complaints from employers, the Ohio Committee on Negro Women in Industry recommended that black women be required to give notice of their intention to quit. The committee recommended that local officials should teach black women proper work habits of "loyalty" and "efficiency."[61]

By the late fall of 1918, African-American workers found that employment of any sort had become greatly constricted. The cessation of the war coincided with the laying off of thousands of workers in steel plants and railroad yards. In the ensuing months, however, few new jobs became available, a pattern that continued into the spring of 1919. Employers reverted to the inclusion of race in help-wanted advertisements, often commenting: "No colored help wanted." Langston Hughes recalled that blacks and immigrants had much in common when it came to scorn, but little in common when it came to job opportunities after the war. "I soon realized that the Kikes and the Spicks and the hunkies—scorned though they might be by the pure Americans—all had it on the niggers in one thing. Summer time came and they could get jobs quickly. A colored boy had to search and search for a job." The postwar upsurge in the economy failed to produce an increase in local employment, and employers hoped that black migrants would disappear as quickly and easily as they had appeared. At a meeting of the Committee on Unemployment for the Cleveland Chamber of Commerce, a member expressed the common hope that blacks would willingly "return to the South, or to former homes." Nonetheless, Negro Welfare Association workers noted that more than 10 percent of the applicants each month had been in the city less than thirty days.[62]

Charles E. Hall, second supervisor to George Haynes in the Division of Negro Economics in the Department of War Labor, remained optimistic that in spite of the loss of jobs, blacks would retain and even expand their presence in industry. In addition to "securing a place in industrial employment," Hall observed that African Americans faced less hostility from white employers and employees than ever before. Equally important, Hall argued that the "gradual elimination of racial objection at 'the gate' or point of hiring" revealed changes in employers' hiring policies overall. At the start of the decade, the optimism that Hall expressed failed to materialize. The reports compiled by the Negro Welfare Association indicated that for increasing numbers of black workers "jobs were hard to find and hard to hold," particularly jobs that black workers had readily obtained during the war.[63] These employment patterns persisted over the course of the decade. African-American migrants entering the city after the war rarely found the abundance of jobs that had marked the war years. They joined thousands of other migrants who had arrived between 1915 and 1920 in the seemingly constant search for work. Those migrants who found or held onto jobs experienced stagnating wages, underemployment, and frequent layoffs.

The constant search for work challenges any characterization of blacks' occupational status as stable. Though the 1920 census reveals that black men had made remarkable gains in manufacturing employment over the previous decade, and though black men maintained a significant presence in these jobs after the war, other evidence from the remaining years of the 1920s demonstrates that over 90 percent of black men labored in unskilled manufacturing and domestic work. Throughout the decade, industrial labor increasingly became vulnerable to the vicissitudes of the economy and competition from white male workers, who found their own job opportunities increasingly circumscribed. The employment data for black women in these years reveals few lasting gains in occupational mobility made as a result of the war. As Kenneth Kusmer has noted, black women's occupational status remained stable—they rarely found opportunities to move out of domestic work. Indeed, their representation in household service returned to prewar levels.[64]

As primarily unskilled workers, blacks experienced bouts of unemployment and long periods of underemployment. In the first months of 1922, the Negro Welfare Association placed just 392 out of 2,142 applicants for work. League officials had greater success after 1924, but throughout the remainder of the decade they struggled to place a minority of blacks in jobs, many of them short-term. Some men still held on to work in the foundries, representing from 10 to 60 percent of the male workers (with an average of 33 percent) in the twelve largest foundries. Though some black men retained or acquired semiskilled positions, most were unskilled and casual laborers. Wage stagnation, technological advances that caused layoffs, and the decline in the rates of reemployment demonstrated trends in African-American workers' industrial experiences generally. Wages fell in steel from the wartime high of seventy-one cents per hour in 1920 to fifty cents per hour in 1922. Wages rose to sixty-three cents per hour in the midtwenties, but would never approach the wartime highs.[65]

Paradoxically, however, employers noted that after the war and the close of immigration, black workers were "the best buy in the labor market." While many employers simply relied on a "reserve army" of unemployed men, others consciously sought to ensure that black laborers would remain cheap and available with skills that could be used in a variety of work settings.[66] Throughout the 1920s, the large employers in the city banded together to coordinate how they recruited and hired workers. Under the auspices of William Frew Long, Cleveland employers organized the American Plan Association connecting management of black workers to their broader effort to manage the city's labor supply.[67] In the 1920s, Cleveland employers stood at the forefront of the open-shop drive, trumpeting its success throughout the decade.

Manufacturers managed the city's unemployed through the State-City Employment Bureau and other offices devoted to documenting and managing workers who sought jobs. Reorganized in 1920, the bureau allowed the unemployed to apply for work free of charge. As during the war, African-American workers found that they had to apply through this agency or with the Negro Welfare Association. Richard Feiss, whose family owned and managed Joseph and Feiss Company, served as director of the bureau. Years earlier he and his brother, Paul Feiss, had become "fervent admirers of [Frederick W.] Taylor," and had initiated the local drive to adopt scientific management principles; in the half decade before the war, they pushed to coordinate the implementation of welfare capitalism. As the largest employer of immigrant garment workers, Richard Feiss came to believe that employers could hire workers scientifically. Through his welfare work with the Welfare Federation of Cleveland and the State-City Employment Bureau, he believed that unemployment could be managed as well. Though Joseph and Feiss did not hire black workers, Paul and Richard Feiss sat on the executive board of the Negro Welfare Association and participated in coordinating employers' hiring of black workers. That these men vehemently excluded black workers from their own factory significantly shaped the management of Cleveland's labor market.[68]

National Malleable provides a case study in these postwar policies. The company had employed African Americans before the war, but by 1918 they comprised more than half of the company's work force of common laborers. Though a much smaller group, some black men worked in semiskilled positions as molders, core makers, and locomotive crane operators. A few blacks held positions as general and assistant foremen. What made black workers most appealing in the postwar years to J. W. Houze was the apparent willingness of a significant number of men to return to the plant each time when it reopened after a prolonged layoff. The "unreliable Negro worker" of the World War I years had become reliable in its aftermath because there was less competition for black workers. Despite their reliability, Houze admitted that personnel managers believed that black workers needed greater supervision in skilled positions than other groups of workers did.[69]

Employers in the large open-shop plants, therefore, did not simply rely on the vagaries of the economy as the means to maintain their labor supply. Rather, companies with a significant number of black workers hired personnel managers to place them through the help of the State-City Employment Bureau and the Negro Welfare Association. The Cleveland Hardware Company, which boasted the largest drop forge plant in the United States, had readily shifted from making metal parts for carriages and farm wagons in the late nineteenth century to making crankshafts and step rods for automobiles by the middle of the second decade of the twentieth. The push to increase profits accelerated the company's shift toward more mechanized production and the use of unskilled labor. The close of immigration forced the company to shift its work force from primarily eastern European immigrants to southern blacks. By 1920 it was one of the largest employers of black workers in the city, and personnel managers estimated that black workers would easily comprise 75 percent of its two thousand employees by the end of the decade. But the shift in work force did not come easily. Edgar E. Adams, one of the owners of the company, hired sociologists to manage his new labor force. With these experts, personnel policies could get at "the truth about the Negro" and not become "beclouded by the sentimental persons who have made a cult out of the Negro." Instead, the company increased its supervision of black workers. Both Cleveland Hardware and National Malleable used personnel staff to visit black workers' homes when they did not show up for work, echoing the "shackrousters" in the South.[70]

By middecade a number of Cleveland's manufacturers viewed the ready availability of casual laborers whose skills fit a variety of jobs as a triumph of efficient managerial practices. A. S. Rodgers, president of White Sewing Machine Company, boasted that employers had access to a large supply of labor, just as they had access to coal. When faced with an urgent need for labor, employers could find a fluid supply of workers in line at the employment agency. Rodgers commented that the abundance of unskilled labor had been a feature of Cleveland's business assets since 1923. Whether working in the mills or in the streets unloading and carrying, these unskilled workers made up what business leaders defined as "an indefinite class of labor." Their strength could be commandeered for "the heavy disagreeable work of the community, working here and there, unloading extra cars which have temporarily swamped regular factory gangs, or cleaning snow from our streets after winter blizzards." The state-run employment agency advertised that it had an available "class" of workers when anyone needed a "man to work around your yard, or two hundred strong backs to help out a large plant in an emergency."[71]

African-American men's relegation to unskilled work and temporary employment reveals shifts in the management of Cleveland's labor market. The economy of the 1920s in Cleveland replicated that of the national economy in its dependence on a migratory reserve of common laborers. According to the historian David Montgomery, "common laborers were not an archaic vestige of pre-industrial society. In fact, their employers included the most highly capitalized industries: railroads, steel, chemicals, mining, and metal fabricating." Cleveland employers depended on the unskilled status of these workers, and despite the dissimilarity between manufacturing and nonmanufacturing employment, the work processes in the shops and on the streets and docks had remarkable similarities.[72]

Throughout the 1920s, jobs in steel, automobile, and related industries had seasonal fluctuations that typically occurred in early winter and again in late summer. Only garment workers had managed to secure a contract guaranteeing work for most of the year through the International Ladies' Garment Workers' Union, one of the few remaining unions in the city with any power. Despite the diverse manufacturing base in Cleveland and the homogenization of skills, when workers were laid off from industrial work they often found it difficult to find similar work. One study on the fluctuations of employment in the city found that "few except the lowest paid unskilled workers have skills or abilities that can be used in other industries with peaks at different times." Only those who worked lifting and carrying or cleaning could "pass readily from foundries and auto body factories to printing plants and bakeries." Though this may seemingly have provided opportunities for black workers to capitalize on their location in unskilled job categories, many frequently found themselves in competition with white workers who considered common labor "emergency work." Moreover, the increasingly protracted periods of seasonal layoffs in manufacturing, which occurred between September and December, coincided with the peak of unemployment in service positions, especially those in hotels and restaurants.[73]

The experiences of black men in Cleveland's fluctuating job market suggest that the managerial triumph was unevenly distributed. Unlike in Pittsburgh and Detroit, where black men typically left to look for work elsewhere, increasing numbers of black men in Cleveland moved between hard casual labor in the steel mills to casual labor in transportation and services. Alabama migrants Daniel Jerome and Vincent Easter easily found work as common laborers in Cleveland steel mills during World War I, but by the early 1920s the high wages and steady work soon evaporated. Neither man could find steady industrial work, and for the rest of the decade both men cobbled together a variety of jobs as common laborers. They then took jobs as garbage collectors but found the work sifting and hoisting waste arduous and distasteful: Jerome discovered a severed infant's head dumped in the trash; Easter found that the stinking garbage made him constantly nauseous. By mid-decade both joined gangs of black men who cut and lifted fifty-pound blocks of ice from Lake Erie, later sold for home iceboxes. The icy winds and sudden thaws made the work dangerous. In contrast, white workers labored in the ice houses, where they loaded and delivered the ice.[74] For both men, finding and keeping work dominated the decade.

Both men's participation in transportation and service work reflects the continuing importance of these occupations to black men. From the start to the end of the decade, African-American men shifted from laboring on or around horse-drawn carts and wagons to loading and working with trucks and cars. Though the number of railroad workers declined after 1920, the number of workers employed in transportation increased from 22,706 in 1920 to 34,495; the number of black men employed in transportation rose from 1,561 in 1920 to 4,625 by 1930. Much of this growth came in the moving and carrying of goods on trucks; the number of blacks working in garages and filling stations increased in proportion with the number of cars and trucks. The majority of black men—53 percent—did not find work operating vehicles, but as laborers on the roads and railroads. By 1930, 38 percent of black transportation workers held helper's positions in the movement of people and goods (1,764). Just how many black men labored as chauffeurs and how many operated trucks is difficult to ascertain since both occupations were combined in the census. As chauffeurs, black men frequently performed household service as butlers and valets as well. Black porters had a fluid job description. Selmer Prewitt, for example, worked as a porter for a drugstore. His work included stocking shelves, holding the door for customers, and delivering prescriptions on foot.[75]

Increasing numbers of black men labored in personal service, while hundreds of others moved in and out of this occupation when industrial opportunities diminished or increased. Few black men labored in private households, but personal service replaced janitorial as the second largest category (922 workers in 1910 compared with 608 in 1920). Though jobs in stores and hotels predominated, many black men found such work only during strikes; others filled positions vacated by whites in search of better-paying industrial jobs. Unlike workers in the steel plants, white workers had successfully maintained unions with whites-only policies in many of the large hotels and restaurants in the city. During the summer months of the 1920s, however, numbers of black men found work as waiters and kitchen help in the seasonal restaurants and small hotels that opened along Lake Erie for vacationers. In other instances, employers hired black men for specific jobs—not because they were nonunion but because of the image of servitude their race represented. Chester Himes found work as a busboy at the Wade Park Manor, "a chichi hotel overlooking Wade Park." Though Wade Park departed from the pattern of the other hotels in Cleveland and allowed black men out of the kitchen, as elsewhere, white workers had the best-paying and least servile jobs. Even then, Himes became "tense and nervous and afraid" from the competitive jockeying for position among black workers seeking tips as porters and elevator operators. Department stores occasionally hired black men as porters, elevator operators, or shoeshiners; at Halle's, the most exclusive of the downtown stores, Langston Hughes operated the dumbwaiter.[76]

Though black men continued to labor in the service industry, they did not work exclusively in any single position. What made black men's labor experiences different from those of white workers was that during seasonal layoffs of industrial employment, they had to compete with whites for jobs in other sectors. In addition, black men and women competed with one another for jobs as porters and elevator operators. Even in positions where employers rarely used whites, blacks faced barriers because of the shade of their skin, marital status, and age. Murtis Taylor recalled that a friend lost his job at a foundry and went to find work as a red cap at the train station. Though the station manager regularly hired black men, Taylor's friend was told that he was "too black, too dark." By the 1920s, expectations of black male servility on Pullman cars had extended to the platform, where dark skin put many black men at a disadvantage.[77]

While employment opportunities appeared to have improved somewhat in the midtwenties, by the last three years of the decade layoffs in manufacturing and construction led to considerable unemployment of black men. The Cleveland Urban League repeatedly rebuked blacks' demands for industrial and building trade work and urged them instead to return to domestic and household service. The league encouraged blacks to accommodate themselves to the demands of employers and the contraction of employment opportunities. But such exhortations were disingenuous since low wages and competition from white workers made service employment as precarious as industrial work.

By the late 1920s, investigators for local social welfare agencies documented the growing presence of black men living in tent camps and abandoned buildings; members of the various committees created to study the problem increasingly perceived these men as irresponsible and undesirable. They viewed men who moved in and out of jobs as "loafers" and "slackers" and repeatedly blamed unemployment on transience. Many of the men in these makeshift camps were actually migrants in search of steady work. Unlike in other cities, however, in Cleveland men found casual employment more readily available. Thus they chose to live in tents because established homeless shelters subjected them to long religious services, tests, and courses on how to find work, making it difficult for them to look for jobs.[78]

African-American women's wage experiences in the postwar years contradicted any claims of "Coolidge Prosperity." The hundreds of black women who applied daily for work at the Phillis Wheatley Association and the Urban League attest to the narrowed employment opportunities of black women at a time when women's access to new occupations in industrial and white-collar positions had greatly expanded. The war had offered some black women temporary access to work beyond domestic service, but these few opportunities evaporated. After the war, the most distinctive characteristic of black women's employment experiences between 1920 and 1930 was their increased participation in household service as the importance of this occupation for white women declined overall. During these years, the percentage of black women wage earners relegated to domestic service steadily rose from 77 percent in 1920 to 86 percent by 1930. Their presence in household work increased from less than one-tenth to nearly one-third of the domestic workers overall. More distinctly, despite the occupational expansion of domestic service, black women remained confined to the most despised and lowest paid of the domestic service jobs: household service and laundry work. In both occupations more than half of the workers were black women.[79]

The second most distinctive characteristic of African-American women's employment during this period was the decline in the participation of married women, a curious shift given the expansion of married white women's presence in wage labor generally. In Cleveland, the percentage of black married women in wage-labor participation was lower than that of married black women in other northern cities. Despite the decline, fully one-third of married black women joined single black women in wage labor. This decline in married women's wage labor has been explained as a result of black men's increased presence in industrial labor, which allowed mothers, wives, and daughters to stay home. Yet black women's participation in wage work, as well as their wage-labor patterns, did not simply emerge as a by-product of black men's employment patterns. Rather, black women, regardless of marital status, found little employment beyond household service. As a group, black married women sought daywork, rather than live-in work. Certainly marital status and household responsibilities affected black women's work experiences, but they also experienced job loss more readily than any other wage-earning group.[80]

Black women's narrowed access to a range of occupations and their increased participation in household work differed markedly from the wage work experiences of white women in Cleveland. Although white native-born and immigrant women had long participated in household service, the overall importance of this occupation to these groups diminished after 1915. New wage opportunities in light industrial, clerical, and retail work provided higher-paying alternatives to domestic service. Although the occupational structure in domestic service expanded in the decade after the war, the percentage of women who labored in household service declined. At the same time, numbers of white women shifted out of household service and into work as beauticians, waitresses, and charwomen—all better-paying positions. By 1930, nearly two-thirds (18,431) of native-born white and immigrant domestic workers labored as beauticians, waitresses, and charwomen. In contrast, black women comprised nearly half of the total 12,950 women working in household service—a percentage disproportionate to their percentage of the population as a whole. Yet, while white women abandoned household service, they nonetheless returned to this employment during periods of job scarcity in other occupations. Thus, in the segmented labor market black women found that even the most scorned of employment—daywork and laundry work—often did not remain theirs alone.[81]

After the war black women watched the gains some made during the war slip away. Though the increase in the number of black women laboring in clerical, department store, and telephone employment had been almost imperceptible, their access to these occupations was nonetheless a hopeful sign. As one contemporary observer of the 1920s noted, "probably the severest difficulties in securing positions are faced by the Negro woman, because the occupations from which she is barred are among those in which white women most frequently engage." For no one was this more evident than for the few black telephone operators. Between 1920 and 1930, the number of black women employed as operators crept up from one to eight, all of whom were employed in black-owned hotel and apartment buildings. Black women who completed high school, whether longtime residents or recent migrants, found few job opportunities in clerical work; those who did tended to work in black-owned businesses and small offices for insurance agents and attorneys.[82]

Department store work, which drew large numbers of white women, was virtually closed to black women. By 1920, white women considered department store work as the most desirable, most respectable, and best paid employment available to women. Just as they had perceived women who were visibly working-class or immigrant, store managers considered blacks undesirable as clerks in department stores that catered to the white middle and upper classes. Susan Porter Benson has noted that though selling merchandise could induce displays of behavior that resembled a "well-trained lady's maid," white department store workers generally rejected work and uniforms that bore any hint of household servility. The presence of black women may have alleviated tensions around work that resembled household service. Department store employers may have claimed that they did not hire black women as counter clerks, but scattered evidence reveals that in several instances black women claimed to be white and found work as clerks. While many of these women deliberately fooled their employers about their racial status, they lived openly as black women in their own communities, which in turn supported the subterfuge. In other instances, employers sought out light-skinned black women for employment as bundle wrappers, stock girls, and elevator operators, complicating the qualifications for specific jobs. Henry Pointer recalled that the black women who worked in department stores "were real fair." Managers preferred that the women's racial identity not be obvious and they required women to wear black dresses with white aprons as they cleaned, dusted, and organized the merchandise. Though the women could not have contact with white customers, the tasks they performed resembled those of servants in private homes.[83]

The evidence suggests that employers relied as heavily on the hue of black women's skin as they did on race, but each criterion proved to be highly flexible. White workers moved in and out of jobs held by blacks and vice versa. While some of this movement could spark violence, as when black workers took hotel jobs normally held by white union members, in other instances employers defined and shifted the racial boundaries by which workers had to abide, even if only temporarily. Black workers came to understand that employers replaced one group of workers with another, depending on the labor market. Skin color was just another way to segment labor when black workers were readily available. They came to understand that if employers could construct race along the lines of the labor market at different moments, they, too, could alter how they identified themselves to fit their economic needs. That some black women presented themselves as white workers and lived as black women in their own communities is a dramatic, but not an uncommon, construction of individual economic identity. The willingness to pass to get work and its acceptance by other blacks suggests a form of resistance to employers' arbitrary construction of the categories of race and skin color.[84]

Employers played with the boundaries of sex as well, but most often with jobs they passed back and forth between black women and men. Denied employment as clerks, black women continued as elevator operators, commonly called "up and down girls"; they had gained access to these positions during the war as black men moved into industry. After the war, store managers considered black women "more courteous and just as snappy as men, if you get the right kind." In stores that had primarily white female clients, employers considered black women to be less threatening because they were not "saucy and noisy" like young black men. These employers considered young black women less likely to seek other employment and easier on the machinery then men. These perceived gender and racial characteristics aside, employers paid women less and required them to clean more than male workers. As one observer noted, black women found "little chance of promotion to a more highly skilled or better paid occupation, there is no incentive to learn other kinds of work, there is rarely any competition in the actual performance of the work, and there is seldom any reward for efficiency beyond a reasonable security of tenure of the job." Despite the characterization of elevator tending as a "blind-alley occupation" without much occupational mobility, black women continued to seek this position because it paid more than domestic work.[85]

But black women did not easily breach the barriers of sex. Even when employers preferred black women, postwar protective labor legislation required that women work fewer hours than men and have access to separate washrooms. In addition, laws prevented women from handling large packages and luggage; women could not work as bellhops, jobs they coveted because of the tips. Given these barriers, employers had to weigh the lower wages paid to black women against the limitations placed on women workers generally. Consequently, when given the opportunity, employers hired older black men.[86]

Though the proportion of black women laboring in mechanized laundries climbed over the course of the twenties, the majority continued to take wash into their homes. Laundry owners explained these patterns as a circumstance of customers' preferences to have their clothes handwashed. Home laundry provided many women with the means to earn wages while they continued to perform household work and care for children. Sallie Hopson remembers that the married women in her neighborhood did hand laundry at seventy-five cents a load. Scattered evidence demonstrates that widows, single mothers, and women with small children regularly or at least occasionally took in laundry. Other black women washed and hired others to help with the ironing. Collective effort, rather than machines, may have made home laundry competitive.[87]

By the mid-1920s, most African-American women, like Alabamian Margie Glass, found that household service "was the extent of employment." Glass came to the city to visit her grandfather and uncles in 1923, but stayed to attend school. By early 1924, Glass needed to earn wages but found only occasional daywork. In addition to competing with thousands of black women confined to similar work, Glass learned that white employers "wanted mulattos; nobody wanted dark people." The literary critic Mary Helen Washington recalled that throughout the 1920s her professionally trained mother and aunts "found every door except the kitchen door closed to them." Josephus Hicks remembered that his college-educated mother and sisters, all of whom had taught school in Alabama, could find only domestic work in a "private family."[88]

Though most black women wage earners continued to labor in laundry and household service, they experienced this work in different and subtle ways than they did in the prewar years. The majority of black women had labored in household service before the war, but they did not make up the majority of those in the occupation. After the war, however, black women comprised the majority, and they received an inordinate amount of attention by white and black social workers seeking to train them. Both the confinement to household work and the efforts to inculcate efficiency and deference shaped black women's work experiences, but they sought to shape and control their own daily experiences as well.

As increasing numbers of black women entered into, returned to, or continued to participate in household service after the war, they tended to labor as dayworkers and not live-in servants. Historians have explained black women's shift to daywork after 1910 as an outgrowth of their desire to meet both their reproductive and productive goals. A significant portion of African-American household service workers lived in or had households of their own, indicating the continued participation of married women and women with children in wage labor. More to the point, the long hours, employer scrutiny, and limited proximity to the black community inhibited women's care of their households and families, regular church attendance, and participation in community organizations. Emma Thomas, for example, eschewed live-in work because it did not allow her time to care for her own children, who had spurred her move to Cleveland. As a group, single women did not perceive living where they worked as an advantage. Many rejected live-in work because it isolated them from the black community, demanded too much work on Sundays, and forced them into constant contact with employers. Bertha Cowan and her many young women friends wanted time for church, social clubs, and each other.[89]

At the same time, the arbitrary hours and wages of daywork presented innumerable problems for women who shouldered the burden of a household alone. Some women turned to family and neighbors to help with the care of small children, but many others could not do so. Carrie Hughes Clark, Langston Hughes's mother, worked in a household after her husband left Cleveland in search of better wages; Clark paid a significant portion of her wages each week to a woman to care for her young son. Unable to stretch meager wages, women like Louise Pattengall's mother turned to alternative forms of child care when relatives or friends could not fill the void. Pattengall went to the library after school each day to wait until her mother finished work. "I became quite a reader from that," Pattengall said.[90]

Both married and single black women in Cleveland pursued daywork because they found that the conditions, particularly the low wages and long hours in household labor, undermined any advantages of living with employers. The majority of these women had done household work in the South, but many had not lived with employers. Many black women rejected live-in work because it duplicated the servile relationships with whites in the South that they found distasteful. Instead, many women hoped that several employers, rather than just one, would allow them flexibility in hours but provide greater control over where and how they labored.[91]

White women's increased demand for part-time and temporary household servants significantly dictated black women's movement into daywork. Between 1915 and 1930, white employers made thousands of requests each year to employment agencies for dayworkers. The postwar expansion in the number of smaller homes and apartments in Cleveland's eastern suburbs reflected the emergence of a middle class with incomes high enough to hire dayworkers but not full-time live-in servants. Most important, occasional help increasingly allowed employers to organize household labor and minimize expenses. Ruth Cowan has argued that gas stoves, washing machines, and carpet sweepers removed some of the drudgery from cooking, washing, and cleaning, but many women continued to use domestic servants despite limited incomes and technological changes in household work. Washing machines eliminated much of the heavy hauling of wet clothing, but they "did not go through their cycles automatically and did not spin the clothes semi-dry." A vacuum cleaner had wheels, but it was also heavy and cumbersome. Rather than employ several household workers for specific tasks, these women sought one general houseworker or occasional help to perform the heaviest, most arduous, and tedious labor. In addition, workers were frequently required to assume some or all of the child care responsibilities as well. Others hired black women as "mother's helpers" to perform only child care tasks. This work paid lower wages even though some workers frequently had to assist with other household tasks. Equally important, employers wanted household laborers who could perform a multitude of tasks in the least amount of time, preferably with skill and efficiency.[92]

While these demands may not have differed from those dictated by white women in the South, many black women nonetheless found northern employers too demanding. Unlike in the South, northern employers did not intend to "train" black women to their needs; rather, they expected the women have some familiarity with the new household appliances and northern diets. Ironically, many employers failed to save labor themselves through these machines, but they believed their servants would expend less effort and get more done. Consequently, expectations around household appliances and their growing availability became a means to lower wages and increase the demand for work. Many white women complained that black household workers had little experience with northern expectations and they particularly did not know much about basic household machines. Other employers claimed that their workers could not take care of good woodwork, wash fragile dishes, or prepare meals and tables for parties. How often black household workers balked at employers' expectations and habit of lowering wages by refusing to use the machines or claiming ignorance about how to work them may never be ascertained. Scattered but consistent evidence in employment agency records and from black women's personal narratives suggests that confrontations over how household work was to be done and how much it was worth were frequent. In the end, employers claimed victory by linking the lack of skill with lowered wages, an ironic assessment given the appliance marketers' claims that the machines did not require skill. For many black women, therefore, experience in domestic work prior to migration did not readily translate into a smooth transition into northern employment.[93] Finally, while some women chose daywork in order to have greater control over their own time, they also faced lower wages and precarious employment.

If northern employers had different expectations about black domestic workers, black women entered household work with expectations of their own. Many black women found that daywork in private families necessitated continued forms of deference to whites, patterns of behavior that they had hoped to escape when they migrated north. Instead, many of the women had to use separate entrances and toilets in basements that resembled indoor outhouses. Black women repeatedly noted that northern employers did not supplement low wages with leftover food and considered it dishonest to take it anyway. White women in Cleveland expected to have their needs and desires anticipated in keeping with servitude, but simultaneously expected their workers to accomplish tasks in a set amount of time like efficient industrial workers. Conversely, black women deplored the lack of respect, arbitrary hours, low wages, and elastic job descriptions. Bertha Cowan discovered that "it was [her] place" to be accommodating, and she was expected to accept it or go without a job. Cowan often chose the latter, deciding that if domestic work was all she could find, she did not intend "to be submissive." Yet other women like Sara Brooks took a more assertive stance. Brooks had employers who asked her to use basement toilets despite the availability of bathrooms upstairs. Brooks told these women that she had arthritis "and I ain't goin downstairs to the toilet."[94] The hoped-for distinctions between southern servant and northern employee remained elusive, but black domestic workers sought to make them.

Throughout the 1920s, black women competed for daywork with white women during seasonal layoffs from industries, hotels, and department stores. During these periods of unemployment, many employers used the availability of white women as a means to lower black women's wages, demand more work for less money, and exploit work conditions. The lack of minimum standards for wages and hours, compounded by the private relationship inherent in household service, meant that employers regularly and arbitrarily added tasks and hours without compensation. Sara Brooks recalled that she did not make much for a day's work, but even after an employer agreed on the wage, "when the day end up" she often received less. She had to either accept the offered money or find other work. Although Brooks began daywork in Cleveland in 1940, her experiences illustrate the conditions of household employment in the previous two decades.[95]

Both the complaints of employers and the repeated appeals for jobs by household workers alarmed professional social workers, particularly Jane Edna Hunter. A migrant from South Carolina, Hunter founded the Phillis Wheatley Association (PWA) in 1911 with the dual purpose of providing rooms and employment for single black women. When Hunter arrived in Cleveland in 1905, she became puzzled by whites' disinterest in hiring her as a private nurse—a common occurrence in the South—and approached a white physician. He told her to go back to the South, since "white doctors did not employ 'nigger nurses' in Cleveland." Unable to find employment in her profession, Hunter cleaned offices instead. She claimed that her contacts with wealthy "altruistic whites" helped her find temporary work as a private nurse, though she continued to rely on domestic and laundry work to make ends meet. The inability to find steady work, along with her training in racial uplift at Hampton Institute, propelled Hunter to push for a home for black women. Just as manufacturers had turned to the Negro Welfare Association to help accommodate black men to the needs of employers, the PWA became the location for a prolonged debate on the ways to overcome the "household labor problem" and induce black women to labor in more efficient and accommodative ways. Hunter received her greatest support from whites committed to saving young women from the streets and to racial segregation. As founder and executive secretary, Hunter fused accommodationism and race uplift with the new professions of social welfare and personnel management. Throughout the 1920s, Hunter repeatedly sought to train efficient household servants, instill habits of accommodation, and provide white women with efficient servants.[96]

Hunter encountered scathing criticism from other African Americans, who charged that the PWA provided little more than a Jane Crow employment agency.[97] Undaunted, she made much of the fact that the majority of employment agencies showed little concern for the plight of black women. Publicly she countered such criticism by claiming that the PWA provided important services in a restricted labor market and trained future black housewives. Although reluctant to admit that the PWA supplied white women with black household workers, Hunter nonetheless viewed the ready supply of unemployed black women as a means to solve white women's demand for household labor. At the same time, she sought to alleviate some of the financial problems that constantly plagued the PWA by forming a relationship with wealthy white women interested in trained live-in servants.[98]

Given Hunter's goals, black women's repeated demands for labor and employers' acceptance of daywork undermined the solvency of the PWA. Hunter viewed dayworkers as a nuisance and a challenge to the PWA's efforts to train efficient homemakers and professional domestic servants. She perceived these women as delinquent and feeble-minded, hardly worth having as the professional servants she hoped to train. Moreover, finding work for these women squandered the PWA's limited resources, which could be better spent on younger women who sought permanent employment as live-in servants. Hunter acknowledged that daywork might meet the needs of *some* women with household obligations and *some* employers without the room for live-in servants. But she attributed black women's frequent appeals for such work to their unwillingness to be trained and employers' inattentiveness to such training. Hunter did not appear to explore whether black women's repeated demands for work may have stemmed from the structure of the job market and the nature of the work itself. Instead, Hunter repeatedly urged the executive board of the PWA to focus on the training and placing of young women in permanent live-in positions.[99]

By early 1926, Hunter had convinced the board that the overabundance of "untrained" dayworkers ruined the professional image that the PWA sought to cultivate. Consequently, the executive board voted to discontinue accepting applications for such work. The PWA then attempted to implement a training program to foster live-in and long-term placements. At first, Hunter worked to establish intensive domestic training with a small group of women handpicked to enroll in the course. She attempted to attract young women with promises of references as long as they agreed to work without pay for a period of time at the PWA. This policy expanded to include laundry, a move that greatly pleased Hunter because it allowed the PWA to get linens washed "at a reasonable price." In spite of these efforts, most black women refused to pay the twenty-five-cent charge for each of the ten lessons required. Hunter continued to push for a domestic training program, but limited funds and women's lack of interest stymied her efforts. Always resourceful, Hunter required women who applied for daywork to take and pay for lessons in household service. Despite these repeated efforts, Hunter was unable to establish a complete program until the dearth of employment during the Great Depression forced women to comply.[100]

As Hunter sought to train black women, she hoped to train potential employers about what to expect from their servants. Concerned with the image of professionalism, she proposed that the PWA focus its attention on training the employer and employee to accept proper work relationships. For Hunter, a well-trained servant needed to display deference and attentiveness to an employer's needs, a return to the ideal of the master-servant relationship found in both the South and in turn-of-the-century northern households. Her idea of domestic training focused more on instilling behaviors rather than on teaching skills needed for household tasks. When board members wondered if the women would balk at domestic training, Hunter announced that if the women did not "fit themselves for work they [could] not come to the Phillis Wheatley Employment Office for work." Hunter remained purposely less clear about an employer's responsibilities. Some members on the Employment Committee suggested that the association establish standards; they concluded that if an employer did "not wish to meet the standard, a good girl should not be sent to them." Just what those standards may have been never received any attention.[101]

Hunter's focus on the behavior of African-American women, however, did not segue into the formation of policies to protect them as wage workers. Elsewhere, middle-class white women began to take a more critical look at how many of them exploited private household workers in their own homes. According to Phyliss Palmer, "middle-class women needed to clean up their own workplaces if they were to be credible moral leaders in the society at large." Unlike these tentative moves, the PWA made few efforts to require that employers abide by maximum hours for work, provide time off, or pay equitable wages. In the end, neither Hunter nor the executive board offered a sustained critique of the conditions that domestic workers faced. The board reasoned that establishing any criteria might alienate employers. Hunter did, however, encourage employers to mimic southern forms of paternalism by training young black women to meet employers' demands at significantly reduced wages. She then urged the board to establish wage rates that undercut those earned by white household workers. By failing to set minimum wage standards, Hunter hoped to forge long-term philanthropic obligations with white employers. Even when faced with evidence of exploitation, Hunter did not push the executive board to investigate.[102]

But Hunter's approach did not stem solely from a pragmatic desire to avoid alienating employers or to keep the PWA solvent. Hunter clearly held competing attitudes about black women's need for jobs and her own vision of proper household servants. Her failure to push employers to observe minimum standards grew out of her genuine belief that black domestics needed to adjust to their limited occupational prospects and acquire the necessary skills to become compliant workers. In this perspective, Hunter departed from others such as Nannie Burroughs in that she rarely called for the need to instill dignity in black women's domestic work. In private talks with black women, Hunter sharply scolded and criticized them for their failure to anticipate employers' needs and their lack of commitment to learn the skills that, in her mind, would make them appealing household workers and therefore competitive with white workers. She firmly believed that the racial dynamic would make black women indispensable in white women's homes.[103]

Black household workers' continued demand that the PWA provide daywork, along with their repeated refusal to be trained as servants, expose the ways in which they resisted Hunter's policies and perspective. A migrant from South Carolina, Hunter viewed black women migrants from the Deep South states of Alabama and Georgia as backward, marginally educated, and therefore unsuited for much more than household work. As director of the PWA, Hunter sought to cultivate wealthy white women as supporters of the PWA and employers of black women. Hunter may have seen live-in work as the most appropriate means for black women to fashion amicable relationships with white women, but the pervasive belief that migrants from the South lacked skill and intelligence made it all the more implausible that anything but paternalism would result. Moreover, during the decade, the demand for dayworkers far outstripped the demand for live-in servants. The logo on the PWA stationary, which depicted a black woman with bowed head pushing a vacuum cleaner, in the end suggested the habits that Hunter attempted to instill.

More generally, black working-class women openly resisted middle-class women's efforts to narrow their job opportunities. Single women and young women graduating from Cleveland high schools armed with clerical training hoped that paid household labor would be nothing more than a necessary route to nondomestic employment. Thus, while social welfare professionals lamented domestic workers' refusal to view household service as a profession, dayworkers were well aware that they performed tasks that their employers did not want to do. Unlike in the South, white women worked in "private families," too, but black women earned less money because of their race. Most important, black household workers balked at Hunter's insistence that they be servants white women could exploit.[104]

In the face of these intolerable work arrangements, African-American women turned to a variety of strategies to protect themselves. The most immediate recourse remained quitting. Brooks recalled that one employer "tried to work me to death one day." The woman later called to ask how Brooks felt and promised not to demand so much in the future. Brooks,

however, did not believe her and told the women, "I'm not comin back. I
didn' go back, neither." Brooks, like many other black women, took some
comfort from her ability to exercise the one option available to her; she recognized that her employer had to find another household worker. On the
other hand, the constant search for employment became an incessant reminder of paternalism and its attendant exploitation. Women went to the
Phillis Wheatley Association, the Cleveland Urban League, and the State-City
Employment Bureau, where their status as the most despised of workers was
constantly reinforced. They waited in offices segregated by gender, race, and
occupation, often for hours or days; typically agents directed black women
to daywork, the lowest-paying and least desirable positions. Frequently, the
women went for interviews with employers who often refused to pay for car
or trolley fares.[105]

In an effort to mediate the indignities that surrounded the search for
work, black women turned to their own networks. As a very young woman,
Bertha Cowan felt particularly vulnerable to the whims of the domestic labor market and turned to older black women and men for contacts with
"good employers." Men working in hotels often provided leads for domestic work, which they offered primarily to kin and friends. At other times,
Cowan went to work with an older live-in worker who needed extra help for
parties and holidays at her employers' home. In these settings, Cowan and
other black women met and looked over future employers. By the 1920s, black
women established their own employment offices in their homes. When Sara
Brooks arrived in the city in 1940, she found this system well-established.
"They would get these jobs," Brooks recalled, "and you pay them and we'd
be at the employment office forming a line outside in order to find a job."
Black women depended on friends and ministers to direct them to jobs where
they "would be protected."[106] When black women encountered abusive employers or those who paid them too little or not at all, they continued the
practice widespread in the South of informing one another about employers' habits and behaviors. They made public complaints at employment agencies. In the emerging small migrant churches, for example, black women frequently used prayer to announce the abuse of particular employers. Whether
public or private, through their complaints and lists black women sought
both to document and counteract the indignities they encountered in employment agencies and white women's homes.[107]

The increased employment was deceptive, however, since many black
workers knew that by the fall they would probably be without work. By the
eve of the Great Depression, the combined percentage of black men who held
service positions in transportation and domestic work nearly equaled that

in manufacturing. And, just as in manufacturing, the majority of men in these jobs were common laborers.[108] Thus, despite the gains made in industrial employment during World War I, the majority of black men and women continued to work as domestic and common laborers even though they had moved into new sectors of employment. Throughout the erratic economy of the 1920s, African Americans in Cleveland watched a stagnation and then a reduction of their occupational mobility, and the constant search for work was a critical feature of their wage experiences.

Yet African-American workers did not act passively in the face of employers' collective and organized efforts to limit their access to work. Daily resistance in workplaces and social welfare agencies took on a visible character as black workers quit, slowed down, talked back, challenged "the color line," and refused to live in. Certainly these efforts underscored black migrants' desire to acquire better work conditions, but such strategies highlight black workers' rejection of the efforts to accommodate them to a segmented labor market based on race and gender. However resistant blacks may have been to employers' hiring policies, represented by their high turnover rates, or their demand for work rhythms in keeping with household needs, the vagaries of the economy greatly undermined individual and collective acts of resistance. Moreover, when black workers sought to shape the work processes or prevent wage cuts and job losses, they faced not only white employers but also organized white workers for whom black activism was perceived as a threat, rather than a display of solidarity. To understand the varied responses black workers mounted in their search for remunerative labor, we need to explore more fully the range of relationships between black and white workers and their often fitful, antagonistic efforts at biracial labor organization during the 1920s.

THREE

"Join a Union": African-American Workers and Organized Labor, 1915–30

My dad always told me that anyplace you go,
where you are working, if anybody is organizing a
union, a gutter union or even a dog union, join the
union. That was his philosophy for me. I appreciated
that, because when I was growing into a man, I could
understand what he was talking about.

—Admiral Kilpatrick, 1980

JOHN MALONE ARRIVED IN Cleveland in 1916 to work for the New York Central Railroad. Born and raised in Alabama, Malone had migrated to Kentucky to work for the Illinois Central Railroad in 1911. Though he intended to return to the South, his wife, Mabel, and their children came to Cleveland and pressured him to stay. Mabel Malone liked the city, her ability to find work cooking for the skilled white workers in the yard, and the chance to keep her youngest son in school. By 1921, the Malones' oldest son found work in the yards as well. Work with the railroad put the Malone family squarely in the midst of the shopcraft strike that immobilized freight lines in the summer of 1922. When thousands of white shopcraft workers went out on strike, Mabel Malone and other black women cooked for the men, women, and their children. Though unorganized, African-American yard workers supported the strike with aggressive and successful efforts, preventing the railroad employers from bringing in white and black strikebreakers. In both the Collinwood and Lindale yards, black men refused to load and unload freight, letting meat spoil in the hot sun. Since railroad employers imported white and black workers to replace those on strike, race never appeared to become an additional point of contestation. Yet African-American workers' self-organized support for the strike generated little attention or comment from either the labor or African-American presses in the city. Years later, Eddie Malone, who continued to work for the railroad and joined a union, noted that his father "never spoke of unions; unions were for the white people and the Colored men did not talk about them too much that I can remember." Absent from Eddie Malone's memory or John Malone's conversations was any mention of the segregated Freight Handlers, Local No. 17210 that claimed hundreds of black members in the 1920s.[1]

The experience of John Malone captures the paradoxical relationship other African-American workers had with workplace struggles between the late 1910s and the early 1920s. Most remained excluded from craft unions because of their race. White craft locals' displacement of African-American workers in Cleveland from biracial unions for the building trades and musicians, along with the continued sharp and often violent exclusion from other unions, echoed patterns documented in other cities. As elsewhere, organized white workers' exclusion of African-American workers in Cleveland had a significant impact, and at the close of the decade black workers remained as unorganized as they had been at its beginning.[2] Added to these difficulties, employers mounted an aggressive effort to battle all unions, often pitting white and black workers against each other and importing blacks as strikebreakers. Added to this anti-union tenor, middle-class blacks tended to denounce unions generally as both impractical and unprincipled.[3]

While John Malone viewed unions as organizations for whites only, not all black workers during and after World War I were indifferent to trade unionism. Just three years earlier, thousands of African-American steelworkers in Cleveland sought to affiliate with the Amalgamated Association of Iron, Steel, and Tin Workers; hundreds joined the radical International Mine, Mill, and Smelter Workers. In the decade that followed the war, black sanitation workers pursued biracial unionism. Black workers in the construction trades encountered locals with policies that ranged from violent exclusion to cooperative biracial efforts, but they sought affiliation whenever possible. African-American hotel and restaurant workers sought affiliation with white locals; when faced with policies based on racial exclusion, black workers organized separate associations and called for recognition as organized workers. At the close of the decade, as employers aggressively sought to dismantle labor unions and while most organized white workers excluded black workers from their unions or relegated them to separate and unequal locals, black workers organized themselves.

Change had occurred in African-American workers' attitudes about organized labor. Black workers participated in several biracial unions before 1915, which provided an important countertradition within a larger pattern of exclusion. Many migrants arrived in the city having witnessed or participated in workplace struggles in the South, and they often built upon those work and organizational experiences.[4] Throughout the war and the decade that followed, African-American workers—overwhelmingly migrants—centered their workplace struggles around wages, hours, and dignity.[5] In these efforts they staged a dual approach to gain access to employment and claim recognition as organized workers. In whatever guise this new activism took, black workers signaled the desire to act on their own behalf. These instances of autonomous organization, however, did not lead to joint efforts by black and white workers to organize or to white workers' abandonment of discrimination. Rather, some of the bitterest strikes in the late twenties pitted independently organized black workers against organized white workers.

As the active participation of Cleveland African-American workers in unions and workplace struggles suggests, therefore, neither the model of their exclusion from nor their indifference to unions and workplace organizing adequately captures the range of their encounters with unions and workplace struggles. In addition, the varieties of organizations that black workers participated in does not reveal a bias toward biracial or segregated unionism.[6] Most of the recent attempts to capture the many tangled strands of the labor movement during the 1920s have focused on the South. Work on northern black workers' attempts to challenge exclusion in unions and their simultaneous pursuit of workplace goals remains incomplete.[7] In this chapter I consider the range of experiences African-American workers had with workplace organizations between 1915 and 1929, their patterns of participation as organized workers, and their self-organization.

Beginning in the 1870s, skilled white workers engaged in a vibrant effort to organize, and the city soon emerged as a center of union activism with a strong base of craftworkers. The Knights of Labor began the movement toward organization and reform. With the formation of the American Federation of Labor (AFL) in the 1880s, unions for machinists, those in the building trades, railroad workers, those in the typographical trades, and musicians emerged in rapid succession; some later established their international headquarters in the city. These craft locals first formed the Cleveland Central Labor Union in 1887, which was soon rivaled by the United Trades and Labor Assembly; the two merged to become the Cleveland Federation of Labor (CFL) in 1910. By that time over one hundred unions belonged to the CFL, three-quarters of which were affiliated with the American Federation of Labor. The Socialist Labor party also provided an important imprint. Max Hayes, a member of the Typographical Union and head of the national Socialist party, had earlier established the labor paper, the *Cleveland Citizen,* in 1891. Over the next decade, Hayes and his newspaper greatly aided the organization of the labor federation; Hayes used the newspaper to espouse cooperation between Socialists, their allies, and the more conservative AFL. After 1905, the Industrial Workers of the World (IWW) emerged to form the third strand of organized labor in Cleveland. Born in Cleveland, Admiral Kilpatrick recalled attending the meetings as a child with his father, a migrant from the South, and a IWW organizer in the city.[8]

But the route to a powerful labor federation was neither cohesive nor inclusive. First, the skilled building trades dominated the CFL, and they favored a marked conservatism after 1902 that remained in place until the 1930s. With the most members, the building trades union typically turned to boycotts rather than strikes, relied on the language of exclusion, and engaged in frequent jurisdictional disputes that inspired rancor rather than unity. Second, employers signaled an aggressive counterattack to skilled crafts workers with an increasing reliance on minimally skilled female laborers and unskilled immigrant men. Between 1880 and 1910, the International Association of Machinists (IAM) responded to these changes with bitter attacks against unskilled and immigrant workers. Other skilled workers formed agreements with employers, eschewed militancy, and established policies barring immigrant workers, women, and blacks.[9] Even after 1910, despite the dramatic increase of foreign workers, anti-immigrant attitudes prevailed. One historian of this period concluded that skilled workers "recognized the threat which the unskilled workers presented, but, burdened by their own prejudices, they were unable to seek their cooperation."[10]

The conservatism of the CFL and the power of Cleveland's employers were displayed in the garment strike of 1911. By 1910, thousands of immigrant workers labored in large factories and outside shops producing garments that placed Cleveland in fourth place behind New York City, Chicago, and Boston in garment production. Over one-third of these garment workers were women who were typically young, single, and immigrant and labored in low-wage, sex-segregated employment. In 1911, these workers joined the International Ladies' Garment Workers' Union (ILGWU), rejecting the long hours, low wages, poor work conditions, and seasonal unemployment that typified jobs in the apparel industry.[11]

After the creation of a masterly coalition that overcame ethnic and workplace schisms between older Czechs in outside shops and younger Italians and Jewish women employed in the large inside shops, the workers called a strike in June. They first took to the streets to demonstrate a powerful solidarity that crossed ethnic, skill, and gender lines; these orderly and festive parades sought to win the sympathy of the city's black and white middle classes. But the first wave of euphoria and support dissipated when the cloak manufacturers moved to split the fragile coalitions through the importation of strikebreakers, the use of spies, and the incitement of violence. By July, police violence, along with injuries and arrests of garment workers, overshadowed the issues of fair wages and hours. By mid-October, unable to acquire external sympathy and support for the strikers, the ILGWU announced the cessation of the strike. At no time did the CFL call for a general strike in support of the garment workers, and when violence emerged, the older craft unions distanced themselves from the women and the ILGWU. Unlike the other garment strikes elsewhere, cross-class alliances between workers and middle- and upper-class people did not emerge in Cleveland. The lack of this coalition converged with the widespread criticism of the violence. In the end, as one historian observed, the "escalating violence indirectly advanced the goals of the intransigent employers, legitimizing their unyielding position toward union recognition and worker demands." The loss of the strike dealt a blow to the ILGWU, and by 1915 fewer than two thousand workers belonged to the five garment unions.[12]

Prior to the war, employers generally used immigrant workers as strikebreakers, but they occasionally used African Americans as well. As elsewhere, white craftworkers perceived blacks as threats to the skills and honor of native-born white laborers. They charged that black workers depressed wages, particularly in the hotel and building trades. Consequently, organized labor in Cleveland followed in the historic paths of organized labor elsewhere and aggressively opposed black union participation through clauses in constitutions or relied on apprenticeship programs with prohibitive fees. In addition, many unions used threats and violence to intimidate and harass blacks.[13] Given the racial antipathy, white workers viewed the increasing presence of unskilled black labor as an economic threat.

In the decades before 1915, a handful of African-American and white workers either had joint organizations or belonged to separate locals. In the 1870s, black workers belonged to several locals in the building trades unions. Though the number of men who had memberships before 1915 was small, the carpenters', brickmasons', plasterers', and latherers' unions reportedly claimed black workers. What organizational forms these unions took is not clear, but little if any discrimination in wages and job assignments occurred. African Americans' memberships in other locals, however, did not go unchallenged. The newer building trades, such as the electricians' and paperhangers' unions, vigorously excluded black workers. In the freight handlers' and porters' unions, African Americans had separate locals.[14]

Even when organizations tolerated integration, segregated locals later emerged, following the national trend. The Musicians' Mutual Protective Organization, first established in 1887, exemplified this pattern. Charles Mc-

Afee and Anderson W. Bowman, two black musicians, were instrumental in the formation of the union. By 1901, the organization had become the American Federation of Musicians, Local No. 4. Bowman served as its delegate to the CFL and as the local's delegate for the Labor Day committee. Yet African-American musicians frequently received lower wages than white musicians; because of the increased segregation in many hotels and halls, they were also barred from playing. By 1910, the earlier history of biracial cooperation had dissolved into rancor, as white members failed to protest the discrimination against black members. The union broke into two separate locals divided by the color line.[15]

The need for labor during the war variously challenged or heightened these patterns of exclusion. During the war the American Federation of Labor's tepid commitment to organize blacks on a national level barely received any notice in Cleveland. State and local labor federations exhibited the elitism typical of the craft unions, and the rhetoric of containment and exclusion of black workers from the crafts abounded. In the labor press, skilled white workers argued that the newly arrived black migrants made not only unfit workers but also inadequate union members. In the arguments against the organization of African Americans, race and southern origin converged to cast them as backward. By the close of the war, editorials from skilled workers regularly expressed their contempt in sharp racial terms. One union member derisively wrote: "In some sections of the South the colored folks have got the notion, that the streets of the cities in the North are paved with gold. Stories of the fabulous earnings have also been circulated by employment agents and it is probable that when the warm weather comes the darkies will be coming along in train loads."[16] As national appeals for the organization of black workers continued, AFL state secretary Thomas Donnelly sought to bypass the call and instead suggested the organization of skilled Ohio-born blacks in segregated locals, a disingenuous suggestion given the limited number of blacks who were both native to the state and employed as skilled workers. Union leaders stressed to their memberships that black workers were ignorant interlopers and dupes of employers.[17]

In the midst of the war, the AFL claimed that locals had "no bar here to unionizing colored men." John G. Owens announced that "Cleveland labor unions have been admitting colored workers both skilled and unskilled into their organizations for years." And then Owens asserted something quite remarkable—something that would have astounded black workers in the city: "I venture to say there are between 4,000 to 5,000 colored men in labor organizations here. I do not believe there is a single union in Cleveland that has been opposed to taking efficient colored men into its membership." If

Owens was correct, than the majority of black workers in the city belonged to some union.[18] While Owens's claims had no basis in fact—and certainly were not challenged at the time in the local press—their reprinting in black newspapers in the South tended to escalate, rather than challenge, the sense that better jobs and fewer union barriers awaited them in the North. Certainly the CFL placed little pressure on locals to organize black workers. Indeed, throughout the war skilled white workers were highly likely to continue their exclusion and to walk out whenever employers sought to place black workers in skilled jobs. In other instances, white workers readily embraced anti-black sentiments when employers replaced them with black workers. At Otis Steel, for example, white workers went out on strike over the right to organize in 1918. When the company imported strikebreakers, many of them black men, the struggle worsened and white workers sharpened their attacks on the company. At no time did the white workers attempt to organize the black workers.[19] What black workers thought about such responses did not get documented.

Yet African-American men's desire to participate in workplace organizations was highly pronounced during what would become known as the Great Steel Strike of 1919. Efforts to organize steelworkers began a year earlier in South Chicago and quickly spread to the other steel districts. In the months before the strike when postwar layoffs affected thousands of men, eleven new chapters of the Amalgamated Association of Iron, Steel, and Tin Workers emerged in Cleveland, many with at least a thousand members. The International Mine, Mill, and Smelter Workers organized two thousand blast furnace and coke oven workers. After a year of organizing, the rank-and-file members demanded action from the leadership to stop the firing of workers and the lowering of wages.[20] Union officials, however, refused to endorse a strike, and the newly organized workers responded by abandoning the union in droves. After a meeting in July, a committee report warned that "the men are letting it be known that if we do not do something for them they will take the matter into their own hands. Where they are not threatening to strike they are taking the positions that they will pay no more dues until they can see some results from their efforts." By July 20, 1919, a strike vote was taken and union membership increased by 50 percent.[21]

The ensuing steel strike was part of the massive strikes taking place nationally in 1919.[22] The steel strike began on September 22, 1919, in the Pittsburgh districts, and by the close of the day most of the mills were shut down in Cleveland. Over the following several days three hundred thousand steelworkers virtually halted steel production nationwide. In Cleveland, eastern European immigrants, joined by thousands of blacks, rejected the deplorable work conditions and the unilateral decisions of the steel managers. They responded to organized labor's "battle for the fruits of democracy" and connected the larger political meanings to communal and personal interpretations. Immigrant workers responded to the political events taking place in their native homelands. By the second day of the strike, all but one of the sixteen steel plants closed, and nineteen to twenty-five thousand workers in Cleveland joined in this dramatic display of unskilled workers' strength.[23]

From the onset of the strike, employers used the specter of violence to intimidate supporters and instigate aid from the state to use its resources to reestablish "law and order." They simultaneously heightened anti-immigrant and antiblack attitudes and fear of violence. The local newspapers printed long lists of workers arrested for disorderly conduct, taking particular pains to identify the ethnicity and race of those involved. Street scuffles did occur, knives and guns were drawn, and bricks were thrown at streetcars carrying strikebreakers to and from the plant. The source of these attacks, however, remained largely a mystery, since witnesses refused to point out the suspected attackers.[24]

Steelworkers counterbalanced the tactics of employers with an immediate effort to quell street brawls. Chiding employers for importing strikebreakers and thereby inciting violence, strikers met arriving workers before they entered the plants and tried to persuade them not to accept employment. They pushed city officials to prevent the importation of strikebreakers. Mayor Harry L. Davis, a former steelworker, responded to the workers' appeal, and in contrast to other cities, the police arrested strikebreakers as "suspicious characters." Equally important to the strike's success in the first weeks, city officials did not halt workers' meetings, a successful tactic used by employers elsewhere. In sharp contrast to events in Pittsburgh and Chicago, Cleveland steelworkers held open, nightly meetings throughout the city. These meetings in schools, parks, and union halls drew support from the neighborhoods and unorganized steelworkers into the union.[25]

Black men actively participated in shop floor organization, street activism, and efforts to deter the importation of strikebreakers. Black coke oven workers affiliated with the Industrial Workers of the World at McKinney Steel Company overwhelmingly decided to honor the strike and then sought membership with the International Mine, Mill, and Smelter Workers. Once outside the company, they continued this organization, preventing violence and the influx of black strikebreakers. Their quick action appears to have dissuaded company officials from importing black strikebreakers, a highly divisive tactic used by employers in other districts. At plant after plant, blacks honored the strike, joined in the street demonstrations, and turned back strikebreakers with a minimum of violence. As the strike continued, black workers helped form the backbone of the union locals that rapidly emerged. These actions indicate a particular effort by blacks to prevent the association of race and "scab" that so readily leapt from the lips of labor organizers and middle-class observers in the other steel districts. Though a heterogeneous group of strikebreakers eventually found its way into some mills, unlike in other areas black workers in Cleveland were not primarily labeled as scabs.[26]

Yet African-American workers' support for the strike was not nearly so unequivocal as their widespread activism suggests. Like African-American leaders, workers expressed a variety of anti-union sentiments, underscoring their tradition of exclusion from unions and skilled employment. Even as the black press documented the numerous and widespread struggles black workers engaged in between 1916 and 1919, it also endorsed the Negro Welfare Association's efforts to prevent union efforts amongst black workers. Once the steel strike began, the *Cleveland Gazette* erroneously described the participants as "foreign workers," but it noted a widespread belief that black workers had finally found access to better jobs. Such expressions of ambivalence took on a more organized display at National Malleable, where long-time black employees, shamed by the behavior of black strikers, reportedly approached the managers and claimed to be "entirely satisfied . . . and [did] not want to see any of those troublemakers across the way come into our shop and cause trouble." These workers gave the names of both black and white strikers so that the company would not hire them at a later date. One of the managers, J. O. Houze, noted black workers "appreciated the fact that we were endeavoring to give them a square deal and they showed their loyalty" when they presented the list.[27]

Accounts associating black workers with scabs in other cities repeatedly appeared in the city's newspapers. The warning from the *Cleveland Citizen* suggested the negative impact: "Pay no heed to the shameless efforts that are being made by disreputable politicians, certain newspapers and other hirelings to sow dissension among them by injecting racial, religious, or political differences." The rumors and innuendoes repeatedly published in local papers about the return of immigrant workers to the plants and the repudiation of the unskilled by the skilled eventually divided the strikers. Though the union did not collapse until the following January, scores of workers returned to the mills and foundries as early as September. Despite the union's demise, African-American workers viewed their participation in the strike as an important gain in the city's labor movement.[28]

Whatever interracial cooperation was displayed during the strike, state leaders at the October 1919 meeting of the Ohio Federation of Labor remained committed to segregation in Ohio's AFL locals. Delegates from the United Mine Workers and Sanitary Drivers and Helpers' Union urged the adoption of a resolution in support of state legislation that would impose fines for discrimination against blacks in public places. At the onset of the debate, AFL state secretary Thomas Donnelly heatedly argued against consideration of the bill on the grounds that the delegates had not "properly" considered its implications for organized labor. Two days later the debate continued and Donnelly shifted to the claim that labor should address only industrial and not social issues. His stance incited an uproar; supporters of the resolution reminded the delegates that they had favorably considered women's suffrage and should give the same consideration to blacks' social rights.[29]

Unable to table the resolution, Donnelly then explicitly appealed to whites' racial identity as an embattled working class. "We cannot afford," he declared, "to take up a question that is without our pale." The demand to end segregation in public places would "bring about a positive injury to the class of employe[e]s in and about public places, namely the hotels, restaurants, and engineers and boilermakers and iron workers, *and all of the people that go to make up the public.*" Donnelly concluded his statement with an argument that not only spoke to organized labors' fears but also sounded the language of exclusion. Organized labor, he argued, could ill "afford to divide ourselves. We cannot afford to lose any part of our organizations; we cannot afford to lose any of our white organizations, nor can we afford to lose any of our white employers upon a question that is not a labor question."[30]

Though contradictory, Donnelly explicitly indicated that organized labor must avoid endorsement of legislation that infringed on the social rights of whites. He linked protection of white social prerogatives to protection of white wage earners; support for the bill could eventually mean that white workers would have to recognize African Americans' social rights. Most dramatically, protection of blacks' civil rights meant that white workers could no longer claim that organization of black workers was impossible because whites did not want to serve or be served by them. Finally, his careful efforts to distinguish "social rights" from "industrial rights" revealed that white workers implicitly recognized the economic benefits they gained from discrimination against blacks. That Donnelley's perspective eventually prevailed underscores the ways in which whites' racial ideologies undermined the creation of working-class solidarity.[31]

Though other components of Cleveland's organized workers did not readily accept the stance of the Ohio Federation of Labor, the policies of AFL locals set the tone for the decade that followed. The renewed racist convictions held by organized labor recognized, rather than ignored, the presence of black labor, made more permanent by the close of immigration in 1924. Overlaid with the rhetoric of black inferiority was the language of self-preservation of skilled white workers' unimpeded access to employment without competition from blacks. Faced with the precipitous decline in membership, powerful employers' organizations, and an antiradical political climate, organized labor hunkered down. Though protracted strikes still occurred, craft locals increasingly turned to boycotts and enforcement of exclusionary policies to hold onto their gains. Such weapons, however, did little to rein in employers; on the contrary, these efforts were leveled at unorganized workers, particularly blacks. Articulation of the right to control the workplace, joined with the exclusion of black workers, emerged as a conscious effort to combine racism with class consciousness. This vigorous antiblack response by the white working class constructed an image of black workers as tools of capital and unfit for union participation. In this context, racism and class consciousness were not at odds with one another; rather, they reinforced each other.[32]

African-American workers' active participation in the steel strike of 1919 meant that their indifference to unions could no longer be assumed. But losing the strike dealt a heavy blow to the possibility of biracial unions in steel and limited subsequent influence on organizing in other industries. First, the union's failure to organize unskilled workers in the strike's aftermath generally checked black participation in industrial labor unions.[33] Second, thousands of blacks lost jobs in the city's foundries and steel shops.

But the actions of antilabor black leaders proved equally detrimental to African-American workers' participation in industrial organizations. During the war, the Negro Welfare Association placed black workers in large, open-shop plants. With the visible support of black workers for the union, Negro Welfare Association officials scrambled to placate employers and remind them that blacks were "reliable workers." Several local social welfare workers argued that blacks could replace more expensive and potentially organized whites. In workplaces and church meetings, social workers warned blacks that association with labor agitators would cost them jobs in the only place where employment was still available. Barbershop owner George Myers proclaimed in print and to customers—many of them directors of the large plants in the city—that organized labor was "inimical to the Negro."[34] Such claims came at a time when employers sought ways to regain control of the workplace from what they perceived as the stranglehold of organized labor. Thus the various arguments leaders made linked black workers' employment needs to employers' desire for the open shop.

Few black community leaders expressed sympathy for the battles waged by organized labor. Throughout the war and after, the local African-American press and the pulpit viewed unions generally as not in the best interests of African-American workers. During and after the war, Negro Welfare Association officials actively supported efforts of management to discourage black participation in labor unions; facing pressure from white trustees, Executive Director William Conners did not detour from this path. Black workers found others to be equally disparaging of unions. In keeping with his public pronouncements, George Myers did not allow men in his barbershop to participate in the black barbers' union. These local assertions received support from national black leaders. In the pages of *Crisis,* W. E. B. Du Bois offered scathing assessments of the AFL, which, he declared, "is not a labor movement. It is a monopoly of skilled laborers, who join the capitalists in exploiting the masses of labor, whenever and wherever they can."[35]

In many ways, the Negro Welfare Association's financial ties to the city's business elite meant that its efforts were at odds with those of the NAACP to integrate black workers into the trade union movement. Abram L. Harris argued that "the advantaged Negro's hostility or antipathy to organized labor is as much attributable to his inheritance of bourgeois temper and training in American institutions as to the racial discrimination practiced by trade unions." Yet some leaders did express support for unions in principle, making careful distinctions between the right for workers to organize and the racist practices of most unions. At the 1919 NAACP national conference in Cleveland, J. E. Spingarn declared, "The challenge is the oppression of the colored man [*sic*]." The gathered representatives concurred that the greatest impediment to black workers' access to employment, skilled positions, and better wages came from the exclusionary tactics of white labor unions. Though Spingarn acknowledged that political agitation might "remedy discrimination," African Americans would be better served by "the economic strike of America's 12,000,000" black workers.[36] Black organizations and newspaper editors generally took an anti-union stance throughout the 1920s. While the violent riots in Chicago, East St. Louis, and other cities never occurred in Cleveland, individual attacks by organized white workers against black workers were not uncommon. Such occurrences fueled anti-union sentiment. In Cleveland, as elsewhere, many black workers joined the elite in viewing the "open shop as an avenue of escape from union discrimination and a means of immediate economic advancement."[37]

Large, open-shop employers hoped to use this anti-union stance to their advantage. Under the auspices of the American Plan Association (APA) formed in the aftermath of the bitter strikes that swept through the city's workplaces during the war, employers conducted a highly coordinated effort to dismantle organized labor. As the general manager of Associated Industries, William Frew Long became head of the APA. Virulently antilabor, Long intended to prevent union "lawlessness" and alter public opinion to favor the closed shop. Throughout the wave of strikes that rocked the city between 1920 and 1922, the APA stoked the fires of anti-union sentiment, which had gained momentum. Through public talks and advertisements, Long depicted unions as inherently violent and linked the closed shop to un-Americanism. Wherever possible, the APA exploited anti-immigrant attitudes amongst native-born white workers and the city's black and white middle classes.[38]

As part of the organized effort to dismantle unions, some of the largest employers shifted to new corporate welfare policies.[39] Managers endorsed workers' right to have representation and they sought to create a "family" based on personal relationships between employers and employees. On the one hand, some of these policies, such as opportunities to buy company stock and form company unions, were easily criticized as maintaining managerial power through binding employees to the interests of employers. As one historian noted, "workers themselves criticized welfare programs as poor substitutes for higher wages and a demeaning intrusion into their private lives." On the other hand, the health, athletic, social, and savings programs received high praise from social welfare reformers.[40] In many instances, however, the programs intruded into workers' lives, such as the policies established by the Joseph and Feiss Company through its Employment and Service Department. As the company's personnel manager, Mary Barnett Gilson not only made decisions about hiring and dismissals but also established home visits and admonished workers on their conduct and dress beyond the workplace. She hoped to eradicate the ethnically diverse workers of their native cultures and their predilection for "cheap amusements and attendance at cheap dance halls and movies" not because such pastimes harmed the work process but because she thought them vulgar.[41]

The new welfare policies were intimately connected with the maintenance of segregation. National Malleable, for example, sponsored benefit associations and clubs, provided entertainment, and encouraged scrap yard workers to plant flowers. Through the pages of its company magazine, National Malleable touted these social and educational activities as cementing "the family spirit in the shop." Similarly, the company sponsored separate monthly social gatherings for black workers, where "they have a general good time in games and dancing." But these clubs were segregated, just as surely as the shops and yards were. In addition, the company allowed only black workers with seniority to belong to these clubs.[42] These connections between segregation and welfare were repeated in other companies in the city. The May

Company department store used more subtle means to separate black and white workers at annual picnics, but achieved similar results. Dates for the outings were based on jobs, and since blacks and whites did not hold the same jobs, the picnics were segregated.[43] Yet the ambiance of family, rather than segregation, may have prevailed, and these social events frequently took on an air of neighborhood gatherings.

APA employers' attempts to reinforce individualism and discourage unions, regardless of their employees' race, had similar patterns. The long battle to halt labor turnover during the war had become one of their central goals in the 1920s. Just as employers made appeals to white workers about the material benefits of steady employment, managers attempted to instill desires for the new consumerism in black workers. In the employee magazine published by National Malleable, management defined the most desirable worker as a man who realized his social responsibilities. One article emphasized the relationship between steady work and social and material advancement: "A man's job is his best friend. It clothes and feeds his wife and children, pays the rent and supplies [him] with the wherewithal to develop and become cultivated. The least a man can do in return is to love his job."[44] In an article entitled "Take Care of Me, I'm Your Job," managers of the W. S. Tyler Company entreated employees: "From me you get food, clothing, shelter, and such luxuries as you enjoy. If you want me badly enough—I'll get you a twelve cylinder automobile."[45] These labor practices had one primary result: they apparently diminished labor turnover.

Other employers simply made the most of the long bouts of unemployment that marked the first years of the 1920s. An employment manager at National Malleable boasted that despite the closure of the plant for eleven months during 1921, black workers "came back more than ninety percent" from at least seventeen states. He was vague, however, on whether these workers were the same ones who had been laid off or if the number of current black workers had merely matched the earlier number. His praise underscored the double meaning of reliability; in the topsy-turvy labor market of the postwar years, employers depended on flexible and mobile labor. In turn, black workers with few industrial opportunities may have returned to employers known to hire blacks. But these policies did not halt absenteeism, which required that personnel managers continue visiting homes whenever employees failed to come to work.[46]

African-American workers viewed employers' efforts from their vulnerable positions in the labor market. Some black workers felt the companies that sponsored social activities were "dependable" and "fair," rather than paternalistic. In an interview with Horace Cayton and George Mitchell, a black worker stated that when the companies "made plenty of money [they] took care of their men. They are loyal to their colored help. They have helped them in hospitals and made loans."[47] As jobs became scarcer by middecade, those employers known to regularly hire blacks appeared to have been more concerned about them than were unions with exclusionary policies. Indeed, many blacks felt the segregated gatherings at National Malleable spared them from the open display of white workers' racism. Yet the company fostered such displays. At a dinner for white workers, for instance, the company held a minstrel show during which a "black-faced" white actor "performed in good darky drawl."[48]

Other African-American workers, however, viewed employers' welfare efforts less favorably. Most of the company plans required continuous employment for an extended period of time. Most employers allowed only the most senior black workers into the clubs. Many blacks became well aware that company policies revealed a desire to take advantage of their workplace vulnerability rather than any genuine concern for their welfare. Many blacks undoubtedly felt like William Davenport, who chose to remain at a laundry, despite the low pay, because of the frequent layoffs in the steel plants. He readily recognized that his employer relied on unemployment elsewhere to foster acquiescence. Moreover, as the *Cleveland Gazette* reluctantly admitted, many employers' preference for black workers arose out of a backlash against white laborers' higher "standards of living and wages." Finally, corporate welfare policies that made appeals to blacks' personal fulfillment did not challenge workplace segregation of labor. For African Americans, therefore, saving a paycheck to buy a car rarely meant a challenge to racialized hiring, placement, and firing practices. In the end, a steady job, not welfare policies, bound black workers to particular employers.[49]

The few African-American women employed as common laborers were subjected to some forms of corporate welfarism. The Cleveland Hardware Company, which made metal parts, hired both black men and women. Edgar E. Adams, one of the company's vice presidents and once an officer for the APA, hired black women in supervisory positions and implemented programs to adjust black workers to industrial labor. In contrast, companies like National Malleable found that while their welfare policies may have stemmed black women's turnover rate, they tended to take more days off than white women did. Personnel managers remained baffled at this tendency. Yet National Malleable had frequent layoffs and gave black women the least desirable work, and thus it is likely that these women took in laundry or had casual daywork as a buffer against forced unemployment.[50]

Employers' highly organized efforts to halt unions and strikes included screening black workers to discover any union involvement or strike activity. While many employers had attempted to use blacks as strikebreakers, the daily self-organization of blacks and their highly visible activism during the steel strike of 1919 delivered a warning to those who assumed black workers were antilabor. In an effort to ensure that such activism would stop in the postwar years, the APA Employment Department instituted mechanisms to screen black workers. By 1923 it had "paid considerable attention to the placing" of black workers as substitutes for organized white workers; it also coordinated these efforts with other organizations "looking after the welfare" of blacks. Throughout early 1920, the Negro Welfare Association helped to place blacks in numerous plants and laundries reportedly to "adjust differences between employer and employees," as well as to prevent strikes.[51] Such efforts revealed the intimate connections between the anti-union backlash and the presence of black workers in the industrial setting. Organizations such as the Negro Welfare Association took on new importance to the success of the APA.

Efforts to organize suggested that blacks were embracing their own workplace concerns, but they could do so by simultaneously endorsing workers' right to organize unions and denouncing racist ideologies used to exclude blacks. Influenced by a radical organizing tradition, Admiral Kilpatrick learned from his father and other black IWW members in the teens and twenties "that anyplace you go, where you are working, if anybody is organizing a union, a gutter union or even a dog union, join the union."[52]

Even when employers and unions agreed to relegate black workers to unskilled positions, exemplified by actions of the railroad unions, it was no guarantee that strikes would diminish or that blacks would remain disinterested bystanders. Black laborers for the New York Central in the Collinwood yards had long been excluded from the Maintenance of Way Employees union, and black men were confined to the most menial of jobs. Black men who were members of the segregated Freight Handlers' local did not join white railroad workers during the strike of 1922. Within the context of growing community support for the strike from union and unorganized workers, black men's scattered refusals to unload perishable livestock and freight sent an important message of solidarity. Black women joined in the most visible and demonstrative of union support: they set up large tents outside the railroad yards and cooked for the striking white workers and their families.[53]

Unlike the steel strike of 1919, however, shopcraft workers, families, and sympathizers could not gather together in or near the shops, so many turned to individual acts that took on a collective appearance. Railway workers confronted, attacked, or appealed to unemployed black and white men who arrived as strikebreakers. Women joined in harassing strikebreakers and urged them to return home. Wives and daughters of New York Central workers organized a house-to-house canvass urging them to stay home. Other women appear to have engaged in some physical attacks against strikebreakers and were subsequently arrested. Because so many workers and their families lived near the roundhouses, neighborhood organizations and individual efforts became critical to limiting the influx of strikebreakers. These tactics had some effect, and railroad employers found few responses to their appeals for replacement workers.[54]

Whatever African-American workers thought about unions, employers' efforts greatly curtailed and then crushed workers' collective power. Even when garment employers signed agreements with the ILGWU and other garment unions in 1922 to minimize layoffs during slack periods and retain wage levels, organized workers remained but a small fraction of industrial workers in the city. As a result, the Cleveland Chamber of Commerce stated with confidence in 1922 that out of 749 manufacturing plants in Cleveland, 73.0 percent had open shops, only 16.8 percent had closed nonunion shops, and 2.1 percent had closed union shops. Less than 100 plants had shifted to representative negotiations for individual contracts. Thus, out of 127,371 workers, 99,149 labored in open, nonunion plants.[55]

After the collapse of the Amalgamated Association of Iron, Steel, and Tin Workers in 1919, the APA began a long, bitter struggle to dismantle the building trades unions, which formed the heart of the AFL's strength in Cleveland. Taking advantage of the wartime building boom, unions secured higher wages, closed shops, and shorter hours. The unions reduced the use of laborers and greatly controlled the number of apprenticeships. By the close of the war, 90 percent of the building trades workers were organized. In the aftermath of such gains, the building employers and the Building Trades Council engaged in a bitter and violent battle over wages, hours, and work rules. Just as the city began to thaw in the spring of 1921, the building trades responded to the APA's efforts with a five-week strike. Anxious to begin building, the employers yielded and the local won wage hikes. The Cleveland Chamber of Commerce then launched a protracted campaign to associate high union wages with higher home prices. In its 1922 report, the chamber of commerce vowed to pursue the open shop, claiming that the Building Trades Council's "own selfish interest" was "in defiance of the public interest."[56] For the next several years the APA published incendiary newspaper advertisements that linked high rents with anti-American activities; these advertisements also appealed to those workers shut out of the building trades. Union cards, they argued, forced nonunion workers to "pay for the right to earn bread." Instead, they charged men must "have the free right to work."[57]

Citing a need to counteract the postwar efforts by the Building Trades Employers' Association, the CFL reinforced its exclusionary practices. To ensure that nonunion labor neither competed with nor replaced union workers, the building trades frequently resorted to intimidation and violence against nonunion workers. In the end, Cleveland's building trades maintained closed shops even in the face of this relentless campaign by the APA to dismantle the scaffolds of the organized.

Despite efforts from organized workers, African Americans increased their presence in the building trades during the war and the decade that followed, but primarily in unskilled positions. By 1930, despite the onset of the depression and the scarcity of jobs for all building trades workers, only particular crafts, not all building trades, excluded blacks (see table 1). Moreover, in many of the trades where they did not make gains, black workers still retained their presence. Throughout the 1920s, blacks faced white workers, whose racial antipathy toward them became part of the conflict with white employers over wages and the closed shop. Elaborate work rules and qualifications joined with constitutional clauses, high union fees, and restrictions for apprenticeships to prevent blacks from obtaining and continuing membership in unions.[58]

The newer craftworkers that labored inside, such as plasterers, paperhangers, and parquet floor layers, were frequently the most violent in their efforts to exclude blacks. In 1920, only 24 blacks held positions as paperhangers; by 1930, this number had grown to 112. Given that the total number of paperhangers had nearly tripled, the gains were more than proportionate. But the overwhelming majority of the black paperhangers labored in nonunion repair jobs or as maintenance workers for the railroads. In the late 1920s, Paperhangers, Local No. 128 triumphantly declared that blacks had not been allowed to join for "thirty-seven years." Whenever the question of black membership arose, members raised a "storm of protest." The local claimed that some years earlier blacks had been used as strikebreakers, which had "weakened the morale of the skilled [workers]." Yet the attitudes against their exclusion were equally influenced by "the fear of personal contact" with blacks. The local had never attempted to organize black workers, though blacks had expressed an enthusiastic "desire to join." The business agent added that the older members of the local realized the necessity of including black workers, but they concluded such an effort might "jeopardize the union's following."[59] Members of Parquet Floor Layers, Local No. 1242 were

Table 1.

	1920		1930	
	Total	Black	Total	Black
Brick and stone masons	2351	107	2209	110
Building laborers	4768	1124	5705	1755
Carpenters	9510	220	7107	251
Electricians	3304	21	3090	33
Helpers	842	174	—	—
Painters	2967	62	4778	241
Paperhangers	396	24	969	112
Plasterers	703	206	889	18
Plumbers	2741	23	2362	48
Sheet metal workers	1395	6	1545	9
Structural iron workers	592	8	548	11

Sources: U.S. Census, *Fourteenth Census;* U.S. Census, *Fifteenth Census.*

more emphatic in their reasons for excluding blacks. Though the local had admitted blacks, the members claimed that, based on one man's earlier experience in a nonunion shop, customers would not countenance black members. The local's secretary concluded: "I have been at this trade 32 years, [and] I can only remember one instance in which the firm for whom I worked employed a negro, and he was more of a mulatto than anything else." Customers, he argued, might object to the presence of black workers in their homes. In both of these locals, antiblack attitudes, rather than particular concerns about competition from unorganized workers, prevailed.[60]

Similarly, the electrical union prohibited blacks from membership and ensured that nonunion members could neither find nor complete jobs. Because it was one of the newest crafts in the building trades, locals' efforts to exclude blacks became a form of organized violence. Elmer Thompson's job experiences and his encounters with the electrical union fully illustrated the tactics. In 1914 Thompson graduated from East Tech High School. As a student, he had learned something of the trade just when electricity was being installed on a large scale. "Nobody was an electrician," but Thompson could not find a contractor that hired blacks. Frustrated, he convinced a white electrician to show him how to wire a whole house. Despite his new and uncommon expertise amongst all building workers, Thompson could not find work with or gain entrance into the union "because my face was black." Throughout the 1920s, he "had the unions to worry with," but he took advantage of their general refusal to accept employment in old houses or work between May and September because "it was too hot." Thompson said, "I'd go up in the hottest attic there is, Fourth of July if I got paid for it."[61]

Even these jobs had to be done quickly and with stealth. During slack periods, union members cruised the neighborhoods in search of nonunion workers making repairs. In an effort to avoid retaliation, Elmer Thompson learned to "take up the floor and put them back down fast so that there was hardly any notice." After too many violent encounters, he learned to keep a hammer nearby in case someone asked for a union card. Though he halted such inquiries with his forceful responses, the union still managed to sabotage his work. "I'd have to ease back and watch that job," Thompson said, "go there and stay until dark to see if they were going to come and clip the wires." By the midtwenties Thompson shifted to work on neon signs for small shop owners. These jobs, undertaken with nonunion Jewish workers, invited union retaliation as well. "The unions got so that they would take a piece of cable that you supported with, bent it like a walking cane, hit the top of the sign and break right through each piece of glass." Though in need of the extra work, he stopped constructing the signs because his presence made them all identifiable as the products of nonunion labor. "I was too easily identified so I got out of it entirely."[62]

Though other craft locals in the building trades did not display such retaliatory or exclusionary policies, blacks nonetheless encountered barriers. The United Brotherhood of Carpenters and Joiners, Local No. 182, for example, had fifteen black members, of which thirteen had joined after the war. Although previously it had been a German-language local, one of the two earlier black members was "a German speaking Brother." With the shift to English, more blacks joined, all of whom played active roles and frequently served as delegates for the CFL. Two black members had helped to "work out new by-laws" for the local.[63]

The lathers', scaffold builders', and bricklayers' unions included black workers, but high fees, limited job assignments, and workers' racial attitudes circumscribed the mobility of most and excluded others. The bricklayers' union had a vacillating policy of inclusion until the turn of the century. With the growing number of black bricklayers, masons, and plasterers, however, the national concluded "that discrimination against Negroes had retarded the organization's progress." Then the union firmly reprimanded locals that excluded blacks. Southern locals, in observance of segregation laws, forced black workers to secure jobs wherever they could. Northern locals reported similar circumstances. In Cleveland, Frank Smith discovered that the high fees and job discrimination in the lathers' union made it virtually impossible to find steady work, just as his father, also a lather, had found. But Frank Smith's pursuit of skilled work demonstrates the way that some black sons followed their fathers into the building trades. Similarly cut out of job assignments, S. J. Plummer, a member of the scaffold builders' union, criticized the business agent and was later severely beaten by union members. Not to be intimidated, Plummer took the union to court and won eight hundred dollars in damages. Only the bricklayers' local, newly affiliated with the AFL in 1916, appears to have minimized job discrimination against its black members.[64]

This expanded presence of blacks in some building trades locals makes it difficult to assess their general status in the organized construction trades. On the one hand, long-standing animosity and the reinvigoration of racist ideas legitimized many locals' policies of exclusion even when black workers posed an economic threat. In addition, white workers were genuinely loathe to extend membership to blacks, though competition and employers' anti-union efforts suggested biracial unionism would be advantageous. In other instances, however, building trades workers maintained, sought, and encouraged black membership. Blacks were the backbone of the asphalt workers' union; and the Hod Carriers, Building, and Common Laborers Union had "the largest number of Negro members." Nationally, one-fifth of the union consisted of black workers, and in Cleveland, a strong local boasted a membership at least 50 percent black. But even so, it was difficult to "maintain wage and hour scales" because the work assignments were frequently temporary.[65] Contrasting sharply with electricians and paperhangers, bricklayers and the handful of carpenters' locals that included black members tended to view brotherhood from a pragmatic perspective as much as from any commitment to egalitarianism. Even when relations between black and white building trades' workers were strained and fractious, the existence of mixed locals at all represented countervailing trends in the construction trades. William Middleton, for example, had decided to migrate to Cleveland because he had heard that he could continue to belong to a bricklayers' union. As a member of a segregated local in Kentucky, Middleton had found only limited skilled work. Once in Cleveland, however, Middleton joined the union and found skilled, steady work throughout the 1920s. In his neighborhood, other black members of the local had had similar experiences.[66]

Blacks' increased presence in the transportation and service trades, particularly in restaurants and hotels, challenged organized labor. Beginning in 1920, the growth of mechanized interurban transportation, especially trucks, bolstered the Teamsters' Union. Though it did not exclude blacks, prohibition and battles with small shop owners greatly impeded the organization of effective biracial unions. Moreover, the blurred lines between transportation workers and service workers were exacerbated by the increased presence of black workers. Long employed in jobs that necessitated backbreaking labor, such as in ice and coal, blacks frequently worked alongside whites or independently from wagons and push carts. With the arrival of mechanized trucks, however, white drivers sought to distinguish their labor from that of African Americans. Most locals relegated black workers to the status of helpers who had no route of advancement to become drivers. In turn, the increasing power of the unions shut blacks out as food, milk, and beverage drivers.[67]

Yet African-American men did make inroads into organized labor through work deemed undesirable by whites. As in other cities, the Sanitary Drivers and Helpers' Union had long included black workers, apparently on a more egalitarian basis then most locals in the city that had black members. In July 1922, the workers called a strike because the city no longer accepted closed shops. Perhaps influenced and heartened by the APA, the mayor, a former police chief, hired strikebreakers and forced the union members out of city-owned housing. Street battles between union members and strikebreakers pitted blacks against each other. After more than six months, the sanitation workers lost their union and black workers lost yet another biracial union. Blacks' access to jobs in the sanitation department now depended on whatever political party controlled the mayor's office. By 1930, a black man served as sanitation supervisor, and blacks held nearly 75 percent of the positions. Despite such power, blacks controlled neither workplace conditions nor trash pickup, thus the black neighborhoods lacked adequate service.[68]

Such tentative biracial efforts did not extend to the rapidly expanding hotel and restaurant trades, where black workers had an increasing presence. The exclusionary policies based on race were clearly evident in the Hotel and Restaurant Employees' Union (HRE), Local No. 106, which had replaced the Cleveland Waiters and Beverage Dispensers union. This earlier union, organized in the late nineteenth century, did not admit blacks because they had apparently "worsted" the local as strikebreakers, "working for less wages, and longer hours." Years later Local 106 continued the policy of exclusion based on this strike. During a 1917 strike, the local used violence and intimidation to force black waiters out of several hotels. Local 107, comprised of waitresses, also joined in the strident opposition to blacks. This policy contrasted with the international's constitution, which allowed for the separate and segregated organization of blacks "where no colored locals existed." The HRE allowed for the organization of black workers into segregated locals when white workers agreed. The bylaws did contain a clause allowing blacks to be accepted into white locals on a segregated basis when there were too few blacks to create a separate local. In areas where this policy was practiced, blacks were relegated to the lower-paid, unskilled occupations. As marginal members of white locals, black workers rarely had access to the benefits of the union. Similar tactics were constructed to divide locals along gender lines to protect white female waitresses' dominance over higher-paying work. When it came to extending the benefits of separatism, however, white women demanded that African-American and Asian women affiliate with men along racial lines. Given that employers invariably sought black men before black women, white women helped to ensure that black women would receive the worst—if any—jobs. As a union stronghold, the Cleveland locals appeared to represent the nation's sentiments.[69] Other nonhotel-based waiters' unions did organize blacks, but with mixed results. The Marine Cooks and Stewards' Union of the Great Lakes had African-American men as members, but this had not stopped white men from calling a strike when the union leadership formally ended segregated eating and socializing.[70]

Wartime confrontations further exacerbated relations between black and white workers in other service trades. Employers quickly used black workers to replace white workers who dared organize. At the Statler Hotel, for example, blacks could obtain jobs only as temporary replacements for workers out on strike. Pushed by the Negro Welfare Association, the management agreed to hire thirty-six black men for thirty days. Managers stipulated that once the strike was settled, ten of the men would be retained as elevator operators. This concession was not a victory since employers had found it difficult to keep white workers from leaving for higher-paying jobs in war-related industries anyway. In addition, in the event of another strike, the use of black workers served as a warning to white workers that management could once again replace them.[71]

Yet black workers persistently pursued affiliation with the HRE despite the locals' policies of exclusion. In 1927, Local 106 began a boycott against the Terrace Garden Restaurant, located eleven miles outside of Cleveland, because of the owner's unfair labor policies. This boycott mirrored those taking place elsewhere as Dana Frank revealed in her study of Seattle. White workers infused the language of class with the language of racism: pro-union meant pro-white. The replacement of organized white workers by unorganized black workers constituted "unfair[ness] to organized labor. But the owner of the restaurant challenged the efforts of Local 106, claiming the boycott was racially motivated. Apparently the owner of Wills' Terrace Garden had hired black workers in 1926 and paid them according to union scale. He claimed that he hired black workers not because they were cheaper but because white union members would not tolerate "the distance of the place from the city of Cleveland and his intermittent and irregular demand" for labor.[72]

The union did not respond until 1927 when the owner rehired the black workers, who then attempted to join Local 106. Outraged at the dismissal of white workers and fearful of black attempts at inclusion, Local 106 called for a boycott; true to long-standing policies, the HRE in Columbus denied black workers' request for a charter. Local 106 demanded the employment of whites only, but the owner refused to comply since he had signed a contract with members of the newly created black local. The owner then sought an injunction against the boycott by Local 106, which the court granted on the grounds that the union had no evidence of violations in wage or work conditions. Instead, the court issued an unexpected reasoning for its decision: "In its last analysis [the boycott] is a case of white men opposing colored men. As this court sees it the only information these defendants could properly and truthfully give the public about plaintiff is that he employs colored people." The court then claimed that the vice president of Local 106 had conceived the campaign against the restaurant because he "wanted to be re-elected custodian, rather than any desire to protect the rights of union labor."[73] Despite the injunction, neither local altered its policies nor allowed for separate black locals in the city.

African-American waiters' attempts to organize on their own behalf, yet in accordance with union work rules, grew out of a general self-organization by black workers. Motivated by A. Philip Randolph, black sleeping car porters began a national unionization drive in 1926. Though there were few Pullman porters residing in Cleveland, black workers were nonetheless supportive of Randolph's call for union membership.[74] Although blacks could join some unions for unskilled workers at this time, the continued exclusion of black waiters, along with the retrenchment of the AFL toward black workers in general, greatly undermined biracial unionism. Indeed, by the midtwenties the *Cleveland Federationist* loudly denounced attempts to organize black workers as communist efforts "to stir up revolution among the backward colored races" and supported attacks against the AFL organization of blacks. In addition, the CFL sponsored parades and picnics at city parks that excluded blacks.[75] The National Negro Welfare Association found that the AFL had failed to sustain black membership and consequently lost its credibility among black leaders. Certainly in the aftermath of the war the AFL was little more than a shell of its once-powerful self. The attacks on black organization, however, signaled the atavistic tendencies that repeatedly emerged in the last half of the decade.

During this period white workers gradually constructed a new vision of themselves that linked racist attitudes and a working-class consciousness, even when they organized black workers. For many white workers in Cleveland, the war presented their first experience with black workers brought in to combat white activism. The efforts by the molders' union during and after the war exemplify the "challenge of oppression" that African-American men faced. Beginning in 1916, employers imported black workers to replace skilled white laborers, prompting an immediate strike. The molders, however, had "no fear of the Negro as strikebreakers" because the new workers had little, if any, experience with casting molds. The molders, aware that blacks had been imported to "discourage" the strike, received great satisfaction when they realized the castings made by the new workers could not be sold. In the aftermath of the strike, all of the strikebreakers were fired. The union, however, could not halt employers' hiring of other blacks. As more employers successfully pursued open shops, the molders then began to organize black workers, most of whom were helpers. By 1926, however, out of three thousand members only twelve were black. The business agent for the union explained with a tone of satisfaction that the low number was an indication that many of the black workers had "misrepresented themselves and could not hold a job. Naturally, they dropped out." Never did the union admit that its and the employers' tactics had limited blacks' access to jobs.[76] Frank Evans, a member of the AFL Molders' Union local during the 1920s, later went to Detroit to organize blacks to join the United Auto Workers. Evans found that the attitudes of the union had prevented greater black participation and job mobility. In the end, Evans concluded, the possibilities of unionism were "undermined by the cleavage between the white skilled workers and the mainly black helpers."[77] Organizing a heterogeneous laboring population remained impossible in a world where white workers clung to racism and participated in the maintenance of barriers against black workers even as employers devised new tactics to dismantle unions generally.

African-American workers' experiences in the railroad brotherhoods demonstrated these patterns as well. Independent black organizations did not develop in the railroads in Cleveland since blacks had been relegated to unskilled occupations with rigid work rules. The new conservative rhetoric from white unions that emerged in the aftermath of the war allowed for blacks' exclusion or the containment of blacks in federal unions and segregated locals. The latter trend was evident when black workers were organized as a federal union in the Freight Handlers, Local No. 17210. The white brotherhoods considered this concession a necessary attempt to contain black workers in separate organizations with weak bargaining positions. Such an incorporation of blacks in segregated and weak locals, along with their relegation to menial positions in the yards, tended to preclude strong, independent black labor activism. It also meant that in such constricted organizations blacks could rarely challenge the segregation that characterized their work lives. Black yard workers remained isolated in company-owned boxcars and excluded from the Collinwood neighborhoods of railroad workers.[78]

In response to their limited inclusion in unions, African-American workers more frequently pursued self-organization. This trend was particularly prevalent in service workers' associations that included waiters, sanitation employees, red caps, and barbers. The Forest City Benefit Association, an organization of black sanitation workers, appears to have offered little more than social gatherings. Other organizations, such as those of the red caps, participated in collective displays of resistance to racism and job exclusion. When African-American bell boys at the exclusive Hollenden Hotel were replaced by whites, they found work as red caps at the train station. They apparently attempted retribution because the hotel management later complained that the black red caps directed arriving passengers to other hotels. However ephemeral these organizations might have been, displays of workplace resistance continued. The *Cleveland Gazette* regularly reported displays of workers' activism, and scattered anecdotal evidence suggests that such actions may have persuaded other black workers to act similarly.[79]

More than any other group, African-American women workers were the least likely to have access to workplace organization, but self-organization nonetheless occurred, suggesting black women's own patterns of self-organized resistance and workplace activism. When told to use the freight elevator at the W. B. Davis department store, black bundle wrappers immediately organized. After the management refused to change the policy, the women went out on strike. The store managers, however, wasted little time in replacing them. Black women formed associations of nurses and stenographers; still others participated in and served as officers of the black musicians' associations.[80] Generally, however, such organizations did not emerge where the overwhelming majority of black women worked. Certainly male workers' indifference about organizing women generally, and black women's location in household service and laundry work, prevented their organization in unions. Historians have suggested, however, that black women displayed individual forms of resistance within the context of community patterns of activism.[81] Just how community labor associations in the North shaped women's workplace resistance is only suggested in oblique references in newspapers and institutional records. How women's resistance may have been legitimized by the general display of black working-class organizations needs more research.

Waiters' organizations emerged as the most visible black community labor associations. The Caterer's Club formed during the war in response to the increased exclusion of black workers from the better hotels and restaurants. At first the club had difficulty organizing because prospective members felt the name suggested a club of servants. By the midtwenties, however, other waiters' organizations joined the club. By 1924 the Waiters' Association at the Union Club of Cleveland secured a contract for its members. At a celebration, W. H. Chaney, who was both head waiter and the association's president, led the parade of workers to the thunder of congratulations offered by families and friends. The Union Club was a private club for many of the most powerful industrialists, professionals, and business owners in the city. Ironically, organized black waiters served these male club members, many of whom feverishly worked in their own companies to prevent their employees from joining unions.[82]

Ultimately, HRE's policies of exclusion and segregation collided. By 1929, the National Association of Colored Waiters and Hotel Employees joined the growing number of community-based black workers' associations. In the spring of 1930, the organization acted quickly when the Cleveland Hotel Association, the organization of hotel and restaurant employers, announced it would no longer recognize the HRE locals. Instead, workers in five of the largest hotels would have to sign individual contracts. All three of the HRE locals of waiters, waitresses, and cooks rejected the managers' plan and announced they would strike if necessary. Before the unions could call a strike, however, the hotel employers ordered the workers out. On July 15, 1930, over three hundred workers wearing white sashes with red letters proclaiming "lockout" took up pickets. With the scarcity of work, the hotel owners had little trouble finding workers, and most of the hotels immediately employed nonunion members, many of whom were black waiters in the newly organized National Association of Colored Waiters. By the close of the decade, this union claimed hundreds of members in both Cleveland and Chicago. In addition, black women who labored as chamber maids had affiliated with unions.[83]

After years of agreements between the locals and the hotel and restaurant employers, the lockout had ominous implications in the midst of an expanding and devastating depression. In the closest thing to a general strike the city had seen, though one galvanized by white workers' racial antipathy toward black workers as much as by employers' actions, the locals immediately received support from the Cleveland Labor Council (formerly the Cleveland Federation of Labor) as well as the international. Shortly after the picketing began, truck drivers, musicians, engineers, and maintenance workers called strikes in support of the white waiters. Though hundreds of white workers acted as strikebreakers, the presence of black workers meant the strike became framed in racial terms. Ralph M. Rowland, president of the black local, explained African Americans' willingness to cross the picket lines as a rejection of the HRE policy of racial exclusion. Throughout the ensuing weeks, the striking workers avoided confrontations on the picket line with the self-organized black workers, but Rowland had a twenty-four-hour po-lice watch on his home because of threats of violence.[84]

Throughout the protracted strike, which lasted until the following sum-mer, black leaders had little sympathy for black workers' struggle to be rec-ognized as a union. At the start of the strike, the black local demanded that the needs of black waiters be addressed in the efforts to settle the strike, in-cluding the removal of barriers to HRE membership. As politicians chose sides, the black local made direct appeals to blacks in the working class "to vote in their own interests and protect black workers." Unwilling to work on behalf of the black waiters, black leaders instead pursued employment for them as unorganized workers. In the end, African-American politicians and community leaders were unable to secure permanent employment for some of the black waiters. The worsening depression ultimately helped the hotel employers, and the strike ended when all black workers were removed from the hotels. The defeated white locals returned to work without contracts and with much lower wages.[85]

The continued racial exclusivity of organized labor in the postwar years was partly in response to employers' power to threaten or use black workers to dismantle the house of labor, but organized white workers created their own racial views independent from those precipitated by their employers' actions. As employers sought to reestablish the open shop in the 1920s, white workers attempted to retain their wartime gains through the exclusion of black workers. Yet just as surely as white workers organized around wages, hours, and work conditions, they also sought to advance perceptions of their own racial prerogatives in the workplace. They actively participated in the making of their own racism, which significantly impeded the construction of a biracial working-class consciousness and movement. White workers' racism and their continued view of African Americans as a threat to their jobs frequently led to the conscious collusion with employers to exclude blacks from the workplace. In the end, despite pronouncements by the national leadership of the AFL to the contrary, an active and violent exclusion of black workers from unions remained the norm.[86]

While not all unions were racially exclusive, possibilities for biracial union-ism were limited in the 1920s. First, organization in one workplace rarely served as a model for organization in another. Second, biracial unionism emerged in the midst of a heightened white working-class consciousness shaped by racism and employers' own racialized hiring policies. The narrow focus of most craft locals on work rules meant that unions ensured the loca-tion of blacks in the lowest job categories, as seen in the railroad yards. By the end of the decade, white workers, whose worlds still encompassed close links between work and home, lived in segregated neighborhoods, which made it difficult to raise support for biracial unions. In the workplace and the neighborhood, the language of racial exclusion as a basis for white working-class identity suggests that biracial unionism did not translate into a multiracial class consciousness or an attack against racism beyond the workplace. Conversely, such racism only strengthened blacks' mistrust of unions. Most critically, biracial unions rarely provided black workers an opportunity to shape the labor movement. Nor did they provide a foundation for a biracial activism that could extend beyond the workplace to take up issues crucial to the African-American community.

The experiences of exclusion and the limits of inclusion taught black workers that they needed to organize on their own behalf. Over the course of the decade, many black working people realized that neither antilabor attitudes nor participation in antiblack unions served their needs. In their separate labor associations, black workers were better able to meld workplace needs with their needs in the community. Further, independent African-American working-class organizations challenged racial exclusion and forced white trade unionists on a city and federation level to face the consequences of exclusion. But independent organizations came with a price. Indeed, when black workers acted "in their own interests," as the waiters' efforts reveal in 1927 and 1930, they encountered an aggressive response from white workers. Conversely, white workers perceived independent black labor organizations not as an expression of working-class solidarity but as a direct challenge to their prerogatives predicated on the exclusion of blacks from the workplace.

As African-American workers sought to craft a community for themselves, they encountered countervailing arguments from black leaders for a concentration on a racial consciousness shaped by middle-class values. That black workers engaged in such vibrant workplace self-organization served as testimony to their willingness to challenge the internal efforts to discourage labor associations. Indeed, the self-generative impulse to organize around work was fueled by their household and community experiences as working people. Just as anti-unionism did not prove to be a viable option for them, they found that African-American churches, clubs, and institutions dominated by elites and professionals sympathetic to white employers failed to meet their needs. The experiences of migration, household formation, and associational life in the 1920s—conjoined with the experiences of the workplace—provided the underpinnings for the emergence of a new form of militant community-based working-class activism in the 1930s.

Unidentified protesters at the Woodland Market and Woolworth boycott, 1938. (Courtesy of the Western Reserve Historical Society, Cleveland)

"Alabama Bus Strike Recalls Hectic Days of Cleveland Boycott Fight." Ralph Matthew's charcoal and ink drawing (ca. 1956) links the street protests of the 1930s and 1940s with the protests in Alabama while reminding African Americans in Cleveland of their Alabama origins. (Courtesy of the Western Reserve Historical Society, Cleveland)

Undated gathering of officers in the Future Outlook League. John O. Holly is the second from the right in the first row. Beatrice Stevens Cockrell is at the left in the second row. (Courtesy of the Western Reserve Historical Society, Cleveland)

Allen Cole's promotional photograph of the Future Outlook League's Employees' Union. Cole often printed captions on his photographs that he sold as promotions for his services. (Courtesy of the Western Reserve Historical Society, Cleveland)

Bishop James Askew and his Church of God in Christ congregation. Located in the Central Area, this church was one of the first Church of God in Christ churches in Ohio. (Courtesy of the Western Reserve Historical Society, Cleveland)

Elmer W. Brown's depiction of a rent party in 1930s Cleveland. *Gandy Dancer's Gal,* 1943. (Courtesy of the Western Reserve Historical Society, Cleveland)

The Live Wire Club, one of the many social clubs of African-American migrants in Cleveland, circa the late 1920s. (Courtesy of the Western Reserve Historical Society, Cleveland)

FOUR

A New World in the City: Making Homes in Cleveland

NOT LONG AFTER A MIGRANT had arrived from Alabama, he wrote a letter to his rural relatives informing them that he found Cleveland "a fine place to make money." Yet, while he and his wife had jobs with good wages and steady work, he did not like what the city had to offer his children: he could not care for them "like they should be" in a city of strangers. He poignantly worried about their well-being because he lacked "surrounding friends" to give him support, comfort, and advice. Faced with their absence, his confidence about the possibilities of making a home for his family began to waver and he had "seval nochants of" returning south.[1] No evidence remains about how this migrant resolved the struggle between earning higher wages and providing a suitable home for his children in the city. In contrast, Bertha Cowan earned much higher wages in Cleveland than she had in the South and, like many migrants, she soon visited her family to show off her success. She arrived "down home" wearing "the city show, went back all polished." Her apparent success initiated a steady stream of family and friends migrating to Cleveland. Though Cowan watched the high wages of the World War I years quickly evaporate in the 1920s, the presence of family and friends anchored her to the city: "This is when the South all came up here and it turned into a new world."[2]

These personal accounts, along with numerous others, provide important insight into the pressing concerns besides work that migrants faced: finding places to live, establishing ways to care for children, and retaining kin and friend connections that had shifted in the wake of migration. Certainly many migrants were temporary sojourners, staying only long enough to work for several months before returning home or migrating again. For those migrants intending to stay in the city, finding and keeping work became intimately linked to remaking households in Cleveland. But as these two migrants' experiences suggest, African Americans often had to balance crafting the bonds of "surrounding" family and friends against earning wages. Making a home in Cleveland mattered to migrants as much as finding jobs with higher wages, and they wanted to live among familiar faces. Many found that the arrival of family and friends bound them to the city even if wages declined or better jobs could no longer be found. But, just as many had struggled to find and keep work, the tasks of making a home and establishing kin and friend networks necessitated new strategies as well.

As successive waves of African-American migrants entered the city between 1915 and 1930, they encountered varying opportunities to find adequate housing, reestablish kin and friend networks, and create neighborhoods. Mounting white racism became manifest in prohibitions against black renters and buyers as they sought more desirable housing. In addition, many African Americans found that their unskilled and frequently irregular employment in the 1920s further narrowed their housing choices. As a large and concentrated population of African-American migrants settled on the east side of Cleveland, where and how they lived came under increased scrutiny from social welfare workers. Over the course of the 1920s, migrants confronted social welfare workers committed to policies of segregation that were neither casual nor benign. The cold winds from Lake Erie that blew through the cracks of the apartments and homes in the Central Avenue district where many migrants settled offered a chilling reminder that making a home in Cleveland would be difficult.

Yet migrants like Bertha Cowan sought to "make a whole world" for themselves in the city. They turned to family and friends for help and guidance in choosing places to live and reestablishing networks of emotional and economic support. Many hoped that the social relations they created in their new households and links to kin and households in the South would enable them to escape the poverty and segregation in the South and serve as bulwarks against the continued economic precariousness and segregation they faced in the North. The choices migrants made about households and their neighborhoods, while crafted in the context of individual needs and circumstances, nonetheless highlight general patterns of rebuilding family and friend networks.

Until 1910, Cleveland's African-American population numbered less than 8,500. The few migrants in this overwhelmingly northern-born longtime population had origins in the border states of Kentucky and West Virginia. The wartime demands for employment and employers' greater use of unskilled black workers in steel, transportation, and service work led to dramatic increases in migration. By 1920 the African-American population had swelled to over 34,000, an increase of 308 percent. This enormous growth propelled the city into second place behind Detroit for the largest increase in the black population. Though the dramatic influx of migrants waned by the spring of 1919, casual observers noted the renewed brisk pace of arrivals from the Deep South between 1923 and 1927. Indeed, by 1930, the black population had again more than doubled to over 71,000. Over half of these new arrivals came from Alabama and other states in the Deep South.[3]

The shifting demographic character of the black population between 1910 and 1930 reveals how the availability of jobs appealed equally to men and women and their families from the Deep South states. While the sharp expansion and contraction of the black population in the summer months during the war suggested that a significant number stayed only temporarily, many migrants did settle permanently. A preponderance of men and women between the ages of eighteen and fifty-four, with nearly 67 percent over twenty-one, came to Cleveland. Throughout the two decades of population growth, men predominated, but unlike in Pittsburgh, women made up a significant portion of the new arrivals after 1920. By 1930, the population of black women roughly equaled that of men. Adult blacks had slightly higher rates of marriage than did native-born whites or immigrants; black women were less likely than white women to be single (19 percent compared with 27 percent). On the other end of the marital spectrum, black women showed the highest rate of widowhood of all groups. Between 1920 and 1930, the number of households with children under the age of ten increased significantly from the previous decade. The number of African-American children entering the Cleveland public schools between 1921 and 1923 climbed dramatically, attesting to the familial character of the migration.[4]

The dramatic and rapid growth of the African-American population during these years altered their proximity to other groups. By the turn of the century a small African-American community lived among newly arrived, predominantly eastern European immigrants who clustered around the Haymarket district that fringed the commercial and industrial sections on the east side of Cleveland (see map 1). Throughout the next decade, the majority of African Americans continued to live on or around Central and

Cedar Avenues. With the rapid increase in the African-American population after 1915, distinct neighborhoods of black residents appeared and expanded northward between Central and Euclid Avenues and to the south
and east along Scovill and Woodland Avenues. As the migration continued,
blacks moved into every ward in this area, with 60 percent clustered between East Fifty-fifth Street and Euclid Avenue (see map 2).[5]

At the beginning of the twentieth century, African-American migrants
from the Deep South coexisted with a diverse, large, and shifting population
of immigrants. The foreign-born population numbered 97,095 in 1890; over
19 percent of this total had come from southern, eastern, and central Europe.
By 1910 those of foreign birth had increased to 196,170, with 57 percent of these
a result of new immigration. Slavs, Italians, Romanians, and Eastern European Jews formed the largest groups of these new residents. While the latest
arrivals tended to live in neighborhoods loosely defined by ethnic origins and
national lines, they, too, were concentrated in neighborhoods on the east side.[6]

African-American migrants looked for housing in a tight and increasingly
segregated market as the wartime influx of workers and families greatly constricted the already limited choices. Unlike in other cities where similar population explosions had occurred, few of Cleveland's business owners provided
housing for their workers. Because of the shrinking availability of rentals,
property owners quickly subdivided older homes. Despite the continuing
problem, large tenements did not flourish, and instead overcrowding became
common in the much smaller subdivided rooms and apartments. Through
the war years, blacks and immigrants competed for scarce rentals clustered
in older neighborhoods on the near east side of the city. Before the war, northern European immigrants abandoned older neighborhoods and joined native-
born whites in the rapid move to newly built homes on the edges of the city.
This flight led to segregated residential patterns.[7]

A 1914 report on housing conditions revealed both the scarcity and the
precarious condition of the houses and apartments that blacks were forced
to rent. Despite earlier slum clearance efforts, "inadequate and unsanitary
conditions" continued to "exist in one of the principal Negro communities
of the city." Nothing had been done to compel landlords to fix or maintain
these older dwellings, thus African Americans continued to live in the "worst
square mile of housing in any civilized community." The housing conditions
between the east bank of the Cuyahoga River and south of East Fifty-fifth
were exacerbated by "unnecessary lot overcrowding."[8]

While most recently arrived unskilled immigrant workers found adequate
but affordable housing difficult to obtain because of their low wages, as a
group African Americans encountered additional prohibitions because of

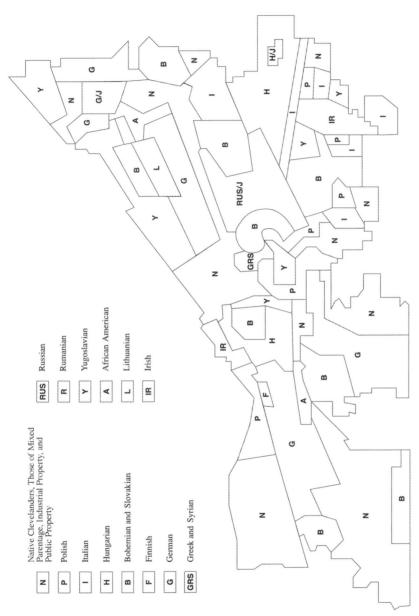

Map 1. Ethnic communities, 1915. Based on Welfare Federation of Cleveland, *Cleveland Area Social Study* (Cleveland: Welfare Federation of Cleveland, 1944).

Legend:

N — Native Clevelanders, Those of Mixed Parentage, Industrial Property, and Public Property

P — Polish

I — Italian

H — Hungarian

B — Bohemian and Slovakian

F — Finnish

G — German

GRS — Greek and Syrian

RUS — Russian

R — Rumanian

Y — Yugoslavian

A — African American

L — Lithuanian

IR — Irish

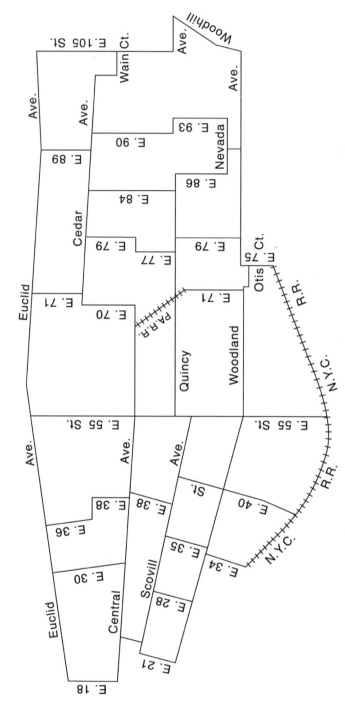

Map 2. Central Area, 1930–40. Based on Welfare Federation of Cleveland, *Cleveland Area Social Study* (Cleveland: Welfare Federation of Cleveland, 1944).

race. Some landlords had refused to rent to African Americans before the war, and others quickly adopted similar racial proscriptions that significantly limited migrants' choices. Aware of the policies of surrounding property owners, landlords increased the rent for the new arrivals. As Langston Hughes recalled of his youth in wartime Cleveland: "White people on the east side of the city were moving out of their frame houses and renting them to Negroes at double and triple the rents they could receive from others. An eight-room house with one bath would be cut up into apartments and five or six families crowded into it, each two-room kitchenette apartment renting for what the whole house had rented before."[9] Investigators conducting wartime surveys found that blacks spent a disproportionate share of their income on rent when compared with native-born whites and immigrants in similar housing in adjacent buildings and neighborhoods. In an apartment house on Central Avenue, for instance, blacks rented five-room suites for thirty-one dollars a month; in contrast, whites paid twenty-two dollars for similar space. This dissimilarity led some migrants to designate the high rents as "the colored tax." Other African Americans perceived landlords as avaricious, but found little recourse to ameliorate their plight.[10]

Black migrants coped with these limited housing choices in a variety of ways. Since rents remained high and living space became scarcer, people lived in hallways, sheds, garages, storefronts, and railroad boxcars. The Malone family, newly arrived from Kentucky, moved into boxcars provided by the New York Central Railroad in its Collinwood yards. Each boxcar was hoisted on top of bricks and partitioned into three rooms. Each car had a coal burning stove; the coal was provided, free of charge, by the company. All of the families shared two water pumps and several outhouses. Despite the inconvenience, black workers chose the boxcars over the company's rundown tenements. In an effort to house the new migrants as quickly and cheaply as possible (and perhaps to diffuse competition with white workers searching for housing), the Welfare Federation of Cleveland suggested the establishment of tents in the city's parks. Eventually some blacks did pitch tents farther north and east on the outskirts of the suburb of Mt. Pleasant. Some white women, concerned about migrants' well-being, allowed black women to use their kitchens and washtubs.[11]

After the war, the African-American community was firmly established in the Central Area of the city. Howard Whipple Green, a longtime statistician of the changes in Cleveland's demographics, found an important difference between the residential patterns of African Americans and white immigrants after World War I. During and after the war, a growing number of white established immigrants with steady employment and relatively high wages sought and found better homes to rent or buy in less congested areas. In contrast, longtime African-American residents and new white migrants in similar economic circumstances found few opportunities to make similar choices. Instead, blacks remained concentrated in adjoining neighborhoods in older industrial areas; new migrants joined them in adjacent areas. These residential patterns, Green found, mirrored those in other cities where "the colored populations are the last to inhabit an area, and . . . they are replaced only by industrial or commercial enterprise." Casual policies hardened into rigid racial proscriptions. Residents in the areas that ringed the city quickly erected barriers against newly arriving Jews and Italians and all African Americans.[12]

But black migrants' settlement in the oldest, most blighted areas was also shaped by their concentration in the lowest occupations and their irregular employment patterns. Precarious employment and frequent layoffs after the war prevented the overwhelming majority of blacks from moving to or purchasing better housing.[13] The desire to turn a profit meant owners continually subdivided dwellings, failed to maintain them, and did not make upgrades; most buildings in the Central Area lacked indoor plumbing and running water. By the 1920s, investigators noted that landlords regularly exploited African-American renters. Even when blacks lived in the same areas and occupied similar dwellings as other groups, they paid more rent out of much smaller incomes.[14]

The external circumstances that demanded African Americans' overwhelming concentration in specific areas of Cleveland's east side rested on their particular economic circumstances and white hostility and racism. As several historians have shown us, the complex interplay between structural factors, white racism, and the economic experiences of urban black workers resulted in a variety of patterns of ghetto formation in northern cities between 1900 and 1930.[15] When Kenneth Kusmer compared the pattern of African-American settlement in Cleveland to that in larger, similarly sized, and smaller cities, he found that Cleveland represented the middle ground between the extremes of African Americans' forced concentration. Neither extreme nor benign, the departure of white immigrants from deteriorated neighborhoods resulted primarily from a greater range in affordable housing and their higher-paying steady employment. In contrast, an unwillingness to live among hostile whites and a need to live close to industrial employment shaped many African-American migrants' choices about where to live. Most important, the desire to live near kin, friends, and community led many to settle in or near the Central Area. The increased segregation and concentration of poorly paid blacks in the Central Area contrasted with the movement of more affluent blacks to neighborhoods abandoned by whites.[16]

Kin and friend networks proved critical in expanding housing options for migrants. Like other migrants, William Murdock's parents discovered that high rents and bouts of unemployment kept them in homes "worse than those" in the South. Throughout their first two decades in the city, the Murdocks depended on kin to help them find more adequate housing; as relatives and friends bought or moved into better housing, the Murdocks joined them. Other migrant families appear to have made housing choices based on household connections and needs. Economics and family ties, in addition to race, shaped decisions in more subtle ways. Sallie Hopson's father worked for the railroad on the west side of town, but her mother insisted on living near other newly arrived relatives and friends from Georgia on the east side.[17]

The few black professionals and business owners who could afford to buy homes outside of black neighborhoods found that builders, real estate developers, and loan companies actively prevented even the most economically solvent from purchasing them. Residents in the eastern suburbs of Garfield Heights, Cleveland Heights, and Shaker Heights were, as Charles Chesnutt noted in 1930, "resistant to [blacks] advent, sometimes by intimidation or violence." He dryly concluded that "it is about as difficult for a Negro to buy property on the Heights . . . as it is for the traditional camel to pass through the eye of the traditional needle." Bombs and threats became the typical response to blacks' attempts to move into white neighborhoods. Robert C. Weaver found, however, that some blacks "could and did acquire desirable and used property in new areas." But he conceded that such efforts often came through subterfuge: "The technique most often employed was to buy through a friendly white, since most white owners would not sell directly to Negroes. Usually, also, the colored purchaser had to pay cash or get a loan from an individual since financial institutions seldom made loans to Negroes in white neighborhoods." More than several blacks secured loans through the aid of the black funeral home director J. Walter Wills.[18]

Such support from within segments of the black elite meant that as the visibly migrant and working-class population expanded in the Central Area, distinct neighborhoods marked by class and region emerged within Cleveland's black community. More affluent African Americans' move eastward represented an attempt by an increasing number to distance themselves physically from the expanding population of black working-class renters with few resources. Before the war, the old elite clustered along East Fortieth Street south of Quincy. By the middle of the 1920s middle-class and professional blacks purchased or rented homes east of East Seventy-ninth Street; others moved east along Kinsman Avenue into Mt. Pleasant, a rapidly growing area of upwardly mobile immigrants at the edge of the city. In these neighborhoods, which were at the outer edge and not the center of the black community, Charles Chesnutt noted, blacks could "purchase or rent and occupy property without objection and many of them own their own homes." Pockets of working-class black home ownership appeared between East Fifty-fifth and East Eighty-ninth Streets, where many skilled workers in the building trades lived alongside white immigrant homeowners. In the 1920s, Elmer Thompson finally found a home to purchase, but he and his family had to move out of Cleveland. He joined eighty black families in Miles Heights, known for its resemblance to Alabama. Though the area lacked paved streets, sewers, and streetlights—services that would not be provided until the 1950s—the families welcomed the privacy, the space, and the opportunity to have large gardens, porches for visiting, and the sense of being "back home." These families, along with a few whites, elected a black mayor. Their efforts at autonomy ended, however, when the city of Cleveland claimed the area in 1929.[19]

Confronted with restrictions on *where* they lived, many African-American migrants intended to make the most of how and with whom they lived. While the social relations African Americans established in their own households might offset low wages, irregular employment, and limited housing choices, such choices equally demonstrated their desire to retain and recreate familial and communal connections, structures, and values. In the rural South, migration patterns made black households quite elastic, as they expanded and contracted according to various needs. Historians generally agree that the long-distance migration and increased urban residency that took place between 1880 and 1930 changed the size of black families and the configuration of black households. Households based on marital and blood ties predominated, but the presence of unrelated members remained high, making the average number of people per household higher than that in other groups.[20]

Although African Americans had many unrelated people in their households, this did not significantly change the power structure of their families. Urban black households remained overwhelmingly headed by men.[21] Significantly, between 1920 and 1930 the percentage of female-headed households in Cleveland rose only slightly higher among blacks than among other groups and nearly equaled the percentage of female-headed second-generation immigrant families. In other northern cities, the percentage of black female-headed households remained equal to or lower than those in the urban South. Over the course of the last decades of the nineteenth century and the first third of the twentieth, the proportion of black female-headed households in the city increased by a mere 2 percent. Within this population, female heads of households were more frequently widowed, divorced, or deserted rather than women who had borne children out of wedlock.[22]

Though working-age black men predominated as heads of households and households typically included family members, the composition of these households was shaped by patterns of migration and a variety of economic and noneconomic needs. The need to care for children and aging parents, for example, had to be balanced against a family's ability to stretch incomes; the desire to maintain family connections and to help kin moved blacks to create a variety of flexible housing arrangements. A close look at why and how African-American migrants pursued various household arrangements will frame a range of goals and values.

Child care needs motivated some migrants to encourage younger or older female relatives to join them.[23] Single black women with children found it especially difficult to work, and they often had limited access to private and public charity. The necessity to work for wages led them to seek help from family members. Geneva Robinson left Hodges, South Carolina, in 1921, accompanied by her grandmother. The women's trip had been arranged by family members in response to a cousin in Cleveland who needed to work and requested household and child care help. Ray Dennis was just four years old when his widowed father sent for him to come to Cleveland. Dennis's father turned to the sister of his father's brother's wife to accompany his son to the city and care for him. Once in Cleveland, Dennis lived with this woman and her family; a year later she became his stepmother.[24]

Without migrating themselves, some southern black families sent children to Cleveland for education, which necessitated some elaborate household arrangements. Families with older wage-earning children made calculated decisions to send younger children north to live with siblings or other relatives. In the late 1920s, fourteen-year-old Linton Freeman and his twin brother left rural Alabama to attend high school in Cleveland. The two boys had three older sisters living in the city, all of whom were single and employed as live-in household workers. The arrival of the boys, however, required the establishment of a permanent household. The boys lived alone, but their sisters moved in and out of the household on their days off. Until the boys finished school, they returned each summer to Alabama to help on their parents' farm, a common pattern for migrants. In 1923, young Margie Glass arrived from Alabama to visit her grandfather, but her stay soon became permanent because of the better schools. Later, her three unmarried uncles arrived from other cities to join their father and niece in establishing a household. Their presence eventually drew other members of the family to the city.[25] In these and other instances, however, the move north meant that parents sometimes lost authority over their children.

African-American migrants without friends or family in the city found their housing choices extremely limited. Cleveland's white working men had access to an ever-increasing number of rooms in boarding houses, low-cost restaurants, and public bathhouses. Although wartime wages increased many single black men's ability to rent rooms, high rents and too few housing options imposed great hardships. Employers found that more than any other group of workers, black unskilled men found it difficult to get housing near their jobs. Many men spent several hours each day walking to work; others spent nearly as much time traveling on streetcars. The desire for better and more accessible housing compelled many men to seek work elsewhere. During the war, few employers maintained company-owned bunkhouses for single black men; workers with access to such beds found the conditions crowded and deplorable. Charles E. Hall, supervisor of Negro Economics in Ohio during the war, reported that black men on the night shift typically returned to boarding houses maintained by large companies to sleep in beds "just vacated by the men going on the day shift." Investigators of the railroad camps found the conditions of tents, outhouses, and eating facilities undesirable for the thousands of black men employed during the summer months between 1916 and 1918. During the 1920s, because of the decreased availability of work and the continued limited choices in housing, black men without families formed a more conspicuous population of tent camp dwellers and squatters in abandoned buildings and vacant lots.[26]

Similarly, single black women did not have access to the increasing number of affordable boarding houses available to single white women. Contemporary observers generally agreed that before 1905, regardless of race, most women could not afford to live on their own. But as the population of single women living in Cleveland grew in the decade before the war, a number of low-cost boarding houses were constructed.[27] Few, if any, of these new boarding houses rented rooms to African-American women, however. In 1905, young and single Jane Edna Hunter arrived in Cleveland with little money and few palatable options for housing. Her first tentative inquiry led her "unknowingly [to] the door of a house of prostitution." After a prolonged search, Hunter finally found a place that consumed most of her weekly wages; she had to pay extra for laundry and gas privileges or clean the place in exchange. Women rarely had access to bathing facilities and instead turned to the dangerously unsanitary public bathhouses. Hunter concluded what other women soon discovered: "A girl alone in a large city must . . . know the dangers and pitfalls awaiting her." She eventually found temporary accommodations through a job as a live-in nurse; when her patient got better, Hunter found herself once again without a respectable place to live.[28]

Given the limited housing options available for working-class migrants without kin and friends, many turned to boarding in private homes rented or owned by other African Americans during and after the war. In turn, many African-American households took in boarders because they needed extra income. A 1919 investigation of thirty families by the local Urban League found that twenty-two depended on boarders who paid two to five dollars per week for a shared room. By 1930, over one-third of black households had boarders, compared with less than 10 percent of native-born white and 17 percent of immigrant households with them. The prevalence and continued expansion of boarding in African-American urban households after 1915 has been correlated to a variety of economic roles unrelated household members played. Unrelated boarders, however, played a variety of noneconomic roles as well.[29]

Though the conditions were often crowded, boarding arrangements enabled new emotional opportunities and relationships. Many migrants missed the patterns of visiting, reciprocity, and familiarity of southern households and eagerly welcomed visitors from the South. In one household a parade of boarders passed through for almost two decades, some related, others merely friends and acquaintances. Few paid rent, but these sojourners provided companionship for a family homesick for the rhythms of the South. Conversely, leaving kin in the South and arriving alone in a city was often emotionally traumatic for migrants. Some eased these difficulties through the creation of surrogate families that sometimes grew out of economic relationships forged through boarding. Older women in particular became absorbed into households as fictive aunts, godmothers, and grandmothers to help care for children and allow mothers to work for wages outside the home. These fictive ties appear to have subtly shifted relationships that began as economic exchanges into affective relationships knit by emotion. In turn, these enriched social relationships deepened the sense of responsibility to exchange monetary and household help during times of need.[30]

Census data provide little insight into the complex bonds that often emerged in African-American household and family arrangements in the wake of migration. Indeed, what census enumerator could recreate the pattern and importance of family and boarding relationships in the Davenport household from one census to the next? William Davenport left Montgomery, Alabama, in 1919 to work in a Cleveland foundry. On his arrival he settled with his father's brother and wife, both of whom had migrated some years earlier. By 1923 the household included not only Davenport but also pregnant and recently widowed Ocelie Johnson and her two small children. This arrangement, however, was not simply an impersonal economic one; Johnson had known the family of Davenport's aunt. By 1924, Johnson had married William Davenport.[31]

Children old enough to work sometimes minimized the need to take in boarders by providing a safety net during periods of parents' unemployment and keeping some black mothers out of wage employment altogether. In an analysis of the differences between black and immigrant working-class households before 1930, John Bodnar, Roger Simon, and Michael P. Weber have asserted that black parents encouraged their children to be independent more than immigrant parents did. Because African-American parents faced greater economic deprivation than did either immigrant or native-born white parents, black parents had little to offer their children except the value of self-sufficiency. In turn, black children were not expected to provide financial aid for parents, siblings, or other family members once they became workers. Evidence from Cleveland suggests that such a conclusion needs careful reassessment. Black parents encouraged their children both to attend school and to have jobs; this dual expectation simultaneously instilled work habits and family economic obligations. During the 1910s, Elmer Thompson and his siblings began to work at a young age, even as they continued to attend school. Until he married and had children of his own, Thompson gave his wages to his parents—not an uncommon pattern for black men and women of his generation. As soon as Louise Pattengall finished her day at school, she helped her uncle in his small store.[32] These experiences suggest that wage-earning children were fundamental to the maintenance of households; through this arrangement children were schooled in habits of hard work and economic interdependence and parents reinforced their authority.

Once in the city, migrants hoped to return home for visits, but many found this goal nearly impossible. Because of their higher incomes, middle-class migrants had more opportunities to travel south, as seen in the social pages of the city's black newspapers. For many working-class blacks, however, the trip from Cleveland to Alabama or Georgia was expensive. Because of tight budgets, many migrants simply never returned "down South" to visit loved ones. The sudden death or illness of a relative or friend still in the South heightened the sense of distance and made the loss all the more difficult. Fearing that she would never see her parents again, Myrtle Wiggins moved her aging and ill parents from Birmingham to Cleveland and cared for both until they died.[33]

The inability to visit reinforced many migrants' desire to retain family ties however possible. Willa Davenport Thomas recalled that her mother, Ocelie Johnson Davenport, could not afford frequent trips home to see relatives, but she and her sisters in Cleveland helped to ensure that at least one of them made a trip south. When their own large families demanded more time and money, they pooled their resources and brought their aging mother north. Until her grandmother's move, Willa Thomas had seen her only once, but the frequent stories that her mother told her had maintained the family connection. Many migrants relied on friends and extended kin already in the North to send word home to family. Though many wrote letters or sent announcements to local southern black newspapers, taking and sending pictures became another important and lasting way to visually document their success and dignity in the North. As Vertamae Smart Grosvenor has noted, migrants everywhere displayed an eagerness "to have the camera catch their likeness to send home so everybody could see how well they were doing in the promised land." By the 1920s, having a picture taken became affordable for increasing numbers of African Americans; still others made the sacrifice at least once. For many migrants sending pictures "down South" was the only means to share a marriage or the birth and growth of children. Similarly, pictures sent North maintained connections to place and kin in the South. The brisk businesses that Allan Cole and other black photographers in Cleveland established in the 1920s testify to the ways in which black Clevelanders marked and maintained family connections.[34]

While many adult migrants found it difficult to visit the South, it was not uncommon for them to send their children instead. The continued presence of relatives in the South provided parents with care for younger children out of school in the summer months and relatives with labor during the planting and cultivating of crops. Older children sometimes found it difficult to find wage work in Cleveland during the summer and instead returned to pick cotton in the South; others provided labor for aging grandparents who owned or rented farms. The experiences of Linton Freeman and his brother, both of whom returned to their parents' farm each summer to work until they finished high school, were fairly common. Their regular returns to rural farms maintained their economic obligations to family still in the South. Many migrant parents, however, intended to provide their children with more than just a chance to learn how to farm. Older relatives could teach and nurture visiting children in southern black culture or introduce them to their geographical roots.[35]

Migrants who returned to the South viewed their trips as a paradoxical reminder of what had been left behind: loved relatives and hated Jim Crow. Even for children the differences in treatment were thrown in sharp relief when they entered the South. As a child, the playwright Adrienne Kennedy made yearly trips to her grandmother's home in Georgia in the 1930s. Although Kennedy "loved [her] grandparents immensely" these trips were fraught with the contradictory emotion of humiliation when she changed trains in Cincinnati and boarded "the dirty Jim Crow car." Her younger brother expressed his feelings in a more visible manner: "As soon as the train pulled out of the Cleveland Terminal Tower he started to cry and he cried all the way to Cincinnati. Night would come while we rode into the South and he cried with his head on my shoulder. . . . I tried to interest my brother in the magazine, but he kept sobbing, 'I want to go home.' I put my arm around my brother, looked out of the dirty double-paned windows and clutched the *Modern Screen* magazine with [Clark] Gable on the cover."[36] Migrants left the South to escape segregation, and thus many were unwilling to return, even for short periods. Henry Pointer's mother, for example, "never lost anything after leaving Nashville, Tennessee. She never went to visit relatives."[37] Others insisted, instead, that relatives visit Cleveland, often with the hope that the visit would become permanent.

Within the variety of responses to separation from relatives and the South, migrants made great efforts to maintain their southern connections in Cleveland. Some sustained links by living close to relatives who had recently migrated. S. Davis recalled that the people on her block had lived in the same town in Alabama. Patricia Ashford's relatives lived in apartments in a building owned by a relative. After each family found a home, another family of relatives arrived from Bessemer, Alabama. This practice began before World War I and continued until the 1960s. But shared blood ties and origins moved beyond residential proximity and obligations of kinship to include the conscious retention of southern values and patterns of behavior. Families continued to take and raise each other's children, and it was fairly common for people from the same place to marry one another after they arrived in the city. They joined the same social organizations and became members of the same churches, where migrants quickly organized southern state clubs. These social organizations created around household, neighborhood, church, and work connections satisfied emotional needs previously fulfilled by families. Through these new relationships, migrants reestablished support networks and retained their sense of being southerners.[38]

Connections with families, friends, and other transplanted southerners lessened many migrants' sense of isolation, but the process of family and household formation and settlement was often long. Darlene Clark Hine has asserted that especially for women migrants, relinquishing ties to the South was an "incomplete process" because they had left immediate family members behind. She has suggested that when migrants left loved ones in the South, "psychological and emotional relocation was much more convoluted and, perhaps, more complicated than heretofore assumed."[39]

The process of migration and the distance from kin in the South tested familial relationships, often resulting in altered, severed, or new perceptions of family ties and obligations. As numerous studies have shown, individuals within black families in the South usually occupied gendered roles, with women perceived as caretakers and men as wage-earning heads of households. In the North, however, black men and women frequently encountered new demands as workers and caretakers. While the care of children was often the work of women, migration thrust many men into similar roles. Some men became the sole caretakers of children sent by family members in the South to attend school in Cleveland.[40] During times of prolonged unemployment, others took on the care of children and households as women turned to wage labor. These examples suggest that varied experiences of caring for children must be more carefully examined.[41]

In more subtle ways, many black men carefully weighed job choices against the needs of their children. In a study on Boston, Elizabeth Pleck found that black men had a high rate of absenteeism from their households because of their limited job opportunities, though black men with young children were the least likely to leave.[42] Robert Griswold has noted that more than immigrant working-class fathers, black men were likely to be absent from their children's lives. Kenneth Kusmer has noted that black men had a greater rate of occupational stability in Cleveland than did black men in other cities.[43] On the other hand, numbers of black men found that work in the steel mills, though higher paying than other jobs, could also be sporadic. Just how the needs of a family may have impacted job choices, migration, and work patterns may never be clearly revealed, but first-person narratives are nonetheless suggestive. Black men expressed a great deal of grief when they had to leave their children to find work. Elmer Thompson recalled that his father quit a well-paying, year-round job as an asphalt layer because it demanded he be separated from his children for extended periods of time. Other black men chose jobs in the service and transportation trades instead of better-paying ones because they tended to provide steady employment.[44]

The 1920s economy in Cleveland periodically forced many married black men out of work, which necessitated that black women seek paid work. Though many married black men, out of pride, insisted that their wives not work for wages, unemployment or illness made this arrangement impossible. In 1925 Henry Pointer's mother, for example, persuaded her husband to buy a Maytag washer instead of a "shiny black Ford." Her fear of losing her husband's wages proved prescient: suddenly widowed four years later and left with two small children, she used the washing machine to clean nurses' uniforms from a hospital near her home. Many black women became the primary wage earners in their households, despite the presence of husbands and sons, which required role changing. For other men, pride compelled them to earn enough to prevent their wives from working. Elmer Thompson reveled in removing his wife's labor from whites' kitchens and keeping it confined to his own. Similarly, Paul Glenn's mother was not allowed to work full-time for wages outside of the home. She occasionally took part-time positions, however, which was a source of conflict in the Glenns' marriage. Eventually, with the aid of her children, she kept her wage work a secret from her husband.[45]

The move north and the creation of new family networks enabled some black women to redefine their roles as daughters, wives, and mothers. As Darlene Clark Hine has noted, some black women found that family migration provided them with an opportunity to free themselves from their abusive households in the South. While still in high school, Flowree Robinson married and soon had two small children. Though Robinson experienced regular abuse from her alcoholic husband, embarrassment and lack of money kept her in the marriage. The migration of her brother to Cleveland gave her new choices. Determined to escape, Robinson wrote her brother, who sent her money but stressed that he wanted Robinson to make her own decision; the enclosed money, however, spoke volumes about his feelings. Others had little more than family support, but even the encouragement and relatives' willingness to take care of children was enough to propel many abandoned or abused women northward. Moreover, as with Robinson, the earlier departure of other family members provided many women with the financial and emotional support necessary to leave the South.[46]

For some women, paid work and migration allowed them to reassess their immediate marital and maternal roles. Pressured to protect her propriety, the vaudeville performer Carrie Davenport married another performer. Although unhappy for several years, she did not end the marriage until she arrived in Cleveland. Davenport's decision appears to have been motivated by her ability to acquire steady work, which gave her economic autonomy. Another woman, however, did not have such an easy time extricating herself from a marriage: when she announced her intention to depart once she arrived in the city, her husband stabbed and killed her. Some women left children with relatives and went in search of the highest wages elsewhere. Others abandoned children and simply disappeared, only to be found later, traveling from one northern city to another.[47]

In many instances, however, migration reinforced familial roles based on gender and age. Myrtle Wiggins wanted to marry, but her aging and ill parents required care. Because she was the only child, Wiggins called off her engagement and moved her parents from Birmingham to Cleveland. In addition, she changed her job, moved closer to a streetcar line, and ceased traveling with a musical group. The unequal gender dynamics in the household did not allow William Murdock's mother an opportunity to dispute or prevent her husband's decision to migrate. Murdock recalled that his mother "was displeased about leaving a good home in Montgomery [Alabama] and moving to Cleveland." He maintained that while she did not openly quarrel with her husband about the move, her anger "was reflected in her thinking a long time."[48]

The experience of migration usually sustained, rather than severed, economic obligations and emotional connections between family members in Cleveland. Low wages and periodic unemployment often limited what adult children could offer their parents or siblings, but evidence shows that many helped whenever possible. Family members migrated to the same or nearby cities precisely because they could share resources. Louise Pattengall's mother and two brothers followed Louise's father from Birmingham to Pittsburgh in 1916, though he died not long after their arrival in the city. Now dependent on the wages of her barely adult sons, Pattengall's mother struggled to provide for her family. The death of one from pneumonia forced the mother to think about returning to the South; her mother's sister and family had migrated from Birmingham to Cleveland, and Louise and her mother soon joined them. Though the house was crowded, family became all "those who lived together," and all shared their resources, enabling Louise to complete high school and her family to stay together. Pattengall's family maintained an interdependence, sustaining ties throughout their adult lives.[49]

Instead of strengthening them, the strain of finding work and reestablishing a life in Cleveland frayed the bonds in some families. For some men, the inability to find work and maintain a sense of dignity caused marital strain and separation. Langston Hughes's mother and stepfather suffered through years of upheaval caused by the difficulty of maintaining a household during a period of economic uncertainty. Similar strains were apparent in the marriage of Chester Himes's parents; both were bitterly disappointed to discover racial relations characteristic of the South in a northern setting. After years of unhappiness, they separated. Repeated unemployment led other men to disappear altogether.[50]

New relationships between African Americans and new immigrants also served to replace lost ties to kin in the South. By the late 1920s, African Americans dominated some neighborhoods in the Central Area. While some migrants were perceived as intruders, other evidence suggests that, at least on an informal and neighborhood level, blacks often had cordial and even deeply intimate social relationships with other groups. Moreover, despite the increased concentration of black migrants in particular neighborhoods, Cleveland's near east side had large populations of Jewish and Italian immigrants, two groups who faced housing prohibitions as well. Indeed, while 90 percent of the black population resided in the Central Area by 1930, tens of thousands of working-class immigrants lived there too. The common experiences of migration and immigration, along with inadequate housing and irregular employment, forged connections between blacks and their immigrant neighbors. Elmer Thompson remembered that "Cleveland seemed like a foreign country—everybody was speaking Italian or [Yiddish]." He jokingly noted that each time a boat or train arrived, more relatives came to live with immigrants or blacks.[51]

Women often acted as links in cross-cultural exchanges as they canned vegetables, shared produce from gardens, and swapped homemade wine in a mutual effort to stretch limited household budgets. They shared child care and the endless effort to keep rundown homes clean. Some black migrants relied on personal relationships with immigrant landlords to keep rents lower or to gain access to better housing and jobs. Black migrant and immigrant children regularly played together on the streets, even as schools and clubs run by social welfare agencies became more segregated. These intimate relationships led some black migrants to communicate with their neighbors in the immigrants' native tongues rather than in English. One African American recalled his neighborhood as "white and colored . . . mixed together. . . . We all lived together." When he was a child, this man's parents rented an apartment from a German immigrant who taught him German. He recalled his first day at school and the surprise of his teacher: "When I got older they took me to school. The teacher looked at me and talked to me, but I wouldn't answer. . . . She called my mother, 'He won't answer, he won't talk.' My mother said to her, 'Well, I did forget to tell you one thing—he doesn't [speak] English.' My mother said she knew German . . . and I heard my folks talk English, but they never said anything to me. I always talked German."[52]

Numerous changes had taken place in the Central Area between 1915 and 1935. Many blacks viewed their households and neighborhoods through a complicated lens of dignity, pride from accomplishment, and frustration over the increasing segregation. Marjorie Isom-Davis, a young girl in the early 1920s, recalled that her neighborhood "was a lovely, tree-lined place in which to live. The people were very careful of how they swept the front side-walks and they kept their lawns looking nice." Marjorie Witt Johnson described her childhood street as "diversified—it had many different [people]." Willa Thomas corroborated Johnson's depiction of the diverse milieu still evident by the 1930s. Born in 1925, Thomas grew up in a mixed neighborhood of working-class blacks and Italian immigrants between East Thirty-third and East Thirty-ninth Streets, where children played in the streets and neighbors shared food. But she knew that outsiders had started to describe her neighborhood as a ghetto. "Most people did," she said, "because they figured most of the poor people lived in that section." Those who lived in the neighborhood, however, refused to perceive it as "rundown." The people "that were renting, and even owning, they would take care of their property . . . they would plant flowers."[53]

When Josephus Hicks arrived in Cleveland in 1935, he, too, recognized the complexities that Davis, Johnson, and Thomas described. Keenly aware of the growing residential segregation, Hicks quickly learned that *ghetto* was a term used by outsiders to demarcate a "place set aside for blacks." With black residents concentrated in one area, city officials had "less appreciation for what [blacks] needed" and instead turned their attention to other neighborhoods. The city provided abysmal garbage collection and police protection, for example.[54] Carl Stokes, who lived in a neighborhood populated by black migrants, remembered "a real sense of community": "The world we knew ran from East Sixty-Eighth Street to East Seventy-Ninth Street going east, and from Cedar Avenue south to Central Avenue. Everybody in that area knew everybody else, knew what they were doing and most of the time what they were hiding. We had almost no notion of anyone's living beyond the horizons of our narrow patch of neighborhood." This community, however, was based not on flower beds but on poverty: "It was not the kind of community in which people should have to live. There is nothing glamorous about stealing from a delivery truck, or bootlegging, or the numbers racket."[55]

As Carl Stokes suggested, in many neighborhoods the material conditions of African Americans' lives did not reflect the supposed prosperity of the 1920s. Census data and several contemporary studies document that few black homes had private toilets or baths. While the overcrowding of the war years abated somewhat as immigrants and native-born whites found better housing in neighborhoods outside the city, African Americans continued to occupy older housing where privacy was a luxury. Disproportionate numbers of African-American households continued to share water and toilets. Thelma and James Bosley came to Cleveland from Georgia believing they had left behind "one room shacks and wood burning stoves." Both Bosleys worked after they migrated, but saw little change in the way they lived: they shared a toilet with five families. Women typically gathered shucks from corn to sweep the yards and houses and packed eggs in the ground to keep them from spoiling. Alberta Hornsby's family came to the city in 1917 and she remembered that "the window sill was our icebox. During the summer we could not always buy the ice until [my father] came home with the paycheck." As a child, Stokes watched his mother hang the clean, wet clothes to dry in the house since "leaving them outside meant you did not want them."[56]

The financial precariousness of many black households had an impact on African Americans' health. Throughout the first decades of the century, tuberculosis accounted for a significant portion of the death rate, so much so that birth rates failed to keep pace. After 1920, black deaths from disease still remained more than double that of whites; the black infant mortality rate was much higher than that of other groups. The impact of poorly ventilated rooms, colder weather, and inadequate diets undermined health, yet poor wages meant few migrants received adequate medical care. Instead, as Natalie Middleton recalled, migrants continued to rely on southern folk remedies, with mixed results: "Sassafras tea . . . sulfur, molasses, Caster Oil, goose grease and hot irons in the bed. . . . If you could stand all that, you wouldn't be sick very long. You would be either better or dead." During the common influenza epidemics, Middleton remembered the rapid appearance of quarantine: "Seemed as if they grew on the clap board siding of homes." Women also relied on folk remedies to terminate unwanted pregnancies, often with disastrous results.[57]

For single African-American women with children, more limited economic means made their circumstances even more dire. After the death of her husband and infant, one mother of four small children sought aid from a neighborhood social settlement. Settlement house workers sent her to Associated Charities for a mother's pension, but a social worker refused "because of too much delinquency" in the woman's neighborhood. To receive help, the woman was compelled to move to another section of the city "away from the friends who have been her main comfort in the last 4 or 5 months." One month after her move, however, she had yet to receive support. After repeated inquiries, no one could guess when money would be forthcoming, since charity workers were months behind in their paperwork.[58]

Despite their limitations, African Americans within the Central Area strove to maintain their notions of respectability and improve the material conditions of their lives. Some migrants with steady jobs and multiple wage earners had disposable income, which bought much needed clothing, household items, and health care. Uninterrupted wage work and access to company housing with relatively low rents, for example, allowed the Malone family to own a car. High wages from skilled work in the building trades enabled William Middleton to send his daughter, Natalie, to weekly tap dance and piano lessons. "Oh, how I remember the tap dancing teacher," Middleton recalled. "I thought she was Clara Bow in person." Similarly, wage-earning children in the Davenport household meant that their mother, Ocelie Davenport, stayed out of wage work and the younger children occasionally went to the movies.[59]

Because of their family responsibilities, African-American women struggled with the often inadequate housing and city services. In the crowded boxcars, for example, a black woman labored to keep her husband, four children, and three rooms scrupulously clean. In addition, she worked long hours for the railroad. The woman tellingly explained the burdens created by the intersection of race, class, and gender: "I am working with my husband so we can get along," she said. "You know the children have to be dressed better than most people who live in box cars."[60] Although Carl Stokes lived on East Sixty-ninth Street "in a rickety old two-family house," his mother went to similar lengths to overcome the inadequate physical comfort of her home: "We covered the rat holes with the tops of tin cans. The front steps always needed fixing, one of them always seemed to be missing. The coal stove kept the living room warm; we used heated bricks and an old flatiron wrapped in flannel to keep warm in the bedroom."[61] In an effort to limit the number of children, black women attended clinics and demanded to learn about birth control, reportedly at three times the frequency of the population as a whole.[62]

When wage work failed to pay the rent or provide for other household needs, many African Americans turned to their neighborhoods for sources of income. Mable Malone never worked for wages outside the home, but her son recalled "the pay night parties she used to give every payday to supplement my father's wages. She used to give them in our boxcar and my grandmother would have similar parties in hers." John Malone remembered that during Prohibition his parents "used to sell liquor to the railroad men and I can remember several times when the federal agents came to our house. It was very embarrassing, but everyone was doing it."[63] Natalie Middleton witnessed the selling and buying of bootleg alcohol in the back alley behind her house, which became known as "Vienna Court." Increasing numbers of women went from house to house, writing policy numbers. Craps, bootlegging, and numbers running provided income, but frequently made neighborhoods more dangerous. According to Marie Crawford, people came to parties with flasks and went out to the alleys to have them filled. On one such occasion, three people were killed in Crawford's neighborhood "on account of liquor."[64]

By the 1920s, Scovill Avenue, between Fourteenth and Fifty-fifth Streets, emerged, in the words of Chester Himes, as the "Bucket of Blood, one of the most degraded slum streets I had ever seen." Here, prostitutes and pimps coexisted with numbers runners working out of speakeasies. "They gambled for small change, fought, drank poisonous 'white mule,' cut each other up, and died in the gutters. It was nothing unusual to see a black man lying in the gutter, drunk and bleeding and dying."[65] Prostitution, too, sometimes spilled over into violence. In one dramatic display, Andrew Walters killed James Childs for cooking spareribs out in the open and luring potential customers away from Walters's wife's business. A witness reported that Walters "objected to Childs' cooking because his wife was a prostitute and he did not want any cooking in the yard for fear of spoiling her business."[66] Despite the danger and contradictions, Carl Stokes claimed that the prostitutes and gamblers that plied their trades in the neighborhood had a certain charisma. "In a community where people live in despair and denial," Stokes recalled, "the man who defies the rules and is able to make a living becomes a hero."[67]

The dramatic increase and concentration of black migrants alarmed some white elites, who declared them to be "a menace to the community."[68] According to these critics, black migrants created overcrowded and chaotic households; these tendencies in turn undermined the urban order. As in other northern cities, contemporary observers in Cleveland correlated the rise in the black population with crime, disease, and immorality. They then cited such social characteristics to explain the physical deterioration of neighborhoods.

Social workers first pointed to the growth in population and criminal behavior of young African-American women and men as evidence of social disorganization. Throughout the war and postwar years, reports of increased arrests of black migrants, particularly migrant men, became typical in the Urban League's records. By 1917, black men had gone from a fraction to over 60 percent of the population at the Cleveland workhouse. Vagrancy was the most common offense. One jail official admitted, however, that "these men were not of the criminal type, but had been sent to the jail for such minor offenses as loafing on street corners, drunkenness, and for being 'suspicious characters.'" He conceded that the lack of housing and limited recreation, along with the absence of proper clothing and hats, made them suspect and vulnerable to arrest. Such an admission exposed the thinly veiled racial ideologies that informed arrest policies. Equally alarming to city officials was the large and visible population of unattached young men and women who participated in the new urban entertainment located in bars, dance halls, and theaters. Jane Edna Hunter described the proliferation of night clubs, dance halls, and jook joints as the "worst the race has to offer" and little more than brothels.[69]

For black women to display sexual autonomy undermined the diligent efforts within the black community to maintain an appearance of traditional female respectability. Critiques of the social and sexual behavior of white working-class women had been common in the city before 1915, but the historically racist attitudes about black women's sexuality heightened the attention newly directed at unattached migrant women. The streets, saloons, and dance halls, which had become places for blacks to rest and socialize, were popularly perceived as locations for licentious behavior. The shrill and disapproving comments in newspapers attested to the pervasive sense of a population of dangerous women. The newspapers frequently reported the arrests of young women charged with disorderly conduct, "lewdness," and prostitution. Police arrested one young woman, for example, and charged her with indecency because she gave a "public entertainment in an immodest way." Women were publicly warned to avoid such behavior, not as a means to protect themselves from harm, but to prevent criticism of the larger community.[70]

The historian Joanne Meyerowitz argues that single women's participation in public unsupervised leisure with men during the first decades of the twentieth century suggested a shift in the range of economic relationships between young women and men. "The exchange of sexual services for monetary support," Meyerowitz noted, "moved beyond the marital bedroom and the brothel and into a variety of intermediate forms including dating, pick-ups, temporary alliances, and occasional prostitution." Jane Edna Hunter encountered similar transactions between young black women and men when she observed "the strong intimation of the evil influence of this rooming house" after coming upon the "pink silk undergarments of the landlady's daughter who went out regularly every afternoon and returned home quite late at night, and more often, in the early morning." Hunter's Victorian sensibilities were further affronted when she discovered that another young woman received "lovely silk hose" for accompanying young men "to the dives of Hamilton Avenue," which was at the heart of an area known for prostitution. Years after her own experiences, Hunter hoped to eradicate "the evil influence [of] the commercial dance hall." Hunter's abhorrence aside, such behavior should not be perceived as an indication of young women's newfound freedom. Rather, the links between sexual relations and economic exchange emerged as a result of young women's inability to make ends meet.[71]

Young black men's behavior received increased public scrutiny as their social contact with white women became more visible. As both black and white women mingled with young men in bars, vaudeville houses, and dance halls, the historic intolerance for interracial sexual contact increased. During World War I, in a scene perhaps influenced by the inflammatory rhetoric around *Birth of a Nation,* a riot nearly occurred when rumors circulated that a black man had "insulted a white woman" in a saloon. What appears to have taken place was a flirtation between the man and woman that was disrupted by some immigrant men. A crowd quickly gathered and began to beat the man with fists and stones; although the man managed to escape, a crowd followed. With the aid of other blacks, the man escaped, but the crowd, intent on capturing a culprit, spent their rage on another black man. He, too, was eventually rescued when two older black women helped him flee.[72]

This heightened awareness of black men's behavior continued in the 1920s. Highly conscious that the larger society perceived black men's encounters with white women as threatening, Chester Himes recounted his first job as a busboy at the Wade Park Manor and his first opportunity to flirt with young white women: "Two young women sat in a glass booth facing the elevators and checked the trays of the room service waiters before they went upstairs. The young women were good-looking and white. Most of the young black waiters flirted with them; they returned the flirtation to a select few. . . . I don't know whether any of the waiters ever scored with either of them, but if not, it wasn't because they didn't try." Himes and the other young men could look at and talk to these women, but they could not touch them because of a glass barrier constructed to prevent physical contact.[73]

The concern over a visible population of unsupervised young African Americans instigated a public debate about the perceived increase in the delinquency of African-American young adults and children. Before the war, the public behavior of both age groups had received little scrutiny; few black children were even admitted to homes for delinquent children. As large numbers of black migrants arrived in the city, however, attitudes about and services for juvenile delinquency changed. In 1919, the Urban League called for protective work to prevent the delinquency of black girls, primarily because most agencies refused to accept blacks. Consequently, the Home for Delinquent Girls had a disproportionate number of young black women accused of a variety of juvenile crimes ranging from immorality to petty larceny. Most were charged with immorality and impudence or were perceived as uncontrollable. Though what constituted immoral behavior was not specified, one report claimed that more than half the girls had some sexual experience, most at a very early age. Since few girls freely admitted to sexual abuse or rape, for social welfare workers, sexual experience constituted willing assignations.[74]

This increased attention to young black women's delinquency bore the mark of an explicit association between race and female deviance. One historian of social welfare work has noted that social welfare reformers in the first decades of the twentieth century used the definition "sexual delinquency" to include prostitution and other divergences from middle-class norms, "including poverty, dependence, transience, illness and out-of-wedlock pregnancy." In Cleveland, social welfare workers attributed the rise in the number of black unwed mothers to the presence of cultural attitudes that allowed such behavior. This emphasis marks the decided shift of Cleveland reformers away from the protection of women's sexual vulnerability toward the conviction that these young women suffered from sexual deviance. Young men could freely engage in sex but young women who did so were labeled sexual psychopaths.[75]

Social workers clearly correlated the rise in delinquency with the cultural inadequacies of black families, particularly those with working mothers. Such labels clearly influenced the findings in the report Howard Whipple Green conducted for the Cleveland Health Council in the late 1920s. Eighty-nine of the 377 girls in the Girls' Industrial School were black; half of this population of black girls reportedly lived with "father, mother, or other adult who was prostituting, immoral, a drunkard, a gambler, bad tempered, foul mouthed, or had a court history." More than one-quarter of the black girls had parents labeled as "abusive, strict, antagonistic, or a religious fanatic" whose habits of nagging, neglect, irresponsibility, or uncooperativeness supposedly contributed to the delinquency. Yet a careful reading of the records reveals that less than one-quarter of these parents charged with "crimes" had actually been in a court. Rather, the majority of these families were saddled with highly subjective charges of "immorality" or "bad temperament." Eleanor Rowland Wembridge, who wrote the introduction to Howard Whipple Green's report, did not refute Green's racialized assessments of the young women. She explained the disproportionate number of black girls as a correlation of regional origin and household disorganization: "The low economic level of the colored families which have lately moved here from the South makes a working mother more of a necessity. Therefore, more colored children proportionately lack their mother's supervision." Social welfare workers perceived this lack of supervision as neglect that bred sexual permissiveness absent in white homes, where the overwhelming majority of women with children did not work for wages.[76]

White social workers and city officials attributed the rise in disease, delinquency, and death rates to the internal values of African Americans and their tendencies to live "without dignity." Eleanor Rowland Wembridge, who worked in the juvenile court, expressed this view when she claimed that blacks chose to congregate "into small rooms, sleeping with no privacy" in areas ill-equipped to provide homes and services. Such choices, according to Wembridge, produced "indecency and loss of civilized standards." Others shared and expressed this assessment; such cultural views, in turn, were used to explain the social problems that African Americans encountered in the city. Some considered the conditions blacks faced to be a result of the dislocation caused by migration rather than specific structural constraints found in a segregated city.[77]

Social welfare workers such as Wembridge believed that segregation by race was necessary to the social and moral order of the welfare agency, and this perspective significantly shaped policy in social settlements located in black neighborhoods. Since white social workers believed that the problems of modern urban life had been surmounted, their perceptions of disorder in black households, characterized as a mishmash of too many kin and working mothers, revealed beliefs in racial and cultural inadequacies.[78] City officials joined in these perceptions, asserting that black migrants presented a particular threat to an orderly urban industrial environment. The charges made against blacks had been raised against immigrants a decade earlier. In the new climate of white nativism, however, social welfare workers expressed a collective belief that African Americans did not deserve efforts used to help immigrants integrate.

When immigrants had arrived, numerous private and church-based philanthropic organizations emerged to provide resources to counteract irregular employment, low wages, and the isolation attendant with leaving one country for another. Out of the fear that many of these organizations sowed the seeds of urban disorder, sympathy for unions, and political anarchy, professional social welfare workers and the business elite embarked on a vigorous program of Americanization through well-funded neighborhood settlement houses. Though shrouded in claims of assimilation, efforts to Americanize immigrants had been conceived as a means to reorient immigrant cultural identity and national loyalty toward the needs of a powerful business elite who desired low-wage, nonunion workers. In the decade before the war, private organizations funded five social settlement houses on the east side of the city and promoted programs to instill middle-class values of thrift, hard work, efficiency, and individualism. Each settlement house established separate programs for men, women, and children to encourage the use of English. Social welfare workers made minimal efforts to incorporate and encourage native cultures. Though these efforts ranged from coercive to respectful, at the heart of the programs was a fundamental belief that immigrants should be integrated into the social and institutional life of the city. As elsewhere, white immigrants in Cleveland simultaneously resisted and utilized these programs based on familial and group needs.[79]

These private efforts led to the creation of a federation to fund philanthropy in an organized manner. The Federation of Charities and Philanthropy emerged in 1913 to reduce fund-raising costs, establish efficiency, and create professional standards. Equally important, planners hoped to reduce the number of organizations and avoid duplication of services; as a result of these goals, organizations competed with each other for funds from the federation. No longer able to solicit funds on their own, organizations had to prove their legitimacy and worthiness. By the eve of the war, the Federation of Charities and Philanthropy joined with the Welfare Council to form the Welfare Federation of Cleveland (WFC). This merger concentrated social welfare in the hands of business elites and professional social welfare workers, limited the ability of nonaffiliated organizations to appeal for funds, and prevented "radical innovations and threats to the status quo of the business-welfare alliance." In his study of Hiram House, John Grabowski noted that by the 1910s, "the endorsement card became a coveted possession for charitable agencies, since most potential donors refused to consider supporting any agency lacking it." By the late 1910s, the WFC was run like a modern corporation and became a model for other social reform efforts elsewhere.[80]

When it became apparent that the separate facilities created for African Americans had to be supplemented through greater inclusion in the other neighborhood settlements, city leaders and their social worker allies responded to the presence of migrants as a sign of urban disorder. The massive prewar efforts to Americanize the foreign-born population, which had spawned an efficient combination of professional expertise and business philanthropy, evolved after the war into a concerted effort to accommodate black workers to the needs of the industrial urban order. Popular views of inherent racial characteristics shaped the construction of segregated facilities and the creation of programs geared to reinforce racial stratification in neighborhoods, social organizations, and schools.[81]

Even in those organizations forced to extend services to blacks, the policy of assimilation had shifted markedly to one of segregation. The change in policies at Hiram House between 1915 and 1930 provide a case study of the way the practices of a settlement house changed when black residents joined immigrants. Located in the heart of the "Roaring Third," Hiram House first served a large Jewish, and then an eastern and a southern European population. Social workers lamented this shift, noting: "In place of Jews, with their splendid morals and intense family life, we will have the fiery Italians; and the Slavish and the Polish, with their duller minds, their drunkenness and immorality." The war caused a dramatic turnover in the population surrounding the agency. Welfare workers soon mourned the loss of the Poles and balked at the influx of African Americans from the Deep South. By 1918 George Bellamy, director of Hiram House, declared that the settlement house was "in the midst of a colored colony." Hiram House workers no longer clung to the social ideal of assimilation. Settlement house workers had earlier sought to remake immigrants into "respectable" Americans and instill "the highest development of character." With blacks, however, workers set only the limited goal of deterring delinquency.[82]

The separation of immigrants and blacks first came about because of the programs geared toward immigrants. Black children found the emphasis on folk dances and English courses strange; black girls displayed an acute disinterest in sewing clothes for white dolls in the "dolly clubs." Unlike the immigrant cultures, settlement social workers made little attempt to understand or appreciate southern black culture. Instead, first through subterfuge and then through explicit policies, settlements established patterns of segregation. In one report, a social worker proudly noted that "a very successful plan was carried out in the sewing and cooking departments. We were able by registering the colored children for a certain day to keep them separated from the white girls without drawing particular attention to the racial differences."[83] In the end, as one scholar of Cleveland's social reform efforts noted, the tradition of philanthropy gave way to fear of race riots and "many [social workers] embraced the popular belief that racial traits played a dominant role in human behavior." By the early 1920s, George Bellamy declared that the care of blacks was not worth the effort or money, exemplifying what the historian Allen Davis characterized as the leftovers of wartime social reform: "prohibition, immigration restriction and racist hysteria."[84]

That white elites both encouraged and largely funded separate and segregated institutions underscored the limited economic resources in the black community to either insist on integrated facilities or shape private welfare policies. Despite the much larger black population after 1915, Cleveland did not experience an explosion in private, black-controlled institutions such as those found in Chicago, Philadelphia, and New York City. No matter how poorly funded the majority of such institutions might have been, they nonetheless attested to the growing autonomy of the communities that had produced them. In contrast, in Cleveland, as Kenneth Kusmer has concluded, "the effective control of a number of these organizations remained with the whites who controlled indispensable financial resources." The impact of such financial control and racial ideologies reverberated in the policies and programs of the Urban League on a daily basis. White male business elites who hired blacks as low-wage, unskilled, and unorganized workers largely fund-ed the organization. Just as William Conners, the league's executive direc-tor, had advocated that black workers labor efficiently in the workplace, he established programs to push similar values in their homes. Thrift clubs encouraged savings, not so much to purchase homes, but to enable black workers to minimize appeals for charity during their periodic unemploy-ment. Many wives and daughters of the men serving on the executive board of the Urban League had similar positions within the PWA. The wife of Sher-win Williams, for example, was the longtime president. Like the men, these women advocated a paternalistic control over the policies of the association.[85]

Black social welfare workers like Jane Edna Hunter carved professional status and community stature out of the segregation that kept the majority of the black population on the margins. In many ways, Hunter represented this new professional group of social welfare workers who acted as media-tors between the powerful white business elite and black workers seeking private charity. In return for interpreting and acting on the wishes of the powerful, Hunter received funds. Josephus Hicks witnessed the maneuver-ings of Hunter and the responses to her efforts. Hunter, he observed, made the most out of segregation and "was able to see the wants of the higher ech-elon [who] needed a person to do work for them." William Conners never openly challenged the interests of the white business elite and instead aggres-sively impeded black workers' efforts to organize unions. To stifle union or-ganization and encourage adherence to company work rules, he placed col-lege-educated black men and women as welfare workers in plants with large proportions of blacks. Such efforts garnered the continued support of busi-ness owners and the black middle class.[86]

In this period of heightened racial antipathy, Hunter's perspective took on a pragmatism evident in black thought elsewhere. Before the war, Hunt-er justified her segregated organization as female salvation. Thus, the PWA was not a Jane Crow "home for girls," but a "haven for the Negro girl." After the war, her proposal to save these young women from low wages and unsa-vory surroundings seemed reasonable since most blacks were forced to pay high rents and young black women without families had few affordable al-ternatives. Her appeals to female propriety found support from middle-class African-American women who otherwise found Hunter's pursuit of domestic training offensive. By the twenties, as African Americans faced exclusion from much of public entertainment because of poverty or segregation, they eagerly sought the recreational services the PWA offered, such as the camp for chil-dren and sewing and cooking classes. The cafeteria provided lunch for black teachers excluded from the lunch rooms where they worked; the recreation rooms offered locations for dance and music lessons, as well as places for various clubs to meet and socialize.[87]

Yet Hunter's hope to provide the only haven for young black women in the city sometimes took atavistic turns of expression, such as was displayed in the 1921 anniversary celebration of the PWA. Young women, dressed in white, sang about the benefits of the PWA to the tune of "Dixie": "If at night we choose to roam," they sang, "We may as well find another home / Away, away, away from PWA / But if we want to be real good / We will find in her the mother-hood."[88] This transparent reference to Hunter made the goals of the PWA clear. The choice of melody may have buoyed the philanthropic sensibilities of whites, but it certainly must have offended the integrationist sentiments of some blacks.

Throughout the 1920s, the majority of Cleveland's settlement houses and charity agencies practiced some form of segregation or exclusion of African Americans. Neither the Travelers' Aid Society nor the Cleveland Orphan Asylum aided African Americans. At Goodrich House, social welfare workers reported to the executive committee that they had successfully segregated black children at the summer camps by taking them two at a time and carefully separating them in recreational activities. The now famous Karamu House, first organized as the Playhouse Settlement, remained an important exception to these trends. Rowena and Russell Jelliffe created an interracial community center that soon became renowned for its theatrical productions. Through most of its early history, Karamu House struggled to fend for itself, but it remained independent from the strong arm of the WFC. Langston Hughes was an early protégé of the Jelliffes. Later, Hughes and Zora Neale Hurston attempted to stage their collaborative, and subsequently controversial play, *Mule Bone.*[89]

Limited income, time, and space combined with the desire for recreation meant that migrants did look to the settlement houses, but they demanded clubs of their own. While white social workers did not often initiate clubs that appealed to African-American migrants, some began to yield to the autonomy that the new participants demanded. African-American women, for example, approached Hiram House workers for space to hold practices for an all-female band. The women made it clear, however, that their sojourn at the house would be temporary because they preferred to have space of their own. Children, too, sought organizations on their own terms in the settlement houses. In the late 1920s, older black girls and boys took control of the drama club at Hiram House. First they changed the club's name to the Langston Hughes Players, then they sought material written by and about black people. When settlement workers expressed skepticism about the children's ability to perform the more complicated plays, the children remained insistent. Their shows opened to enthusiastic reviews, and they typically performed the plays elsewhere in the city.[90]

Working-class black women reconfigured the segregated mothers' clubs first organized in the settlement houses. Most of the women in the club at the Friendly Inn, for example, lived on the edge of poverty and juggled large households; many generally found it difficult to allocate time to socialize with other women. Though initially organized by settlement workers as a sewing club, the women wanted to make the most of their free time and soon turned their meetings into lively discussions on national and race-conscious topics. Weekly, the women encouraged one another to testify—speak out—about the abuse that African Americans had experienced in the South. Social workers noted that the club sharply contrasted with the other mothers' clubs: "The other [immigrant] members do not seem to be interested in things outside of their homes."[91]

Though city schools remained integrated, an insistence on racial segregation began to pervade education policies. With the large in-migration of blacks, some schools attempted to establish segregated classes, claiming that newly arrived African Americans from the South had much lower levels of literacy. Some school board members claimed black students posed a discipline problem. In both instances, the Cleveland Board of Education altered the curriculum to reflect attitudes about race. By the late 1920s, several schools were nearly all black, reflecting the changing demographics of adjacent neighborhoods. African-American parents complained, however, when their children had to travel to attend the nearly all-black high school even when other schools were more convenient. The expanding segregation was most evident in the technical schools. As the business elite gained greater control over efforts to unionize the building trades, organized craftworkers participated in excluding most young black adults from technical schools. The city's three trade and technical schools either did not admit blacks at all or greatly restricted their access. East Technical High School was in the heart of the Central Area, but only a handful of blacks attended. Carl Stokes recalled the elaborate plan to bring white students from the west side of the city to attend classes. Ironically, these trends allowed for the increase in the number of black teachers, but only for those with northern educations. They found expanded opportunities only in all-black schools. Most were subjected to subtle and blatant forms of harassment and segregation. At some schools, for example, black teachers could not eat in the cafeterias.[92]

The decade following the war provided countervailing trends for blacks in Cleveland. As a group, blacks faced common barriers because of race, but as individuals some found it less difficult to transcend such obstacles because of class, skin color, and northern birth. Many more economically solvent longtime residents blamed what they considered the culturally, socially, and economically impoverished migrant population for the new forms of institutional and informal segregation that emerged in the aftermath of the war. Yet the greatly expanded black population provided some with the opportunities to establish businesses, practice professions, and enter politics. These opportunities laid the foundation for the emergence of a new elite. Within neighborhoods, churches, community institutions, and social clubs, this new elite sought out and found ways to differentiate themselves from the larger community.

But the newly arrived migrants sought to reshape their cultural and social milieu to act on their own behalf. Powerful social and economic forces shaped their settlement in the city, frequently confining them to the least desirable neighborhoods and preventing access to resources. However difficult settlement proved to be, many migrants saw life in the urban North as considerably better than life in the South. Moreover, migrants were not naive about the difficulties they faced. Community, household, and family needed attention, frequently requiring cooperation and ingenuity. But migrants wanted to satisfy more than just their everyday needs for housing; migration north had been born out of a complex set of desires to improve their lives as a people, not simply to acquire higher wages or escape segregation. Many migrants sought to retain ties to a southern past and at the same time create a community that included their new experiences.

FIVE

"AlabamaNorth": A Community of Southerners

I board in Birmingham about half past four
Tell your daddy where I've been gone so long
I've been in Cleveland, I've been sad and gone.

—Dunham Jubilee Singers,
 "My Mama's Baby Child," 1928

BY THE TIME ARTHUR TURNER and the other members of the Birmingham-based Dunham Jubilee Singers recorded "My Mama's Baby Child" in 1928, they had frequently performed in Cleveland. The direct connection made in the lyrics between the two cities, however, was no mere pandering to the enthusiastic audiences that regularly greeted the group. Turner recalled that though his and other quartets from Alabama, such as the Ravizee Singers, the Bessemer Sunset Four, and the Heavenly Gospel Singers, found appreciative crowds in many midwestern cities, few displayed the warmth of crowds in Cleveland. The quartet sang tight harmony and a diverse repertoire of African-American folk songs, spirituals, blues, and the new gospel. In the early 1920s, a talent scout scouring Birmingham had discovered the Dunham Jubilee Singers and signed them to sing on the radio. Soon the quartet joined a growing number of Jefferson County groups traveling to perform for African-American audiences in northern and midwestern cities hungry for familiar music. Songs like "Holy Is My Name" and the sexually explicit "Who Stole the Lock from the Henhouse Door" shared billing in the halls and homes of Cleveland's African-American community. By the time Turner decided to remain in Cleveland in 1929, the city, like Birmingham, had become filled with quartets. "You couldn't find quartets, particularly gospel quartets in Detroit," recalled Turner, "but Cleveland, now there was a quartet on every street corner, just like Birmingham." For Turner and many other migrants, Cleveland had started to look, sound, smell, and feel like Alabama.[1]

Nearly a decade earlier, Langston Hughes, who sold ice cream and other refreshments from a small shop in the heart of migrant neighborhoods during World War I, documented the beginning of this distinctly black southern culture in the city. He described the usual customers as "the gayest and the bravest people possible—these Negroes from the southern ghettos—facing tremendous odds, working, and laughing and trying to get somewhere in the world."[2] On street corners, in streetcars, and in churches, the buzz and hum of southern black voices began to predominate over those of longtime black residents. By the 1920s, Woodland Avenue and East Fifty-fifth Street emerged as the hub of the Central Area, where African-American residents lived, shopped, worshipped, and played. Along Central and Woodland Avenues, small grocery and dry goods stores coexisted with street vendors and hawkers, policy houses, jook joints, and storefront churches all catering to the needs and demands of migrants. The steady influx of people from the Deep South, with more than half coming from Alabama, continually rejuvenated the southernness of black Cleveland, leading many to refer to the city as "AlabamaNorth."[3] By the eve of the Great Depression, the African-American population had become both large and highly visible with a distinctly southern sound and character.

The "whole new world" of family and friend networks that emerged in the midst of African-American migration to Cleveland allowed for the establishment of a familiar associational life rooted in southern black working-class culture. By the 1920s, working-class migrants created separate churches, clubs, and entertainment, where they mediated their regional origins with expectations for and demands of the urban North. Time and space created for worship and play took on deep meanings as migrants melded their cultural, social, and religious past in the South with their experiences of migration and community building in the urban North. The numerous churches, social clubs, and voluntary organizations they created in the years between the war and the start of the depression reflected their desire to fulfill the promises of northern life.

The noticeable nurturance of southern ways did not escape either the attention or the concern of longtime black residents, particularly elites and professionals. As one complained, before 1917 "there were no barbecue joints and storefront churches or jook joints up here until all these Negroes came from down South. Oh, there were a few places way downtown but none to speak of."[4] While African-American leaders and longtime residents applauded the new wage opportunities that the war provided, they openly worried about the impact migrants from the Deep South might have on the social status of all African Americans in the city. An article in the *Cleveland Gazette* bemoaned "that corner 'preaching,' yelling, shouting, monkey-shines, comedian business, etc., etc. Stop it!"[5] As instances of violence and segregation rose after 1916, many longtime black residents correlated these increases with the growth of the African-American migrant population. In turn, these fears and concerns widened the gaps between African Americans along class and regional lines for social and religious activities, patterns not noticeable before 1915.

African-American migrants' attempts at self-definition and self-determination predated the mass departure.[6] Churches, for example, provided spiritual empowerment for working men and women and sometimes legitimized union activism. In a variety of secular activities working-class African Americans articulated concepts of individual, communal, and racial identity. Robin D. G. Kelley has argued that "during the era of Jim Crow, black working people carved out social space free from the watchful eye of white authority, or in a few cases, the moralizing of the black middle class." These secular spaces, he has suggested, became more than just a "refuge from the humiliations and indignities of racism, class pretensions, and wage exploitation"; the spaces for pleasure sustained values of community while encouraging individuality and allowed for hidden and occasionally public critiques of the dominant ideology.[7]

Black migrants did not arrive with these practices or their racial and class sensibilities intact; rather, the northern setting shaped and was shaped by their sense of themselves as migrants and as southerners. Though all black Clevelanders shared the growing segregation that confined them to the Central Area and limited their access to public and private spaces, regional origins, time of arrival, and material circumstances created different and collective experiences that increasingly informed black working-class identities. Migrants' gatherings for pleasure and solidarity at once coexisted with and stood in opposition to a small population of longtime African-American residents and an emerging business and professional class that created its own sense of community. But class divisions did not simply demonstrate clashes over region and differences in material circumstances; nor were they the result of different styles of behavior. Rather, in churches and organizations in the 1920s, black workers—the majority recently arrived migrants—debated with a black middle class over the structure and role of these organizations; at the center of this debate was the continuing meaningfulness of southern black culture.[8] In their separate clubs, churches, and street parades, black workers asserted an ethos that valued their social autonomy, southern origins, and black expressive culture. Equally important, these forms of expression served as visible and vibrant critiques of racial segregation, gender hierarchies, and class subordination within the larger culture. After more than a decade of this rich associational life, working-class African-American migrants would ultimately reshape the leadership and politics of their community.[9]

The differences between Langston Hughes's perceptions of southern migrants during World War I and the more ambivalent views held by the long-time resident echoed the divergent perspectives expressed by black Clevelanders generally.[10] As the large influx began, African-American leaders cautiously welcomed the recent arrivals. Soon, however, the old elite felt outnumbered by what they defined as a "backward" population of African-American workers from Alabama and Georgia "who are proving so harmful to all our people of this community."[11] Many worried that the massive influx of migrants might disrupt the fragile racial peace. Harry C. Smith, editor of the nationally prominent *Cleveland Gazette,* exemplified this concern when he lamented that before the arrival of migrants, "whites had been old friends of the race."[12]

Many African Americans feared that the almost daily occurrence of racial violence after 1916 might escalate into a full-blown war. The two weekly African-American newspapers regularly documented attacks against African Americans and their property. African-American leaders initially linked the showing of the popular and racially derogatory *Birth of a Nation* to the outbreak of violence. Indeed, after the film's release, local white newspapers commonly used inflammatory and derogatory language, racial jokes, and stereotypes to describe the regional and physical characteristics of African Americans. Voicing a growing popular view, the mayor, Harry L. Davis, publicly declared that blacks had an innate tendency toward degeneracy that understandably justified whites' violent responses.[13] After the brutal riot in Chicago, Rev. O. W. Childress, pastor of St. James A.M.E. Church, warned the local papers to cease the similar "veiled threats [against blacks in Cleveland] in the guise of news." Nonetheless, Childress, like many other elites, directly linked the increase in violence against them to African-American workers' participation in the 1919 steel strike. Now viewed as competition in the labor market, all blacks "live[d] constantly in dread of the result of any disturbance between the races."[14] Though its membership was smaller than that of other groups in the state, others cited the rise in prominence of the Ku Klux Klan in Cleveland as evidence of increased antipathy toward African Americans. City officials rapidly enacted city ordinances to prevent large Klan parades like those taking place in other Ohio cities, but suspicious attacks on African Americans' homes occurred. In at least one instance, Klan members bedecked in robes and full regalia paraded in front of a black doctor's home.[15]

In mass meetings, longtime black residents openly expressed both their fears of the violence and their disdain for the newly arrived. As seemingly hundreds of migrants entered the city daily, they were described as "the loud-mouthed individual of color on the streets, in the streetcars and other public places."[16] Though some African Americans assumed a more defiant stance in the face of the violence, others, dismayed over the increased segregation and unable to halt the frequent attacks against blacks on the streets, scrutinized the behavior of the migrants. Harry Smith, for instance, urged the NAACP "to go to the various plants in the city and talk to the newcomers from the South and tell them how to conduct themselves in public places so as to help and not hurt *our* people of *this* community." More than any other reason, Smith linked migrants' behavior with the rising tide of antiblack attitudes. One editorial suggested that an immigrant's declaration that "down south they make the niggers ride in the back end of streetcars and they ought to do the same here" might prove to be prophetic. The *Cleveland Gazette* concluded, "If the loud-mouthed Negro here is not soon curbed, we may wake up some fine day and find this true here." African-American migrants were regularly criticized for public impropriety, such as dressing too gaily for the May Company parade.[17] Over the course of the war, Smith occasionally argued for an aggressive response to the threats and intimidation African Americans faced. After the report of violence at a local park, for example, Smith urged blacks to "purchase a U. S. Army riot gun and plenty of ammunition for it and keep it in your home."[18] Smith's call to longtime residents to inculcate proper behavior among the newly arrived, however, was the norm.

The consternation felt by longtime residents over the perceived problems brought about by the newly arrived migrants continued in the postwar years. The old elite, in particular, sought to distance themselves from the southern origins of the new migrants. In a letter to the Yale historian James Rhodes, George Myers, a longtime leader of the city's black Republicans, articulated these differences: "Many of the Negroes are of the lowest and shiftless class from when [sic] they came. We here 'to the manor born', so to speak, are doing all we can to assimilute [sic] them. Our greatest task is to get them to see themselves from a northern, instead of a southern standpoint and leave their old condition and customs back in the South. Speaking in the vernacular—to quit being a southern darkey."[19] Another longtime resident, Elmer Thompson, ridiculed the too sharply drawn distinctions between the long-time residents and the newly arrived. "You see with me," he said, "it was just a case of one coming sooner than the other. We were all trying to get away from the cotton fields."[20]

As they had done for nearly a century prior to the influx of so many migrants, black churches in Cleveland sought to mediate the community's debates and provide a range of resources. Since the early part of the nineteenth
century, most African Americans in the city worshipped in all-black Methodist or Baptist churches, with much smaller populations belonging to Catholic, Congregational, and Episcopal churches. By 1910, fourteen churches
served the eighty-five hundred African-American residents.[21] Many of these
churches prided themselves on their educated pastors, their well-organized
memberships, and the gentility that both represented. Additionally, ownership of church property indicated the stability of the congregation's finances.[22]
While the black middle class and elites did not belong to any one church or
denomination, membership patterns were nonetheless discernible. Many in
this small population attended either Mt. Zion Congregational Church or St.
Andrew's Episcopal Church.[23] More recently arrived middle-class blacks tended to affiliate with either St. James A.M.E. Church, Shiloh Baptist Church, or
Antioch Baptist Church—the three oldest black churches in the city. Over the
course of the 1920s, the middle and professional classes came to dominate the
leadership roles in the older and larger A.M.E. and Baptist churches.

As migrants arrived, they first turned to the churches in their neighborhoods, adding to these congregations and strengthening their financial bases.
With much larger congregations, many churches could purchase or construct
new buildings. Both Triedstone Baptist Church and Friendship Baptist Church,
for example, struggled after their formation at the turn of the century. By World
War I, each had grown enough to buy larger buildings.[24] By the mid-1920s, the
membership at Antioch Baptist Church had grown from 500 to 1,400, and
Shiloh Baptist gained over 3,000 new members, increasing its congregation to
over 5,000. With larger memberships, both purchased bigger churches from
departing white congregations.[25] Many of these structures had been built at
the turn of the century and had a neo-medieval architecture that at once distinguished the established congregations from the more transient storefront
churches and announced solid financial foundations. Though each congregation would recreate the physical space to meet its needs, a new location nonetheless carried implications of prestige and legitimacy.[26]

Dramatic expansion in church activities followed the explosion in church
membership. Members of St. John A.M.E., for example, saw the arrival of the
migrants as a "new burden." Some churches responded by creating organizations designed to address the needs of the migrants. Women frequently took
the lead in these efforts, drawing on a dense network of private societies and
professional ties. Instead of leaving one church to shoulder the bulk of the
cost, a number of women's clubs from different churches formed the Help-

ing Hand Charity Club in the summer of 1917. Believing a more professional response was needed, Hazel Mountain, secretary of the state Ohio Federation for Uplift among Colored People, organized black women in the city associated with social welfare work. Within these efforts sponsored by the churches, women displayed a keen awareness of the limited resources available from private white welfare organizations. The Traveler's Aid Society, for example, did not typically aid black migrants traveling alone; instead, black women provided for children traveling alone and young women and men who were ill and dying, bereft of family.[27]

After the war, the larger black churches continued to provide resources to meet the religious, social, and economic needs of the community, but the tone of these efforts changed, revealing class divisions. Most of the large churches held a variety of evening and weekend classes to provide migrants with instructions on upright living habits, such as proper hygiene and the use of cutlery. Occasionally churches offered health care for pregnant and nursing women, inoculations for children, and visits with dentists. While migrants with little money for such services eagerly stood in long lines, they frequently received sharp critiques of their poverty, which was assumed to be a manifestation of their backwardness. There was, as several historians have persuasively argued, a conservative and stereotyped shape to the rhetoric of racial uplift. The emphasis on thrift and cleanliness, for example, was not simply an attempt to inculcate values of self-help, but rather an admonition designed to counter a widely shared perception of the "negative practices and behavior" of blacks.[28]

Middle-class black women espoused an older ideology of conservative racial uplift and a new practice of social welfare. At St. John A.M.E., for example, women led discussions on "careful buying, household budgets, conservation of food, thrift and economy." These talks paralleled those given to male workers on the shop floor about the need to behave on the job and save their pay.[29] Yet some black church women remained divided and ambivalent about definitions of appropriate female behavior. The Beacon of Light Girls, another women's organization at St. John A.M.E., typified the efforts in the uplift of young women. The members' weekly discussions of black women's sexuality were limited to older notions of acceptable behavior in the confines of marriage and motherhood. Yet *The Princess of Poverty,* a play performed for the Council of Women, had a plot with hints of female sexual indiscretion, with a surprising warning: the women were counseled "not to exalt ourselves lest we be humbled by our own family skeleton."[30] Unable to move black club women to show interest in the well-being of unwed mothers, Marie Taylor Brown, president of the Women's Clubs in Cleveland, pushed fellow members of the Mt. Zion Baptist Church to organize a home for delinquent girls, where they could make "useful women" out of "bad girls."[31]

However much the tone in some congregations shifted toward a negative assessment of the new arrivals, for many migrants, particularly for live-in domestic workers, church activities became the one opportunity to mingle in the community. Many women sent children off to Sunday schools and received a much needed reprieve from child care. On any Sunday afternoon throughout the decade, black Clevelanders could attend concerts and lecture series at Antioch Baptist Church or debates at St. John A.M.E. Church. In 1927, St. James A.M.E. Church, which had a large population of longtime and middle-class congregants, became known as a center for cultural debate through its weekly literary forums. These social activities attracted working-class young migrants like William Murdock, who wanted to hear W. E. B. Du Bois, George C. Schuyler, Walter White, Mary McLeod Bethune, and Carter G. Woodson, among other prominent speakers. These programs proved so popular that other larger churches with greater resources quickly copied them.[32]

The cultural activities at these churches continued the historic role of black churches as social and educational places. In Cleveland, custom, not law, barred blacks from public spaces. Black clubs and organizations had little, if any, access to spaces owned or frequented by whites; the few amusement parks and dance halls that did admit blacks enforced segregation. Though the social welfare agencies expanded their activities to accommodate the growing black population, they soon replicated the patterns of segregation mushrooming throughout the city. Increasingly, therefore, the larger churches provided space for secular activities, ranging from the meetings of music and drama clubs to those of fraternal organizations such as the Knights of Pythias.[33] The differing resources that the older and larger churches offered strengthened their role as critical institutions in the African-American community.

Even as the older churches expanded their congregations and their activities to accommodate migrants, a long struggle over blacks' sacred lives began. On the surface, much of the debate seemed to be about an uneasiness over migrants' more expressive styles of worship. Editorials in African-American newspapers urged patience and warned against isolating new migrants. Yet these editorials reinforced the belief in the differences between southern backwardness and northern modernity that would divide later debates over black folk culture.[34] As Alain Locke published *The New Negro* in 1925, the association between the "New Negro" and modernity provided a legitimate and discursive focus to firmly reject Booker T. Washington's accommodation to segregation. While the ideology of the New Negro celebrated migrants in search of modern life, Cleveland's black elites found nothing "truthful" or celebratory about southern and rural patterns of expression retained in the urban environment. Both the disdain for migrants' habits and the frustration about the increased segregation led to contradictory renderings of the meaning of migration. The arrival of migrants, many of whom came from the Deep South, brought patterns of expression and dress that many black leaders variously found humorous or objectionable. But the contempt for the migrants emerged not merely out of differences in manners and expression. Rather, the backwardness that migrants represented challenged the habits of self-control that the established community had so assiduously pursued.[35]

These cultural tensions received extensive attention in Cleveland's black churches. Many migrants joined older churches that had eradicated the expressive worship prevalent in rural and smaller urban churches in the South. Even though his parents had just arrived from the South in 1906, Elmer Thompson had witnessed their rapid adaptation to the more subdued worship practices by the end of the decade. The Thompson family was one of a few migrant families during these years, which might have hastened their adaptation. By the time his grandmother arrived a decade later, the contrast between her worship style and that of his parents was sharp. Thompson vividly remembered his grandmother's ecstatic responses to the preaching each Sunday. "Before we went to church, my sister would ask, 'You're not going to shout today, are you?'" Thompson recognized both the class and regional distinctions increasingly evident in the congregation; migrants like Thompson's grandmother sparked renewed efforts to diminish overly expressive behavior during church services. "That was the difference in the black churches. The more education the people had, the less noise you heard out of them."[36] By the early 1920s, many of the church leaders in the older denominations with educated ministers pondered just how to make their congregants less emotional.[37]

In a series of articles in the *Cleveland Gazette* after World War I, Rev. William A. Byrd scolded migrants and proclaimed that "the decorum of the Colored churches should be improved. The wild outbursts of frantic emotionalism should be discouraged." Instead, he urged "the sane presentation of the truth in a dignified" manner. Byrd contemptuously added that since the migration the educated members were forced to suffer the boorishness of the uneducated migrants and their ministers. "The Colored youth of the North receives the same training in thought, language, rhetoric, reasoning and speech that other youths receive. But the greater portion of these youths on the Sabbath day must listen to the ramblings and disconnected discourses, loud and boisterous ravings, ancient emotionalism and cant in addition to the murder of almost every principle of the English language."[38] Byrd recycled critiques raised in the Victorian era of the black South and advocated middle-class values of decorum, intellect, and an educated ministry.[39]

The formation of Lane Memorial C.M.E. Church provides an important case study in the responses of black migrants to northern churches and ministers' critiques. Rev. Frank A. Smith arrived in Cleveland with his parents shortly after the turn of the century. Although a child at the time, Smith recalled that the migrants "were told that they could get employment here in Cleveland," and they left Monticello, Georgia. After their arrival, Smith's family attended Cory Methodist Church located on East Thirty-seventh and Central, but they soon joined seven other migrant families from Jasper County and held prayer meetings in each other's homes. Smith clearly remembered that "they were strangers here and they didn't like the other churches." Most important, Lane Memorial emerged from his family's desire to worship in the manner "they were accustomed to in Georgia." The migrants formed Lane Memorial C.M.E. Church on June 13, 1902, first meeting in a church building purchased from whites, then settling permanently in a church purchased from the First Christian Science Church at East Forty-sixth and Cedar in 1919.[40]

Years after Lane Memorial's founding, Reverend Smith recalled how important it had been for migrants to reject the northern urban demeanor of the A.M.E. churches in Cleveland. "Some of the folks had become sort of sophisticated," recalled Smith, "and didn't have the amens that they were used to." The migrants also felt that longtime church members "didn't want the southern people up here." The style of worship and the cool welcome moved the migrants to build their own church. "So it was a mutual situation. They didn't want us, and we didn't want them." The sentiments of the members struck a responsive chord as other migrants from the South joined the church, swelling the membership into the hundreds by the next decade. Lane Memorial continued to attract migrants while retaining its older population of black southerners still hungry for familiar styles of church worship.[41] Few of the established churches welcomed migrants in such an enthusiastic manner, with many seeking to minimize southern habits instead. Smith reasoned that middle-class ministers and their congregations felt "the Lord didn't need to hear all that shouting."[42]

The prevalence of such denunciations led migrants to create new churches more tolerant of ecstatic worship. Thirty-seven members of the Mt. Haven Baptist Church, dissatisfied with the moderate preaching in the city's churches, left the congregation as a group and organized Second Emmanuel in 1916. The church settled in a storefront, but after a series of rallies that raised thousands of dollars, members soon acquired a building. By 1923, the church had six hundred members and a Sunday school.[43] Other examples of a church splintering over styles of worship occurred at about the same time in the Triedstone Baptist Church. In the mid-1920s, the Alabama Club and the minister at Triedstone began to disagree. By 1926, these disgruntled members—most of them older migrants—formed Mt. Carmel Baptist Church. This congregation soon merged with members of St. Paul Baptist, which had been formed by unhappy members at Shiloh Baptist Church, and together they established Mt. Hermon Baptist Church.[44] Several years later, another group of migrants at Triedstone left over intradenominational differences. In 1931, forty members left Triedstone and organized the New Light Baptist Church; they changed the name to Olivet Baptist Church in 1933.[45]

Many of these new congregations did not have the resources to build or buy churches, so they moved into storefronts, theaters, and homes instead. Such patterns elicited frequent characterizations of these congregations as unstable. Many, however, were remarkably resilient. Organized during the war, Second Mt. Olive Baptist Church, for example, held services in a storefront, but later moved to a school building. The church eventually acquired a library and quickly expanded its membership to more than 400. Throughout all these changes, J. E. A. Wilson remained the pastor.[46] Marie Crawford helped organize a storefront church in 1916. The services took place in a white church until "those good white Christians got tired of us." The members then held their meetings in a room over a nightclub on East Fifty-fifth Street. "And I tell my people in the church never get so proud to think we weren't a storefront. We were up over a storefront. The people that church people called wicked, they welcomed us and treated us better than those dear Christians did."[47] For many of the smaller congregations settling into a storefront remained the only option since neither building nor purchasing a church was possible. A small prayer group of mostly poor migrants from the South found that though they had the land, building Union Baptist Church could be a slow endeavor. Estimating that they needed fifty thousand bricks, they left a sign on the property pleading with passers-by to "throw a brick over the fence" to hasten the process.[48]

Many migrants established churches close to where they lived. As small groups of migrants settled in areas outside the Central Area they found the older churches too distant to attend on a regular basis. In 1919, a small group of foundry workers and their families purchased a building near their homes and work. By the end of the next decade, this working-class congregation at Liberty Hill Baptist Church had grown and needed a larger building.[49] Few African Americans lived on the west side of the city, but during the war a small enclave of migrants came to work for the New York Central Railroad and

National Carbon. Initially, these workers lived on the east side but several families eventually settled in neighborhoods near West Park. Both St. Paul A.M.E. and Second Calvary Baptist Church were established by these workers.[50]

Even in the face of such economic and denominational difficulties, African Americans' church affiliation and participation increased in relation to their increasing numbers. Between 1920 and 1930, the Federated Churches of Cleveland reported that the number of black churches had grown from 54 to 132, with 60 percent of black Clevelanders affiliated with a church. As in the early part of the century, over half the membership belonged to large churches that the congregations either built or bought. While independent storefronts had been but a fraction of the community's churches prior to 1920, by 1930, 56 percent of the churches were storefronts organized by recent migrants. Many of these congregants could be identified as working class. More generally, these newer denominations were more associated with the working class than with the middle class.[51] Some churches either folded not long after their formation or moved frequently, though the city's directories reveal that many attracted members and eventually purchased or built churches after World War II. C. Eric Lincoln and Lawrence H. Mamiya documented this process, noting: "If [the migrants] did not feel comfortable in the large established churches, they helped to create smaller ones by first meeting in homes, then renting storefronts, and later purchasing their own church edifices."[52] Bertha Cowan articulated what many migrants felt when they arrived in Cleveland: finding a "church home" where she would be comfortable was as important as finding work.[53] Indeed, as Viv Broughton has reminded us, working-class church women and men "didn't just build churches, they built homes where they and their God could dwell together."[54]

For many migrants, the splintering and proliferation of churches demonstrated a deep desire to either sustain continuities with their southern past or acculturate into the northern setting at their own pace. That many migrants shifted into or later organized churches that retained southern-style ecstatic worship after they had joined established churches indicates their wish to reestablish their traditions. While some migrant churches slowly encouraged more private displays of spirituality, in other churches the influx of new migrants sustained the shouts, hollers, and fainting as each group helped to reaffirm their roots in the sacred traditions of the rural South. As Lawrence Levine has aptly noted: "Negro acculturation has been a complex process of shifting emphases and reaffirmations: of permitting certain new traits to permeate but of simultaneously re-emphasizing specific traditional loyalties and characteristics."[55] As we have seen, not all migrants left the older churches, choosing instead to acculturate to the subdued and formal styles of northern worship. Some migrants, who had left these churches for new ones, occasionally returned to older churches as they sought to identify as northerners or claimed middle-class social status. This pattern was most evident among the children of migrants who were either too young to remember the South or had been born in the North.

Migrants' insistence on retaining ecstatic worship, however, was about more than just style. Many migrants interpreted the struggle to renegotiate how they expressed their religious beliefs in church settings as an abandonment of religious beliefs deeply rooted in a Christianity informed by African values. Conversion, spirit possession, and divine intervention continued to figure prominently in their religious beliefs. The protracted process of finding work and sustaining families tested blacks' faith, but experience had taught them that migration itself had been part of their prophetic and historical search for autonomy and dignity. For many, the North as Canaan had proven elusive and God's promise had yet to be fulfilled, but they did not need to suffer in Cleveland. More than anything, manipulation of one's environment—the role of human agency—remained the most critical component of black theology. Suffering was not the goal of redemption; rather, black theology rested firmly on a humanism that insisted on the "importance of human struggle" to bring about social transformation.[56]

But agency did not exist without faith and faith demanded the active participation of the individual in a religious community. Prayer and song, both interspersed throughout church services, built on the daily experiences of the converted. The oral histories and narratives of black migrants demonstrate how dreams, prayers, and sacred songs punctuated their daily activities, revealed answers to questions about how they should act, and reaffirmed that their God did not let them struggle needlessly.[57] In short, the black faithful engaged in a daily call and response between their past and their present. Once in church, this dialogue became the basis for devotional prayers, testimonials, and ecstatic responses to sermons. A congregation's imposition of silence, therefore, interrupted a critical public and communal dialogue in which they reminded one another of their historic and divine experiences.

Many migrants, therefore, sought churches or denominations in which chants, shouts, and call and response remained central components of worship. In Baptist congregations that maintained older modes of prayer, devotions at the start of a service were initiated by a lone deacon and the congregation; here, without the minister present, specific personal problems were addressed. Devotions typically included quietly chanted prayer verses spontaneously crafted from lined hymns, gospel songs, scripture, and lines from other prayers. The individuals considered most effective took center stage, leading the congregation. After these prayers, ministers and deacons entered the sanctuary, followed by the choir. Over the next several hours, the congregation moved between prayers, congregational hymns, and hymns sung by the choir. As each of these expressions heightened the emotion, the shouts, cries, and chants of individuals became louder or led some to fall into trances. White-gloved nurses and ushers quickly moved to help these men, women, and children, removing the fallen if necessary. These events came to a close with church announcements and the collection of monies quieting the congregation; when the choir sang more hymns, the congregation would be swept up once again in a collective outpouring of their faith. Ministers with strong singing voices typically engaged in antiphony, linking the shouts of the congregation with the hymns of the choir. Once the latter quieted, the minister would then speak or chant the beginning of his sermon. The anticipated focal point of the worship service, the sermon was at once formulaic and improvisational. The transcriptions and observations of sermons demonstrate how pastors wove together biblical imagery with current concerns. Trains, for example, figured prominently in the everyday lives of migrants, and ministers drew heavily on such imagery as the saints were called to heaven or taken to hell.[58]

Church membership grew most in the Pentecostal, Holiness, Apostolic (originally Ethiopian), and nondenominational Sanctified churches, and by the late 1930s these predominated. Located in former stores, taverns, and theaters, these churches settled in the heart of the Central Area in the midst of the migrant population. Many of these churches literally appeared in the wake of migrants' arrivals, rather than through the conversion of longtime residents. Some new churches formed as a result of disputes with older churches, and the majority of the new congregations were not headed by seminary-trained ministers. Others emerged out of the numerous revivals now common in the city, with itinerant ministers from the South holding tent meetings filled with familiar styles of worship. Large crowds attended these nightly meetings that frequently continued for several weeks.[59]

In these new denominations, church members were obligated to actively participate in church services. As Peter Goldsmith has observed: "Saints are expected to be able to 'testify' in the course of a service, to initiate songs, to pray over an offering and to carry out other ritual functions. Saints cannot attend church for long without being expected to demonstrate these skills, and they must be ready and willing to demonstrate them on the spot."[60] Unlike the older denominations, Sanctified churches used dance and song as part of their worship. Some aspects of these worship practices continued African traditions rarely seen in northern churches. The rhythmic patting of the body, for instance, replaced the drum commonly used in African worship. Jon Spencer has noted that the body, like the drum, acted "as a sacred instrument possessing supernatural power that enables it to summon the gods into ritual communion with the people."[61] Though describing a Holiness church in Chicago, Langston Hughes had just left Cleveland and could have similarly characterized worship in the latter city: "I was entranced by their stepped-up rhythms, tambourines, hand-clapping, and uninhibited dynamics. The music of these less formal Negro churches early took hold of me, moved me, and thrilled me."[62]

Blacks' desire for personal agency in worship legitimized many black women's search for expanded roles as leaders. Within the Holiness and Pentecostal churches, black women formed the majority of the membership and often controlled the finances. But just as the A.M.E. and Baptist churches had prohibited women from pastoring, these new denominations limited women's roles as ministers. Some women rejected these boundaries and formed their own independent Spiritualist churches.[63] In 1931, Addie M. Battle, also known as Madam A. M. Johnson, organized the Mt. Zion Holy Trinity Spiritual Church after a vision instructed her to leave her church and become a "prophet for the Lord." Although she did not envision herself to be like Father Divine or Daddy Grace, she did see herself as one of "God's chosen prophets endowed with the same power and privileges as St. John or Paul, the Apostle." She argued "that the Negro is in reality God's only chosen people" and she was "chosen by God to give the Negro . . . spiritual comfort while here on earth so that he may escape the misery of the world and be able to suffer the hardships longer." Dressed in the required white, she held her services in the kitchen, blending theology and worship practices found in Catholic and Pentecostal churches.[64]

Along with an eclectic theology, Battle offered her largely female congregation a model for resistance in their lives as workers and family members. Communal prayers often focused on retaining dignity in the face of abusive employers. In response to one member's pleas for advice to halt the abuse she regularly received from an employer, Battle urged her to simultaneously "be careful on your job and keep your determination." Offering what was commonly called "motherwit"—a mixture of secular and spiritual wisdom—Battle demonstrated that black ecstatic worship was more than emotional outbursts and otherworldly exhortations. Services like hers enabled women and men to testify openly and collectively about their daily experiences as workers, migrants, and spiritual people. Her advice, in turn, specifically addressed these concerns, while affirming the individual's right to act on her own behalf.[65]

Battle and other women ministers provided particular guidance for women concerned about their roles as mothers and wives. Battle offered consultations, spiritual advice, and comfort for "many worldly problems involving love, money, and marital difficulties." She required only "faith from those seeking her help, plus the proper amount of finance," typically two dollars, to offset the expenses of running the church (and perhaps to supplement her income). She encouraged wives to leave adulterous husbands and she insisted that single women socialize only with male members of the church. The female pastor for the Jesus Only Church of God received no special salary, only donations from the working-class members who attended services in her home. The pastor, guided by other women in the congregation, crafted an elaborate list of prohibitions, including "adultery, fornication, lying and joking, back-biting, whoremongering, smoking, drinking, chewing tobacco, dipping snuff, dancing in public, wearing lipstick, earrings, beads, or short skirts."[66] Since female ministers advanced (and modeled) female independence and leadership, the insistence on restrained female public behavior suggests differences from the patterns of policing found in middle-class churches. Here, working-class blacks may have placed limitations on their own behavior, instead of simply accepting those handed down by the black middle class.[67]

Along with the continuation of ecstatic worship, the preference for gospel music became a divisive regional issue. Before the arrival of huge numbers of migrants, African-American worshippers in the older churches typically sang classical Protestant hymns and anthems. In the Episcopalian, Congregational, and Presbyterian churches, members insisted on regular performances of European-influenced Protestant hymns and not traditional African-American sacred music. In the mainline Methodist and Baptist congregations, some college-educated members from Fisk University had organized jubilee choirs that sang European-influenced spirituals. The growing presence of a professional elite with a northern college education propelled the trend toward highly trained choirs, music directors, and hymnals rather than improvisation and congregational participation.[68]

In sharp contrast, in the Holiness, Pentecostal, and smaller Baptist and Methodist missions, southern rural and working-class sacred music flourished. Noble Sissle, whose father, Rev. George A. Sissle, was pastor of Cory Methodist Episcopal Church in 1906, recalled: "I used to get a great thrill when my father or some member of the congregation would lead us in hymn, reading off the lyrics ahead of us. Then everyone would join in and every foot would keep time, and soon the whole church would be swaying in rhythm or patting their hands and feet. Whenever I sing a rhythm song—even today—I still pat my foot in the same way."[69] Though more traditional, these jubilee spirituals, Baptist "lining hymns," shape-note hymns, and Watts hymns still did not match the highly spirited rhythms and instrumentations of songs in the Holiness and Pentecostal churches. The Holiness churches embraced tambourines, hand-clapping, and ecstatic singing and vocalizations.[70]

African-American workers who arrived from Alabama brought with them a demand for and experience with gospel quartets. The work camps around Birmingham, Bessemer, and other areas of Jefferson County were the seedbed for gospel quartet singing. Though forged in the steel and coal camps, gospel quartet singing had roots in shape-note singing, Watts hymns, folk music, minstrel quartets, and college jubilee singing in the Civil War and Reconstruction-era South.[71] Historians have described gospel quartet singing as influenced by male jubilee quartets formed at Fisk University and Tuskegee. Kip Lornell noted that by the turn of the century while "black quartet singing existed at every level of black culture," it was particularly prevalent among black workers who tended to belong to smaller Baptist churches or the emerging Holiness and Pentecostal churches. Equally important, many of these singers were Baptists and sought to offer more spirited singing than their congregations allowed; their music and performances, however, were more refined than the ecstatic singing in the Holiness and Pentecostal churches. During breaks from the mills and mines, gospel quartets performed and perfected their styles in the segregated steel and coal camps. As they began to perform for local churches, they matched their style to accommodate enthusiastic responses to the music. In these early performances, quartets were influenced by their audiences, creating a folk style that allowed rhythmic movements, vocal embellishments, and greater vocal ranges common in churches and not universities.[72]

Arthur Turner and the other members of the Dunham Jubilee Singers were trained and influenced by R. C. Foster, who had formed the first male quartet in Bessemer, Alabama, after he began working in the mines there in 1915. The Foster Singers performed spirituals and the new gospel hymns published in Charles Tindley's *Gospel Pearls.* By the time the Dunham Jubilee Singers formed their quartet in 1924, the development of local radio programs and the success of traveling black musicians led the group to broaden its repertoire to include secular music as well. Over the next several years, the Dunham Jubilee Singers sang gospel, folk music, spirituals, blues, and work songs in northern and southern cities. Turner sang bass and the group, like many others, had two tenors and a baritone. Known for their tight harmonies, these quartets mesmerized listeners through great skill and meticulous control. Though quartet singing allowed for call and response, an emphasis on close harmony meant that few could tell the voices apart.[73]

Because gospel quartets tended to draw members from several congregations, rather than the same church, and since so many performed around work camps or began to travel, singers were exposed to a variety of sacred and secular styles of music. Though committed to singing "for the Lord," quartets also competed for audiences as they got invited to churches. Members, in turn, paid their expenses and provided eating and sleeping accommodations. To take advantage of the various radio, recording, and performance opportunities, many of these quartets performed both sacred and secular music. In the end, as Lawrence Levine has concluded, gospel music in style and presentation returned to "the sounds and structure of the folk spirituals, work songs, and nineteenth-century cries and hollers; [gospel singers and composers] borrowed freely from the ragtime, blues and jazz of the secular black world."[74] Gospel also included the sounds and experiences of migration.

The organized resistance to southern and working-class ecstatic worship, the growing presence of Holiness and Spiritualist churches, and the increasing difficulties of southern quartets to finance tours in the late 1920s gave rise to Cleveland-based gospel-only quartets and choirs. Unable to find steady work in the South, Turner decided to settle in Cleveland and join the Shield Brothers. This quartet and the Live Wire Singers were influenced by Turner and other singers from Alabama. By the midthirties more than two dozen gospel quartets, both male and female, sang in or around Cleveland. The female quartets, like the Deep River Songbirds, the Bright Stars, the Eley Sisters, and the Elite Jewels, sang secular music as well, differing dramatically from the emerging female hard gospel groups such as the Roberta Martin Singers and the Davis Sisters.[75]

The Cleveland Colored Gospel Quintet, one of the city's earliest all-gospel groups, was organized by migrants in 1920 who had joined the Christian and Missionary Alliance Church. Some of the members had performed with local well-known minstrel groups such as the Musical Magpies. By the late 1920s, H. D. Dodges, Spurgeon R. Jones, Floyd H. Lacy, Alexander E. Talbert, and J. W. Parker had religious conversions, abandoned the secular stage, and regularly sang at churches, revivals, hospitals, and street meetings in the Midwest and Canada. In the 1930s, the group had made several well-received European tours. Their precision harmonies, ability to sing in several languages, urgent testimonials of spiritual salvation, and wide-ranging repertoire of spirituals, shape-note hymns, and gospel helped sustain their popularity until the deaths of several members in the 1950s.[76]

Much credit has been given to Thomas Dorsey's inarguably prominent role in shaping hard gospel music, and he was the leading figure in gospel composition. Yet a decade prior to Dorsey's efforts, local and traveling gospel quartets, gospel choirs, and gospel singers made gospel popular and acceptable through their close harmony, dignity, and personal testimony. In a single program, quartets like the Dunham Jubilee Singers answered the ironic secular blues songs of despair with the sacred songs of hope. Using the double-voice common in black expressive culture, their song "Your Mama's Baby Child" depicted a son who missed the South even as he made the choice to leave, but the group's "Lord Don't Pass Me By" contained the hope and faith of migration, like the hope for heaven, as a continuing possibility. Moreover, as many quartets began to sing just gospel songs, members typically began their programs with testimonials of their salvation from sin and their faith "in Jesus." Arthur Turner recalled that the harmony of groups like the Dunham Jubilee Singers and the Shield Brothers was so good, that "seems as if the notes could be heard in the room the next day." The tight harmony of gospel quartets was so popular in Cleveland that the hard gospel singing started by Dorsey and Mahalia Jackson did not gain ground until after World War II. The famous Kings of Harmony, a Birmingham group that settled permanently in Cleveland, brought the hard sound to the city in the 1940s, but the smoother style of the Shield Brothers remained popular.[77]

Before the late 1930s, gospel quartets and groups struggled to be heard in either large or medium-sized Baptist churches. Because of its close links to secular music, especially the blues, many ministers viewed gospel music as sinful and they attempted to stop it by refusing to allow quartets and small groups to perform in services at all. But migrants' willingness to leave one church or denomination for those willing to include gospel music began to challenge many ministers' prohibitions. Some ministers attempted to dampen gospel music's influence by relegating groups' performances to late afternoons, presumably hoping church members would tire from having already spent the day in services. Arthur Turner recalled that in the early 1930s, the Shield Brothers sang one afternoon in a church, drawing hundreds of listeners. The minister noted that more people came to hear the group than regularly attended his services.[78] By the time Thomas Dorsey began selling his gospel music, Cleveland's gospel quartets had become so popular that however much ministers and the longtime members of the traditional black denominations may have found gospel to be too influenced by secular performance practices, they conceded that it had displaced other forms of African-American sacred music.

Precipitated by the organization of Wings over Jordan by Rev. Glenn T. Settles, pastor at Gethsemene Baptist Church, many ministers in the Baptist congregations had started to accept gospel music. By 1937, Wings over Jor-

dan had become the most well-known of Cleveland's African-American sacred music choirs and spawned a number of gospel choirs. Though Settles
formed the choir, its members had been singing gospel in other churches.
James Tate, the first choirmaster, trained members and arranged the new
group's music. As Wings became a regular feature on national radio, some
churches changed the time of their services rather than compete with the
popular broadcast.[79]

However much gospel music eventually ushered in a host of star singers
who traveled and recorded, on the local level the highly participatory character of African-American religious institutions meant that small and large
congregations allowed many members to sing along. In addition to singing,
many blacks took part in church activities all week long. Even small congregations had Sunday schools and boards to assist the pastor. Often, these committees, trustee boards, deacons' boards, mothers' boards, missionary societies, and choirs were established along lines of gender, age, and length of
membership.[80]

Migrants' affiliation with a church continued a southern pattern of receiving spiritual sustenance, social contact, and entertainment at places of
worship. For young women in particular, rural churches provided one of the
few opportunities to meet young men under the watchful gaze of parents.[81]
In Cleveland, migrants sought to continue these patterns, with the added
pleasure that churches were in their own neighborhoods and ministers held
services each week. While many initially attended established churches in
their neighborhoods, they often found themselves marginal to church activities. Elizabeth Clark-Lewis noted in her study of Washington, D.C., that black
migrants in the city's churches "felt relegated to the periphery of activity."[82]
African-American migrants in Cleveland found that some churches helped
them adjust to the city by providing contact with other migrants. But these
new urban dwellers intended to make the city their own and therefore they
wanted to become active and not passive participants in churches. In the
larger, mainline churches, middle-class congregants typically held the most
prominent positions; working-class migrants found it especially difficult to
become leaders of deacons', trustees', and mothers' boards, the most prestigious organizations.[83]

As churches separated along class and regional lines, so too did secular
activities. As early as 1914, African-American workers noted the sharp demar-
cations along class and skin color lines within the community. The elites, one
man noted, had exclusive supper clubs and fraternal organizations. At the
same time, settlement houses offered few options, as they had either excluded blacks or imposed segregation in recreation. Some women and young

children had access to clubs, but working-class men felt the most excluded. With little money, men's leisure time was centered around either churches or saloons. Dancing, which had been the pastime of working-class young adults, had been under attack beginning in 1912 by both white and black social welfare workers. Jane Edna Hunter described these dance halls: "Here to the tune of St. Louis voodoo blues, half-naked Negro girls dance shameless dances with men in Spanish costumes, while daughters from highly respectable families, attended by escorts, clap their dainty, white hands and shout their approval. The whole atmosphere is one of unrestrained animality, the jungle faintly veneered with civilized trappings."[84]

Elite and middle-class blacks' participation in fraternal and mutual benefit associations—much in evidence before 1915—continued in the postwar decade. Attracted by the quasi-religious, quasi-militaristic rituals and parades, men continued to join the Masons, Odd Fellows, Knights of Pythias, and Knights of Tabor, which instilled the ideology of middle-class life. Since dues and uniforms were part of the membership, most if not all of these groups were led by the more economically solvent members of the community; the rank-and-file were usually equally affluent. Even if they could afford the dues, lodge members generally considered migrants from the Deep South less educated and less well mannered than they and, therefore, ineligible for membership. In one publication, a Masonic lodge attested to its long-standing relationship to the "'old' families" considered to be the most prominent.[85] Many fraternal organizations had women's auxiliaries that thinly veiled their patriarchy. Though some women carved out distinct roles in these affiliates, they were nonetheless made clearly aware of their subordinate status.[86]

Higher education or a middle-class economic or professional position did not immediately confer status or prestige, however. Certainly more than in any previous period, in the 1920s African-American men with steady work acquired some standing in the community. While their occupations widely ranged from small business owners to Pullman porters, all had held their jobs for some years, which enabled some to purchase homes and keep their wives out of wage work. Men with these relatively stable and better-paying positions typically labored in hotels as head waiters and chefs, as Pullman porters, or in the post office sorting mail. Sampson Keeble, for example, worked in the main city post office, eventually becoming a foreman in 1929. This enabled him to purchase a home in Mt. Pleasant; he also rose to the upper levels of the Masons. By 1930, the officers for one chapter of the Masons included a carpenter, a barber, and a machinist.[87] These men did not acquire their offices simply by their economic standing, however, since each had been subjected to the rigorous screening process of the lodge's Investigatory Committee to determine whether they adhered to acceptable notions of propriety. Charles Wesley noted that the tradition of such scrutiny began in the late nineteenth century when "Ohio was thus engaged . . . in organizing the selective, well-qualified few among colored Americans." Hence, the Investigatory Committee was, as one historian of the organization surmised, "designed to rigorously exclude those who deviate[d] from acceptable bourgeois behavior." Such attention to patterns of behavior ensured that the poor, recent migrants, the young, and those considered morally wayward would be bypassed in favor of sober "first-class human beings."[88]

Middle-class and professional African-Americans separated themselves from working-class blacks in leisure activities. African-American women's sororities, garden clubs, reading clubs, bridge clubs, and singing groups flourished in the 1920s. Men's social clubs were similarly organized around advanced education and professional status. The Royal Vagabond Club, organized in 1925, required that applicants be recommended by two members, meet standards of citizenship, and document contributions to the community. Despite its rigorous admissions policy, the club filled social needs and its members refused to engage in discussions considered divisive. Given that many social clubs required adherence to a middle-class economic and social status, they probably heightened the class differences within the black community. The children of working-class migrants discovered that by the mid-twenties even high school clubs reflected the hierarchies of region, color, and class.[89]

The self-conscious orientation of the black middle and upper classes aside, the ideology of the New Negro coexisted with a radical economic and cultural critique that provided avenues for black working-class participation. A. Philip Randolph and Chandler Owen, editors of the *Messenger,* depicted migrants as agents of their own destiny, a reinterpretation of Alain Locke's representation of "the folk" seeking modernity. Randolph and Owen labeled the movement of blacks out of the South a "product of the same world-wide forces that have brought into being the great liberal and radical movements." Most tellingly, this " 'New Negro' unlike the 'old Negro' was not to be lulled into a false sense of security with political spoils and patronage." Instead, Randolph's vision was of politically active black workers standing in solidarity with white workers, all concentrated on "the getting of more wages, shorter hours, and better working conditions."[90] Langston Hughes was more perceptive when he wryly noted that "the ordinary Negroes hadn't heard of the Negro Renaissance. And if they had, it hadn't raised their wages any."[91] Hughes did not dismiss black workers, but instead offered a critique of the musings of black intellectuals, which he felt rarely translated into prosperity for the masses. Hughes concluded that the "real New Negro . . . is one who understands that he is primarily a worker, agricultural or industrial."[92]

Black workers' perceptions of themselves as distinct from the black middle class emerged from a complicated interplay between race and class. Certainly African-Americans confronted class in the workplace, whether as unskilled workers in foundries or as household workers in the homes of white employers. These distinctions, however, accompanied a racial consciousness of themselves as blacks in a segregated society, views they shared with the middle class. Yet African-American workers recognized class differences within their own community. Their exclusion from private middle-class social clubs stemmed from distinctions in class and increasingly region. Thus, in their own clubs, as in their churches, black men and women of the working class shared experiences as former southerners.

Just as in their self-organized labor associations, the explosion of voluntary and social organizations created by working-class migrants during and after the war signaled their desire to determine their own boundaries of life and behavior. Voluntary associations and social organizations, like the migrant churches, structured the rhythms of daily life in black working-class neighborhoods. Migrants with roots in the urban South arrived with knowledge of, and participation in, black voluntary associations. In sharp contrast, those migrants from southern rural areas had only infrequently had an opportunity to participate in organizations beyond church and burial societies. For many, distance, along with work patterns and household obligations, had greatly limited even these activities.[93]

Despite their unfamiliarity with them, migrants from rural areas eagerly joined those from urban areas in the creation and recreation of community organizations. A number of secret societies with southern origins formed; the United Order of True Reformers, the United Brothers of Friendship, the Grand Samaritans, and the Daughters of Samaritans offered insurance and burial benefits. Though the Masonic lodges typically attracted middle-class black men, the Independent Benevolent and Protective Order of Elks of the World became dominated by working-class migrants since the organization did not shun those with little education and low wages. Working-class black women, in particular, sought new opportunities for expression, despite the incessant demands of their households and their jobs. Women joined the Glenara Temple, which served as the women's affiliate to the Elks.[94] Black working-class women organized street clubs that differed from leisure activities like middle-class women's garden clubs. Aware of low incomes and neglectful landlords, these women instead aided in the care of rented homes and economically insolvent families. Building on the intimate relationships established through shared household and child care responsibilities, some of these street clubs drew in immigrant women as well.[95]

Though some of these new clubs were organized around age and marital status, the majority had both male and female members. More typically, these new clubs drew lines along places of origin and neighborhood settlement in the city. Migrants from Alabama, Tennessee, and Georgia each created separate clubs. Sometimes these social clubs established funds to send members home for visits. Many clubs chose provocative and enigmatic names, such as the Alien Club, suggesting a secretive element long part of the black social club movement. Most, however, sported names that reflected the members' social intent, such as the Gaylords, or the Mae West Club. Many organized their members as singing quartets with names like the Live Wires. Other forms of conviviality drew specific clubs, such as card playing and reading; young men who played baseball but did not participate in the Negro Leagues formed clubs. Finally, many clubs were formed by workers who shared a place of employment or an occupation.[96]

In the face of increasing segregation, the clubs provided much desired social entertainment. The city's movie houses, dance halls, and amusement parks were often segregated or blacks were excluded altogether. Only a handful of rundown movie theaters admitted African Americans. The city's largest amusement park, Euclid Beach Park, refused to allow blacks admittance to many of its attractions (a policy followed until it closed in the 1960s). Catering to the dominant antiblack sentiments, the owners stated that they did not want to offend their patrons by admitting blacks. Luna Park had special nights, usually Mondays, when the owners closed the park to whites and allowed blacks to enter at double the usual admission fee. Similar patterns of restriction took root in public dance halls, popular night clubs, and private dances held at settlement houses. Though the city had attempted to close dance halls prior to the war, in the 1920s public halls once again flourished, generally under segregated policies. Aware of limited space in black neighborhoods, some public dance halls allowed black groups to rent the facilities but at a much higher fee than they offered whites.[97]

Even as African Americans began to attend popular movies and listen to the radio, many raised protests over derogatory representations of African-American life. Black newspapers and social and church clubs provided a forum to discuss—and denounce—the offensive images. In contrast to the racist images on the screen, a parade of African-American stars such as Noble Sissle, Eubie Blake, and Ethel Waters came through Cleveland. Though many working-class blacks could not afford to attend their shows, they tried their best to see these stars perform on Cedar Avenue. Bertha Cowan recalled the arrival of "all the stars, blues singers, church soloist[s]—we stretched our neck to try to go to all those things." It would be the churches, private clubs, and live performances, not the movie screens, that provided migrants with visions of African-American dignity.[98]

Though nightclubs provided highly respectable dancing and big-city entertainment, admission was expensive and prohibitive to the working class. During the decade preceding the war, elites typically held balls, usually sponsored by political groups through membership clubs, a pattern that continued through the 1930s; during Prohibition, these membership clubs also featured gambling and liquor. The Elks Lodge, for example, held dances, typically after hours. Men's social clubs held "smokers" that combined vaudeville, boxing, and singing. Despite the veneer of respectability, these events were not immune to police raids. The Autumn Leaf Club, for example, held a dance at the Elks' Cabaret, a nightclub located in the basement of the Elks Lodge. A police raid uncovered that the married, middle-class members were in violation of Prohibition.[99]

Working-class blacks, too, created social clubs to provide for their entertainment needs. These efforts reflected their economic vulnerability and their unprotected status as unskilled laborers. Low wages and high rents led to rent parties, which had southern origins that grew out of the jook joints—private parties—and the church socials organized to pay ministers' salaries. Variously known as "chitlin' struts," "blue Monday affairs," "house shouts," and "too bad parties," rent parties provided low-cost entertainment and redistributed migrants' incomes. The proliferation of honky-tonks, buffet clubs, and after-hours joints that catered to African-American workers enabled a folk culture to continue to flourish. In all of these settings, itinerant and occasional blues musicians and vaudeville performers played "for a good meal and liquor."[100] Working-class clubs and associations held numerous private dances and parties. The Waiters' and Chauffeurs' Clubs—perceived as working men's clubs, unlike the Caterers' Association—sponsored dances as well.[101]

Many of these working-class gatherings drew hundreds, but others were small and intimate. Elmer Thompson, though not a waiter, had friends who worked in hotels. He fondly remembered the "three full-dress affairs" his friends held each year. The waiters "knew how to take care of" all the niceties expected and lavished their attention on friends. For young men and women, who were excluded from the majority of clubs and restaurants, these private gatherings provided affordable luxury and dignity. Such displays of expertise by the waiters also showed the value of service employment. Equally important, the entertainment at many of these gatherings instilled race pride.

Numerous traveling African-American blues singers and gospel quartets performed "without objectionable" mannerisms characteristic of white vaudeville entertainers in blackface.[102]

Working-class social clubs, in particular, provided much needed services. The black wing of the American Legion organized the Service Men's Social Club to provide good literature and an employment bureau. The Caterers' Club led the effort to discourage blacks from using Luna Park.[103] Community organizations sponsored events that allowed for the presentation and discussion of issues ranging from literature and movies to Pan-Africanism and black participation in socialist activities. These often spirited discussions reveal the historic efforts working-class African Americans undertook to understand not only their particular needs but also the world around them. Equally important, these self-organized clubs carved out alternative cultural spaces. Activities in the clubs and organizations affirmed black working-class experiences while providing much needed resources and security. Finally, these clubs established privacy absent in the large churches and white-controlled institutions.

The black working class, many of whom had been schooled in the ideology of race uplift and self-help, did not receive rewards for "upright living." Few found success through establishing a business or practicing habits of thrift and cleanliness. At the same time, the intellectual tones of W. E. B. Du Bois stirred many, though most men and women found access to higher education severely circumscribed. From this vantage point, neither strict adherence to accommodation nor pursuit of integration had any real merits for the thousands of migrants whose lives were spent maintaining households in precarious economic circumstances. What had long sustained the black community, regardless of region, was a commitment to self-help shaped by mutuality, reciprocity, and notions of justice.

The Universal Negro Improvement Association (UNIA), with its emphasis on self-help, personal empowerment, and formal pageantry, constituted an alternative to middle-class notions of individualism, acquiescence, and decorum. Marcus Garvey's shouts of "Up You Mighty Race" thrilled the large and appreciative audiences in Cleveland. Garvey's enthusiastic call for race pride, black self-organization, and an end to black subservience quickly drew six thousand members in Cleveland by 1919; four years later the organization had expanded to include over fifteen thousand men and women. Though a few ministers and men with political aspirations joined the UNIA, the overwhelming majority of the Cleveland division, as elsewhere, was composed of laboring men and women. From its inception, the UNIA quickly pulled in African Americans frustrated by the limited activism of other protest organizations and their exclusion from labor organizations. In Cleveland, the UNIA drew blacks from the maligned IWW. Those men and women who joined—and remained members long after Garvey's deportation in 1925 and death in 1940—appreciated the structured organization and opportunity for leadership roles. Still others learned from its militant and separatist stance, which would later serve as a springboard for participation in other militant organizations in the 1930s and 1940s.[104]

Garvey and other upper-echelon members of the UNIA made frequent stops in Cleveland during the heyday of the organization. Large crowds typically packed churches and theaters to hear about the "Destiny of the New Negro"; crowds lined the streets for UNIA parades. While Du Bois and Randolph dismissed Garvey as a buffoon and a clown, Garvey's pageantry left a very different imprint on others. As one Clevelander recounted: "I remember as a lad in Cleveland during the hungry days of 1921, standing on Central Avenue, watching a parade one Sunday afternoon when thousands of Garvey Legionnaires, resplendent in their uniforms marched by. When Garvey rode by in his plumed hat, I got an emotional lift, which swept me above the poverty and prejudice by which my life was limited."[105] Another observer corroborated this assessment of the large and enthusiastic crowds that typically greeted Garvey in the various churches. "The masses are with Garvey," the observer reported. "It is a fact that cannot be denied." A Federal Bureau of Investigation informant noted that hundreds typically joined the UNIA after these church meetings.[106]

According to an analysis of 140 members of the UNIA who regularly paid dues from 1923 to 1929, most were married men and women with jobs as common laborers and household workers. Married women who identified themselves as housewives were typically married to laborers or had sons in such occupations. Most resided in some of the poorest neighborhoods in the Central Area and had arrived in the city after 1915. The next sizable group of members were men who labored in the building trades and were excluded from unions, such as paperhangers and sign painters. Only four of these men could be identified as professionals.[107]

The Cleveland division proved to be durable throughout the 1920s, but like other radical organizations it faced an antiradical backlash. Garvey's conviction for mail fraud along with the taint of radicalism meant that aspiring leaders frequently found publicity more cumbersome than helpful. The prominent dentist Leroy Bundy, charged with murder and conspiracy for the East St. Louis riot of 1917 but later acquitted, was elected president of the Cleveland division. Denounced as disingenuous in both his association with the UNIA and the use of its funds, Bundy was forced out; he then pursued political office. He was rewarded for his persistence when he won a seat on the city council in 1928. S. V. Robinson, a sanitation worker, replaced Bundy and apparently brought a more working-class frame of reference to the UNIA leadership. Though black workers would soon hold 75 percent of the jobs in the sanitation department, they would depend not on a union, but on the good fortunes of black politicians to extract patronage positions.[108]

In the end, the limitations of the UNIA meant that African Americans did not abandon their churches and fraternal and voluntary associations. With so few separate institutions, blacks did not willingly publicly criticize either the Urban League or the NAACP. But historians who have compared the UNIA's membership with those of the traditional organizations missed what was well-known among black Clevelanders: when they entered the Urban League's door workers had to become members before they could fill out job applications. Faced with few alternatives, black workers joined the Urban League *and* attended UNIA meetings. In private, the NAACP acknowledged its limited influence outside of the middle class. One of the local's officers candidly wrote in the mid-1920s that "if the Cleveland branch is typical of other branches, then the NAACP is in bad shape. We hold practically no mass meetings throughout the year. Consciously or otherwise, the Negro leaders take a high-brow attitude toward the Negro masses and no effort is made to interest them in the affairs of the organization."[109]

African Americans' community-based associational life of the 1920s had a mixed legacy. In their separate churches and social organizations, workers had acquired critical opportunities to develop an associational life that retained religious values and an expressive culture rooted in their experiences as migrants from the South. For many, however, exclusion from most unions along with limited economic means undermined the numerous community efforts to help them. Parties might have enabled some to pay their rents, but they did little to alleviate narrow housing choices created by segregation. Similarly, black workers found it difficult to sustain social clubs and churches in periods of unemployment. While organizations such as the Chauffeurs' Club attempted to merge workplace with community needs, the dignity that many may have found in the privacy of their own homes and community did not easily transfer to the workplace. Finally, the UNIA called for small business ownership, not for a movement of workers to find work or fair wages.

Nonetheless, African-American workers' autonomous social and workplace organizations in the 1920s, along with their desire to acquire adequate employment during the Great Depression, fueled an unprecedented community-based protest of the unemployed in the 1930s. As many middle-class leaders and social workers urged African-American workers in Cleveland to accommodate themselves to the exigencies of the Great Depression, unemployed men and women, many of them migrants from Alabama, launched a militant boycott movement to halt their exclusion from employment in white-owned stores in their neighborhoods. As the new organization attracted thousands, many members who had gained jobs turned to the creation of a labor association that would address their needs as workers. While these efforts precipitated a protracted discussion of organized labor's new effort to include them, blacks' self-generated effort must be perceived as more than a precursor to their involvement in a reinvigorated labor movement. Even as black workers created a labor association within the boycott efforts, they battled AFL and CIO locals. At the close of the 1930s, this new community-based organization was the largest movement of black workers that the city had ever seen, but it neither aligned with middle-class black leaders nor readily accepted unions that did not address African Americans' exclusion from employment because of race.

SIX

"The Future Is Yours": Store Boycott Campaigns and Black Workers' Militancy

The Future Outlook League
Appeals to Negroes everyday
To not spend any money
Where your color draws no pay
These merchants will abide
Because the League is unified
We'll get those jobs today.

—to the tune of "Glory Hallelujah,"
    Birmingham Jubilee Quartet,
    May 21, 1938

IN FEBRUARY 1935, African-American men and women in Cleveland met at the home of John O. Holly to form a boycott organization that would win employment for them and others in neighborhood stores. Holly, influenced by black boycotts in Chicago and black labor activism in Detroit, urged the group to form a direct-action organization that would rely on the picket and the boycott. The group would target white-owned stores in the Central Area that depended on African-American customers but barred them from employment. In response to the frustration over too few jobs and the dearth of leadership in the community, Holly declared that "the future is yours" to make, establishing a sense of agency that soon became the organization's mantra. Holly was elected president and the new organization was called the Future Outlook League (FOL). The small cadre of members then turned to recruiting others, but few responded.[1] Undeterred, the FOL set up pickets, vocally badgered shoppers to boycott, and announced to store owners they were just the first wave. Their tactics, however, overshadowed their success in obtaining a handful of jobs and the criticism from the black middle class was swift and sharp. Turning their backs on these critiques, FOL members escalated their aggressive tactics and soon attracted other unemployed men and women to the picket lines and the boycotts. Over the second half of the 1930s, thousands of employed and unemployed African Americans, many of them migrants, were schooled in independent radical activism under the aegis of the league's boycotts and meetings.

The continued high unemployment that had quickly settled in the black community at the start of the Great Depression in 1929 fueled the league's emergence. With so little employment available to African Americans, especially industrial work or openings in the newly created Works Project Administration projects, the FOL intended to seek out jobs in their own neighborhoods. Holly's previous employment in a West Virginia coal mine and a Detroit auto plant familiarized him with aggressive workplace tactics. Charismatic and combative, Holly privately hoped that the placement of African Americans in stores would give them the necessary experience to establish businesses of their own, eventually becoming "the merchants of tomorrow." In a letter to a friend, Holly expressed his initial hopes for the FOL: "These men and women who are being placed in various stores will take the places of the white man and be the merchants of tomorrow with the experience acquired under the white man's instructions."[2] Indeed, several members of the league did establish businesses and the FOL helped to anchor other struggling companies.

But the African-American men and women drawn to the FOL sought jobs. While some employed men and women joined the picket lines, the majority of the FOL's initial membership were unemployed. As the activism continued, the black Left and working-class southern migrants, rather than professional or middle-class African Americans, played prominent roles in shifting and shaping the league's policies and tactics. By the late 1930s, members came to the meetings and participated in the picketing because they hoped to gain not only jobs but also dignity, fair wages, reasonable work hours, and better conditions. By the late 1930s, the FOL moved from direct-action boycotts to labor activism and functioned as a bargaining agent for service workers rather than as an organization of future merchants. As the CIO began to gain momentum in the city, the league challenged antilabor black leaders and goaded the AFL and the CIO to organize African Americans. At the same time, as members of the FOL reshaped their organization into a labor association, they vocally expressed skepticism and concerns about a labor movement that did not fundamentally address their inability to obtain work.

The numerous direct-action boycotts that swept through African-American communities during the Great Depression exhibited an urgency and a militancy not typically seen in earlier efforts.[3] Before the 1930s, African Americans had historically used economic boycotts as a powerful form of protest against racial and economic discrimination.[4] In a broad consideration of African-American economic boycotts in the 1930s, August Meier and Elliott Rudwick have argued that the boycotts waged by blacks in the 1930s "contrasted sharply both quantitatively and qualitatively with the history of such tactics during the entire preceding century, and achieved salience in black protest that would not be equaled or surpassed until the late 1950's and 1960's."[5] The FOL shared some characteristics with the other coalitions of the war years, most noticeably its dramatic street confrontations, its charismatic leadership, and its inclusion of members with a variety of viewpoints. At the same time, the league did not stumble under the weight of internecine battles that plagued some of the boycott movements. Unlike the efforts in Harlem, for example, the Cleveland movement managed to meet the immediate employment needs of its members and respond to their additional and diverse interests over time. As Cheryl Greenberg concluded about the boycotts in Harlem, African-American "leaders sought to create one coherent movement, but the diversity of Harlem's population proved an obstacle."[6] Whereas more radical leaders and ideas tended to undermine boycotts elsewhere, the FOL in Cleveland grew more militant over time.

The FOL's ability to shift successfully from a boycott organization to a radical labor organization made it unique among its counterparts of the period. While the FOL's predecessors originated in the historical tendency of African Americans to use the boycott as a weapon against racial and economic discrimination, it also had important links to the struggles of black workers to organize and participate in unions in the two decades before 1935. Indeed, African Americans had struggled continuously for participation in the city's labor movement since 1910. The stalled attempts to build biracial unions in the 1920s left blacks largely excluded from organized labor. The reenergized labor movement of the 1930s had yet to include blacks in any appreciable number. Thus, the league provided self-organization that enabled its members to mediate the deleterious impact of employers' and organized labor's segregation.

Any analysis of the FOL must consider the multiple roots of its members and the milieu in which it continued to thrive. In particular, the activism of the league must be linked to the general swirl of radical action by black workers and the movements of the unemployed in Cleveland between 1929 and 1935. Several of the key organizers of the FOL, most notably Maude White, had been members of the Communist party (CP); others, like Admiral Kilpatrick, witnessed the shop floor and street struggles of black and white workers in Cleveland and elsewhere. The radical tone of some black newspapers and magazines, along with the outspoken criticism of traditional black leaders and tactics from black radicals, such as A. Philip Randolph, greatly altered the general tone in the city.

Another important ingredient giving stability and direction to the league was middle-class blacks' seeming distaste for direct-action approaches to solving black unemployment in Cleveland. Some black leaders had attempted to organize boycotts of neighborhood stores as early as 1931, with sporadic efforts through 1935. All of these attempts faltered whenever black politicians and leaders called for their cessation. This new movement did not capitulate in the face of similar demands largely because the tactics of the league and Holly's personality did not attract the black middle class. Under the auspices of the FOL, the working-class membership melded their earlier experiences of autonomous social organizations and the tradition of separate black labor associations with mass, direct-action efforts.

While the league's origins sprang from the exigencies of the Great Depression, its transformation into an independent African-American community-based labor association can be traced to the particular workplace experiences of its members and the autonomy they demanded. In the meetings and the streets, the members of the FOL had a dramatic impact on the direction of the organization. Most urgent is an understanding of the ways in which the highly visible protest of black workers signaled their claims of autonomy from middle-class efforts to mediate employment issues. Finally, the formation, action, and transformation of the FOL's purpose must be seen within the larger context of working-class responses to the deprivations of the Great Depression and African Americans' sustained push for a more egalitarian labor movement.

The massive unemployment fueled by the stock market crash of 1929 began in Cleveland early. As one of the largest cities in the nation, Cleveland had experienced unprecedented industrial growth and expansion of its working population. Yet steady employment eluded a significant portion of the wage-earning population, particularly black workers, during the 1920s. In late 1928, the growing number of business failures and layoffs in stores and factories cast ominous signs for the end of the decade. By 1930, an estimated 41,000—one-seventh of the working-population—were unemployed; one year later, unemployment had skyrocketed to nearly 100,000—one-third of the previously employed.[7]

The Central Area, home for 90 percent of the 84,000 African Americans in the city—many of them newly arrived—had one of the city's highest concentration of jobless people. Male job displacement was particularly evident in unskilled and semiskilled industrial employment and the building trades.

As early as 1929, the Urban League documented widespread unemployment in construction and foundry employment, the two sectors where black men found most of their jobs as unskilled workers. Additionally, with nearly one-quarter of white males unemployed, few blacks retained their nondomestic employment in the other sectors, such as in transportation. Overall black male unemployment rates dramatically increased, and many of the remaining job holders were constantly subject to layoffs or underemployment. Social workers noted that at the onset of the depression many of these men went each day in search of work, but by 1932 most had become discouraged and had ceased to look any longer. Many men had hitchhiked to other cities in search of work, but they, too, appeared to have given up and returned home.[8]

The experience of the Middleton family typified that of many African Americans who had managed to stave off deprivation during the twenties. Steady work as a skilled bricklayer and cement finisher had enabled William Middleton to purchase a home on a block populated with similarly employed black and immigrant workers. The loss of work, however, "just about devastated" the Middleton family, and they nearly lost their home. Throughout the 1930s, William Middleton found only a few odd jobs; Nellie Middleton, who had not been in wage work for more than a decade, found daywork in domestic service. She occasionally washed dishes in a restaurant and took in boarders. The Hill family was in similar circumstances, but they rented the upper portion of their two-family home, which paid the mortgage. In addition, the oldest son, twelve-year-old George, ran errands and delivered groceries.[9] Like many black men, regardless of skills, Middleton and Hill became vulnerable to the constriction in employment and the widespread availability of whites willing to work at jobs previously dominated by blacks.

The precariousness of married African-American men's employment meant that increasing numbers of women sought full-time or part-time work. Urban League officials noted that many of these women had not been in the wage labor force for some time. Dottie Smith, whose husband was employed no more than two days a week, continually sought daywork, which she managed to find just one day a week. Her pursuit of employment became more urgent when her three married daughters and their families arrived to live with the Smiths, which swelled the household count to fourteen. Out of eight adults, not one held a steady job. Because of her husband's irregular employment Eleanor Walls Grist, too, sought work. Her marital status, however, prevented her from finding work. "They assumed that if you were married, your husband had a job. . . . But black men only had a piece of a job."[10] Both women's experiences typified those of many black women whose plights were documented in institutional records.

African-American women, regardless of marital status, found it difficult to secure and retain employment because of their location in the labor market. Increasingly confined to low-wage household and laundry work in the 1920s, black women found new competition for even these jobs from white women pushed out of industrial and better-paying domestic work. Numerous reports from the Cleveland Urban League and the Phillis Wheatley Association confirm that the downward occupational mobility of white women displaced black women from jobs as stockroom attendants, bundle wrappers, and elevator operators.[11] With the exception of laundry work, the unemployment of white women had the greatest impact on black household service workers. The increased availability of white women meant that black household servants, especially dayworkers, experienced a sharp decline in wages and job placements. By 1934, wages had fallen to $2.50 a week. For many women, low wages made car fare to an employer's home in the suburbs prohibitive.[12]

Even as white women claimed access to black women's work, they demanded exclusive control over jobs they deemed "white women's work." Using work stoppages and other forms of protest, white women increasingly objected to black women's limited employment in industrial occupations. For instance, at the Max B. Wertheim Company, which manufactured women's blouses, skilled white women workers threatened to quit and demanded the dismissal of unskilled black women workers. Fearing the loss of the "best workers among the white girls," the personnel manager fired the black women.[13]

Workers' inability to financially cope with the growing unemployment was keenly evident in the sharp increase in demands for charity. The number of cases aided by the Associated Charities increased only incrementally between 1927 and 1929. With high unemployment after 1929, however, requests for food, clothes, and rent assistance greatly depleted private agencies' available resources. By late 1932, the limited reach of private charity organizations was wholly inadequate. Black churches, too, struggled to feed the unemployed, but because they depended on the economic solvency of their membership, they were quickly overwhelmed. Several churches took steps to reduce the salaries of ministers. Ohio epitomized states bound to antiquated views of aid and poverty; until well into the midthirties, local governments and private organizations were disproportionately burdened with dispensing aid. Even with the infusion of federal aid, the state's deep distaste for intervention led to the implementation of a hodgepodge of relief legislation. This led to poor coordination of direct relief efforts, despite high expenditures on the federal, state, and local levels.[14]

With limited work prior to the depression, few African-American workers could depend on savings, insurance, or private relief. Out of necessity, families turned to a variety of means to offset the loss of meager wages. Women regularly visited markets to retrieve rotten food; husbands and children peddled rags and paper; children ran errands and sold newspapers for pennies and scavenged for coal and food at freight yards. But for those families whose economic position had been precarious before the depression, these efforts did little to provide sustenance or stave off deprivation. The impact of unemployment and precarious relief was evident in the Avery family, whose plight came to the attention of Hiram House workers in 1930. Mr. Avery had been without regular employment for five years, which eventually made him despondent. With five children to care for, Mrs. Avery found it impossible to leave the house to work for wages. The scarcity of money forced the Averys to turn to burning battery boxes for fuel. As a result, the children got severe lead poisoning and two of them subsequently died. Relief workers initially provided the father with paper to resell, but by 1931 the Averys were in worse condition. The two oldest sons, both under the age of sixteen, had been arrested for going into vacant houses to remove pipes and bottles to sell.[15]

The newly established Works Progress Administration (WPA) had done little to provide relief to unemployed African Americans. While the WPA had made important inroads in white male joblessness in the city, much of the work offered to black men was short-term, unskilled labor. Federal entrenchment of blacks' exclusion from work and racial segmentation of jobs where they did find work was rampant in Cleveland. The Cleveland Urban League reported that black men's assignment to skilled and semiskilled work would be based on their proportion of such positions in the 1930 census. Given that less than 4 percent of African-American men held skilled positions then, they had little hope of any but unskilled positions through the WPA.[16] Ray Dennis's work experiences on the WPA typified those of many other black men. Laid off from Standard Oil in early 1930, Dennis migrated to Port Huron, Michigan, in search of a job. Unable to find even temporary work, Dennis returned to Cleveland. For the remainder of the decade, Dennis "never had a decent job." Instead he moved between jobs as a porter shining shoes and "wherever I could find some form of employment." In the winter of 1934, Dennis found work with the WPA "doing just common pick and shovel work." For several years after that he worked only eight days a month, always performing unskilled labor.[17]

African-American women found the least amelioration of their unemployment through federal programs. Excluded from New Deal legislation,

African-American service workers found no brake for their downward slide in wages. Black women frequently discovered that minimum wage laws tended to push them out of nonservice work altogether. Moreover, since WPA work was typically confined to heavy labor and factory jobs, black women had few opportunities to find employment at all. Some young black women who had received clerical training in high school found work through the National Youth Administration, but even in these positions race and gender barriers relegated them to the least desirable jobs and inadequate wages.[18] Natalie Middleton applied for numerous clerical positions through the administration in Cleveland, but found work only in Columbus. Though she had earned a high score on her test, like other black women, she received a much lower job classification and earned half of what white women earned with similar scores. Prevented from typing or counting money, Middleton and other black women worked in an attic sorting discarded files. A sense of personal dignity and pride compelled these women to wear skirts and starched white blouses to work. At the end of the day, the women left covered with dust and grime. "We looked as if we had been laying railroad ties," Middleton remarked.[19]

By 1934, 80 percent of the black population received either direct or indirect relief.[20] Superadded to the disproportionate burden of unemployment, those African Americans on relief did not receive cash like white recipients; instead, blacks had to buy from stores authorized to fill orders. In justification, the Cuyahoga County relief administration claimed that African Americans "would prove unable to properly manage their affairs" if they gave direct payment to the poor.[21] The sharp decline in the community's economic stability extended to business owners who had depended largely on black patronage. *Call and Post* writer Charles Loeb described the dismal economic conditions of black Clevelanders: "Fifteen percent had a gross family income of less than $1000 per year. Business and professional classes averaged around $3000 per year. . . . Negro business places . . . numbered less than fifty establishments worthy of mention."[22] Sixty-four percent of the black-owned businesses were small food stores and restaurants with yearly sales of less than $5,381 each. Their economic instability meant black-owned businesses employed only 161 men and women in full-time positions and another 34 in part-time work.[23]

The onset of the depression, however, halted the dispersion of white Central Area merchants to outlying neighborhoods. Both the large and the small stores depended on black customers, but less than 100 blacks found employment in more than 3,000 stores. Many were small family-operated grocery and dry goods stores, pharmacies, dress shops, and shoe stores. Blacks rejected store owners' claims that they employed only family members; instead they pointed to the visible and extensive presence of chain stores such as the Newberry Five and Ten, Atlantic and Pacific markets, F. W. Woolworth, Fisher Brothers, and Marshall Drugs, all of which either did not employ blacks or relegated them to menial, part-time work. "The significant point," the attorney Harvey Johnson explained, "is that so many people had businesses in the black areas, and all white clerks and all white help. And 98 percent of their patronage was from black people." When questioned about these policies, some owners claimed that white customers would not tolerate black hands touching food they intended to purchase. Those few blacks who did find work in white-owned stores and restaurants often labored in shops that limited black patronage. Some owners, according to Harvey Johnson, "wouldn't let [blacks] go into the stores. It was wrong, illegal, unlawful and vicious."[24]

Beginning in the late 1920s, African Americans in several cities across the United Stages began to mount boycotts to challenge exclusion from employment in stores where they were the majority of the customers. By the 1940s these efforts had expanded to at least thirty-five cities, ranging from boycotts in Chicago to trade agreements in New York City to pickets in St. Louis.[25] Each of these boycotts extended from black organizations that hoped to find employment for blacks in white-owned stores that depended on black consumers. In New York City, for instance, the Negro Industrial and Clerical Alliance picketed stores. Although it had little initial success, the alliance affiliated with the Greater New York Coordinating Committee for Employment eventually obtained an agreement with the merchants of Harlem to ensure hiring of blacks when jobs opened up. The alliance's efforts incurred the wrath of many black Harlemites and Jewish merchants, who perceived the boycotts as anti-Semitic. Sufi Abdul Hamid, the leader of the alliance, was dismissed by other black leaders as a dishonest, self-interested "menace to the best interests of Harlem."[26]

As the depression worsened, African Americans in Cleveland organized to boycott stores that would not employ blacks, but these efforts were immediately denounced by black leaders as "untimely and selfish."[27] In 1931, members of the Shiloh Baptist Church joined the church's pastor and his wife, Reverend and Mrs. Boston J. Prince, in forming the Economic Race Development Society. Their slogan—"Don't Spend Your Money Where You Can't Work"—wedded direct action with unemployment. "Feeling that the community's major leadership agencies were not adequately dealing with the crucial problem of unemployment," the Princes called on blacks to use their collective power as consumers to obtain much needed jobs. After successfully obtaining jobs at several Atlantic and Pacific stores, the Economic Race Development Society collapsed in 1932 when Boston Prince suffered a stroke.[28] Others suggested that Prince had been warned to stop the picketing. That same year, Lily Mason and Mary Windsor, members of the East End Political Club, obtained jobs for blacks in the Kroger Food store. Mason and others soon charged, however, that black city council representative Clayborne George, who had initially supported the effort, pressured members to stop the boycotts out of his own fear of political repercussions.[29]

Through Housewives' Leagues, organized in 1932, middle-class black women attempted to promote black businesses. Many of the members were wives of businessmen, though some had small shops of their own. In association with the Cleveland Board of Trade, a consortium of black businesses, the Housewives' Leagues held exhibitions and taught modern techniques of shopping and proper home management. In these venues, black women combined promotion of black businesses with their new roles as urban consumers.[30] Perhaps sensitive to the charges of self-promotion, the women announced that they were "determined to wage war on extreme poverty and general unemployment" by supporting black-owned stores.[31]

This focus on the internal black economy prompted organized collective action when black garbage collectors had their wages cut in 1934. The Housewives' Leagues dumped garbage in the streets as a response to both the wage cuts of black garbage collectors and the pileup of rubbish.[32] In the summer of 1934, Housewives' Leagues from several states, including those from Detroit, met in Cleveland to discuss the creation of a national organization. The women discussed the lack of industrial jobs for black women and the need to "dignify household employment." There is no report of a discussion of boycotts against white-owned stores. The women did, however, announce their intention to boycott stores of landlords "who ousted Race merchants."[33]

African-American leaders of welfare institutions and black business owners cautioned against labor militancy and instead made a variety of appeals for individual improvement. Faced with efforts by white workers to organize black gas station attendants at seven of his Sohio stations, Alonzo Wright announced that it would be foolish for the men to join a union that he believed offered nothing but segregation.[34] Black business leaders appealed to race consciousness and called for "patronage" of black-owned stores, "making possible jobs for our own men and women who are turned down by the other group." In an extension of this stance, others turned to traditional ideas of self-help and community solidarity around race. In an inversion of the call for "Don't buy where you can't work," William O. Walker suggested that blacks spend money where they could work.[35]

The rhetoric of accommodation expressed by African-American leaders attested to the strained resources of community institutions and the inability to dismantle the structural barriers many black workers faced because of race. William Conners, director of the Urban League, urged black workers to be efficient "and to develop a higher appreciation of their work." Jane Edna Hunter blamed the loss of domestic service jobs squarely on the behavior of black workers. "Mr. Fat Job," she declared, "once extended a welcome hand to Mr. Negro, but he now has a book of complaints stacked up." She suggested that "it may be necessary for some of us to return to the farms." Those workers with jobs "must become more efficient, dependable, cooperative and greatly indispensable to our employers." With such exhortations it is little wonder that neither the Urban League nor the PWA proved capable of stemming the widespread dismissal of black workers and the sharp decline in wages for the employed. Privately, the Urban League admitted that it could no longer "handle the pressing problems of the colored group."[36]

In local politics, African-American Republican council representatives had little of the political leverage they had enjoyed in the previous decade. Though African Americans shifted their support toward the Democrats in national elections, they still remained fastened to the Republican party in Cleveland even as they witnessed diminished returns for their votes. In the 1920s, the three black Republican council representatives had often cast pivotal votes in meetings, which had translated into city jobs for African-American workers. In the 1930s, this pattern was disrupted by the renewed clout of the Democrats bolstered by the election of Franklin D. Roosevelt. By 1932, African Americans in Cleveland agreed with Walter White's assessment of the Republican party platform as "flapdoodle" because it failed to support civil rights legislation. Elmer Thompson sneered at the party's lack of interest on the local level, noting that "Republicans would still pat you on the back, but they wouldn't give you a damn thing to eat." But the growing black support for the Democrats on the national level had yet to translate into new power on the local level, since the party focused on the ethnic working-class neighborhoods and exerted little effort among black voters. In turn, African-American voters continued their support for local Republicans.[37]

The newly formed Unemployed Councils, established by the local CP, captured the attention of many unemployed African Americans. Beginning in December 1929 and running through the bitterly cold months of 1930, the Unemployed Councils organized marches of the jobless through the streets of the east side and onto Public Square near the recently constructed Terminal Tower, built to symbolize the city's economic prowess but whose owners had gone bankrupt in late 1928. Though city leaders dismissed the marchers as a "motley throng" of red-led unemployed workers, the city's response to the thousands gathered for the frequent and loud demonstrations was violent. Police on horseback typically charged into the crowds, swinging nightsticks and the rumps of horses. In response to these repeated demonstrations, the mayor and officials of various private charity organizations called for patience from the jobless and greater contributions from the wealthy to depleted relief organizations. By March 1930, local efforts of the unemployed were linked to worldwide demonstrations. Ten thousand unemployed workers "moved in peace" through downtown streets and then gathered around the monument to Cleveland's progressive past, the statue of Mayor Tom L. Johnson. The thousands of jobless, many of them African Americans, roared: "We demand work! We demand food!" The mayor admitted to the crowd that the city lacked the resources to respond to the demands. Afraid of the political repercussions, the mayor ordered the police to wait until most of the demonstrators had left and then use brutal force.[38]

Under the aegis of the Trade Union Educational League (TUEL), the CP held weekly meetings in neighborhoods and organized demonstrations against unemployment and evictions. By 1931, the city had at least eight Unemployed Councils, one of which was located in the heart of the Central Area on East Forty-seventh Street, near Woodland Avenue. Morris Stamm, one of the organizers for the TUEL in Cleveland, helped with the almost daily activities of the Unemployed Councils. Helping people get on welfare "was the bread and butter" of the movement. He helped "rally the neighbors where an eviction had taken place and organized them to help put the furniture back in the house." As unemployed African Americans received soup and bread, they heard the demand for relief, jobs, and unemployment insurance; they witnessed the efforts to prevent evictions; they heard whites call for an end to racial discrimination. Len De Caux, a participant in these street demonstrations, found that blacks "were . . . among the first to get the message when Communists spread among the jobless urging them to demonstrate, march, picket, sit down, sit in, fight back."[39]

By 1931, the street-centered activities of the Unemployed Councils had elicited considerable participation from African Americans. On October 5, 1931, hundreds of unemployed African Americans marched on city hall to gain access to a city council meeting to protest the continuing increases in joblessness and the decreases in charity. Despite several arrests, hundreds more gathered the next evening to prevent an eviction on Woodland Avenue, not far from the Unemployed Council office. Armed police reported being attacked by a "howling, screaming mob of negroes"; though no demonstrators carried weapons, the police wounded four and killed one. One of the wounded later died. Over the next several days, the police elaborated their claims of an armed, dangerous crowd led by Communists. They then maintained that the dead had been carrying incendiary Communist literature, and one had an open pocketknife. Outraged at these charges, residents around Woodland Avenue displayed solidarity. To the tune of "The Internationale," thousands buried the dead at the Woodhill Cemetery. Volunteers wearing scarlet armbands prevented the police from entering the neighborhood.[40]

White and black leaders downplayed the growing approval for the Unemployed Councils and the local CP. Len De Caux recalled that despite the widespread unemployment, newspaper editorials claimed "the colored" had become "victims of economic maladjustment" and had then fallen under the spell of "Communist agitators." But De Caux argued: Blacks "didn't have to be indoctrinated with Marxism-Leninism to know they were exploited not only as workers but also as blacks; that they were not only oppressed workers but also an oppressed people. Looking around the world, they could compare their subjugation with that of any colonial people under the thumb of imperialism."[41] De Caux linked blacks' desire for self-determination to earlier black nationalist movements of the 1920s, such as that led by Marcus Garvey. "What was wrong," he asked "with national liberation here, with running things at least where they were a majority?"[42]

What De Caux recognized then and perceptive historians have come to appreciate now is that the Unemployed Councils tapped into what Robin D. G. Kelley has called the African-American "culture of opposition." Communist publications carried articles on the international struggle for black liberation rarely found in the black press. The educational component of the CP appealed to the black tradition of self-education long built into its social and church clubs. In 1933, for example, the interracial Cleveland Workers' School was established. In addition to taking courses, school members debated and held interracial gatherings and picnics. The weekly street demonstrations featured speakers, often black, who denounced class oppression and called for racial equality. While most blacks did not actively participate in the CP, the press and street nonetheless served as locations to link their deprivation and struggles to those of others. Speakers on behalf of the League of Struggle for Negro Rights and the International Labor Defense (ILD), champions of both the Scottsboro Boys and Angelo Herndon, provided sustenance to the CP's antiracist appeals. In Cleveland, ILD lawyer Yetta Land defended blacks arrested in the eviction marches.[43]

African Americans organizing Cleveland's CP-sponsored activism lent credence to the party's commitment to black equality. Abraham Lewis, Admiral Kilpatrick, and Maude White, all three of whom moved between the CP and black organizations, were particularly prominent. Born and raised in severe poverty in Alabama, Lewis moved to Cleveland and labored as a laundry worker for several years. He soon joined the CP, became district organizer for the ILD, and wrote for the black newspapers. He combined his CP activities with traditional organizations in the black community, such as the NAACP and the black church. Admiral Kilpatrick represented the historical association between black nationalism and an international perspective. By 1930, Kilpatrick had been a longtime member of the Socialist Party and a veteran of political and labor activism. Born into a radical family, Kilpatrick joined the IWW as a teenager and helped organize against the Palmer Raids and in support of Sacco and Vanzetti. Active with the local Unemployed Councils at their inception, Kilpatrick left for the Soviet Union to attend the Lenin School in 1931. Howard University graduate Maude White went to the Soviet Union in the 1920s, returning to the United States to become a prominent organizer in Harlem and to write articles for the *Daily Worker.* By 1933 she replaced Cyrill Briggs as editor of the *Harlem Liberator,* but soon left to organize in Cleveland. In 1934, at the age of twenty-eight, White posed a "triple threat" as a black woman, a veteran organizer, and a theoretician; she eventually worked with the Trade Union Unity League and the National Negro Congress.[44]

Black workers, however, needed little encouragement to display their outrage over too few jobs and insufficient relief. Black organizations of building trades workers, barbers, beauticians, laundry workers, and plumbers, along with the unemployed, emerged "to protect and promote [black] interests."[45] These efforts coincided with the numerous social clubs blacks created to redistribute incomes. Black women repeatedly expressed anger at food clerks who cheated them out of food when they attempted to have relief orders filled at specifically designated stores. In the heat of July in 1934, for instance, this anger spilled over into several riots at the Quincy Cut Rate Market.[46] The demonstrations and protests over limited relief and evictions in 1934 built on nearly a half decade of militancy. In a jointly sponsored protest by the ILD and the Unemployed Councils, Abe Lewis led a parade down to the relief office. Officials once again sent police to terrorize the crowd, resulting in the death of several demonstrators, one of whom was a black woman.[47]

Blacks in and affiliated with the CP occupied visible roles in these new organizations and efforts. Maude White, for example, organized the Neighborhood Committee to protest the lack of black employees in the A and P stores. White, along with other women, protested the segregated pools in the Mt. Pleasant area.[48] Her participation in boycotts against white-owned stores marked a shift from the CP's earlier denunciations of the Harlem boycott as campaigns against foreign workers. Those boycotts had been portrayed as a collusion between "Negro reformists" and "the white ruling class." Though similar objections were raised at the CP's 1934 convention, months later the CP encouraged interracial picketing and the placement of blacks without the displacement of white workers. The CP, discouraged by the low number of black CP members, clarified this position in early 1935 and directed members to "shift the scene of our attention to the existing mass organizations among Negroes, no matter what." As part of this united front, White, joined by Abraham Lewis and recently returned Admiral Kilpatrick, moved quickly to join and help organize the FOL.[49] The involvement in the league of key figures from the black Left provided additional evidence that the renewed pursuit of employment in neighborhood stores had taken a decidedly working-class and radical direction.

African Americans' demands for jobs in Central Area stores emerged, therefore, out of complicated origins. After the topsy-turvy labor market of the 1920s, blacks wanted steady employment. Considered respectable, work as clerks and cashiers held the hope of wage increases and job mobility, something not found in the positions blacks typically held. By late 1935, the WPA played an important role in the reduction of black male unemployment, but work was typically short-term and unskilled.[50] Federal entrenchment of racialized job segmentation and black exclusion were rampant in Cleveland. For African-American women, the pursuit of nondomestic jobs was particularly urgent. Few women willingly chose domestic work, though there was a concerted effort by federal, city, and community agencies to limit other wage opportunities. Black women wanted jobs where white women predominated: clerical and department store work. Increasing numbers of young black women had clerical training in high school, despite the efforts to discourage them. Unable to obtain office work, black women turned to the FOL in search of white-collar positions.[51]

John Holly resembled many migrants whose efforts at finding steady work had been hampered long before the onset of the Great Depression. Born and raised in Tuscaloosa, Alabama, Holly had worked in a Virginia coal mine, at the Packard Motor Company in Detroit, and then as a chauffeur. In Detroit, he met his wife, Leola. While there, he was influenced by his father's efforts to organize black workers in the auto industry. At the start of the depression Holly migrated to Cleveland, found work as a porter at Halle Brothers, but was laid off in 1930; he finally found work as a shipping clerk at the Federal Sanitation Company, a chemical manufacturer.[52]

In 1933 Holly drove his employer to Chicago; while there he attended the World's Fair, where he witnessed blacks with jobs and managerial positions that had been won through boycotts against white-owned stores. Holly must have heard the excited buzz that fourteen inexperienced black employees hired at the South Center Department Store had multiplied to become 60 percent of the 185 employees. Perhaps Holly read *Opportunity* magazine's boast that "no exhibit in the Fair . . . could have had the interest for Negro visitors that is contained in the South Center Department Store." Since the *Chicago Whip*'s call for the boycotts, jobs had been won and black-owned businesses had multiplied. Whatever Holly gleaned from what he saw, heard, or read in Chicago enforced the idea that change had taken place only through the collective power of African Americans.[53] In Cleveland, Holly linked the widespread use of the "Don't Spend Your Money Where You Can't Work" campaign to the collective power of the black unemployed providing for their own needs.

M. Milton Lewis and Harvey Johnson quickly responded to Holly's plan because of their inability to carve out professional careers in small business. Like Holly, both men were raised and educated in the South; unlike Holly, both had gone on to obtain higher education. Johnson received a law degree from Western Reserve Law School, but like other black lawyers he was excluded from white law firms and found it impossible to attract black clients who had money. Educated in business, M. Milton Lewis followed the route of many college-educated black men when he turned to selling insurance. An assistant manager for the Atlanta Life Insurance Company, Lewis had earlier attempted to organize the Douglass Laundry Company, but failed. Johnson, too, pursued self-employment and organized an employment bureau for women in his office. When both heard about Holly's idea to boycott stores, they attended the initial organizational meeting. Holly, Johnson, and Lewis linked together the boycotts of stores with the establishment of black businesses in their formation of the FOL. Lewis served as vice president and Johnson provided legal counsel. Though Johnson rarely received fees, he nonetheless eventually built "a fairly good practice" through his involvement in the FOL.[54]

As president, Holly simultaneously repelled the black middle class and drew in the working class and the unemployed. At the league's inception, Holly's insistence on direct action in the streets, rather than talk, was widely perceived as "rabid." Whether or not he desired support from the educated black middle class was not fully clear; from the start of the FOL, middle-class leaders described him as a "foreigner" unused to patience and more genteel negotiations that had characterized white and black relations in the city during the previous decade. Yet Holly was both ambitious and attuned to the shifting sensibilities of the black unemployed. From the beginning, Holly remained singularly committed to the organization of African-American workers on their own behalf. Though he lacked a formal education and was diminutive, the black unemployed responded to his commanding presence and urgent eloquence.[55]

Even as the FOL faced skepticism and widespread disinterest in its initial efforts, it gained an important ally when it received an endorsement from William O. Walker, the new editor and owner of the *Call and Post.* Walker had few advertisers to appease and enthusiastically announced and supported the activities of the FOL. He offered a prescient assessment of the community when he argued that the older black organizations no longer proved "the haves in the time of economic storms they should be. The Negro masses, exploited both from within as well as without, segregated and discriminated against, are going to find a way out or make one." He suggested the time had come to ignore the "moss back reactionary" views of the "sickly old thinkers" and make way for the "young Negro who is looking to the future." He used the pages of the newspaper to denounce the league's critics and advertise its efforts and successes. He had his news editor, Charles Loeb, work as the publicity manager for the league.[56]

Middle-class hostility for the league meant that the majority of the leadership came from the working class. The inclusion of Robert Warren, who would eventually lead the FOL toward a labor association, infused the members with a working-class militancy that eventually predominated. Within the weekly meetings Warren expressed support for the most radical action. "Warren walked left," Harvey Johnson recalled, "he did lean over the edge, you know; he was a little bit radical." Whether Warren had participated in radical organizations prior to the FOL is not clear. It is evident, however, that his perspective was bolstered by the participation of Admiral Kilpatrick, who had returned from the Soviet Union in time for the FOL's debut. Abraham Lewis, another member of the local CP, became a member of the executive board. Although men occupied the primary leadership positions, women held important roles. Maude White, one of the organizers for the CP, served on the executive board and had the central task of teaching FOL members how to organize a picket line. Beatrice Stevens and Ruth Harper worked as secretaries, becoming the only paid workers for the league, though they frequently had to wait for donations on the picket line to provide their paychecks. Stevens and Harper relayed critical information about the time and place for the boycotts and made arrangements for pickets and jobs. Other women served on the executive board, acted as speakers, organized new members and fund raisers, and headed committees that investigated discrimination in jobs and housing.[57]

The membership, like the leadership, formed a rich mosaic. While African-American leaders continued to denounce the league, little by little the unemployed, migrants, black radicals, housewives, and newly graduated high school students responded by participating in the boycotts, providing donations, and joining the organization. Women made up an important element of the membership. Indeed, according to Marge Robinson, "black women were the FOL." In numerous ways, black women came particularly prepared to participate in the league's direct-action campaigns. First, the FOL made direct appeals to black women as the primary purchasers of food and clothing. Second, whether married or single, many black women had the common need to secure employment and the FOL provided an opportunity to obtain nondomestic work. Isabelle Shaw, for example, became a member of the Investigation Committee, which visited stores and questioned owners about their hiring policies. The large female membership joined radicals, migrants, and students in moving the FOL away from becoming an organization of business owners.[58]

In the two years after its start, the FOL developed a highly choreographed system of investigating stores and organizing pickets. Robert Warren and Milton Lewis, later joined by Isabelle Shaw, examined store practices and met with owners. In the beginning, store owners "were just amazed that we should ask to put a Negro in [their] stores." Despite threats of boycotts, owners "were pretty much set in their ways; they weren't going to hire any blacks." The league chose Saturday, the biggest shopping day in the Woodland Avenue and East Fifty-fifth Street area, to conduct pickets. FOL members gave soapbox speeches while others "walked sandwich" between placards that said "Fools Trade Where They Can't Work" and "Don't Buy Where You Can't Work." This took courage, Isabelle Shaw remarked. In the beginning, few people cheered or joined the picket lines, but many did withhold their purchases, which quickly persuaded store owners to hire blacks. The league's efforts against Hoicowitz Department Store, Simon's Grocery, and Bender Shoes were short in duration and without violence. Even efforts against the much larger chain stores, like Newberry's and the Atlantic and Pacific Tea Company, required only short protests and negotiations. Within hours, blacks had jobs behind counters.[59]

After these successes, organization for the league took place on the picket lines, which had become "the key" and "lever" to garnering black support. Many blacks, when confronted with signs that spoke to the common experience of unemployment and job exclusion, immediately responded by refusing to make purchases. But the most successful means of organization was the limited duration of the boycotts and the immediate reward of a job, often given to a recently recruited picketer. This latter aspect provided a tangible and dramatic demonstration of the feasibility of the FOL's tactics and the impact of collective action. Equally important, the success of these street demonstrations provided a resounding rebuttal to claims that the FOL was nothing more than a racket.[60]

Throughout late 1935 the league continued its pickets and boycotts, but these efforts took on a more confrontational air. The downturn in the economy undoubtedly led to a renewed scarcity of employment. In meetings, Holly demanded jobs and offered the dreaded picket as the only alternative. In turn, store owners responded to picketers with armed police. The FOL faced its first injunction at Barnes Grocery Store on East Seventy-third and Kinsman. Frank Barnes, a southerner, announced he intended to take the money of black people, but refused to give them any as employees. When pickets appeared, Barnes immediately sought an injunction; he argued that since no labor dispute existed and since the league was not a legal labor organization, a boycott violated the law. He then placed ads in city newspapers claiming the picketers were "armed thugs." Though the only guns seen were those carried by the police, shortly after these ads appeared bricks were thrown through the store windows. When the FOL placed pickets around the Fisher Brothers store on Quincy Avenue, its management sought an injunction. The court granted both injunctions, but Fisher Brothers later withdrew the request when management agreed to hire some black workers in December.[61]

Faced with an injunction and the potential loss of sympathy, the league reiterated its commitment to aggressive boycotts against racial discrimination. Although forced to remove the picket line, FOL sympathizers distributed flyers and conducted an effective house-to-house canvass, which eventually drove Barnes out of business. A statement from the FOL emphatically denounced the injunction and criticisms of the boycotts: "Laws and legal technicalities and decisions of judges that will allow other groups to picket in any other part of the city, and at the same time prevent Negroes from using the same method in demanding their economic rights will never be obeyed or recognized by the Future Outlook League."[62] The use of the injunction against the FOL, however, became a recurring threat to dissuade boycotts and diminish community participation. Indeed, the courts' repeated support for injunctions against boycotts in the first half of the decade increased indifference toward and defiance of the boycotts by many blacks in the community. Second, because injunctions took time to be heard and appealed, the league became dependent on sympathizers to help continue the boycotts. Though this method had noticeably diminished Barnes Grocery Store's clientele, it also led to the use of sabotage that fueled claims that the FOL preached and practiced violence. Though many in the league suspected that those at the store instigated the thrown bricks, the specter of violence served to reinforce negative assessments of the FOL.[63]

Rumors of such violence surrounded the boycotts between 1936 and 1938. What was once considered "a neighborhood affair" became a confrontation between merchants, shoppers, and large crowds of picketers requiring police intervention. During meetings, FOL members reported rumors of female customers carrying pistols to protect themselves from the picketers. Such claims dampened enthusiasm, especially of women, to participate in the boycotts. M. Milton Lewis, however, urged members to stop behaving like "sheeps." "We need to institute some wolf into our everyday life," he argued. FOL member Selmer Prewitt did not relish the air of violence, but he expressed what others believed: blacks had to let the merchants and uncooperative consumers know "that we meant business." The league, however, neither advocated nor used violence against recalcitrant merchants. But the combative nature of the pickets led to some displays of guns by police. Moreover, sympathizers sometimes used threats and sabotage. Harvey Johnson dryly noted that "sympathizers of the League . . . would work wonders from time to time." Rumors, the confrontations with police, and the chaos that sometimes erupted around the pickets often swayed small store owners to quickly capitulate. By 1937 the FOL claimed to have become "a thing of bare knuckles and no blows barred."[64]

With the increased threat of violence, women remained reluctant to take part in the pickets. During the pickets, their large presence made them more vulnerable to be "seized and roughened by police." Some of the boycotts ended with tear gas and arrests. The league depended on veteran organizer Maude White to teach the women how to hold pickets and organize other women to withhold their purchases from the stores. To ensure safety, the FOL held sessions to train all members how to participate on picket lines where violence might occur. Such recruiting and training paid off: during boycotts black women sent food to picketers, withheld their purchases, and served as "shock troops" to strengthen picket lines when gaps appeared. Such militancy propelled women into highly visible and frequently dangerous roles.[65]

That violence surrounded FOL activities signaled both the league's particular vulnerability in the city's political landscape and an embracement of self-defense strategies long endorsed by African Americans, particularly workers. By the 1930s even the rumor of violence meant the presence of the police. During the evictions of the early 1930s, for example, the Urban League stepped in to mediate between landowners, black tenants, and the police. This approach had intended to halt what the Urban League reportedly called "communistic propaganda." As more blacks joined or endorsed the CP, however, the Urban League refused to intervene. Similarly, without the support of prominent black leaders, the FOL could not count on their help to prevent police harassment or picketers' arrests. While the FOL did not publicly endorse the use of violence or sabotage, the organization could appreciate how the threat of violence worked in its favor. Since some of the rumors and actual violence did appear to come from supporters of the FOL, boycotters appeared to have utilized both the rhetoric and the practice of self-defense measures. Bringing weapons to the picket line made sense to men and women raised in the small towns and rural communities of the South, where such actions were quite common.[66]

Faced with injunctions and opposition from African Americans, the league turned its attention to the Haltnorth Theater in August 1936. The management, emboldened by the mounting criticism against the FOL, refused to meet with the investigation committee. Despite heavy rains, the FOL conducted five days of spirited, but peaceful, picketing that eventually elicited support from other organizations. Frustrated at the loss of moviegoers, the theater management obtained an injunction, but the Union Social Club, sympathizers of the league, continued to picket. The theater then brought charges of contempt against league officials. Undaunted, sympathizers swarmed the chambers of the judge presiding over the case. Unable to halt the growing sympathy for the FOL and the loss of customers, the Haltnorth struck a compromise: the theater agreed to hire black ushers in exchange for the FOL's removal of the pickets. Over the next several years, the league placed African Americans in other area theaters.[67]

Internal community conflicts over FOL tactics flared during the battle with Telling Belle Vernon. In November 1936, the league requested the placement of black men as drivers of milk delivery trucks. The company, the city's largest distributor of milk and ice cream to small stores, many of them in black neighborhoods, did not employ black delivery workers or drivers. Owners claimed that because of seniority clauses, the Teamsters' local would not allow the employment of black drivers and, therefore, they could not hire any. Finding that 90 percent of black shoppers purchased Telling Belle Vernon products, the league immediately called for a boycott. Initial responses were lukewarm, however, largely because of an effective counterattack by the company. Members set out to hold mass meetings at churches, but when they attempted to distribute flyers disputing the company's supposedly good intentions, some ministers refused to allow them to do so. One minister, in response to both the company's campaign and the league's call for a boycott, indignantly retorted that "churches should not allow literature to be circulated thru their memberships on Sunday mornings [to attack] some big firm that has donated thousands of dollars . . . in the past few years. It seems foolish to break up somebody's business that has millions back of them, and you have not a place to lay your head. It looks like you want to starve to death."[68]

Committed league women continued to organize boldly throughout an unusually bitter November. They distributed flyers intended to shock the community and goad them into support of the boycott. One flyer, for example, read in bold print "THE TELLING BELLE VERNON MILK IS POISON! and in small print "to our economic well being." They began a house-to-house campaign, persuading women to participate in the boycott by placing No Milk Today notes in empty milk bottles. They provided names of smaller distributors that employed blacks. Often they met with "slammed doors" and "unprintable" remarks and insults. Some small stores, having faced earlier boycotts of the league, cooperated. Growing consumer support and store owner cooperation eventually began to have an impact on the company's sales.[69]

Five weeks into the boycott, violence flared. Despite muted support for the boycott from some white drivers, FOL supporters threw bricks at delivery trucks and overturned others. The league claimed no responsibility for the violence and called for its cessation. In addition, its attempts to negotiate with the company and the union were thwarted by several ministers who promised the end of the boycott in exchange for the hiring of two black drivers. In a meeting, Milton Lewis firmly reiterated the league's position: "The boycott would end when the officials of the Telling Belle Vernon company [met] officials of the FOL and promised definitely to put on five drivers and within 30 days add the others."[70] The company agreed to these terms.

Although the FOL credited black women with the successful outcome of the boycott, its organization efforts based on class and gender in addition to race initiated conflicts. Throughout the neighborhood campaigns, women had drawn on associations not only as consumers but also as members of women's organizations. Women who belonged to both the FOL and the Glenara Temple, for example, had used the tactics of ward precinct organizers to ensure that not a house in the neighborhood was left unorganized. As Sharon Harley has noted, such settings allowed for community consciousness-raising around "shared interests and the articulation of work-related concerns."[71] When middle-class women in Cleveland began to organize through the Housewives' Leagues in an effort to support black-owned businesses, they hoped it would lead to the employment of other blacks. They united as wives and mothers in support of racial solidarity, but the placement of blacks in white-owned stores had never been an issue for them before. In contrast, when working-class black women participated in boycotts led by the FOL, they were sharply criticized by middle-class leaders for failing to support African-American businesses and raising the ire of white businesses supportive of black institutions.[72]

Working-class black women's participation in the boycotts and on the picket lines emerged as a highly visible display of their individual and collective power as consumers. After weeks of meetings and training sessions at which they spoke openly about their experiences, women then turned to the picket lines, where they badgered, taunted, ridiculed, and scolded other women not to spend their money in stores where they and other black women could not work. Many women had learned how to appear threatening through their songs, shouts, and closely connected bodies. When women sang the league's song—sung to the tune of a popular black gospel hymn—they dared both white store owners and black customers to defy their efforts. While many women did not cross the lines, others did so. Whether out of anger over the noise or out of disgust over the aggressive tactics of the picketers, middle-class black women insisted on their right to patronize these stores and entered anyway. A bag of groceries came to represent the differences of class, which undermined the common experiences shaped by gender and race. Rather than support the boycotts—and unwilling to face loud crowds—many middle-class women sought ways to undermine the effort without entering stores. The ability to afford a phone, for example, meant that some of these women had groceries delivered to their homes. In response, league women began to follow the delivery trucks and then set up picket lines around the transgressors' homes.[73] In short, economic self-determination heightened African-American women's sense of class identity and conflicted with the call for a racial solidarity based on middle-class interests.

These tensions were clearly evident during the most volatile boycott of the period. Spurred on by the new wave of unemployment, the league announced a boycott against the two largest stores in the area, Woodland Market and F. W. Woolworth.[74] Though the FOL had initially secured an agreement with the Woolworth store in 1936, the management had not kept its promise to increase the number of black workers. The market, located at the junction of several streetcar lines in the heart of the black neighborhoods on East Fifty-fifth and Woodland, housed independent vendors, many of whom employed nonfamily members. Selmer Prewitt was incredulous: "Fifty-Fifth and Woodland, no blacks."[75] The league had approached the management of the market three years earlier, but had been rebuffed. Once again in 1938 the vendors refused to respond to the league's request for a meeting; this time drivers in the Teamsters' local announced they would aid the shop owners in the event of a black boycott.[76]

The battle waged between picketers, consumers, and police at the Woodland Market had a more combative and dramatic character than any of the previous boycotts. On the morning of the boycott, hundreds of FOL members blocked store entrances. As shoppers arrived, many joined the pickets; other blacks loudly proclaimed their lack of sympathy. "The thing that really got me," Prewitt remarked, "was when we picketed the Market, those blacks [said] 'You have a picket?' Oh we had a picket line all around the place. And blacks would go *break* that picket line and go in and out with their groceries *as if we meant nothing.*"[77] The wife of Gordan Simpson, who was the manager of the Outhwaite Housing complex, emerged triumphantly from her morning's shopping. She apparently flaunted her purchases, which soon ended up in the street. As cabbage, apples, and chicken rolled, Simpson screamed that she had been attacked. No one actually saw the attack against Simpson, but the police nonetheless arrested Holly and turned tear gas on the twenty-five hundred picketers.[78]

Despite Holly's arrest and the violence, the Woodland merchants conceded defeat. Their acceptance of the FOL's demand for jobs had an immediate impact on nearby store owners. Selmer Prewitt recalled that store owners "knew about the pickets . . . and they knew that any store that didn't hire blacks in that area was targeted."[79] In addition, the league resolved long-standing disagreements with the Woolworth store. Bolstered by victory, the league announced that its office—and only its office—would be responsible for job placements in the market. The FOL received an added boost by the U.S. Supreme Court ruling that allowed for black boycotts and pickets against stores denying them employment. Black leaders and workers, according to August Meier and Elliot Rudwick, "correctly assessed [the ruling] . . . as a landmark decision." Throughout the nation's black communities, boycotts against discriminatory hiring practices began anew. In Cleveland, the league cemented its position as an organization that got results.[80]

Success and legal legitimacy had a particularly positive impact on the FOL and new members flocked to the meetings. Between 1936 and 1939, the league claimed its membership climbed from ten thousand to eighteen thousand.[81] How many members actually joined the FOL has not been clearly reconstructed, but minutes from the weekly minutes document that throughout the last years of the 1930s the membership steadily grew into the thousands. Between five and ten members joined at each weekly meeting and many did so after a successful picket. Social clubs and fraternal organizations sometimes joined en masse. In June 1938, for example, five hundred members of the Elks lodge joined.[82]

These patterns prompted the league to boast that the city's entire African-American population had joined. Such bravura was not entirely misplaced, since waves of black men and women appeared to spontaneously join in the pickets and the boycotts. When confronted with a gun-wielding store owner, Milton Lewis once announced with confidence, "you will face 80,000 Negroes."[83]

Such confidence, however, belied the difficulties the FOL faced in collecting its membership dues. From the start the league had a fluid membership of unemployed and employed workers who neither attended meetings nor paid dues regularly. The constant struggle to solicit dues suggests that few members regularly contributed to the treasury. Active members—those who paid each week—probably numbered in the low hundreds. When faced with an empty treasury, members solicited sympathetic ministers and church congregations, such as Antioch Baptist Church and Second Mt. Sinai Baptist Church. In addition, organizers constantly sought creative methods to enroll new members and raise funds through building drives, picnics, and workplace solicitations. They held frequent contests among the members to see who could bring in the most recruits. Several members sold insurance and solicited members at the same time. The league advertised on the radio and in the *Call and Post*. In an effort to both encourage new members and retain those who did join, the Speaker's Bureau, the Legal Defense Committee, and the Entertainment Committee were organized.[84]

The number of black women who joined after 1937 began to outpace that of men. Between March and June of 1938, the FOL registered ninety-four new members; sixty-seven were women. During several boycotts in this same period, a significant portion of the dozens of new members who joined on the picket line were women. By May 1939, women were so numerous that they proposed the creation of a women's auxiliary to provide them with additional social opportunities. Instead, they decided to head various committees to raise funds and recruit new members, two activities that typically had been done through social events.[85] Women's greater participation after 1938 can be explained as a result of the legitimation of the league's boycotts by the 1938 Supreme Court decision. Indeed, after May 1938, the threat of violence from police dissipated, making the picket lines safer.

But the style and content of the weekly meetings became a critical component to enticing and retaining members. Several hundred members attended weekly meetings that began with "I Shall Not be Moved" followed by "Lift

Every Voice and Sing" and often concluded with a song from the CP or the labor movement. Like the community organizations and social clubs of the 1920s, the FOL sponsored numerous events that allowed for the presentation and discussion of African-American literature, politics, and culture. They invited Garveyites, Republicans, Democrats, Communists, and Socialists to speak and supported black nationalist efforts. These forums included political activities that members pursued. In 1937, the FOL learned about Admiral Kilpatrick's and Abe Lewis's participation in the Abraham Lincoln Brigade.[86] Many members viewed Mary McLeod Bethune and A. Philip Randolph as heroes and role models. In addition, the league organized numerous events to raise money as well as provide social activities for its members. They held balls, teas, and auctioned off radios, lamps, and hams. These spirited meetings and events reveal the historic desire of African Americans to understand the world around them and the FOL's efforts to provide affordable entertainment for an economically vulnerable membership.

FOL flyers announced activities and boycotts that appealed to "Race Pride." But within the context of the league's activism, a racial consciousness was increasingly shaped by the black working class. Members used the meetings to argue that though segregation had created structural barriers to employment, "some Negroes have been working against" those blacks who "must fight hard for [their] living." While league officials pursued the creation of black-owned businesses, they were not bound to a separate black economy or separate black institutions. Yet, after years of white-controlled institutions created for African Americans, interracialism did not mean that whites would have preference at the expense of blacks. The FOL displayed an aggressive racial consciousness: when white store owners requested clerks with light skin, the league sent only those with dark complexions.[87]

Even though a handful of league members went on to establish successful businesses in the early and middle forties, they did not do so under the auspices of the FOL. Throughout the first several years of the league's existence, some of the leadership continued to hope for the creation of a cadre of black small business owners. John O. Holly, M. Milton Lewis, and Harvey Johnson attempted or ran businesses in the late 1930s. In late 1937, Holly began to market his Sure Death fly spray. After several failed attempts to run a laundry business, Lewis began to organize his Booker T. Washington Laundry, hoping that the better economic stability of the late 1930s might give it an added boost. Though Harvey Johnson received few fees, he did manage to build a solid clientele by advertising his legal work for the FOL in the *Call and Post*.[88] Most members expressed deep ambivalence about the benefits of capitalist accumulation for workers' welfare. "The truth was," the league announced in its 1937 yearbook, "American business is ruthless, without ethics, without honesty. It recognizes only one thing—force."[89] Viewed alongside their boycotts, this analysis sharpened the FOL's opposition to laissez-faire policies.

Though league members launched few businesses, the patronage of league shoppers anchored many struggling stores and shops owned by both blacks and whites. African-American business owners typically came to meetings to advertise new businesses and services; many business owners began to hire more black workers because of the FOL. Advertisements in black newspapers urged blacks to "spend your money where you can work."[90] In meetings and in its newspaper, the *Voice of the League,* the FOL urged its members to patronize businesses that provided support and jobs. In exchange for their support, some black-owned stores provided "special purchase credits" to league members. Its most successful support went to the Crayton Baking Company. After the demise of Kritzer's Bakery, Leroy Crayton began making Crayton's Brown Girl Bread. Its advertising—"Demand the loaf made by brown hands, delivered by brown boys with the smiling brown girl on every loaf"—appealed to a renewed race pride. Conversely, Holly denounced community leaders who "mistreated black businesses" but felt free to claim the league hurt the "best interests of the race." Jane Edna Hunter, for example, refused to serve Crayton's Brown Girl Bread.[91]

Holly and others initially intended to form alliances with black business and professional organizations, but other league leaders and members continually repudiated these efforts. In one such discussion, members disapproved of appeals to racial solidarity because they feared the potential obfuscation of the needs of the black working class and the rights of workers. One woman announced that any alliance with black business owners might yield to the interests of employers, not workers: it "would cause our employees to work longer hours than employees of the other races." When Holly attempted to steer such discussions back to issues of racial solidarity, the members continued to rebuff an affiliation with black merchants. When asked later to consider a black business owner as a full-fledged member, the rank-and-file rejected the request. Instead, they called for an eight-hour-day drive in all places blacks worked, regardless of the employers' race. Meetings typically began with questions about raises, hours, and workplace conditions, not race.[92]

Responses by African-American businesses to the FOL's distinctions between employers and employees were evident in the advertising in the yearly anniversary books and the *Voice of the League.* L. Slaughter, for example, advertised that she sold fresh food and delivered groceries for free. She made it clear that she, too, was a migrant and "employed four to five men receiving adequate salaries." To cement her goodwill, Slaughter added: "I wish to thank the public for continuing with me and I intend to carry on with your co-operation."[93] Though it rejected employers as members, as the league became more influential it accepted contributions from store owners. This practice apparently became so widespread that the league had to prevent blacks who posed as members from soliciting donations.[94]

The refusals to align with black merchants and the careful appeals made by black businesses contravenes one historian's argument that the league was nothing more than a trumpeter for Washingtonian economic self-help.[95] On the one hand, the FOL practiced self-help and racial uplift through its job-training instructions during weekly meetings: "Points such as honesty in dealing with employer and patrons, punctuality, neatness and courtesy were stressed incessantly, and members were encouraged to assimilate rapidly all possible knowledge of their occupations."[96] On the other hand, the FOL eschewed Washington's accommodationist stance and readily criticized the "'handkerchief-head' attitude of certain so-called Negro leaders." The short-lived newspaper *Voice of the League* provided the forum to critique the institutional efforts to train blacks for domestic work, such as at the PWA.[97] Finally, the use of radical, direct-action protest was contrary to the ideology of accommodation. Within this framework of radical protest, ideas of economic self-help took on a more confrontational air. Indeed, Beatrice Stevens, the office secretary, often found it necessary to inform skeptical employers that FOL members had been trained to work in stores.[98]

These differing ideas made for potentially uneasy alliances within the league, but incipient strife faded as it concentrated on obtaining jobs. The FOL appealed to Isabelle Shaw, for example, because it attacked structural barriers to black employment, something not accomplished by other organizations: "Of course we didn't call it civil rights, we didn't use those terms then, but it was really about civil rights." Shaw, who had the misfortune of graduating from high school during the depression, became a member of the executive board in 1936 and drew her friends into the league and onto the picket lines. Though Holly and Lewis talked about the need to establish black businesses, Shaw felt that would "be a dream—almost as if you died and went to heaven." Shaw, like most members, did not think about owning a business; youth and unemployment meant it was not possible. For these members, the issue was jobs, not business ownership. Speaking for the majority of members, Shaw said "a j-o-b was necessary."[99]

For many others, the radical actions of Holly, along with the opportunity to get a job, pulled them to support the boycotts. Only thirteen, Henry

Pointer got a job at a meat market because of Holly, whom he described as "that short, energetic man." For African-American migrants from the Deep South, long accustomed to disparagement for their limited formal education, southern ways, and dark skin, Holly represented a dramatic shift in black leadership. Holly, however, was not the only one to make an imprint on blacks' perspective of leadership. Robert Warren, Maude White, and others provided styles of protest and leadership absent in similar organizations. As they articulated their needs, black workers highlighted the class differences within the black community. People became aware that there was a problem and that collectively something could be done to eradicate structural inequities.[100]

But the increasingly militant demands of black workers were often discordant with those of the black middle class and elites. While some prominent blacks, such as William O. Walker, owner and editor of the *Call and Post,* and Rev. Wade Hampton McKinney, pastor of Antioch Baptist Church, regularly supported the league, the majority of black leaders either ignored or criticized—often in vociferous terms—the leaders and the boycotts. Many feared that the protests would offend white philanthropists. Linton Freeman succinctly described this perspective: "[Blacks] were always afraid [the FOL] was going to create bad relations with the whites. Those black folks are always concerned about their relationship they would have with white people and they were afraid that if [blacks] obeyed our instructions by behaving in this way it would create some kind of feeling between them."[101] Most leaders argued that social welfare efforts, not street radicalism, would be best for African-American workers. As one minister intoned in the *Cleveland Gazette,* black radicalism would be destructive to the larger needs of the community, and black workers needed to turn to "the established social agencies" for this objective guidance.[102] But William O. Walker endorsed the league's tactics and ideology in an editorial: "White participation in our affairs . . . has served to keep the race from developing a real militant program of action."[103]

After the success at the Woodland Market and the 1938 Supreme Court decision allowing boycotts, some black elites began to mute their public critiques of the tactics and ideology of the FOL even as they held private misgivings. The organizational weaknesses of the NAACP, in which African-American elites had traditionally claimed authority, meant that it could not provide an alternative. Though publicly supportive of the league, NAACP board members L. Pearl Mitchell and Perry B. Jackson argued privately to Holly that they found the possibility of removing white workers from jobs and the boycotts against some Jewish store owners "distasteful." FOL members countered, however, with the argument that whites could get jobs where they could not. Moreover, they were quick to note that they never singled out a store owner because of his or her race or religion. Some of the stores were owned by Jews, but the boycotts in Cleveland never took on the anti-ethnic and anti-Semitic pall of those in Harlem. Indeed, the league actively discouraged any public or private expression of anti-Semitism. The FOL bolstered this assertion with an appeal to local hero Jesse Owens's experiences in the 1936 Olympics.[104]

From its inception, the league included political discussions in its weekly meetings that moved from support for all parties to partisan support for the Democrats. The first efforts were bipartisan and the members wanted the issues, rather than specific candidates, discussed. Members refused to participate in rallies for candidates. Such policies appear to have been developed as a means to forestall divisiveness in the weekly meetings. By 1936, however, the FOL took a more visible stance during elections, perhaps because it recognized that the issue of jobs had political relevance.[105] Candidates for the fall election had access to the meetings, but the pattern of bipartisanism still predominated. Republicans, Democrats, and Communists were given equal time. Because of the early involvement of CP member Maude White and Robert Warren's radical sentiments, the FOL included support for the CP and other radical causes. ILD attorney Yetta Land, along with her son Jerry, helped picket; in several instances Yetta Land served as an attorney for the league. In 1937, however, the bipartisan approach to politics ended. Holly ran for city council as a Democrat. Though he lost, the FOL became the forum for the Democratic party by the end of the 1930s. In subsequent elections, league members campaigned for Democratic candidates, though some continued to be sympathetic to the CP.[106]

Very quickly after organizing, league members struggled to sustain the interest of members placed in jobs. In early 1936 the FOL created an affiliated, but separate, Employees' Association (EA) to encourage the continued participation (and financial contributions) of employed workers. Those men and women who obtained jobs had to become members of both the FOL and the EA. This new organization intended to provide a solid financial base for the league and tie those who obtained jobs to the league's core stability. The EA was not successful in getting these new members to pay dues, however. Just as unions resorted to collecting dues at the gates, the EA began going to places of members' employment. In addition, they fined members for tardiness and missed meetings.[107]

The complaints of members about wages and hours soon breathed new life into the EA. In meetings, EA members complained that employers did not abide by the initial contracts signed with the FOL. They received lower wages and worked longer hours than was promised or were soon fired. By late 1936, the task of the EA shifted from sustaining the interest of employed workers in the FOL to monitoring their wages, hours, and workplace conditions. Headed by Robert Warren, the EA began to revisit employers to verify that they did not hire FOL members for "practically nothing so that it will seem that they are complying with the demands." In turn, EA members sought out placed workers to ensure that they were not being coerced by unscrupulous employers. Shelton Baines discovered that some blacks had seemingly colluded with employers and accepted low wages "to help [the employer] fake the picture of Race justice." In other instances, the coercive tactics of store owners were remarkably similar to those of landowners' in the South. One store owner hired a young black man whose mother owed money; with no one to stop him, the owner then took the debt out of the young man's pay. When Baines came to collect dues, the owner claimed his employee had gone for lunch. Suspicious, Baines chatted for a half an hour; teeth chattering, the threatened (and endangered) young employee finally emerged from the freezer where he had been hiding. The EA organizers found that employers frequently and arbitrarily reduced the hours of workers the league had placed. At the Atlantic and Pacific, for example, several young men worked part-time, some for only one day a week. The EA demanded full-time employment, and after a brief boycott, the managers complied.[108]

The enforcement of African-American workers' wages, hours, and work conditions expanded to include those not affiliated with the league. Many of these labored in the building trades, as part-time barbers, and in their homes as beauticians. Unorganized and subjected to the sabotage of white union members or small shop owners, they increasingly appealed to the FOL. In the summer of 1936, seventy-five home-based beauticians organized and affiliated with the FOL to protect themselves from the encroachment of white-owned beauty shops. Erma Lee, one of the few shop owners, was elected as president and then became a member of the FOL executive board. Two years later, the barbers' association asked for similar affiliation and support. That same year, independently organized building laborers asked for affiliation and support for a boycott of St. James A.M.E. Church, which had hired white workers in the AFL to help build its new wing.[109]

Despite these union-like activities, members expressed muted interest in affiliating with either the AFL or the CIO. Certainly the historic exclusion of blacks from craft locals precluded an endorsement of the recent turn toward interracial unionism in AFL locals. But as the FOL emerged, the CIO's promises of "an industrial union for every worker, every worker in an industrial union" without regard to race appealed to Cleveland's unorganized black

workers long used to exclusion. But both the AFL's and the CIO's equivoca-
tion on the inclusion of an antidiscrimination clause in the Wagner Act did
little to assuage fears that blacks would "be sacrificed to Jim Crow unionism."[110] Most important, despite the rhetoric of antidiscrimination, neither
the AFL nor the CIO pushed employers who refused to hire blacks to change
their policies. Black workers were highly aware that they needed work before
they could be organized. In many instances, they viewed the AFL as the greatest impediment to finding and keeping work.

When local unions made overtures toward black workers, some black
leaders undermined the efforts. Black clergymen expressed the most vehe-
mence, many using the pulpit and the press to openly denounce the CIO's
call for interracial unionism. Instead, ministers advocated continued affiliation with employers. Others were skeptical of any union that had "not as yet
indicated any change in its vast polic[ies] regarding Negro workers."[111] Some
pointed to the numerous newspaper accounts of violence and sabotage that
unions reportedly instigated. In particular, the taint of communism made it
impossible for many leaders to endorse unions.

After years of criticism of the exclusionary policies of white organized
labor, the black press greeted the arrival of the CIO with lukewarm endorsements. Despite the failure of the unions to back the NAACP antidiscrimination clause in the Wagner Act, the critical organizing drives in the steel and
auto industries helped to assuage fears about a wholesale exclusion of black
workers. William O. Walker's frequent endorsements of the CIO in the *Call
and Post* significantly swayed the black working class. One of his editorials
baldly stated: "Unless Negro workers get into these various unions, they will
soon find themselves completely locked out of all decent and desirable jobs."
Walker strongly urged support for the CIO despite the history of white-dom-
inated unions' protection of economic gains at the expense of blacks. The
organization of industrial workers meant new economic opportunities for
blacks previously unimagined in the craft unionism of the AFL. He added
that "the Committee for Industrial Organization, which is the Lewis group,
has been fairer to Negro Workers. There is more merit to industrial unions
than in crafts." Weekly articles by David Pierce in the *Call and Post* added to
Walker's appeals: "What is to be done here at home about the thousands of
unemployed? The first correct move, I believe, is the rallying call issued by
the Cleveland CIO unions." But the unemployed could not join unions until they had jobs, and Cleveland's large unemployed black population had no
alternative except to organize through the FOL.[112]

Simultaneously bolstered and threatened by this period of vibrant labor
organizing, members of the FOL made it clear to the black community that

they sought jobs, fair wages, and an end to racial discrimination in employ-ment practices, all of which white unions had failed to secure. The EA ex-pressed the sentiments of many: "The employees [in the EA] believe in union-ism," the FOL yearbook announced, "because it is the trend of the working class today. . . . The day has passed when Negroes will be used to break strikes." Though racial unity was important, the separate organization of black workers "meant the end of a situation which had long been of advantage to whites: the use of the Negro to break down wages, to cushion the blows of an increas-ingly powerful unionism in the U. S., to act as strikebreakers."[113]

The repeated use of injunctions against league boycotts increased discus-sion of affiliation with either the AFL or the CIO during the later part of 1936. Beginning with the injunction sought by Frank Barnes in late 1935 and in each subsequent request, employers' claims that the FOL did not constitute a la-bor organization had dissipated community support and incited the wrath of recognized labor unions. In a September 1936 meeting, Holly called for the necessary data to seek affiliation with the AFL. One month later, Holly ap-peared more in favor of affiliating with "the Lewis CIO." Why the switch occurred cannot be determined, but by the summer of 1937 the league had yet to pursue an affiliation. Holly, instead, warned the members "not to be swayed too much by the labor movements of the day and to be especially wary of falling in line one way or the other." To punctuate Holly's "warning," Robert Warren informed the members that blacks had been dismissed from a drugstore and white workers had taken their jobs. It is not clear whether white unions had influenced the dismissal, yet Warren's point was clear: only the FOL would act on behalf of black workers. Members unanimously de-cided that the drugstore must be closed as soon as possible.[114]

The league's hesitancy is illustrated in the debates that arose in the exec-utive board meetings, which forestalled an alliance with either the AFL or the CIO. Several board members argued that before the FOL could affiliate with the AFL, all privileges must be extended "for the Colored." Despite the more egalitarian rhetoric of the CIO, FOL members feared that union leaders could not ensure that white workers would fight for black workers.[115] Certainly, the bitter reactions of local white-controlled unions to the inclusion of blacks did not lead to an easy alliance. Most important, the duality of the league's purpose—the battle for employment and protection of black workers with jobs—amplified the tentative efforts of the unions on behalf of African-American workers. Thus the FOL never moved to affiliate with the large unions and instead chose to remain independent; throughout the late 1930s, the FOL's call for interracial unionism remained at the level of rhetoric.

Yet African-American members demanded a response to their needs as black workers and instigated action to ensure they would be met. In April 1937, black waitresses at the Rainbow Cafe demanded an increase in their five-dollar weekly salary and an end to twelve-hour days and seven-day work weeks. The waitresses "put down their aprons and trays" and walked out. Sympathetic customers put down their drinks and forks and joined the women on the picket line. FOL pickets had placed the women in the cafe, but this time the women called their protest a strike because this was the weapon workers used to gain better conditions. Less than one hour later, "patron, picket, and public" returned to the cafe to raise a toast to the new agreement that ensured shorter hours and higher wages. Such a dramatic and united display of workers' rights pushed the FOL to begin to organize the other waitresses it had placed. For the next seven years the league urged other non-FOL waitresses to aid in the improvement of hours, wages, and job protection.[116]

The confrontation with union drivers at the Woodland Market in 1938 compelled the league to function like a labor union. After the Woodland Market boycott, the EA created a labor board to monitor working laws, wages, and conditions. It then changed its name to the Employees' Union and announced the new goals of the organization: "To establish the fact that the Negro can and will organize themselves into a strong labor movement, thereby putting the Negro on equal footing with other labor movements."[117] Several months later when employers attempted to fire blacks and reduce the hours of others, the league placed the FOL label on the stalls of merchants who continued to comply with the agreement. In addition, flyers urged blacks to buy only from stalls bearing the FOL label. Within days new agreements were signed.[118]

The internal transformation of the EA into the Employees' Union (EU) was unique to African-Americans' boycott campaigns. In its new incarnation the organization intended to act as a bargaining agent for workers. Born out of necessity and success, the EU quickly sought to legitimize its organization in the community. Throughout the fall, members of the EU used the pages of the league's newspaper to carefully delineate its distinctiveness and purpose as a union of black workers. J. W. Dowden declared that blacks "for your own protection . . . should join the union. It is not wise to stand off nor wise to stand and squat." But blacks faced a dilemma since white unions denied them "equal opportunity." Until the CIO displayed "outward manifestation of an inward policy," it was necessary for blacks to protect their own rights as workers.[119]

The EU made it a policy to picket stores that did not hire blacks and those that did not pay wages stipulated in the contracts of organized white workers in comparable jobs. After the EU picketed a store because it hired non-FOL members, an editorial in the conservative *Cleveland Herald* accused the league of deliberately misleading the community: "How many know that the League was organized along union lines with practices of the CIO?" The editorial then demanded, "We ought to know now what to expect—whether the League is organized to secure economic justice for the race along broad lines, or whether its theory and practice are those of a labor union?"[120]

While the FOL's actions may have startled some, its endeavors had been nurtured by the new coalitions formed between labor, the Left, and civil rights organizations. Just as the league found its stride in early 1936, the National Negro Congress met to organize a broad coalition of groups committed to advocacy of blacks' rights in their communities and workplaces. Members from the FOL joined hundreds of delegates from fraternal organizations, churches, labor organizations, and Communists. Throughout the congress's existence, the league sent delegates. Other representatives were sent to meetings held by the Steel Workers Organizing Committee; in a display of solidarity, some black women in the league joined its strikes in Youngstown. Such coalitions continued with the league's push to provide affordable and adequate housing for the black community; it protested the segregation in the newly built housing projects. These efforts, along with the success of the FOL, resulted in the establishment of other leagues in Akron, Canton, Toledo, Springfield, Warren, and Youngstown, Ohio, as well as in Philadelphia.[121]

The growing strength of the EU provoked conflicts over whether the league would be a union or an organization of future merchants. The FOL's initial successes came from the placement of blacks in jobs, but employed members increasingly demanded more aggressive protection of their needs as workers. In an attempt to solidify this shift, Robert Warren, through the backing of the EU, attempted to oust Holly and become president. Hoping to reaffirm the commitment to business ownership, M. Milton Lewis also attempted to take over, receiving support from a handful of members who sought to own businesses. While Holly had tried to allow both sentiments to coexist in the league, he, too, recognized the necessity of a union to ensure blacks' rights as workers. Yet he also argued that the league needed to continue finding jobs for unemployed blacks. Holly won reelection, but the members had sent a warning through the second-place Warren: the EU had become the center of power in the league. Lewis's few votes underscored once and for all that the league was not an organization of future merchants.[122]

In many ways, the league encroached upon the traditional base of support for the older black organizations by effectively organizing around race and class. More than any other organization in Cleveland, the FOL met the needs of the black working class in Cleveland during the depression. Its success occurred for several important and interrelated reasons. The league did not emerge in a vacuum; it was nurtured by both the resurgence of black militancy and the general wave of labor organizing that began in 1931. Despite the criticism of its tactics, the seeds for its success had been present in the black community since the 1920s. Building upon both labor and community activism, the league did not demand a rejection of unions in exchange for jobs, and therefore challenged the Urban League. Its emphasis on direct action upstaged the legal activism of the Cleveland NAACP.[123] By the eve of the war, the FOL claimed thousands of supporters and had spawned branches in cities throughout Ohio. The league's tactics and ideology influenced the formation of similar organizations throughout the United States. Despite the initial hostility to the FOL and Holly's leadership, black business leaders and politicians reluctantly recognized the league's success and influence.

Though the FOL opened new job opportunities through direct action, it could not adequately address the problems of African Americans' economic marginality. The league had also not been able to mount a campaign to find employment for black women outside of neighborhood stores. As the city's industries once again turned to war production, black workers had yet to tear down the barriers to semiskilled and skilled industrial employment. Faced with labor shortages, employers looked south once again. This time, however, they shunned available black workers and imported white workers from Tennessee and Kentucky. In the face of these trends, the Future Outlook League shifted its attention to industrial employment.

SEVEN

"The Plight of Negro Workers": Federal Initiatives and African-American Working-Class Militancy during World War II

As the great "Tradition Buster"
Ends a "shift" of eight long years,
Negro hearts mus' feel misgivin's
Negro eyes are blurred by tears.
Though they're draftin' Negro manhood
Dixie folks still rule by mob,
While up North . . . "The Seat of Freedom,"
We can't even get a job!

—"The Meditations of Methuselah Brown,
     America's No. 1 exponent of horse sense,"
     Cleveland Call and Post, January 25, 1941

AFTER THE PROTRACTED STRUGGLE for employment during the Great Depression, African Americans in Cleveland hoped the local labor shortages brought about by the war in Europe would provide them with easier access to industrial jobs, particularly higher-paying defense work. "Methuselah Brown's" blues, however, served as the collective outpouring of impatience from black Clevelanders about the paradoxes they encountered in the city's labor market: employers lamented the lack of skilled workers but frequently refused to hire and train blacks. Though such discrimination was not new in the context of blacks' experiences in the city, the local and national effort they waged against it was unprecedented. When A. Philip Randolph, the veteran labor organizer and civil rights activist, carried African Americans' outrage to the White House in 1940, he went with an unequivocal endorsement from black organizations in Cleveland. His subsequent call for tens of thousands of blacks to march on Washington, D.C., to demand jobs and integration of the military met with equal approval and promises of participation by the FOL. In the half decade before the war, thousands of blacks had regularly engaged in militant direct-action protest and they were willing to do so again to obtain wartime jobs. The widespread threat of tens of thousands of black people protesting racial discrimination in the streets just as the nation announced its support of a war against Nazism pushed President Roosevelt to issue Executive Order 8802 in June 1941 and create the Committee on Fair Employment Practice (COFEP), which was reconstituted as the Fair Employment Practice Commission (FEPC) in June 1944.[1]

Despite this new federal initiative, patterns of discrimination on the local level persisted. Several months after Roosevelt's order, Frank G. Jones, City Relief Commissioner of Cleveland, noted the continued "plight of the Negro worker," who remained disproportionately on relief or confined to WPA work. "As yet," Jones observed, "the Negro has not been accorded the opportunity to participate in the program to make America the arsenal for democracy." Two years later, Lawrence W. Cramer, executive secretary of the COFEP, acknowledged that while "it might have been expected that our entry into the war would have brushed aside the luxury of 'prejudice as usual' as it did the complacence of 'business as usual,'" African-American workers continued to face persistent discrimination in many sectors of defense employment.[2] Until the end of the war Cleveland employers used an array of tactics to limit black men's access to higher-skilled industrial work and bar black women from defense work altogether. Moreover, even as white workers abandoned nonindustrial employment in droves, African Americans found that these jobs remained closed to them. Ironically, the threat of mass black protest that had sparked the creation of the COFEP did not bring about a diligent effort by federal investigators to ensure equal access to jobs. On the contrary, community-based black militancy was viewed as an impediment to the war. Black protest may have motivated Roosevelt, but employers claimed it stirred up white workers—whose antiblack tactics were viewed as natural—and impeded wartime production. Repeatedly local employers insisted that blacks confine their grievances to paper, wait for various agencies to investigate, and rely on mediators to plead their cause, if at all.

The tension between the promises and the failures of federal initiatives on the local level, along with the continued intransigence of many nonindustrial employers, elicited a new community-based militancy from black workers in Cleveland. They insisted, as African Americans did everywhere, that victory abroad must include a substantive defeat of racial inequality at home.[3] When the local implementation of the COFEP proved to be inadequate, the FOL channeled blacks' frustration and resentment into vigorous pickets and boycotts against discriminatory employers. Though the threat of a march on Washington gave a new legitimacy to black workers' demands for defense employment, local middle-class black leaders came to perceive the use of pickets and boycotts as counterproductive to the negotiated settlements that federal policies required. While the COFEP proved generally incapable of dismantling employers' constructed racial barriers to jobs, its call for investigation of discrimination nonetheless provided a backdrop for blacks to demand scrutiny of an employer's policies.

When African-American women in Cleveland could not find production work in defense industries, even with the proper training and a call for women workers, they turned to the FOL for investigation and direct action. After months of criticism about its street protests, the FOL brought suits against two of the largest defense employers in the city, hoping to replicate COFEP hearings held elsewhere. The subsequent court battle revealed more than black women's inability to find work because of their race and gender. More to the point, the court battles demonstrated that employers used local racial antipathy *and* an executive order with limited enforcement power to circumvent antidiscrimination policies. But black workers did not simply intend to highlight the inadequacy of the executive order—that it did not prevent discrimination against them was amply evident. Rather, African Americans continued to use confrontational community-based protest to demand that the court compel employers to ensure equality in the workplace. In the process, they pressured unions and local organizations to advocate blacks' civil rights as necessary and permanent in the workplace. In these new local efforts and alliances, black Clevelanders helped define the contours for the modern civil rights movement in the city.

By early 1941, the city's auto, steel, electrical, and chemical manufacturers secured large defense orders. For most companies, these orders made it imperative to expand production and hire additional labor. The shortage of white male workers on all skill levels, with a particular shortage of skilled workers in some machine tool occupations, made it difficult to meet the production quotas. Once the United States entered the war and the local labor market tightened further, many employers went to the South to hire white workers; others appealed to white women to enter industrial work. To accommodate these new workers, large companies retooled machinery and implemented new training programs. As more companies claimed that they had to rely on new groups of white workers, the Cleveland Chamber of Commerce coordinated these programs, obtaining funds from government sources. By late 1941, large companies provided training materials to city technical schools with the stipulation that students would be trained for specific positions.[4] In short, Cleveland employers mounted a massive effort to train white workers.

Such creative and coordinated responses did not expand to include black workers. Agencies that documented the city's labor supply became increasingly aware that employers adamantly refused to hire African Americans. The data collected throughout the war reveal just how limited blacks' access to jobs remained, even as the number of jobs increased. In 1940, African Americans filled less than 5,000 of the 130,000 industrial jobs in the city; black women held less than 200 of these. By July 1942, the number of workers with defense jobs had exploded to 200,000, but blacks held less than 5 percent of these jobs. When questioned about the continuing sharp disparity, two-thirds of the Associated Industries members responded that they intended to stand by their exclusionary hiring policies. Charles Stilwell, president of the Cleveland Chamber of Commerce and Warner and Swasey, set the tone for such policies when he argued that blacks had limited capabilities. Without any evidence, chamber of commerce members argued that the workers still on the WPA rolls, many of them black, were particularly "unsuitable." The *Call and Post* conducted its own survey, discovering that 65 percent of the respondents refused to hire blacks at all or admitted that they discriminated against them. Others claimed that they intended to hire blacks "only when the supply of white workers had been exhausted." Even in those plants where blacks worked, personnel managers refused to hire more, claiming they had filled their "color quota."[5]

Access to industrial employment did not necessarily offer African Americans new occupational mobility. The Urban League found that it could place blacks only in positions traditionally perceived as "Negro jobs," typically in heavy work in foundries and chemical manufacturing. In some companies where black men comprised a significant portion of the labor force, wartime orders and the tight labor market compelled employers to consider greater flexibility in job assignments. But in the majority of plants employers trained white workers instead, and blacks continued to face limited occupational mobility. When pressed, many personnel managers acknowledged that they refused to train African Americans for, or place them in, skilled occupations. The policies followed by Bishop and Babcock Manufacturing Company, which produced 105 mm shells for the army and navy, exemplified this rigidity. Even with a need for skilled labor, the company refused to upgrade black male laborers, continuing to confine them to the heat-treating department.[6]

Evading charges of discrimination, some employers cited the highly restrictive patterns of blacks' employment before the war to explain their continued restrictions in hiring. Some expressed an explicitly racist view, arguing that blacks inherently lacked the ability to acquire the necessary skills. Others, noting the small pool of skilled black workers in industrial jobs before the war, claimed that blacks lacked the skills for the new jobs. Such assertions, however, denied the elaborate training programs employers helped institute for white workers. In many instances, employers shortened training programs, reclassified jobs, and provided workers with on-the-job training. The local branches of the Urban League and the NAACP received constant complaints from African-American workers that instructors discouraged them from taking courses to gain necessary skills. Such policies made a dramatic impact, fueling continued exclusion: by 1942 less than 500 black men and 200 black women had received the training they needed to get defense jobs. Without a doubt, while persistent patterns of discrimination hindered blacks' access to new employment, new patterns took shape as well.[7]

As the military drew more men away from the civilian labor pool, employers began to make direct and innovative appeals to white women. Many of these women were recent migrants from the South. Daily ads in Cleveland newspapers stressed the cleanliness and ease of defense work, as well as its temporary nature. Even with increased access to defense work, white women overwhelmingly entered employment perceived as suitable for them. Though prewar patterns shaped much of the job stratification, new wartime jobs were also assigned according to gender stereotypes and notions of white women's capabilities. The assigning of jobs, however, was not systematic. What employers considered appropriate for men in one sector could be assigned to women in another after a significant number of women performed the work. The preponderance of women, therefore, and not the inherent characteristics of the job, frequently shaped the gendering of occupations.[8] By late 1942, more than half of the defense employers in Cleveland hired white women, especially for production work in plane parts, munitions, and electrical manufacturing. As southern white women comprised an increasing proportion of the respondents, some employers claimed the workplace was "nigger free." With jobs more plentiful, many of these women quit jobs when little more than a rumor suggested an employer intended to hire black workers. Some employers soon discovered that these workers left high-paying defense jobs once they found themselves working alongside blacks. Many white workers came from areas where there had been few black workers, and they expected and demanded segregated work settings. Other whites had some experience with racially segmented work in the mining areas of West Virginia, Tennessee, and Kentucky. Once aware of these patterns, employers and employment agencies shaped the work environment accordingly.[9]

To justify their racialized hiring policies, some employers emphasized white women workers' general enmity toward blacks and their particular fear of black men as sexual predators. But white women rarely competed for the same defense jobs with either black men or women. Since employers concentrated white women in semiskilled machine production in light industries and typically assigned black men to heavy and nonproduction work, sex segregation did not necessarily compromise racial stratification. When an employer hired black men and white women, each group could reinforce rather than compromise the confinement of the other. At White Motors, which made plane engines and parts, the lines of racially and sexually segregated labor were sharply drawn. Black men labored in heavy, nonproduction work and white women were confined to the finishing departments. Even in plants where the lines between white and black men's work were more blurred, white women did not compete for jobs with either group.[10]

While many employers filled labor shortages by hiring white women, growing production demands began to erode the exclusion of black men. As war pulled white men into the military, African-American men had held on to work as unskilled laborers. The continued need for male workers compelled some employers to rethink their promotions, transfers, and integration into production work. Eventually labor shortages, especially in foundries, steel, and chemicals, allowed increased access for black men. By late 1942, black male unemployment began to decline, and some employers actively sought to recruit these men for production work.[11]

The changes in black men's industrial work could no longer be perceived as a temporary shift, but instead represented dramatic alterations in workplace relations. White men aggressively responded to these changes, frequently balking at the hiring of black men. Employers countered by hiring white women instead, but white men equally took issue with this new policy. Employers overcame the dilemma that white women posed by confining them to particular jobs. However much women hoped the new wartime jobs might lead to a permanent presence, employers repeatedly stressed the temporary nature of defense work. Part of the local War Manpower Commission's appeal to push employers to hire local labor rested on this very feature. Given the implications of black men's work, employers and white men often found a common interest in maintaining racially stratified occupations and hiring white women as a means to do so.[12]

Employers' and white workers' efforts to maintain these patterns closed avenues for African-American women in production work, where white women already labored. Unions and employers alike claimed that black women would instigate white workers' objections, "upset local wage scales," or dissuade more desirable workers from applying. Both groups generally agreed that black women would be employed last, if at all. When many black women inquired at personnel offices they found production jobs closed to them because of their race and gender. Indeed, the very act of applying for work served as a reminder of black women's unique exclusion because of race, class, and gender. Employers generally hoped the large pool of available white women could be tapped, making it unnecessary to hire black women except in cafeterias or in cleaning positions.[13] The general reluctance to hire black women for industrial positions despite the widespread shortage of workers appears to lack a coherent logic since many companies hired both black men and white women. Because employers relied on prevailing racial and sexual stereotypes, their decision to exclude black women arose from complicated assignment patterns of black men and white women.[14]

Even in nondefense industries, employers generally continued to bar African-American women. As white women left household service and shifted into higher-paying work, the local U.S. Employment Service (USES) office attempted to prevent black women from making similar moves. Despite black women's requests for defense work, officials confined them to a separate office and referred them to household work only, justifying the policy with the observation that employers would naturally refuse to hire them for production work. Many African-American women did leave or reject household service, but not for defense work. Rather, the majority worked as replacements for black men and white women in nonindustrial employment, all of which paid less than defense work.[15]

Given the restrictions of the labor market, African Americans enthusiastically responded to Roosevelt's executive order. Although not naive about its capabilities, black workers hoped that it would strip away some of the most egregious barriers to their employment. But the order lacked enforcement, thus from the start its supporters had to persuade, not threaten, employers to stop their patterns of discrimination. Cleveland mayor Edward Blythin's appeal represented the limitations of such an approach when he could only "respectfully urge that all employers, labor organizations, and fellow employees within the City of Cleveland do all within their power to give effect to the letter and spirit" of Roosevelt's order.[16] Consequently, African Americans agreed that constant pressure would be necessary to ensure compliance. For weeks the *Call and Post* published directions on how to file complaints at the local COFEP office.[17]

From the start, however, it was apparent that the COFEP suffered from numerous systemic problems that hindered its effectiveness in investigating complaints. Inadequately staffed and underfunded, neither the national nor the regional offices had any legal basis to compel employers to hire blacks. Agents frequently became embroiled in lengthy investigations and negotiations with employers, finding that moral persuasion made little impact. In most instances, local offices relied on tight labor markets to bolster appeals to employers.[18] But the goals of the order were most hampered by conflicts with other government policies. The War Manpower Commission (WMC), for example, which was the agency responsible for the COFEP, maintained orderly production schedules. When employers claimed that compliance with the executive order led to threats of walkouts, work stoppages, and hate strikes that disrupted production, the WMC frequently allowed the delay in, or evasion of, hiring black workers. Where such threats did not occur, companies nonetheless argued that the possibility of white retaliation could hinder production, making it necessary to continue discriminating policies.[19] In many instances, the WMC gained employment for workers from various ethnic groups, but not for blacks.[20]

Simultaneous investigations by other agencies concerned with hiring policies in defense industries hindered the COFEP. A memo from the Greater Cleveland Council on Fair Employment Practice admitted "that there was a great deal of overlapping of effort," which resulted in a repetition of investigations. In one instance, field workers from two agencies attempted to gain compliance from General Dry Batteries, a company that repeatedly refused to hire blacks. After several investigations, the COFEP agreed to cease its investigation if six nonwhites (an evasive tactic since many ethnic workers were classified as nonwhite) were employed. The company, however, did not intend to comply until all other "various government agencies" had completed their investigations, which dragged on for months, allowing the company to continue its discriminatory policies.[21] As a result of such bureaucratic limitations, the director of Region V admitted to little success "in obtaining voluntary compliance" with the executive order. COFEP field agents bitterly complained that the WMC left them with the most difficult cases. As a result, the director suggested that the reason "why fewer cases are closed per capita of examiners" than in other regions was because the WMC handled the easiest cases and pawned the rest off on the COFEP.[22]

In addition, the regional COFEP often found that the USES sabotaged its efforts to place black workers. The USES screened black workers in separate offices, refusing to inform them of available production work. Ignoring the COFEP, USES agents typically complied with employers' requests for white workers only.[23] When asked to help enforce the Order, some companies began requesting older black workers between the ages of forty-five and sixty and then demanded birth certificates. Since most of these blacks had been born in the South where such records were rarely kept for them, they lost the jobs.[24] Although a regional director of the USES attempted to halt this practice in Cleveland, subsequent instructions from Washington, D.C., rescinded the directive and ordered continued compliance with policies considered more conducive to maintaining stable production.[25]

However well intentioned, local COFEP agents were overburdened with cases and thwarted by the actions or policies of other agencies. Field agents found it difficult to proceed with more extensive investigations of companies and unions that practiced discrimination against blacks. At public and informational meetings, the director of the COFEP office in Cleveland admitted to the limitations in personnel, budget, and functions. Field agents, instead, urged individuals and black organizations to gather evidence of discrimination to minimize the investigative process.[26]

Unions often enforced an employers' discriminatory hiring practices or took little action to prevent them. Management at Parker Appliances, for example, adamantly opposed hiring black women. Company officials claimed that union contracts with machinists, molders, electricians, and pattern makers prohibited compliance with federal policies. Moreover, Parker employed eight hundred to nine hundred white women in the plant, which angered white men. The union claimed, therefore, that problems of job assignments and wages "would be greatly exaggerated if Negroes were used."[27] Ohio Chemical Company made similar claims and refused to hire black women in production because white women were required to blow glass with their mouths. The management stated with certainty "that white women would not work on the same assembly line with Negroes." When interviewed, the president of the United Gas, Coal, Coke, and Chemical Workers, Local No. 140 denied that the union tolerated discrimination. He urged the company to send out a letter to each member reiterating union policy, but refused to allow the union to take a more active role.[28]

Many African-American union members were well aware of the intransigence in some locals. William Raiford, a black bricklayer and a member of the AFL local, argued that many unions not only prevented blacks from obtaining jobs in Cleveland, but also stifled the mobility of those with jobs. Although a staunch unionist, Raiford believed that blacks would gain new employment opportunities, not through collective bargaining, but from government contracts that stipulated proportionate hiring practices.[29] One week later, the *Call and Post* reported that an official at the Cleveland General Motor's plant placed the blame on the union, claiming the company would not hire blacks because the "CIO union wouldn't stand for it." When questioned whether this was a case of racial discrimination, the manager responded, "We don't discriminate against Negroes, we just don't hire any."[30]

Despite the deep distrust that such views engendered among many African Americans, the CIO increasingly received black workers' support. Even as the local black press reported evidence of unions' limited efforts to battle employers' discrimination, accounts of CIO activism elsewhere helped to precipitate the growing support for organized labor. In late 1940, 500 workers in Columbus, Ohio struck at the Curtiss-Wright aircraft plant when a black man was promoted to the tool and die department. R. J. Thomas, president of the CIO affiliate of the United Auto Workers (UAW-CIO), immediately removed the local union official who had endorsed the strike and ordered the men back to work. This action won approval from the *Call and Post* as well as from CIO members in Cleveland. In December, the community was rewarded for its continued support. Local 486 of the UAW-CIO at Midland Steel elected Joseph Jackson as its first black president. The union had only three hundred black workers compared with eleven hundred whites, but Jackson received 90 percent of the vote. Local competition for members in Cleveland forced the AFL to openly endorse blacks' right to join the locals. Sam Marable, one of the first blacks to work in a large cleaning firm, was elected to the board of trustees for the AFL Cleaning and Dye House Workers. Marable announced that he decided to join the AFL after assurances that the local "really intended to adopt a more liberal policy with respect to members of my race." Marable was then urged by the AFL to recruit other black workers. Hoping to cement these feelings of goodwill, the AFL affiliate of the UAW unanimously passed a resolution condemning the denial of employment opportunities to blacks working on defense contracts. As an affirmation of this new policy, the AFL-UAW local won reinstatement and back pay for three black employees of the West Steel Casting Company.[31]

Despite new union policies and rhetoric of antidiscrimination, many semiskilled and skilled industrial jobs still remained closed to blacks, and black women found little access at all. A front page article in the *Call and Post* in the late summer of 1941 presented the issues: "While a few Cleveland plants have begun to consider Negroes for unskilled jobs, particularly foundry labor and porters' work, there has been no marked change in the attitude of Cleveland's industries in its seeming determination to keep the Negro out of the skilled and highest paid jobs."[32] Letters from labor organizations poured into the *Call and Post* attempting to disassociate nondiscriminatory union policies from employers' discriminatory hiring practices.[33]

Many union organizers, however, privately claimed that they did not know "what to do" with the large group of white workers both unfamiliar with unions and resistant to black workers. Southern white migrants' hesitant support for unions could quickly evaporate when black workers were hired or upgraded. Many frequently saw unions as subjecting them to unwanted racial mixing. Even when individual CIO unions attempted to advance the workplace needs of African-American workers they encountered belligerent white workers supported by equally recalcitrant employers.[34] The experiences of the CIO-UAW at Thompson Products illustrated such difficulties. Between 1937 and 1941 the union waged a long and unsuccessful battle to organize several thousand workers. The company typically hired young white women, southern white men, and some black men, all the while segregating them. As the CIO made headway, it attempted to endorse mixed shops, only to find union support dramatically decline. In addition, the CIO discovered an active branch of the Ku Klux Klan.[35]

Whatever the feelings of union organizers about the presence of black workers, they often had little choice but to organize interracial locals, particularly where the AFL and CIO competed. Such was the case at the Aluminum Company of America Plant, where the majority of the seven thousand workers had not decided on either an AFL or a CIO affiliation. Taking note of this indecision, the CIO vigorously organized the nineteen hundred workers paying particular attention to blacks. In addition, the CIO helped several black workers gain promotions. Though only a small presence, blacks augmented the white CIO supporters at the time of the union vote. Such solidarity pushed the AFL out and allowed the CIO to form a closed shop.[36]

As the experience of these locals reveal, black workers provided critical support, much of which had been forged before the war. In particular, blacks had been highly active in the Steel Workers Organizing Committee (SWOC) throughout the Cleveland area, and they eventually formed a significant portion of the membership of the United Steel Workers of America locals. While blacks had yet to gain offices on the executive board, they nonetheless had highly visible positions on the SWOC. One historian noted that blacks' presence made the steel strikes between 1937 and 1941 the "reverse of [the situation] in 1919."[37] During the 1937 strike at Republic Steel, half of the black workers joined the SWOC; the company found it difficult to recruit local black strikebreakers. The company then imported black and white workers from the South, armed them with pickaxes, and sent them to attack the strikers at soup kitchens. With blacks and whites on both sides, the struggle for workers' rights was no longer perceived in sharp racial terms.[38]

Other unions aggressively attempted to organize diverse groups of workers, maintain no-strike pledges, and follow antidiscrimination policies set by national and local leaders. Within this context, some locals refused to pander to racism. Early in the spring of 1942, the Ohio CIO Council warned its locals to be aware of employers' divisive racial tactics. A statement from the state council warned shop stewards to move quickly to prevent conflicts. "If any change in employment status occurs in your plant with respect to colored workers," the statement cautioned, "be sure that no stoppage results, and that no harsh words or fighting occurs."[39] Such actions announced a broad-based effort to eradicate discrimination within locals and employers' ability to use antiblack attitudes to dismantle unions. As Michael Goldfield noted, "there is much evidence that solidaristic interracial struggle helped mitigate racist attitudes among white workers and at times led them to support and even join in the battles of African-American workers for equality."[40] Yet such interracial efforts depended on specific local contexts in which charismatic leaders and educational programs worked hand-in-hand. The Cleveland CIO Industrial Council moved beyond mere statements when it pushed locals to institute educational programs promoting the acceptance of black workers on the shop floor. In plants with relatively few difficulties, such as steel foundries, shop stewards pressured management to end discriminatory hiring and promoting practices and demanded improved safety conditions for black workers. These locals then pushed for the elections of blacks to union committees and offices.[41]

But the long history of African-American workers' exclusion from unions, combined with the continued evidence of discrimination in locals and job assignments, made the claims of the CIO suspect. Unlike in packinghouses and auto plants in Chicago and Detroit, where black men had been key to successful organization, the attempts at unionizing in steel plants had been far more difficult. Through the SWOC, blacks in Cleveland joined the CIO at lower rates than they did in other districts and the CIO more generally.[42] At the start of the war, African Americans remained skeptical of unions, especially since collective bargaining often sanctioned job segmentation and inequities in wage rates. Blacks questioned why support for and membership in unions had not provided greater access to defense jobs. Even those blacks supportive of organized labor recognized that unions had done little for black women. Indeed, unions' focus on organizing in the workplace and rarely, if at all, around concerns of blacks' exclusion from industrial jobs demonstrated the limits of CIO leadership's efforts. In sharp contrast, black workers in the 1930s had waged a protracted struggle to challenge employers' hiring policies. The lack of black women's gains in the 1940s would reenergize the FOL and legitimize their confrontational efforts in the streets.

By late 1940, the FOL found that obstacles to jobs in stores had receded, thus their use of pickets and boycotts became infrequent. Although black women had acquired some of these positions, the majority of the placements had gone to men. Women had taken issue with this policy during the depression, when some male members had suggested that men should receive employment first. Others argued that single women should have preference over married women.[43] As defense jobs became more available for African-American men, women found greater access to nondomestic service employment, though they continued to face exclusion from similar jobs outside black neighborhoods. With additional barriers to defense work, women agitated for a return to community-based direct action. Employers' negative responses to calls for negotiations pushed the FOL to "return to the picket" and "test its power outside its tightly-organized backyard."[44]

The league decided to target Ohio Bell Telephone since it employed a large number of white women. The company's refusal to hire blacks had been raised in FOL meetings years earlier, but because the majority of blacks did not have telephones, a boycott was considered unwise.[45] After weeks of conferences in the spring of 1941, the company agreed to hire a few black men to deliver city directories, but refused to hire women. Officials argued that such a concession would cause six thousand white women to leave their jobs.[46] On the morning of May 5, 1941, thousands of black "housewives" picked up their phones and simultaneously dialed the operator. They then asked to speak to company officials to protest the discriminatory hiring policies. The calls were synchronized with the arrival of hundreds of picketers carrying American flags and banners comparing Ohio Bell's racial policy to Hitler's. Within a week, the company agreed to hire black women as elevator operators. When league negotiators called for black women's placement in positions as clerical workers and operators, company officials argued that they would have to work in a segregated office.[47]

Just as the FOL organized a mass protest, A. Philip Randolph strengthened his call for a march on Washington, thus the timing of the boycott proved opportune. Within the context of the national efforts, even the partial success of the FOL's efforts engendered support from the NAACP and the Urban League, both of whom had ignored earlier appeals for aid.[48] African-American women applauded the FOL's efforts, but they also urged the league to recognize that the "objectives in the phone company campaign were not realized." In a letter to the editor of the Call and Post, a woman wrote: "So much has been done to open up jobs for men that, until the Future Outlook League raised the issue with the telephone company, we think the public had generally overlooked the plight of the Negro female worker." She urged the FOL not to compromise "the future of Negro women" by accepting menial employment from Ohio Bell.[49] By the late summer, however, the FOL had made little progress in gaining more than elevator jobs for black women. The continued impasse made it clear that the FOL needed to continue dramatic efforts to obtain employment for black women.[50]

Bolstered by the experience with Ohio Bell, the league shifted its attention to opening industrial employment. The newer efforts focused on negotiations and conferences with company personnel managers. But league members aggressively pursued direct action as well. They wrote letters to companies, published their experiences with discrimination in the newspapers, and sent numbers of women to apply daily at specific companies. They stood outside plant gates, looking for black workers. By the spring of 1942 these efforts had yet to bear fruit, so members demanded a return to the pickets. The FOL chose Standard Tool Company because of its location in the Central Area; equally important, out of more than six hundred employees, only three were black, all of whom worked in maintenance. Testimony from other African Americans revealed that many had repeatedly applied to the company but had been denied jobs. Holly and other executive board members hoped that its location would dramatize the inequities of the company's hiring policies and persuade other organizations to join in the FOL's efforts. On May 1, picketers arrived at Standard Tool carrying signs that equated company officials with Hitler and white workers with Nazis.[51]

The group of picketers was comparatively small in light of earlier efforts, but its verbal barrage proved unquestionably dramatic and confrontational. The ire it aroused in white workers at Standard Tool nearly caused a riot and forced Frank Lausche, mayor of Cleveland, to intervene. He quickly called a meeting with company personnel managers, Holly, black city council members, and NAACP executive secretary L. Pearl Mitchell. He then called for help from the Cleveland Metropolitan Council of Fair Employment, which included members from liberal organizations and unions. Hoping to prevent both pickets by blacks and a counterstrike by angry white workers, the company only tentatively consented to hire black women. In exchange, the FOL agreed not to resume its pickets, but only if Lausche called for meetings with industries located in the Central Area. Well aware that the mayor's interest was little more than a salve, Holly continued to press for meetings. In addition, he sent telegrams to the national COFEP office requesting a large-scale investigation. William O. Walker aided the league by allowing blacks to file complaints with the COFEP at the more conveniently located office of the *Call and Post*.[52]

The league's decision to cease the use of confrontation in the streets came not from a sense of an impending victory but from the pressure it received from other civil rights organizations to desist in mass protest. The NAACP had applauded the boycott against Ohio Bell, but only because L. Pearl Mitchell perceived Holly as "a live competitor." By the spring of 1942, national attitudes embraced the ideology of cooperation for the sake of the war, and in this context local black militancy was perceived as disruptive to war production. What appeared to be at issue, then, was how the demand for jobs should be made and under which organization's behest. The NAACP, and then the Metro Council on Fair Employment, had hoped to act as intermediaries between employers and African-American workers. Through such efforts, they intended negotiation rather than confrontation to persuade employers and prevent retaliation from white workers. Because the FOL had resorted to mass protests, civil rights organizations felt the very purpose of the COFEP and their own goals had been undermined.[53]

Most important to this new strategy, the national office of the NAACP urged its branches to maintain control over the local pursuit of jobs in industry. It then urged branches to cultivate "the continued active cooperation of churches, labor groups, fraternal organizations and others . . . in gathering and checking the facts." Clearly Walter White hoped to rechannel black militancy into the process of investigation and negotiation, but he also intended that these efforts would bolster the legitimacy of the NAACP as leader of the masses.[54] On the local level, L. Pearl Mitchell found renewed interest in the NAACP only because of its focus on jobs. In addition, the new membership came from the efforts of the FOL. For years Mitchell had pursued alignments with black labor organizations but found that the lack of funds and the dearth of "some dramatic events to keep up the interest," along with the dominance of black leaders who served as succors to whites interested in maintaining segregation, impeded progress. The fragility of the NAACP in the late 1930s enabled Holly to usurp some of its power, but he could not displace the trust it engendered. Whatever its limitations, many middle-class African Americans and white supporters still perceived the NAACP as the location for liberal interracial contact. Additionally, the shifts in attitudes about wartime black militancy, especially after the riots of 1943, eroded support for Holly's combativeness. Thus, Holly and others had to work within the NAACP to further FOL goals. But this strategy did not translate into acceptance of a working-class coalition within the NAACP. Though Mitchell publicly welcomed the FOL, she privately found Holly's influence and his tactics counterproductive. Mitchell told White that she had been forced to deal with Holly because the FOL had "someone daily blowing a trumpet about their work." With so little effort made by the NAACP, "Negroes in Cleveland find it difficult to cast their lot with us." Two years later in 1944, Mitchell wrote White that the branch was nearly "swamped" by Holly and the FOL. She confided to Roy Wilkens that "the Future Outlook League prospers because the local branch was not doing what it should" for the workers. While she continued to chastise professional blacks for their failure to make the NAACP do what it should, she nonetheless blamed Holly and the FOL for the bulk of the intraracial struggles, concluding, "there is such a thing as cooperation and [then] burrowing under another group."[55] The struggles within the Cleveland branch suggest that however much the NAACP may have been invigorated by working-class protest politics, even out of pragmatism, the old guard did not readily yield to the style and tactics of the new crowd.

The FOL's tactics during the war instigated varying responses from employers, ranging from the hiring of African-American women in some instances to highly creative barriers in others. Just weeks after the picket at Standard Tool, for example, several companies claimed they feared similar events at their gates would result in riots and decided instead to remove hiring barriers. Others claimed they would have done so earlier but black and white women did not "mix as readily as men of the two races." These companies then used the fear of hostility to institute tightly controlled hiring policies for a limited number of black women in segregated shops. Despite the large pool of trained women, personnel managers hired only those recruited through the Urban League. National Screw, for example, regularly hired white women without skills and trained them for a variety of positions. It departed from this practice when it assured white women that only "twelve well-qualified" black women had been hired for specific jobs on the night shift. Other companies demanded that African-American women have college degrees or take voice tests to ensure they were not from the South; some personnel managers recruited middle-class women and the wives of doctors and dentists. By the fall of 1942, twelve companies claimed they hired black women, few of whom had positions in production.[56]

African-American women continued to press employers and state officials, demanding explanations for their exclusion from training classes and industrial jobs. The director of the Ohio State Employment Bureau responded that he saw no reason to train black women for defense production when industries "had stated they would not accept Negro women in other than domestic capacity . . . and only in separate all Negro departments." Companies that refused to hire black women claimed that they followed federal policies and "did not discriminate in the selection of employees on the grounds of race, color, or creed." These companies pointed to black male employees as evidence of their compliance.[57]

Such unabashed refusals to comply with the executive order heightened league members' demands for direct confrontation with recalcitrant employers, which coincided with the reexplosion of black militancy nationally.[58] However much the local NAACP and other civil rights organizations stressed measured negotiations for jobs, African-American workers still chafed under such a slow and apparently unsuccessful policy. Instead, black workers demanded more immediate action and pursued a campaign for support. Letters sent to the *Call and Post* pressed women to continue demanding jobs in highly confrontational ways. The FOL held mass meetings in the city and toured the state, showing a film of its earlier success at Ohio Bell. It publicly and enthusiastically supported workplace activism of African-Americans in other cities, maintaining that action, not negotiation, led to gains.[59] In print and in meetings, black women continued to detail their exclusion from jobs in an effort to incite further direct action. Despite these efforts, other leaders in the black community pressured the FOL to stay out of the streets and away from plant gates.[60]

The responses by Effie Mae Turner and Claretta Jean Johnson to their own exclusion from production work dramatically altered the FOL's confrontational tactics. After learning to operate lathes and drill presses in government training classes, Johnson applied for work at Thompson Products; Turner, who had completed a similar training course, applied for work at Warner and Swasey. The women received the same response: neither company hired African-American women for production work. Instead, personnel managers at both plants offered positions in either the cafeteria or the bathrooms. Angered that both companies hired lesser-trained white women and black men but excluded trained black women, Turner and Johnson immediately filed complaints at the COFEP.[61]

Turner and Johnson, however, refused to simply allow the apparently ineffective investigative process of the COFEP to take its own course. The two women belonged to the FOL and demanded to know how many other women the two companies had refused to hire in production work. COFEP officials divulged that Johnson and Turner were just two of hundreds of black women who had filed similar complaints against the two companies. Knowing that the COFEP could do little more than make long, ineffectual investigations into their individual complaints, Johnson and Turner decided to take action. They hired lawyers to file claims against Thompson Products and Warner and Swasey; they then informed the league of their intention to seek injunctions against two of the largest defense industries in the city. Holly immediately grasped that the women's initiative would allow the FOL to hold public hearings in court. More critically, the FOL hoped the court would succeed where the COFEP had failed: the state, through the courts, would intervene on behalf of black women and force companies to comply with the executive order.[62]

Charges of racial discrimination in hiring policies for production work against the two companies immediately attracted controversy. The largest producer of turret lathes in the United States, Warner and Swasey hired thousands of white women to replace white men lost to the military. Despite continued labor shortages, the company had hired 216 black men in maintenance, though many of them were qualified to work in semiskilled and skilled positions. The company had only recently hired thirty-three black women to work as maids, cooks, and dishwashers. Several weeks before Turner's suit against the company, the AFL affiliate of the International Association of Machinists followed the pattern elsewhere and voted overwhelmingly to exclude African-American men from the union, foreclosing access to skilled positions. The union successfully demanded that the company restrict blacks to certain washrooms and areas of the cafeteria. Exposing the limitations in pursuing a policy of discrimination, Matt Demore, president of the local, conceded that one by-product of the union's decision was foremen's tendencies to "agitate" white workers by threatening to replace them with black workers whenever conflicts arose.[63] Yet, skilled white workers and the company colluded in these efforts, but for different reasons: the company hoped to stave off future union drives while skilled white workers intended to protect their workplace prerogatives. Both parties hoped to maintain their racism.

To prevent union growth, Thompson Products made the most of a heterogeneous workplace by vigorously stoking white men's fear of women's presence and white workers' collective fear of blacks. By 1942, African-American men comprised nearly 10 percent of the more than fifteen thousand workers at Thompson Products. Unable to find enough white women, the company hired a few black women to work in the cafeteria. Backed by management's support, company unions of skilled white workers played a significant role in determining where and how blacks worked, but in very different ways from the AFL at Warner and Swasey. Their ability to do so had been strengthened by the company as a counterattack to prevent either the CIO or the AFL from organizing. The company's paternalism had resulted in frequent wage increases and job protection for longtime employees. Company dinners, lunchtime dancing, and complicated wage rates created divisions amongst the semiskilled.[64]

In 1937, the UAW-CIO began a long and energetic campaign to organize Thompson Products workers. The large number of women workers angered the skilled men, and the UAW sought to organize the newly hired black men and white women. The company retaliated by refusing to allow the women to talk to each other during work hours and maintaining separation between blacks and whites. When black workers complained, company officials argued it created a necessary competitiveness that increased production. By 1941, however, the UAW-CIO had yet to win a National Labor Relations Board election, largely because of the countermeasures employed by Thompson Products president Frederick C. Crawford, who was also head of the National Association of Manufacturers. Though it was illegal, in the days before elections Crawford gave speeches over the loudspeakers; he then raised wage rates just before the vote. In addition, the company took advantage of the dramatic increase in the number of southern white workers and white women by claiming the UAW intended to organize them as a means to push men with seniority out of work. But labor shortages forced the company to increase the number of black men in maintenance and unskilled nonproduction work. Under the guise of protecting southern white women from black men, the company erected physical barriers to prevent black men from seeing anything except the shoes of white women. Ironically, many women complained of sexual harassment from white men and foremen. The company even tolerated the intimidating practices of a company-based Ku Klux Klan cell. But the company's refusal to place black women in production, as elsewhere, was a calculated ploy to placate and segregate white women.[65]

After years of frustration, the UAW-CIO applauded the FOL's intentions to "air discrimination in court." Though critical of the company's refusal to hire black women in production and resolute in its efforts to organize black workers generally, the UAW-CIO had frequently manipulated white workers' racism as well. This tendency was readily apparent when union organizers declared that unorganized blacks in Thompson Products had acted as "dupes" and "stooges" for managers. UAW-CIO organizers intimated that the hiring of black women would threaten the jobs of unorganized white women. Creating such a combative air underscored the UAW-CIO's intention to outmaneuver management at the cost of African-American workers. In the end, the UAW-CIO decided that it was better to instigate racial antagonism as a strategy for success. Whether this was a pragmatic decision rather than one of conviction is not clear, but organizers repeatedly failed to establish a union at the plant.[66] Now under public scrutiny, company officials charged the union with discrimination and the union countercharged that managers practiced discrimination at the gate and against unions.[67]

Local African-American leaders applauded the league's use of the courts as a legitimate and orderly response, especially when Walter White and the new NAACP legal council, Thurgood Marshall, expressed interest in the case. Several lawyers offered immediate and free legal counsel. Despite the support,

FOL lawyers recognized that building a legal case against the companies based on the discrimination of black women would be difficult. Officials from both Thompson Products and Warner and Swasey openly admitted that they discriminated against black women, but only to expedite production work. Denying any resistance against hiring blacks, both companies argued that they hired black men and white women in production work and, therefore, did not mock even the spirit of the order. To challenge such a defense, FOL lawyers moved to file a class-action suit, ultimately hoping to include hundreds of black women who unsuccessfully applied to the companies. Indeed, other women came forward, claiming that the hiring policies had discouraged them from applying.[68]

Turner v. Warner and Swasey and *Johnson v. Thompson Products* went to Cleveland Common Pleas Court in early December 1942. Both companies based their defense on two issues. First, that the presence of blacks in general, and black women in particular, posed a threat to the war effort. However sympathetic the companies might be to African Americans' particular plight, expanding job opportunities for them would amount to tampering with social relations, thereby causing massive resistance from white workers. Second, they argued that the executive order infringed on an employer's right to establish personal hiring preferences. It was difficult enough, they concluded, for employers to deal with unions. Private contracts between employers and employees, not federal initiatives to dictate hiring policies, ensured that the ultimate goal of winning the war would be achieved. Lawyers for Warner and Swasey argued that the executive order called for the end to discrimination on the basis of race, creed, and color, but did not compel a company to hire a particular group. Moreover, though defense contracts prohibited discrimination on the basis of race they did not on race and sex, therefore African-American women could not constitute themselves as a group separate from black men. Lawyers for Thompson Products argued that because the company hired black men, they did not discriminate against black women simply because they were excluded from production work.[69]

After reviewing the testimony, Appeals Court judge Frank Merrick offered his own interpretation of the order: "Gentlemen, it is important for all of us to keep in mind that advisory suggestions which emanate from time to time from Washington do not have the weight of statutes. The great White Father may suggest that we do this or that but that doesn't make it law." Indeed, he stressed, "no law could be passed to say 'You must hire Negroes in percentage to the population.'" Such a provision would breach the right of companies to make private contracts. These points of jurisprudence aside, he concluded his opinion from the bench with the admonishment that African Americans had no legitimate claims to compel either the courts or the federal government to alter intractable social relations, especially in time of war. Most important, businesses should not be forced to establish racial parity on the shop floor. To do so impaled the war effort; it was better to discriminate for the purpose of victory. He then added comments that the black press later called "The African Jungle Speech." He claimed that because blacks were recently removed "from the jungles of Africa," it was necessary for them to expect discrimination.[70]

Merrick did not make his decision, however, merely out of a disdain for blacks or his respect for private contract. Rather, his decision revealed the inadequacies of the COFEP. The decision was based on the implicit belief that the existence of the COFEP foreclosed blacks' access to the courts. He admonished Johnson and Turner for failing to give the COFEP time to investigate the complaints. The demand that blacks utilize an obviously inadequate process to investigate discrimination on a case-by-case basis meant that the possibility of waging a collective struggle against resistant employers was closed. Merrick's argument had a clear and insidious message: blacks had no right to call for fundamental social change; they had to wait for whites to instigate change, if at all. Certainly the white press supported such a claim, earlier arguing that the executive order placed an undue burden on white workers. Such a perspective anticipated battles that would later emerge in the civil rights movement. Merrick ruled in favor of the defendants and ordered Turner and Johnson to pay court costs.[71]

Though the women and the FOL took the case to the Ohio Supreme Court, they also continued to conduct their grass-roots efforts to dismantle discrimination. The league organized blacks to bombard elected judges with letters detailing their intention to vote against them if the women lost the appeal. The boycotts, investigations, and media exposure contributed to the employment of thousands of black women in defense industries. Ironically, the success on the grass-roots level led to the refusal by the Ohio Supreme Court to hear the case. The justices ruled that since 6,000 black women reportedly held industrial jobs in Cleveland, they had no reason to hear the cases.[72] By late 1943, Warner and Swasey claimed to have quadrupled its number of black workers, of which 149 were women. Thompson Products had reportedly hired black women, but only a handful. In early 1945, the Cleveland NAACP reported that only 4 black women worked at Thompson Products; "no one had seen [black women] working" at Warner and Swasey.[73]

In the end, critical labor shortages, not employers' desire to comply with a federal policy, allowed for increasing numbers of black women to gain access to some defense work. Some employers turned to African-American women, considering wartime employment transitory. The Cleveland Bomber Plant, built in 1942 near the city's airport, represented the new industrial jobs available for white women, southern white migrants, and black men and women, all of whom were considered temporary. Owned by the Department of Defense and operated by General Motors as the Fisher Body Aircraft Plant no. 2, the Bomber Plant soon employed 15,000 workers at the relatively high wage of $.95 an hour. The plant operated twenty-four hours a day, seven days a week, and most workers put in at least fifty-five hours a week. From the beginning, the plant was overstaffed to maximize the defense contract and compensate for the inexperienced workers, though all were required to attend several weeks of training. In addition, managers' quotas dispensed with production quotas. Supervisors allowed the workers, particularly the women, to labor alongside friends and kin; they encouraged workers to name work stations and isles after battlefields. Such efforts undermined shop floor activism and instilled loyalty to the tasks at hand. Though workers belonged to the UAW-CIO, they tended to view the union as "a mystery."[74]

Unlike employers' visible campaign to recruit white women, many black women seeking defense employment depended on the kindness of friends and acquaintances to place a "good word" for them at plant personnel offices. The experiences of Natalie Middleton reveal the prevalence of such practices.[75] In late 1942 Middleton applied at Cleveland Graphite Bronze because she knew one of the personnel directors, who had been a National Youth Administration supervisor. Middleton then became one of the "teaspoonful" of blacks hired so as to comply with antidiscrimination policies attached to defense contracts. Graphite Bronze confined black men to maintenance and black women to the lowest occupations of finishing work. Middleton dutifully joined the Mechanics Educational Society of America (MESA), but, like other women, only occasionally attended meetings. An independent union known for its aggressive use of sympathy strikes over wages, hours, and work rules, MESA struggled to maintain control over a labor force that had tripled in size. Committed to interracial unionism, MESA encouraged black workers to file grievances. This sincerity, however, did not segue into a challenge of black workers' job segregation and segmentation. Thus, from Middleton's and other black workers' perspectives, the union did little to dismantle the major barrier they confronted. Indeed, racial discrimination in job assignments remained in place until the 1960s.[76]

In other instances, however, African-American workers had the backing of unions to challenge discrimination based on race and gender. Unions with black members staged walkouts, work stoppages, and slowdowns to protest companies refusing to hire black women and upgrade black men's positions. Once such protest occurred at Eastern Malleable Iron Company on December 11, 1943. One hundred black and white men left their jobs over the hiring of two black women in the foundry. The men complained that the jobs were not fit for any woman "because of the dirt, heat, and heavy work." In addition, the two women had to use separate restrooms from white women and a white male supervisor carried the key, which the women had to ask for. The men told COFEP field workers that they had been waiting for the day when black women would be hired since they had been refused employment for over a year. The men did not object to black women's employment, but they charged that the social and occupational segregation violated a twenty-year-old union policy barring discrimination.[77] But the men protested as much over the placement of black women in "men's work" as they did the segregation of the women along racial lines.

Ray Dennis, who worked for a company that made aluminum alloy, recalled that black and white male workers raised similar protests around the work assignments of black women. Prior to the war, most of the employees were black or Polish men. In early 1943 the company faced a severe labor shortage and began to hire black women to stack agates—a "job nobody wanted to do because it was so arduous." According to Dennis, many of the men opposed the hiring of women: "They felt it was beneath the dignity of a woman to come in and work in a plant like that." As president of the union, Dennis argued, "wasn't it better for [the women] to come here and make a decent wage than work in some white woman's kitchen washing clothes and scrubbing floors." Ironically, when mechanization replaced hand labor, some of the women earned more money then the men. Black women, however, did not have access to lab or clerical work—jobs that white women performed—because the union did not have any bargaining rights over these positions.[78]

Despite the higher wages, many African-American women did not pursue industrial employment. The limitations on seniority and occupations, together with the general atmosphere of antifemale attitudes, dissuaded them. Because of their historical exclusion from better jobs, they instead sought employment that offered some protection. Black women wanted jobs, not temporary positions. Many chose to take nondomestic service work, postal work, or clerical work in state and federal offices. For these reasons, Eleanor Walls Grist got a job as an elevator operator in the main Cleveland Public Library instead of work in the defense industry. As white women shifted into defense work, Grist quickly moved to the switchboard and later became the supervisor. By the end of the war, she had started training as a librarian. Though many of the women ignored unions, Grist and other black women formed a staff organization, which then affiliated with the CIO. Grist eventually became president of Local 105A and helped to organize similar unions in other city offices.[79]

The changes that the war engendered empowered black workers in both interracial and more radical unions, such as the International Mine, Mill, and Smelter Workers, and in some UAW-CIO locals. Moreover, the continuing black activism in the community resulted in an unprecedented wave of black self-organization that had, in turn, compelled many organized white workers to recognize and fight for the rights of black workers. Generally the CIO locals, and to a lesser extent those of the AFL, increasingly displayed support for the rights of black workers to find jobs and have protection on the shop floor. Such shifts resulted in the coalition of white and union leaders with the FOL. The alliance underscored the greater presence of black workers in industrial, rather than service jobs. By late 1943, some CIO locals publicly chastised employers who persisted in importing white workers from the South to avoid hiring black workers. The shift in white union recognition of racial discrimination against blacks appears to have been significantly more muted than the increasing support black packinghouse workers received from CIO locals in Chicago. Perhaps the more contentious nature of the steel locals might explain the differences.[80]

By 1945, the Cleveland Industrial Union Council of the CIO (CIUC) had moved to join the coalition of organizations committed to eradicate discrimination in the workplace. It issued a resolution as a rebuttal to employers who insisted it was their prerogative "to use their own sound judgment and discretion in selecting loyal and capable employees." The CIUC argued that though government "cannot legislate away the prejudices of individuals," it could nonetheless "pass laws against the discrimination that results from such prejudices. We can through legislation refuse to sanction prejudice." Such a point underscored a stance that many within Cleveland's labor movement had come to realize: employer opposition to fair employment legislation for blacks and other minority workers could allow them to make inroads on the gains of white workers in the industrial setting. The CIUC began its resolution by comparing employer opposition to the fair employment practices legislation with employer opposition to the Wagner Act and the National Labor Relations Act ten years earlier. In making such a comparison, however, the CIUC did not intend a combative stance. Rather, labor hoped to remind management of the partnership that had been forged during the war. As one CIUC leader noted, "The Wagner Act stabilized labor relations and reduced to a minimum strikes caused by discriminatory practices. What the Wagner Act did was to eliminate discrimination based on union activity."[81]

Blacks found hope in the CIUC's call for the cessation in discrimination both at the gate and on the shop floor.[82]

The postwar backlash against organized labor generally, however, would make the antidiscrimination efforts difficult to sustain. The fragility of racial egalitarianism was readily apparent when George Stevens filed a grievance against a racist and abusive foreman at Reliance Steel. Before the hearing, the company fired Stevens, provoking a walkout by black workers. Union officials immediately endorsed the action, and white union members joined in the walkout. Both the leadership and the rank-and-file viewed the issue from blacks' perspective and as an issue of collective bargaining. This marked a dramatic shift in perspective, since earlier objections from African Americans about racist foremen had not won support from whites; rather, blacks' protest frequently raised anti-union responses from whites. Before the postwar walkout was settled, the company laid off numbers of workers, many of them black. This move ultimately broke the union.[83]

What did African-American workers think about unions' efforts to halt discrimination in their own ranks? However scattered the examples of interracial unionism, African-American workers began to hope that these efforts, along with their continued struggles, would eradicate workplace discrimination. At the same time, they understood the larger societal pulls that undermined even the most genuine efforts. Thus, on the one hand, black workers welcomed efforts to open leadership roles to them, to allow their inclusion on committees, and to educate white workers about race, and they applauded whenever white workers walked out in support of black workers. On the other hand, as the court battle waged by the FOL demonstrated, the alliances some unions formed with employers could often reinforce racial discrimination and white workers' prerogatives. Unions would have to consistently embrace black workers' struggle for economic equality as a workplace issue and they would have to demand the end to discriminatory practices in hiring and placement from white employers and workers. Finally, the particular and widespread discrimination that African-American women faced had to be addressed.

African Americans simultaneously sought inclusion in Democratic politics, but with similarly limited results. Frank Lausche won the mayor's race in 1941, but without black support. In this election, Lausche ran on an independent ticket backed by the Democrats, promising to rid the city of racketeering and "a square deal for all minority groups." Despite these appeals, blacks voted for the Republican candidate, though most would vote for Roosevelt in the national elections. By 1943, however, Lausche's rhetoric of fairness, along with his investigations of job and rent discrimination, elicited bipartisan support amongst black voters. Yet organized labor, which increasingly included African-American workers, did not care for Lausche's probusiness attitudes, renaming him "Lousy Lausche." Nor did he fully incorporate African Americans into the Democratic party, leaving party supporters without patronage jobs. Without such ballast, black Democrats were adrift and nearly sank in the 1944 elections. Blacks had little influence in the Republican party, as more voters aligned with Democrats. In short, African Americans found they had less political leverage during the war than in the previous two decades. At the close of the war, leaving the party of Lincoln for the party of the common folk had yet to bear political fruit.[84]

For many black workers, therefore, the war had resulted in few lasting gains, evident in their loss of jobs immediately following the war. Many black men had their positions downgraded or were laid off. Black women had the highest rate of layoffs of any group since so few had acquired seniority. Additionally, the state passed legislation that prohibited women from working in occupations that required heavy lifting, which all but guaranteed black women's displacement from many jobs. Although some women retained their jobs, they remained in positions defined as well-suited for them. "We became," Natalie Middleton recalled, "black blue-collar workers, but there was no upward mobility for blacks in private American industry."[85]

Rather than a personal conclusion, Middleton voiced what many black working-class Clevelanders deduced at the close of the war. Because black women's experiences of finding and keeping work had been incorporated into the overall perspective of black working-class Clevelanders, the belief that gains had been long-lasting was clearly muted. Two black women decided to fight back when they faced both the intransigence of employers and the limitations of an executive order with no broad-based power to ensure enforcement. Perhaps the organized and creative response of these women and the FOL demonstrated just how black Americans had come to view the state's efforts to advance blacks' civil rights: limited at best. In short, the FOL challenged employers and the state; while it failed to make any headway against discrimination in employment, it nonetheless underscored the continuing necessity of community-based protest.

Outside of the FOL, there were few models for racial egalitarianism or mass participation for black working people in Cleveland at the close of the war. In 1946 when Charles Loeb published the history of the FOL he could rightfully claim that it alone was the premier organization for broad-based black protest. But this claim was tenuous at best. As the FOL's struggles during the war demonstrated, black protest could be roundly sanctioned or dismissed when it simultaneously challenged racial discrimination and economic inequality, especially when it did so through mass protest. Efforts to contain this protest revealed the competing claims to leadership within the black community, a struggle that would continue after the war. Even as the league's energy dissipated through the next decade, its members remained insistent that their economic position in American society must be fundamentally changed and that their right to determine and shape that process must be recognized.

CONCLUSION

We Will Make a Way Somehow: The Legacy of a Southern Past in a Northern City

> *I wonder what I have done*
> *That makes this race so hard to run*
> *Then I say to my soul take courage*
> *The Lord will make a way somehow.*
>
> —Thomas Dorsey, "The Lord Will Make a
>   Way Somehow," as sung by the
>   Wilson Jubilee Singers

SARA BROOKS MIGRATED to Cleveland in 1940, found work, and joined a church, where she lived for several years until she saved the money to buy a home. This church anchored her faith and provided permission to engage in purposeful action in her home, community, and workplace. Brooks concluded that while her "husband didn't turn out" and persistent poverty in Alabama had forced her to leave her children and find work elsewhere, her faith brought her "through all this up until now." She left her husband and mothered her children, often over a great distance; she went on to organize a union in Alabama and stand up to abusive employers. She concluded her moving narrative, *You May Plow Here,* with an affirmation of the faith that had pushed her from the South: "But since I was here in Cleveland, I have dreamed about the peach trees out there in the field between the garden and the house. I saw all those peach trees [in Alabama], and they were hanging just so fulla fruit. They were so pretty, and I don't know why, but I didn't get a chance to get any of it."[1]

The oral testimony of Brooks, like that of many other African-American migrants living in Cleveland, expressed a sense of prophecy and agency. That Brooks characterized her move to a northern city as akin to spiritual transcendence should not be construed as overstatement. African Americans had long used biblical imagery and language to articulate their desires as a people. When blacks announced they were heaven bound, they boarded trains headed north. African-American migrants in the urban North continued to link mobility with personal and communal autonomy that had animated decades of movement in the South. Migrants intended to stay in the North, and they meant to make it home. Once they arrived, they attempted to make the city fulfill the promises of freedom. They hoped migration would provide them with the opportunities to escape poverty, earn fair wages, and live without segregation and violence. Brooks juxtaposed her ability to work, buy a home, and reunite her family in the North with her inability to lay claims to the fruits of her labor—symbolized by the ripe peaches on the tree—in a segregated South. Thus, the experiences of migration became intimately linked to her settlement and sense of purposeful activism.

African Americans' expressive culture and activism had retained ties to a southern past. About the time Sara Brooks arrived in Cleveland, Barbara Smith was growing up in the Central Area surrounded by a grandmother and aunts who worked in private families, attended Antioch Baptist Church, and took care of their homes and family. Smith called her grandmother and aunts "old-fashioned" because they still looked to the South for values and a sense of "home" to instill in their children and grandchildren. These "older relatives' allegiance to a place we'd never seen" confused Smith but nonetheless "provided us with an essentially southern upbringing, rooting us solidly in the past."[2] Smith soon discovered that her grandmother and aunts intended that their offspring would not struggle to find work or live in cramped homes.

At the same time, while many migrants still looked to the South for their own values and sense of orientation, they did not describe the South as a place to live, work, or raise their children. Gerald L. Davis has argued that "the U. S. South is a complex, little understood phenomenon in the worldview of African-American people." In the collective minds and memories of African Americans, the South simultaneously represented backwardness and "a secure place of renewal, of contact with humanizing spirits, of communication with the souls of Black folk."[3] For Carl Stokes's mother, it was a place of horror, but her son learned that despite the relentless poverty she faced in Cleveland, the dignity that she had daily demonstrated was rooted in her southern past. LeRoi Jones noted that for many migrants "the South was *home*. It was a place that Negroes knew, and given the natural attachment of man to land, even loved. The North was to be beaten, there was room for attack. No such room had been possible in the South, but it was still what could be called home."[4]

Retaining values from the South, however, did not mean migrants expressed much, if any, desire to return. Scholars have documented the large migration of African Americans to the South beginning after 1975.[5] In the

1940s and early 1950s, however, the local and national black press wrote of atrocities and inequities throughout the South, sparing few details of the violence or humiliation that African Americans encountered there daily. Many migrants continued to tell their northern-born children about lynchings and Jim Crow as both a warning and a collective memory. Carl Stokes recalled that when he decided to join the army and was first stationed in Alabama shortly after the end of World War II, his mother firmly warned him "that in the South the white man could kill any black person he wanted to." Not long after he arrived at a military base, he questioned a white waitress's treatment of black soldiers and was told: "You may not know it nigger, but you're in Alabama now." Despite having heard his mother's "horror stories" of the South, the black Alabama of Cleveland had not fully prepared him for the white Alabama of the South.[6]

To simply argue that black migrants left the South and found a better life in the North underestimates both the struggle and the barriers that many encountered along the way. Smith recalled that "the women in my family, and their friends, worked harder than any people I have known before or since, and despite their objective circumstances, they believed that I could have a future beyond theirs, although there was little enough indication in the 40s and 50s that Negro girls would ever have a place to stand." Only years later did Smith recognize the mixed inheritance of growing up in this southern and northern household, the shame and fear of being black and female, the hope that "she would have a future beyond theirs." Life in Cleveland had given her a better education and her mother a better job than either might have obtained in the post–World War II South.[7] This example, like the many other narratives of African-American migrants, displays the complicated perspectives that many had acquired as they moved from the South to the urban Midwest.

Indeed, in the years between 1920 and 1950 migrants and their children conceded that the city had provided them with mixed opportunities. As in earlier years, the North remained an unyielding place to find work, hardly the refuge that many African Americans had hoped. In the years following the war, many felt they could find only certain jobs since they "were allocated to them as they got into the door, but that was as far as you were going to go." Men and women knew "ahead of time that if you go to this company you're gonna be in the mail department, you're gonna be in the cleaning and maintenance department, and so don't even look for anything else."[8] Rumors, circumstantial evidence, documented investigations, and personal testimony gave credibility to the belief that unions were as likely as employers to segregate them.[9]

Despite the largely successful efforts of the Future Outlook League, African-American workers still remained unorganized and those that belonged to the AFL and the CIO remained excluded from leadership positions. The numerous locals in both the AFL and the CIO would provide, at best, lukewarm efforts to include black workers in the rank-and-file and leadership. African Americans made their greatest gains in unions in areas where many whites no longer worked: custodial care, public transportation, and sanitation. As late as 1949, city newspapers allowed employers to advertise jobs by race.[10] Ironically, as African-American workers became critical to the food, steel, and auto locals in the early 1960s, the city's industrial base began to erode. These large developments await separate studies.

Even as black workers who claimed affiliation with either the AFL or the CIO grew in numbers, their skepticism remained pronounced. Black organizers for the AFL noted that blacks, like many workers, did not immediately recognize the benefits of unions. The tentative support of the Cleveland Federation of Labor (CFL) for black participation was exacerbated by its limited efforts to educate new union members. Moreover, the CFL had done little "to integrate them into the C.F.L. and make of them good, strong and loyal supporters of the Trade Union Movement or why they are really organized." In a manner typical of signifying, Lee Morgan of the NAACP noted that *of course* these new union members "no doubt had been given an honest, wholehearted welcome into their locals' meetings, program, and other activities." But Morgan warned that the CFL could not cease its efforts once an agreement had been reached with employers: "The old adage in Labor, that a contract cannot Union Members make," was as true for black workers as it was for whites. However much Morgan framed his critiques as a general lack of attention to all new workers, he nonetheless intimated that racism played a detrimental role in the CFL's lukewarm efforts to organize African-American workers.[11]

Yet organizers' explanations for the continued barriers African-American workers faced included an analysis of their political and organizational ties within the community that white workers found objectionable. Lee Morgan outlined the dynamics within the black community that had limited the gains they had made in AFL locals and in securing unions' wholehearted endorsements for a national FEPC. Black support for the NAACP's court battles that targeted locals barring blacks dampened the CFL's support. For many white union members, fears of being labeled communists linked red-baiting and race-baiting. These critics also complained that African Americans' alliances with "too many 'so-called' Liberals who died with F. D. R. but haven't been buried" further threatened organizing drives in the city. Yet even as Morgan outlined the CFL's criticism for black workers' too-close alliances with various parties he also acknowledged that organizers "will not restore or build confidence among Negroes unless wholehearted moral, financial, and active support is encouraged by all Locals at once."[12] The gulf between blacks' desires for an egalitarian workplace and society and white workers' much narrower focus on workplace issues that did not challenge their own racial sensibilities remained significant.

In the aftermath of the war, too often white unionists bypassed support of black workers by concentrating on issues of seniority and calling for women's expulsion from jobs. Facing discrimination in the workplace and unable to depend on unions, black workers turned to the NAACP or the FOL to argue their cause. As Horace Huntley has shown, white unionists' successful efforts to dismantle unions that advanced black workers' causes or offered equal participation left them with little recourse except to relocate or continue their activism within their own community struggles.[13]

White racial identity, most often expressed in racism against African Americans outside workplaces, remained a critical fault line for the tens of thousands of Eastern European immigrants and white migrants from the South. After the war, employers successfully baited white workers' fears of "social mixing" in the workplace, even at the expense of economic gains. Outside workplaces, whites demanded all-white neighborhoods, schools, and social activities. Although Cleveland was never as violent as either Chicago or Detroit, when African Americans ventured outside the Central Area for leisure they ran the risk of violent attacks. As Gary Gerstle notes, "we have yet to incorporate into our understanding of post–World War II race relations the anger and violence directed by white working-class homeowners at blacks who attempted to move into their neighborhoods and use their public facilities."[14] Both the AFL and the CIO often held picnics and meetings in areas of the city where African Americans were tacitly excluded or that had a history of segregation, such as Euclid Beach Park.

Even as industrial union jobs remained closed, African Americans nonetheless found steady work and higher wages. These trends, along with white population shifts into the suburbs after 1947, allowed many blacks to move unimpeded into the outermost areas of the city on the east side. By the 1950s, many African Americans who lived in Glenville owned their own homes. A growing population of black small business owners, teachers, city workers, and skilled craftworkers moved east along Kinsman Avenue into Mt. Pleasant, an area that contained similarly employed Italian and Polish immigrants. These integrated neighborhoods, however, were short-lived. Barbara Smith recalled that her family's move from a home on Cedar Avenue near Antioch

Baptist Church to Mt. Pleasant meant "that for the first time we lived near white people." Smith noted that over the next decade, whites in this area "quickly exited." In Thylias Moss's neighborhood, "little by little, the faces all became browner and the cooking smells in the evening were different, though they were always deep, rich smells." Moss, like Smith, watched the smells and sounds of her neighborhood shift to those most recognizable to African-American migrants.[15]

The steady exit of whites from integrated neighborhoods, however, did not prevent Smith and other African-American children from realizing that they and their white classmates had more in common than not. Though white, these students were the children of Polish, Czech, and Hungarian immigrants: "Cleveland was new to their people as it was to ours; the church figured heavily in their lives as both a spiritual and social force; they were involved in close-knit extended families and they were working people." The playwright Adrienne Kennedy recalled Glenville in a similar manner: "Our new neighborhood was Poland, Czechoslovakia, Hungary, and Russia."[16]

The steady eastward drift had an impact on the location of black-owned businesses, churches, and social associations. By the late 1940s, Cory Methodist Church, for example, followed its members and relocated to Glenville, reflecting the residential predominance of African Americans. By the early 1940s, the overwhelmingly southern congregation of St. Timothy Missionary Baptist Church formed over forty committees, including deacons' and trustees' boards, a mothers' board, six choirs, three ushers' boards, a pastor's aid club, a Sunday school, and a laypersons' league. They also formed six state clubs for members from Alabama, West Virginia, Tennessee, Georgia, Kentucky, and North Carolina. In its literature, the church affirmed the commitment to a broad-based participation: "The Church where everybody is somebody," and "If it is to be, it's up to me."[17]

The leisure time of African Americans still belonged to the church. While traditional mainline churches continued to retain their congregations, newer denominations saw their memberships expand significantly as waves of migrants from Alabama and other states in the Deep South arrived. Holiness, Pentecostal, and nondenominational churches—already numerically dominant before the war—continued to grow most rapidly. Like in the World War I period, however, these churches drew primarily newly arrived migrants from the Deep South.[18] Thylias Moss recalled the engulfing world of her mother's place of worship, True Vine Baptist Church: "She was at church for the Wednesday prayer service, for the Thursday and Friday choir rehearsals, for Baptist Training Union meeting, and all day on Sunday, for Sunday school, morning worship, afternoon program, and evening service." Though a child in the early 1950s, Moss was "mesmerized and awed" by the "choir robed in magenta satin and in the presence of all the hats, all the opulence of Sunday finery." The minister, wearing a white robe with sleeves like wings, "with just his voice" made the congregation "shout, writhe, jump, run through the aisles, or simply stand and quiver." The power of language and the collective emotion remained central components of many weekly gatherings.[19]

Gospel music predominated after World War II, and the older male and female sacred quartets remained important in the community lives of African Americans in Cleveland. Alabama-influenced local groups like the Shield Brothers, the Live Wire Singers, and the Elite Jewels regularly attracted large audiences in afternoon and evening performances. In the late forties, these groups were joined by the L and N Gospel Singers, a group that migrated from Montgomery, Alabama. Like the earlier quartets, this new group had its origins in the workplace. Its members had worked for the Louisville and Nashville Railroad in Montgomery in the late 1920s, first singing in the depot; several years later, they formed another group with the same name based in Birmingham. Eventually the railroad hired the group to sing on its line in the South. By the midforties, several members of the quartet migrated to Chicago and Cleveland. Eddie Glover, one of the original members, organized a new group in Cleveland.[20] These gospel performances, while firmly rooted in the church, were opportunities for some men and women to earn extra income. Few had either the funds or the inclination to record, since gospel groups like the Soul Stirrers dominated the tours. For most local noncommercial quartets, then, the gatherings in Cleveland allowed them to display simultaneously their spirituality and their skill to one another. As new churches were built and dedicated, gospel programs featuring as many as twenty groups were not uncommon. Within this context, quartet performers transmitted and maintained connections to the South and the experience of migration.[21]

The artist portrayed the members of the Future Outlook League in 1952 as African-American workers bolstered by claims of militancy and courage, but the canvas also captured the paradoxes of their lives in the middle of the twentieth century. Indeed, as black workers beckoned still more kin and friends from the Deep South into the city, they announced that this journey north did not grant economic stability without a struggle. For the generation of migrants who had moved North between 1915 and 1945, settling and working in the city had extracted a price from them as a people. On the other hand, at midcentury thousands of migrants from the South had crafted, for themselves, a community that placed *them* as the caretakers of their own lives.

NOTES

Introduction

1. Beni E. Kosh (aka Charles E. Harris) may have been the artist. I borrow *multi-sensorial* from Robert J. Powell, who defines the term as encompassing African-American visual, musical, physical, and vocal characteristics that are simultaneously created and recollected in vernacular art, dance, and literature. Sermons, blues, folktales, and biblical stories, Powell claims, "have inspired the works of many [African-American] artists." See Richard J. Powell, "Art History and Black Memory: Toward a 'Blues Aesthetic,'" in *History and Memory in African-American Culture*, ed. Genevieve Fabre and Robert O'Meally (New York: Oxford University Press, 1994), 237.

My understanding of black vernacular, which includes the sacred and the secular, has been greatly aided by Grey Gundaker's *Signs of Diaspora, Diaspora of Signs: Literacies, Creolization, and Vernacular Practice in African American* (New York: Oxford University Press, 1998), 3–6; Henry Louis Gates Jr.'s *The Signifying Monkey: A Theory of African-American Literary Criticism* (New York: Oxford University Press, 1988); Houston A. Baker Jr.'s *Blues, Ideology, and Afro-American Literature: A Vernacular Theory* (Chicago: University of Chicago Press, 1984); and Robert G. O'Meally's "On Burke and the Vernacular: Ralph Ellison's Boomerang of History," *History and Memory in African-American Culture*, 244–60. All, however, have been close readers of Ralph Ellison and Albert Murray. See Ralph Ellison, "Flying Home," in *Cross Section*, ed. Edwin Seaver (New York: L. B. Fischer, 1944), 469–85; Ralph Ellison, *Invisible Man* (New York: Random House, 1952); Ralph Ellison, *Shadow and Act* (New York: Random House, 1964); Ralph Ellison, *Going to the Territory* (New York: Random House, 1986); and Albert Murray, *Stomping the Blues* (New York: McGraw-Hill, 1976). For Ellison, vernacular is a process "in which the most refined styles from the past are continually merged with the play-it-by-eye-and-ear improvisations which we invent in our efforts to control our environment and entertain ourselves. And this is not only in language and literature, but in architecture and cuisine, in music, costume, and dance, and in tools and in technology. In it the styles of the past are adjusted to the needs of the present, and in its integrative action the high styles of the past are democratized. From this perspective the vernacular is no less than the styles associated with aristocracy, a gesture toward perfection." Ellison, *Going to the Territory*, 139–40. For other introductions to black vernacular, especially sacred vernacular, which gets very little attention in many of the above works, see W. E. B. Du Bois, *The Souls of Black Folk* (Chicago: A. C. McClury, 1903); Zora Neale Hurston, *Mules and Men* (Philadelphia: J. B. Lippincott, 1935; reprint, New York: HarperPerennial, 1990); Zora Neale Hurston, *The Sanctified Church* (Berkeley: Turtle Island, 1983); and Dolan Hubbard, *The Sermon and the African American Literary Imagination* (Columbia: University of Missouri Press, 1994).

2. African Americans' constructions of whites as Pharaoh and their hope to escape to the promised land dates to before the eighteenth century. In the twentieth century, blacks continued this enduring association in gospel lyrics, especially those by gospel quartets. "Way Down in Egyptland" was a familiar program piece for these groups. Blacks' view that the South was the location of black oppression and the northern city the promised land had its origins in their migrations after the Civil War. See Hubbard, *Sermon*, 2–3; and Charles B. Copher, "Transforming the Land of Oppression into the Promiseland," in *Preaching the Gospel*, ed. Henry Young (Philadelphia: Fortress, 1976), 25–30. For examples of gospel quartets' use of Pharaoh, see Golden Gate Quartet, "'Way down in Egypt Land," *Travelin' Shoes*, Bluebird 66063–2; and Birmingham Jubilee Quartet, "Pharaoh's Army Got Drowned," *Birmingham Jubilee Singers*, vol. 1, DOCD-5345.

3. In Haiti, Moses assumed the guise of Dunbala. In African-American culture in the United States, Esu assumed the guise of the signifying monkey, the trickster. Lawrence Levine has suggested that by the twentieth century the trickster figure in African-American culture was represented by the "bad nigger," such as John Henry. I want to suggest that this guide could easily represent both sacred and secular characteristics, demonstrating that this image, like African-American texts, has a double voice. See Lawrence Levine, *Black Culture and Black Consciousness: Afro-American Folk Thought from Slavery to Freedom* (New York: Oxford University Press, 1977); on the signifying monkey and double-voiced discourses, see Gates, *Signifying Monkey*, xxiii, xxv–xxviii, 110–13. Few historians, if any, have considered how biblical figures that populate African-American vernacular might represent deities. The figures of David, Daniel, and King Jesus, for example, closely resemble Yoruban deities. The literature on African survivals is voluminous; see, for example, Robert Farris Thompson, *Flash of the Spirit* (New York: Random House, 1983).

4. Robert O'Meally, working through Ralph Ellison's short stories, novel, and papers, demonstrates how the literature of Ellison—at once textual and performative—is steeped in black vernacular and provides the characters and readers "'equipment for living': vernacular-trained Americans can cope with trouble and can remain optimistic enough, as the expression goes, *to keep on keeping on*." O'Meally, "On Burke," 251–52.

5. For help in thinking about the painting as both formal and improvised memory, I turned to Ellison, *Going to the Territory*, 139–40.

6. Charles Loeb, *The Future Is Yours* (Cleveland: Future Outlook League, 1946). The most comprehensive overview of African-American boycotts against economic and racial discrimination remains August Meier and Elliott Rudwick's "The Origins of Nonviolent Direct Action in Afro-American Protest: A Note on Historical Discontinuities," *Along the Color Line: Explorations in the Black Experience* (Urbana: University of Illinois Press, 1976), 307–404.

7. Loeb, *The Future Is Yours*, 15–22, 51, 65–73; Beatrice Stevens Cockrell, interview

by author, Cleveland, Sept. 27, 1991, transcript; Selmer Prewitt, interview by author, Cleveland, Mar. 7, 1991, transcript; Linton Freeman, interview by author, Cleveland, Mar. 7, 1991, transcript; Ruth Harper Freeman, interview by author, Cleveland, Mar. 7, 1991, transcript.

8. Carl B. Stokes, *Promises of Power Then and Now* (Cleveland: Friends of Carl Stokes, 1989), 16–18; Loeb, *The Future Is Yours,* 50.

9. John O. Holly to H. G. Emerson, Feb. 12, 1936, Records of the Future Outlook League, Western Reserve Historical Society, Cleveland (hereafter WRHS).

10. For the exclusion of black workers from hotel and restaurant unions, see Dorothy Sue Cobble, "Sisters in the Craft: Waitresses and Their Unions in the Twentieth Century" (Ph.D. diss., Stanford University, 1986), 155–59; Matthew Josephson, *Union House, Union Bar: The History of the Hotel and Restaurant Employees and Bartenders International Union, AFL-CIO* (New York: Random House, 1956), 180–85; and Department of Research and Investigations of the National Negro Welfare Association, *Negro Membership in American Labor Unions* (New York: Alexander Press, 1930), 51–52.

11. For a description of black politicians in Cleveland prior to Holly, see Kenneth L. Kusmer, *A Ghetto Takes Shape: Black Cleveland, 1870–1930* (Urbana: University of Illinois Press, 1976), esp. 113–54; Willard B. Gatewood, *Aristocrats of Color: The Black Elite, 1880–1920* (Bloomington: University of Indiana Press, 1990); and Stokes, *Promises of Power.*

12. Stokes, *Promises of Power,* 16–17.

13. For the collapse of many of the efforts in Harlem, see Cheryl Greenberg, *"Or Does It Explode?": Black Harlem in the Great Depression* (New York: Oxford University Press, 1991), 115.

14. My reading of the development of and changes in the activism of the Future Outlook League—greatly elaborated on in chapter 6—has been influenced by James C. Scott's *Domination and the Arts of Resistance: Hidden Transcripts* (New Haven: Yale University Press, 1990), 207; and Kelley, *Race Rebels.*

15. Kusmer, *A Ghetto Takes Shape,* 91–154, 235–74; Christopher G. Wye, "A Midwest Ghetto: Patterns of Negro Life and Thought in Cleveland, Ohio, 1929–1945" (Ph.D. diss., Kent State University, 1973); Larry Cuban, "A Strategy for Racial Peace: Negro Leadership in Cleveland, 1900–1919," *Phylon* 28 (Fall 1967): 301–19; Adrienne Lash Jones, *Jane Edna Hunter: A Case Study of Black Leadership, 1910–1959* (New York: Carlson, 1990); Gatewood, *Aristocrats of Color;* Vanessa Northington Gamble, *Making a Place for Ourselves: The Black Hospital Movement, 1920–1945* (New York: Oxford University Press, 1995); Charles W. Chesnutt, "The Negro in Cleveland," *The Clevelander* 5 (Nov. 1930): 3–4, 24–27.

16. *New York Age,* Mar. 28, 1911. For expressions of the loss of status, see the letters and autobiographies of African-American elites, e.g., John A. Garraty, ed., *The Barber and the Historian: The Correspondence of George A. Myers and James Ford Rhodes, 1910–1923* (Columbus: Ohio Historical Society, 1956); Jane Edna Hunter, *A Nickel and a Prayer* (Cleveland: Elli Kani, 1940), 135–49; Chester Himes, *The Quality of Hurt: The Autobiography of Chester Himes* (New York: Doubleday, 1972), 1:15–22.

17. U.S. Bureau of the Census, *Negroes in the United States, 1920–1932* (Washington, D.C.: Government Printing Office, 1935).

18. Kusmer, *A Ghetto Takes Shape.* For a critique of this approach, see Joe William Trotter Jr., *Black Milwaukee: The Making of an Industrial Proletariat, 1915–45* (Urba-

na: University of Illinois Press, 1985), appendix, 264–82. For a critique of his own approach, see Kenneth L. Kusmer, "The Black Urban Experience in American History," in *The State of Afro-American History: Past, Present, and Future*, ed. Darlene Clark Hine (Baton Rouge: Louisiana State University Press, 1986), 91–122; see also Joe William Trotter Jr., "African Americans in the City: The Industrial Era, 1900–1950," *Journal of Urban History* 21 (May 1995): 438–57.

19. Kusmer, *A Ghetto Takes Shape*, 233.

20. Joe William Trotter Jr., "African-American Workers: New Directions in U.S. Labor Historiography," *Labor History* 35 (Fall 1994): 495. Some examples of these studies include Joe William Trotter Jr., *Coal, Class, and Color: Blacks in Southern West Virginia, 1915–32* (Urbana: University of Illinois Press, 1990); Earl Lewis, *In Their Own Interests: Race, Class, and Power in Twentieth Century Norfolk, Virginia* (Berkeley: University of California Press, 1990); Elizabeth Clark-Lewis, *Living In, Living Out: African American Domestics in Washington, D.C., 1910–1940* (Washington, D.C.: Smithsonian Institution, 1994); Rick Halpern, "Organized Labour, Black Workers, and the Twentieth Century South: The Emerging Revision," *Social History* 19 (Spring 1992): 361.

21. The literature on African-American migration and proletarianization is extensive. See, e.g., Nell Irvin Painter, *Exodusters: Black Migration to Kansas after Reconstruction* (New York: Knopf, 1976; reprint, Lawrence: University of Kansas Press, 1986); Trotter, *Black Milwaukee;* Peter Gottlieb, *Making Their Own Way: Southern Blacks' Migration to Pittsburgh, 1916–30* (Urbana: University of Illinois Press, 1987); James R. Grossman, *Land of Hope: Chicago, Black Southerners, and the Great Migration* (Chicago: University of Chicago Press, 1989); Lewis, *In Their Own Interests;* Carole Marks, *Farewell—We're Good and Gone: The Great Black Migration* (Bloomington: Indiana University Press, 1989); Trotter, *Coal, Class, and Color;* Richard W. Thomas, *Life for Us Is What We Make It: Building Black Community in Detroit, 1915–1945* (Bloomington: Indiana University Press, 1992); Clark-Lewis, *Living In, Living Out*, 51–66; and Cindy Hahamovitch, *The Fruits of Their Labor: Atlantic Coast Farmworkers and the Making of Migrant Poverty, 1870–1945* (Chapel Hill: University of North Carolina Press, 1997). For an overview of the debates, see Joe William Trotter Jr., ed., *The Great Migration in Historical Perspective: New Dimensions of Race, Class, and Gender* (Bloomington: Indiana University Press, 1991), 1–21.

22. The literature is extensive; see, e.g., Jacqueline Jones, *Labor of Love, Labor of Sorrow: Black Women, Work, and the Family from Slavery to the Present* (New York: Basic Books, 1985); Dolores Janiewski, *Sisterhood Denied: Race, Gender, and Class in a New South Community* (Philadelphia: Temple University Press, 1985); Darlene Clark Hine, "Black Migration to the Urban Midwest: The Gender Dimension, 1915–1945," in *The Great Migration in Historical Perspective*, 126–46; Darlene Clark Hine, *Black Women in White: Racial Conflict and Cooperation in the Nursing Profession, 1890–1950* (Bloomington: Indiana University Press, 1989); Elsa Barkley Brown, "Womanist Consciousness: Maggie Lena Walker and the Independent Order of St. Luke," *Signs* 14 (Spring 1989): 610–33; Elsa Barkley Brown, "Uncle Ned's Children: Richmond, Virginia's Black Community, 1890–1930" (Ph.D. diss., Kent State University, 1994); Evelyn Brooks Higginbotham, *Righteous Discontent: The Women's Movement in the Black Baptist Church, 1880–1920* (Cambridge, Mass.: Harvard University Press, 1993); Clark-Lewis, *Living In, Living Out;* Tera W. Hunter, "Domination and Resistance: The Politics of Wage Household Labor in New South Atlanta," *Labor History* 34 (Spring–

Summer 1993): 205–20; Tera W. Hunter, *To 'Joy My Freedom: Southern Black Women's Lives and Labors after the Civil War* (Cambridge, Mass.: Harvard University Press, 1997); Stephanie Shaw, *"What a Woman Ought to Be and to Do": Black Professional Women during the Jim Crow Era* (Chicago: University of Chicago Press, 1995).

23. Trotter, *Great Migration,* 2, 148–49.

24. Ibid. In *Land of Hope,* James Grossman, too, documented the importance of southern culture for African Americans who settled in Chicago. Because this study focuses on the World War I era, we learn little of the long-term social and organizational impact of this culture in black people's lives in the city.

25. Gottlieb, *Making Their Own Way,* chap. 1.

26. Hine, "Black Migration," 126–46; Clark-Lewis, *Living In, Living Out.* My understanding of black working-class women's experiences of gender, race, and class as intersecting and differing historical and cultural processes has been influenced by Patricia Hill Collins, *Black Feminist Thought: Knowledge, Consciousness, and the Politics of Empowerment* (Boston: Unwin Hyman, 1990); Elsa Barkley Brown, "'What Has Happened Here': The Politics of Difference in Women's History and Feminist Politics," *Feminist Studies* 18 (Summer 1992): 295–312; Evelyn Brooks Higginbotham, "African-American Women's History and the Metalanguage of Race," *Signs* 17 (Winter 1992): 251–74; Joan Kelly, *Women, History, and Theory: The Essays of Joan Kelly* (Chicago: University of Chicago Press, 1984), esp. chap. 2; Joan W. Scott, "Gender: A Useful Category of Historical Analysis," *American History Review* 91 (Dec. 1986): 1053–75; Angela Y. Davis, *Women, Race, and Class* (New York: Random House, 1981); and Cornel West, "Black Culture and Postmodernism," in *A Postmodern Reader,* ed. Joseph Natoli and Linda Hutcheon (Albany: State University of New York Press, 1993), 390–97.

27. Gottlieb, *Making Their Own Way,* 12–33. Peter Gottlieb's study, for example, focuses on the process, not the range, of African Americans' moves into industrial wage work in the South.

28. For patterns of work in lumber camps, see Steven A. Reich, "Struggle in the Piney Woods: Land, Labor, and Working-Class Formation in East Texas," 4–5, paper presented at the annual meeting of the Southern Historical Association, Nov. 9, 1995, New Orleans; James Green, "The Brotherhood of Timber Workers, 1910–1913: A Radical Response to Industrial Capitalism in the Southern USA," *Past and Present* 60 (Aug. 1973): 161–200. For an important discussion of black life in West Virginia coal camps, see Trotter, *Coal, Class, and Color;* and Gus Joiner, interview by author, Cleveland, Oct. 2, 1989, transcript.

29. Sara Brooks, *You May Plow Here: The Narrative of Sara Brooks,* ed. Thordis Simonsen (New York: Simon and Schuster, 1987), 184–204; Joiner interview; Bertha Cowan, interview by Eleanor Jackson, Jan. 16, 1987, Cleveland, transcript, St. James A.M.E. Oral History Project, WRHS.

30. Joiner interview; Natalie Middleton, interview by author, Cleveland, Feb. 21, 1989, transcript; Brooks, *You May Plow Here,* 171–83; Hunter, "Domination and Resistance"; Hunter, *To 'Joy My Freedom.*

31. Kelley, *Race Rebels,* 1–13. For Kelley's influences, see Scott, *Domination and the Arts of Resistance,* xii–xiii; and Lila Abu-Lughod, "The Romance of Resistance: Tracing Transformations of Power through Bedouin Women," *American Ethnologist* 17 (Feb. 1990): 41–55. For a critique of James C. Scott's general theoretical approach, see Timothy Mitchell, "Everyday Metaphors of Power," *Theory and Society* 19 (Oct. 1990):

545–77; and Robin D. G. Kelley, "An Archeology of Resistance," *American Quarterly* 44 (June 1992): 292–98. For an addendum to Kelley's work, see Kenneth W. Goings and Gerald L. Smith, "'Unhidden' Transcripts: Memphis and African American Agency, 1862–1920," *Journal of Urban History* 21 (Mar. 1995): 372–94. For a provocative explication of passing, see Amy Robinson, "It Takes One to Know One: Passing and Communities of Common Interest," *Critical Inquiry* 20 (Summer 1994): 715–36. For passing as free, white, or straight as a form of resistance to the dominant culture or policing by the state, see George Chauncy, *Gay New York: Gender, Urban Culture, and the Making of the Gay Male World, 1890–1940* (New York: Basic Books, 1994).

32. For works that consider African Americans' participation in organized labor from 1900 to 1929, see Trotter, *Coal, Class, and Color;* Lewis, *In Their Own Interests;* Eric Arnesen, *Waterfront Workers of New Orleans: Race, Class, and Politics, 1863–1923* (New York: Oxford University Press, 1991); Eric Arnesen, "Following the Color Line of Labor: Black Workers and the Labor Movement before 1930," *Radical History* 55 (Winter 1993): 53–87; Eric Arnesen, "'Like Banquo's Ghost, It Will Not Down': The Race Question and the American Railroad Brotherhoods, 1880–1920," *American Historical Review* 99 (Dec. 1994): 1601–33; James R. Barrett, *Work and Community in the Jungle: Chicago's Packinghouse Workers, 1894–1922* (Urbana: University of Illinois Press, 1987); Ronald L. Lewis, *Black Coal Miners in America: Race, Class, and Community Conflict, 1780–1980* (Lexington: University Press of Kentucky, 1987); Jones, *Labor of Love, Labor of Sorrow;* and Paul B. Worthman, "Black Workers and Labor Unions in Birmingham, Alabama, 1897–1904" *Labor History* 10 (Summer 1969): 375–407. For important earlier literature on black wage experiences, see William H. Harris, *The Harder We Run: Black Workers since the Civil War* (New York: Oxford University Press, 1982); William H. Harris, *Keeping the Faith: A. Philip Randolph, Milton P. Webster, and the Brotherhood of Sleeping Car Porters, 1925–37* (Urbana: University of Illinois Press, 1977); Philip S. Foner, *Organized Labor and the Black Worker, 1619–1973* (New York: Praeger, 1974); John H. Bracey Jr., August Meier, and Elliott Rudwick, eds., *Black Workers and Organized Labor* (Belmont, Calif.: Wadsworth, 1971); Charles H. Wesley, *Negro Labor in the United States, 1850–1925: A Study in American Economic History* (New York: Vanguard Press, 1927); Department of Research and Investigations of the National Negro Welfare Association, *Negro Membership;* Sterling D. Spero and Abram L. Harris, *The Black Worker: The Negro and the Labor Movement* (New York: Columbia University Press, 1931; reprint, New York: Atheneum, 1969); Lorenzo J. Greene and Carter G. Woodson, *The Negro Wage Earner* (New York: Russell and Russell, 1930); and Horace R. Cayton and George S. Mitchell, *Black Workers and the New Unions* (Chapel Hill: University of North Carolina Press, 1939). For works that address the difficulties white workers confronted in organizing during the 1920s, see Irving Berstein, *The Lean Years: A History of the American Worker, 1920–1933* (Boston: Houghton Mifflin, 1960); David Montgomery, *The Fall of the House of Labor: The Workplace, the State, and American Labor Activism* (Cambridge: Cambridge University Press, 1987); Lizbeth Cohen, *Making a New Deal: Industrial Workers in Chicago, 1919–1939* (Cambridge: Cambridge University Press, 1990); and Dana Frank, *Purchasing Power: Consumer Organizing, Gender, and the Seattle Labor Movement, 1919–1929* (Cambridge: Cambridge University Press, 1994).

33. For a definition of *home sphere,* see Lewis, *In Their Own Interests,* 5–6, 66–109. For a similar use, see Trotter, *Coal, Class, and Color,* 177–216. Lewis and Trotter sug-

gest that the home sphere provided African Americans with a place to "congregate," creating a racial consciousness that could mute class and gender differences. Yet class identity, as an experience of social reproduction, did take shape in households, churches, and places of leisure. In short, the home sphere provided innumerable opportunities to reproduce social relations and gender imbalances. For alternative takes on African-American cultural and social reproduction, see Brown, "Womanist Consciousness"; and Hunter, *To 'Joy My Freedom*.

34. Gottlieb, *Making Their Own Way*, 49; Hine, "Black Migration." The literature on family history has been helpful; see, for example, Barrie Thorne, ed., with Marilyn Yalom, *Rethinking the Family: Some Feminist Questions* (New York: Longman, 1982); Elizabeth Faue, *Community of Suffering and Struggle: Men, Women, and the Labor Movement in Minneapolis, 1915–1945* (Chapel Hill: University of North Carolina Press, 1991); Elizabeth Faue, "Facing and Effacing Difference: Reproducing the Narrative of Class Struggle in Labor and Working Class History," paper presented at the annual meeting of the Organization of American Historians, Mar. 31, 1995, Washington, D.C.

35. My analysis has been influenced by Laura Tabili's *"We Ask for British Justice": Workers and Racial Difference in Late Imperial Britain* (Ithaca: Cornell University Press, 1994); Faue, "Facing and Effacing Difference"; and Elsa Barkley Brown, "Negotiating and Transforming the Public Sphere: African American Political Life in the Transition from Slavery to Freedom," in *The Black Public Sphere*, ed. the Black Public Sphere Collective (Chicago: University of Chicago Press, 1995), 111–50.

36. For a discussion of African-American migrants' encounters with established institutions, see Trotter, *Black Milwaukee;* and Gottlieb, *Making Their Own Way*, 183–210.

37. Kelley, *Race Rebels*, 47–48.

38. Lewis, *In Their Own Interests*, 137–43; Bruce Nelson, *Workers on the Waterfront: Seamen, Longshoremen, and Unionism in the 1930s* (Urbana: University of Illinois Press, 1988); Michael K. Honey, *Southern Labor and Black Civil Rights: Organizing Memphis Workers* (Urbana: University of Illinois Press, 1993), 117–44; August Meier and Elliott Rudwick, *Black Detroit and the Rise of the UAW* (New York: Oxford University Press, 1979), 34–107. For another view, see Michael Goldfield, "Race and the CIO: The Possibilities for Racial Egalitarianism during the 1930s and 1940s," *International Labor and Working-Class History* 44 (Fall 1993): 1–32.

39. For the relationships between African Americans and communists, see Mark Naison, *Communists in Harlem during the Depression* (New York: Grove Press, 1983); Robin D. G. Kelley, *Hammer and Hoe: Alabama Communists during the Great Depression* (Chapel Hill: University of North Carolina Press, 1990); Nell Irvin Painter, *The Narrative of Hosea Hudson: His Life as a Negro Communist in the South* (Cambridge, Mass.: Harvard University Press, 1979); Theodore Rosengarten, *All God's Dangers: The Life of Nate Shaw* (New York: Avon Books, 1974; reprint, New York: Vintage Books, 1984); Gerald Zahavi, "Passionate Commitments: Race, Sex, and Communism at Schenectady General Electric, 1932–1954," *Journal of American History* 83 (Sept. 1996): 514–48.

40. For an example of this debate, see Goldfield, "Race and the CIO," 1–31; for a response to this, see Judith Stein, "Response: The Ins and Outs of the CIO," *International Labor and Working-Class History* 44 (Fall 1993): 53–63. For an absence of any

discussion of discrimination in the CIO, see Walter Galenson, *The CIO Challenge to the AFL: A History of the American Labor Movement, 1935–1941* (Cambridge, Mass.: Harvard University Press, 1960); and John Raymond Walsh, *C.I.O.: Industrial Unionism in Action* (New York: W. W. Norton, 1937). For a more critical view, see Herbert R. Northrup, *Organized Labor and the Negro* (New York: Harper and Brothers, 1944); Horace R. Cayton and George S. Mitchell, *Black Workers and the New Unions* (Chapel Hill: University of North Carolina Press, 1939); Judith Stein, "Southern Workers in International Unions, 1936–1951," in *Organized Labor in the Twentieth Century South,* ed. Robert Zieger (Knoxville: University of Tennessee Press, 1991), 183–222; and Middleton interview by author.

41. Stein, "Response," 55.

42. Stokes, *Promises of Power,* 48.

43. Ibid., 16–18; Judge Jean Murrell Capers, interview by author and Patricia Miles Ashford, Cleveland, Aug. 8, 1991, transcript.

44. For a discussion of this inclusive approach, see Miranda Miles and Jonathan Crush, "Personal Narratives as Interactive Texts: Collecting and Interpreting Migrant Life-Histories," *Professional Geographer* 45 (Feb. 1993): 84–94. For a more detailed discussion of my methodology, see Kimberley L. Phillips, "Oral History: Some Guidelines for a Community Project," *Ohio Council for the Social Studies Review* 30 (Summer 1994): 21–27.

45. "Identity, Dignity, and Community: Black Religious Experiences in Cleveland," July 27, 1996–Sept. 30, 1997, WRHS.

Chapter 1: "Pins" North

1. Josephus Hicks, interview by author, Cleveland, Nov. 14, 1990, transcript.

2. W. E. B. Du Bois, *The Philadelphia Negro: A Social Study* (Philadelphia: Publications for the University, 1899; reprint, Schocken Books, 1967); John Daniels, *In Freedom's Birthplace* (Boston: Houghton Mifflin, 1914; reprint, New York: Arno Press, 1969); U.S. Department of Labor, *Negro Migration in 1916–1917* (Washington, D.C.: Government Printing Office, 1919; reprint, New York: Negro Universities Press, 1969); Carter G. Woodson, *A Century of Negro Migration* (New York: Russell and Russell, 1918); Emmett J. Scott, *Negro Migration during the War* (New York: Oxford University Press, 1920; reprint, New York: Arno Press, 1969); Thomas J. Woofter, *Negro Migration: Changes in Rural Organization and Population of the Cotton Belt* (New York: W. D. Gray, 1920; reprint, Negro Universities Press, 1969); Chicago Commission on Race Relations, *The Negro in Chicago: A Study of Race Relations in a Race Riot* (Chicago: University of Chicago Press, 1922; reprint, New York: Arno Press, 1968); Louise V. Kennedy, *The Negro Peasant Turns Cityward: Effects of Recent Migrations to Northern Cities* (New York: Columbia University Press, 1930); Edward E. Lewis, *The Mobility of the Negro: A Study in the American Labor Supply* (New York: Columbia University Press, 1931; reprint, New York: AMS Press, 1968); Clyde V. Kiser, *Sea Island to City: A Study of St. Helena Islanders in Harlem and Other Urban Centers* (New York: Columbia University Press, 1932; reprint, New York: AMS Press, 1967); William Tuttle, *Race Riot: Chicago in the Red Summer of 1919* (New York: Atheneum, 1970; reprint, Urbana: University of Illinois Press, 1996); Florette Henri, *Black Migration: Movement North, 1900–1920* (Garden City, N.Y.: Anchor Press, 1975); Elizabeth H. Pleck, *Black Migration and Poverty: Boston, 1865–1900* (New York: Academic Press, 1979); James Borchert,

Alley Life in Washington: Family, Community, Religion, and Folklife in the City, 1850–1970 (Urbana: University of Illinois Press, 1980); Elizabeth Rauel Bethel, *Promiseland: A Century of Life in a Negro Community* (Philadelphia: Temple University Press, 1981); Allen R. Ballard, *One More Day's Journey: The Making of Black Philadelphia* (Philadelphia: Institute for the Study of Human Issues, 1984). For comparative studies of black and white migration out of the South, see Gene B. Petersen, Laurie M. Sharp, and Thomas F. Drury, *Southern Newcomers to Northern Cities: Work and Social Adjustment in Cleveland* (New York: Praeger, 1977); Neil Fligstein, *Going North: Migration of Blacks and Whites from the South, 1900–1950* (New York: Academic Press, 1981); and Jacqueline Jones, *The Dispossessed: America's Underclasses from the Civil War to the Present* (New York: Basic Books, 1992).

3. Peter Gottlieb, "Rethinking the Great Migration: A Perspective from Pittsburgh," in *The Great Migration in Historical Perspective: New Dimensions of Race, Class, and Gender*, ed. Joe William Trotter Jr. (Bloomington: Indiana University Press, 1991), 68.

4. Ibid.; Peter Gottlieb, *Making Their Own Way: Southern Blacks' Migration to Pittsburgh, 1916–30* (Urbana: University of Illinois Press, 1987), 1–62; Carole Marks, *Farewell—We're Good and Gone: The Great Black Migration* (Bloomington: Indiana University Press, 1989); Neil R. McMillen, *Dark Journey: Black Mississippians in the Age of Jim Crow* (Urbana: University of Illinois Press, 1989), 269–70; William Cohen, *At Freedom's Edge: Black Mobility and the Southern White Quest for Racial Control, 1861–1915* (Baton Rouge: Louisiana State University Press, 1991).

5. Trotter, *Great Migration*, 2.

6. Peter Kolchin, *First Freedom: Responses of Alabama Blacks to Emancipation and Reconstruction* (Westport, Conn.: Greenwood Press, 1972); Joseph P. Reidy, *From Slavery to Agrarian Capitalism in the Cotton Plantation South: Central Georgia, 1800–1880* (Chapel Hill: University of North Carolina Press, 1992), 231–32; Robert Higgs, *Competition and Coercion: Blacks in the Postwar Economy, 1865–1914* (Cambridge: Cambridge University Press, 1977). On the role of black labor in the New South, see Robin D. G. Kelley, *Hammer and Hoe: Alabama Communists during the Great Depression* (Chapel Hill: University of North Carolina Press, 1990); Tera W. Hunter, *To 'Joy My Freedom: Southern Black Women's Lives and Labors after the Civil War* (Cambridge, Mass.: Harvard University Press, 1997); Daniel Letwin, *The Challenge of Interracial Unionism: Alabama Coal Miners, 1878–1921* (Chapel Hill: University of North Carolina Press, 1998); Brian Kelly, "Policing the 'Negro Eden': Racial Paternalism in the Alabama Coalfields, 1906–22, Part One," *Alabama Review* 51 (Summer 1998): 163–83.

7. The sociologist Charles S. Johnson described the mass migration as a "leaderless movement." Quoted in Tuttle, *Race Riot*, 93.

8. U.S. Bureau of the Census, *Negroes in the United States, 1920–1932* (Washington, D.C.: Government Printing Office, 1935), 55 (table 10); census data on gross migration is not available for 1910, 1920, and 1940. For a helpful discussion, see John Temple Kirby, *Rural Worlds Lost: The American South, 1920–1960* (Baton Rouge: Louisiana State University Press, 1987).

9. For an overview of the transition from slavery to freedom, see Alex Lichtenstein, "Was the Emancipated Slave a Proletarian?" *Reviews in American History* 26 (Mar. 1998): 124–48.

10. Robert J. Norell, *James Bowron: The Autobiography of a New South Industrialist* (Chapel Hill: University of North Carolina Press, 1991), 244–45.

11. Thavolia Glymph, "Freedpeople and Ex-Masters: Shaping a New Order in the Postbellum South, 1865–1868," in *Essays on the Postbellum Southern Economy,* ed. Thavolia Glymph and John Kushma (College Station: Texas A&M University Press, 1985), 48–72; Roger L. Ransom and Richard Sutch, *One Kind of Freedom: The Economic Consequences of Emancipation* (Cambridge: Cambridge University Press, 1977); Kolchin, *First Freedom,* 3–29; Reidy, *From Slavery to Agrarian Capitalism,* 142–43, 157, 195–96.

12. Gerald David Jaynes, *Branches without Roots: Genesis of the Black Working Class in the American South, 1862–1882* (New York: Oxford University Press, 1986); Glymph, "Freedpeople and Ex-Masters," 49; Reidy, *From Slavery to Agrarian Capitalism,* 138–41, 156–57; Leslie A. Schwalm, *A Hard Fight for We: Women's Transition from Slavery to Freedom in South Carolina* (Urbana: University of Illinois Press, 1997), 263. Other historians have noted black men's turn toward more patriarchal views of black women's roles in the family and community. See Elsa Barkley Brown, "Negotiating and Transforming the Public Sphere: African American Political Life in the Transition from Slavery to Freedom," in *The Black Public Sphere,* ed. the Black Public Sphere Collective (Chicago: University of Chicago Press, 1995), 111–50.

13. Reidy, *From Slavery to Agrarian Capitalism,* 209–12, 215–41; Lichtenstein, "Was the Emancipated Slave a Proletarian?"; Melinda Meek Heenessey, "Political Terrorism in the Black Belt: The Eutaw Riot," *Alabama Review* 46 (Jan. 1980): 35–48; Michael W. Fitzgerald, "'To Give Our Votes to the Party': Black Political Agitation and Agricultural Change in Alabama, 1865–1870," *Journal of American History* 76 (Sept. 1989): 503–5. For an overview of political terrorism, see Edward Ayers, *Promise of the New South: Life after Reconstruction* (New York: Oxford University Press, 1992), 35–54.

14. Kelley, *Hammer and Hoe,* 1; W. David Lewis, "The Emergence of Birmingham as a Case Study of Continuity between the Antebellum Planter Class and Industrialization in the 'New South,'" *Agricultural History* 68 (Spring 1994): 62–79. For a different view, see Jonathan M. Wiener, *Social Origins of the New South: Alabama, 1860–1885* (Baton Rouge: Louisiana State University Press, 1978), 186–221. For a discussion of the continuity between antebellum and New South racial and labor policy, see Alex Lichtenstein, *Twice the Work of Free Labor: The Political Economy of Convict Labor in the New South* (New York: Verso Press, 1996), chap. 1.

15. Kolchin, *First Freedom,* 184–86; Reidy, *From Slavery to Agrarian Capitalism,* 215–21; Fitzgerald, "'To Give Our Votes to the Party,'" 491; Schwalm, *A Hard Fight for We,* 187–233.

16. C. Vann Woodward, *Origins of the New South, 1877–1913* (Baton Rouge: Louisiana State University Press, 1951); C. Vann Woodward, *The Strange Career of Jim Crow,* 3d ed. (New York: Oxford University Press, 1974); J. Morgan Kousser, *The Shaping of Southern Politics: Suffrage Restriction and the Establishment of the One-Party South, 1880–1910* (New Haven: Yale University Press, 1974); Ayers, *Promise of the New South,* 304–9; Cohen, *At Freedom's Edge,* 216–20; McMillen, *Dark Journey,* 35–71. For the emergence of Jim Crow in the urban South, see John Dittmer, *Black Georgia in the Progressive Era, 1900–1920* (Urbana: University of Illinois Press, 1977), 8–22; and Hunter, *To 'Joy My Freedom.*

17. Reidy, *From Slavery to Agrarian Capitalism,* 221–27; Cohen, *At Freedom's Edge,* 248–73. For an early, but important discussion, see William Cohen, "Negro Involuntary Servitude in the South, 1865–1940: A Preliminary Analysis," *Journal of Southern History* 62 (Feb. 1976): 31–60; Lichtenstein, *Twice the Work of Free Labor;* Pete Daniel,

The Shadow of Slavery: Peonage in the South, 1901–1969 (Urbana: University of Illinois Press, 1972); Lewis, "The Emergence of Birmingham as a Case Study," 72–73; Jack Leonard Lerner, "A Monument to Shame: The Convict Lease System in Alabama" (M.A. thesis, Stanford University, 1969).

18. Ayers, *Promise of the New South,* 208–10; Margaret Pace Farmer, "Furnishing Merchants and Sharecroppers in Pike County, Alabama," *Alabama Review* 23 (Apr. 1970): 143–51; Harold D. Woodman, "Post–Civil War Southern Agriculture and the Law," *Agriculture History* 53 (Jan. 1979): 319–37; Fitzgerald, "'To Give Our Votes to the Party,'" 489–90.

19. Reidy, *From Slavery to Agrarian Capitalism,* 242–48; Jones, *The Dispossessed,* 73–103; James Little quoted in James Seay Brown Jr., *Up before Daylight: Life Histories from the Alabama Writers' Project, 1938–1939* (Birmingham: University of Alabama Press, 1982), 147.

20. Cohen, *At Freedom's Edge,* 229–46 (first quote on 229; second quote on 246).

21. Reidy, *From Slavery to Agrarian Capitalism,* 225, see also 222–24; Daniel, *Shadow of Slavery.*

22. Jones, *The Dispossessed,* 107; Ransom and Sutch, *One Kind of Freedom,* 61–64; Theodore Rosengarten, *All God's Dangers: The Life of Nate Shaw* (New York: Avon Books, 1974; reprint, New York: Vintage Books, 1984), 103–9.

23. Rosengarten, *All God's Dangers,* 212–13, 228–29 (quote on 213).

24. Sydney Nathans, "'Gotta Mind to Move, a Mind to Settle Down': Afro-Americans and the Plantation Frontier," in *A Master's Due: Essays in Honor of David Herbert Donald,* ed. William J. Cooper Jr., Michael F. Holt, and John McCardell (Baton Rouge: Louisiana State University Press, 1985), 208; Fligstein, *Going North,* 15–16; Cohen, *At Freedom's Edge,* 263.

25. Rosengarten, *All God's Dangers,* 183–85; Sara Brooks, *You May Plow Here: The Narrative of Sara Brooks,* ed. Thordis Simonsen (New York: Simon and Schuster, 1987), 102; Selmer Prewitt, interview by author, Cleveland, Mar. 7, 1991, transcript.

26. Brooks, *You May Plow Here,* 46–48 (quote on 46); Charles S. Johnson, *Shadow of the Plantation* (Chicago: University of Chicago Press, 1934), 101.

27. Rosengarten, *All God's Dangers,* 15, 36–41, 184–85, 212–13 (quote on 36); Carl Kelsey, *The Negro Farmer* (Chicago: Jennings and Pye, 1903), 48; Charles S. Johnson, *Growing Up in the Black Belt: Negro Youth in the Rural South* (Washington, D.C.: American Council on Education, 1941).

28. Minnie Brown, "Black Women in American Agriculture," *Agricultural History* 50 (Winter 1976): 202–12; Richard Westmacott, *African-American Gardens and Yards in the Rural South* (Knoxville: University of Tennessee Press, 1992), 23–27, 87–89; Brooks, *You May Plow Here,* 27–29; Gus Joiner, interview by author, Oct. 2, 1989; Naomi Morgan, interview by Emily Lasiter, Cleveland, Dec. 12, 1986, transcript, St. James A.M.E. Oral History Project, Western Reserve Historical Society, Cleveland (hereafter WRHS); D. Dewitt, "Family Oral History" (undergraduate paper, Cleveland State University, n.d.); Sarah Rice, *He Included Me: The Autobiography of Sarah Rice* (Athens: University of Georgia Press, 1989), vii, 16–47; Johnson, *Shadow of the Plantation,* 91, 115; Arthur Raper, *Preface to Peasantry: A Tale of Two Black Counties* (Chapel Hill: University of North Carolina Press, 1936), 50. I have used Johnson's documentation of sharecroppers' diets with caution. Most of his information highlighted the deprivation brought on by the Great Depression. Nonetheless, some of

the informants for his study indicated more varied diets prior to the depression. Of the 612 families he interviewed, 513 had gardens. Arthur Raper noted a different trend in his study of North Carolina: as cotton prices fell, particularly after 1927, black farm families depended more, not less, on gardens. He suggested that prior to the 1920s, black farm families did not or could not subsist on their gardens.

29. Kelsey, *Negro Farmer*, 45; Brooks, *You May Plow Here*, 164; Rice, *He Included Me*, 55–56; Annie Jones, interview by Madelyn Lee, Cleveland, Oct. 19, 1986, transcript, St. James A.M.E. Oral History Project; Carrie Turner, interview by Emily Lasiter, Cleveland, Aug. 27, 1986, transcript, St. James A.M.E. Oral History Project.

30. Brown, "Black Women in American Agriculture," 202–12; Jacqueline Jones, *Labor of Love, Labor of Sorrow: Black Women, Work, and the Family from Slavery to the Present* (New York: Basic Books, 1985), 81–99, 200–220; Brooks, *You May Plow Here*, 86–90, 162; B. Clark, "Family Oral History" (undergraduate paper, Cleveland State University, 1984); W. E. B. Du Bois, *The Negro American Family*, Atlanta University Publications, no. 13 (Atlanta: Atlanta University Press, 1908), 138.

31. On the imbalance of power in black rural households, see Elizabeth Clark-Lewis, *Living In, Living Out: African American Domestics in Washington, D.C., 1910–1940* (Washington, D.C.: Smithsonian Institution, 1994), 1–52; Kelley, *Hammer and Hoe*, 36; and Rice, *He Included Me*, 51–52. Any section of Rosengarten's *All God's Dangers* will reveal such imbalances; see especially Seay, *Up before Daylight*, 148; and Brooks, *You May Plow Here*, 153–70.

32. Rosengarten, *All God's Dangers*, 184.

33. Brooks, *You May Plow Here*, 86.

34. Ibid., 68, 114; Annie Jones interview; Louise James, "Family History of Thelma and James Bosley," n.d., Ursula J. Honore Papers, WRHS; B. Clark, "Family Oral History."

35. Johnson, *Shadow of the Plantation*, 136–49; Rosengarten, *All God's Dangers*, 24–26, 216–21; Prewitt interview. McMillen notes that white landowners in Mississippi had similar perceptions. See *Dark Journey*, 72–108.

36. Horace Mann Bond, *Negro Education in Alabama* (New York: Atheneum, 1939; reprint, New York: Atheneum, 1969). For an overview of black education in the South, see James D. Anderson, *The Education of Blacks in the South, 1860–1935* (Chapel Hill: University of North Carolina Press, 1988); Hicks interview; Prewitt interview; Johnson, *Shadow of the Plantation*, 136–49; Rosengarten, *All God's Dangers*, 216–21.

37. L. Echols, "Family Oral History" (undergraduate paper, Cleveland State University, 1979).

38. Brooks, *You May Plow Here*, 86–87.

39. Du Bois, *Negro American Family*, 138; Rice, *He Included Me*, 19, 28; Annie Jones interview.

40. Seay, *Up before Daylight*, 147; Brooks, *You May Plow Here*, 34–42, 102–8; Rice, *He Included Me*, 35.

41. Rice, *He Included Me*, 17.

42. For a discussion of the contracts, see Kelsey, *Negro Farmer*, 46–49; Rosengarten, *All God's Dangers*, 131, emphasis added; and Seay, *Up before Daylight*, 147.

43. Kelsey, *Negro Farmer*, 45 (quote), 48; Johnson, *Shadow of the Plantation*, 113–14.

44. Thomas F. Armstrong, "The Transformation of Work: Turpentine Workers in Coastal Georgia, 1865–1901," *Labor History* 25 (Fall 1984): 519–21; Chriss H. Doss,

"Cullman Coal and Coke Company Railroad," *Alabama Review* 37 (Oct. 1984): 243–56; Woofter, *Negro Migration,* 52–68; Rosengarten, *All God's Dangers,* 193–97, 216–17; Sallie Hopson, interview by Antoinette Kindall, Cleveland, Aug. 26, 1986, transcript, St. James A.M.E. Oral History Project.

45. Carter Goodwin Woodson, *The Rural Negro* (Washington, D.C.: Association for the Study of Negro Life and History, 1930), 89, 106; Du Bois, *Negro American Family,* 134–35; Raper, *Preface to Peasantry,* 16; Rice, *He Included Me,* 2. For an overview of the development of Southern industries, see Ayers, *Promise of the New South,* 105–31; and Jones, *The Dispossessed,* 127–55. For industries in Alabama, see Ronald L. Lewis, *Black Coal Miners in America: Race, Class, and Community Conflict, 1780–1980* (Lexington: University Press of Kentucky, 1987).

46. Gottlieb, *Making Their Own Way,* 22–33; R. Flowers, "Family Oral History" (undergraduate paper, Cleveland State University, 1981); Rosengarten, *All God's Dangers,* 193–97. For patterns of rural migration in Georgia before 1915, see Woofter, *Negro Migration,* 97–104.

47. B. Clark, "Family Oral History"; Joiner interview; Rosengarten, *All God's Dangers,* 193–95; Doss, "Cullman Coal and Coke Company Railroad," 253; U.S. Department of Labor, *Negro Migration,* 84.

48. Rosengarten, *All God's Dangers,* 193 (quote). For patterns of work in lumber camps, see Steven A. Reich, "Struggle in the Piney Woods: Land, Labor, and Working-Class Formation in East Texas," 4–5, paper presented at the annual meeting of the Southern Historical Association, Nov. 9, 1995, New Orleans; James Green, "The Brotherhood of Timber Workers, 1910–1913: A Radical Response to Industrial Capitalism in the Southern USA," *Past and Present* 60 (Aug. 1973): 161–200; and Doss, "Cullman Coal and Coke Company Railroad," 252–253. For a discussion of the kin and friend networks that provided information about work, see Charles Tilly, "Transplanted Networks," in *Immigration Reconsidered: History, Sociology, and Politics,* ed. Virginia Yans-McLaughlin (New York: Oxford University Press, 1990), 79–95.

49. Edwin L. Brown, "'. . . To Make a Man Feel Good': John Henry Mealing, Railroad Caller," *Labor History* 27 (Spring 1986): 262; Eric Arnesen, "'It Aint like They Do in New Orleans': Race Relations, Labor Markets, and Waterfront Labor Movements in the American South, 1880–1990," in *Racism and the Labour Market: Historical Studies,* ed. Marcel van der Linden and Jan Lucassen (Bern: Peter Lang, 1995), 77; Johnson, *Shadow of the Plantation,* 113.

50. Joiner interview.

51. F. Cheney, "Family Oral History" (undergraduate paper, Cleveland State University, 1981); B. Cross, "Family Oral History" (undergraduate paper, Cleveland State University, 1986); Bethel, *Promiseland,* 158; V. Davis, "Family Oral History" (undergraduate paper, Cleveland State University, 1985).

52. For a description of the extraction of resin, see Woodson, *Rural Negro,* 91–100; and Ayers, *Promise of the New South,* 124.

53. Eric Arnesen, "'Like Banquo's Ghost, It Will Not Down': The Race Question and the American Railroad Brotherhoods, 1880–1920," *American Historical Review* 99 (Dec. 1994): 1619–20. For other accounts, see Ayers, *Promise of the New South,* 125–26; and Brown, "'. . . To Make a Man Feel Good,'" 257–58.

54. Green, "Brotherhood of Timber Workers," 164–67; Deryck W. Holdsworth, "'I'm a Lumberjack and I'm OK': The Built Environment and Varied Masculinities

in the Industrial Age," in *Gender, Class, and Shelter,* ed. Elizabeth Collins Cromley and Carter L. Hudgins, Perspectives in Vernacular Architecture no. 5 (Knoxville: University of Tennessee Press, 1995), 14.

55. Zora Neale Hurston, *Mules and Men* (Philadelphia: J. B. Lippincott, 1935; reprint, New York: HarperPerennial, 1990), 84, 269.

56. Ibid., 264. For numerous examples of work songs, see Howard W. Odum and Guy B. Johnson, *Negro Workaday Songs* (Chapel Hill: University of North Carolina Press, 1926), 118–34. For the meaning of work songs among black men, see Lawrence Levine, *Black Culture and Black Consciousness: Afro-American Folk Thought from Slavery to Freedom* (New York: Oxford University Press, 1977), 202–17, esp. 214–17.

57. For discussions of integrated work settings and segregated jobs, see Jones, *The Dispossessed,* 127–47; Eric Arnesen, *Waterfront Workers of New Orleans: Race, Class, and Politics, 1863–1923* (New York: Oxford University Press, 1991); Trotter, *Coal, Class, and Color,* esp. 65–88, 102–11; Lewis, *Black Coal Miners,* 191–93; and Letwin, *Challenge of Interracial Unionism,* 31–40. For a description of integrated work and racialized wages, see Rosengarten, *All God's Dangers,* 193–95. For a discussion of racialized industrial work in the South, see Charles H. Wesley, *Negro Labor in the United States, 1850–1925: A Study in American Economic History* (New York: Vanguard Press, 1927).

58. Trotter, *Coal, Class, and Color,* 78–79; Ronald L. Lewis, "From Peasant to Proletarian: The Migration of Southern Blacks to the Central Appalachian Coalfields," *Journal of Southern History* 60 (Feb. 1989): 78–82; Joiner interview.

59. Joiner interview; P. Chance, "Family Oral History" (undergraduate paper, Cleveland State University, 1985); Marks, *Farewell,* 149–55; Lewis, *Black Coal Miners,* 79; Trotter, *Coal, Class, and Color,* 76–80.

60. Lewis, *Black Coal Miners,* appendix, 191; Kelley, *Hammer and Hoe,* 1–6; Paul B. Worthman, "Black Workers and Labor Unions in Birmingham, Alabama, 1897–1904," *Labor History* 10 (Summer 1969): 376–81; Esther Lowell, "Housing for Negro Employe[e]s, United States Steel Corporation," *Opportunity* 7 (Aug. 1929): 247–49; Sterling D. Spero and Abram L. Harris, *The Black Worker: The Negro and the Labor Movement* (New York: Columbia University Press, 1931; reprint, New York: Atheneum, 1969), 246. On Alabama coal, see Lewis, *Black Coal Miners,* chaps. 3, 4; and Daniel Letwin, "Interracial Unionism, Gender, and 'Social Equality' in the Alabama Coalfields, 1878–1908," *Journal of Southern History* 66 (Aug. 1995): 519–54. For employers' control, see Trotter, *Coal, Class, and Color,* 65; and Joiner interview.

61. Joiner interview; Icabod Flewellen, interview by author, Cleveland, July 2, 1995, transcript.

62. Joiner interview.

63. Lewis, *Black Coal Miners,* 86; M. Davis, "Family Oral History" (undergraduate paper, Cleveland State University, 1988).

64. Joiner interview; Hicks interview; Natalie Middleton, interview by author, Cleveland, Feb. 21, 1989, transcript; Arnesen, "'It Aint like They Do in New Orleans,'" 76–80; Letwin, "Interracial Unionism," 519–54.

65. Trotter, *Coal, Class, and Color,* 17, 110–15.

66. For the debate, see Herbert Hill, "The Problem of Race in American Labor History," *Reviews in American History* 24 (June 1996): 189–208; Herbert Hill, "Myth-Making as Labor History: Herbert Gutman and the United Mine Workers of America," *International Journal of Politics, Culture, and Society* 2 (Winter 1988): 132–200.

For important rebuttals of Hill's assessments, see Nell Irvin Painter, "The New Labor History and the Historical Moment," *International Journal of Politics, Culture, and Society* 2 (Spring 1989): 367–70; and Alex Lichtenstein, "Racial Conflict and Racial Solidarity in the Alabama Coal Strike of 1894: New Evidence for the Gutman-Hill Debate," *Labor History* 36 (Winter 1995): 63–76. For critiques of white working-class racism, see David Roediger, "Race and the Working-Class Past in the United States: Multiple Identities and the Future of Labor History," *International Review of Social History* 38 (1993, supp. 1): 127–43.

67. Brooks, *You May Plow Here*, 144–45; Hicks interview; Joiner interview. Connecticut farmers, working through the National Urban League, recruited hundreds of black southern college students to work in tobacco fields. Josephus Hicks worked in this network. See also James R. Grossman, *Land of Hope: Chicago, Black Southerners, and the Great Migration* (Chicago: University of Chicago Press, 1989), 69.

68. Gottlieb, *Making Their Own Way*, 27; Prewitt interview; Brooks, *You May Plow Here*, 171–96; Hicks interview; Flowree Robinson, interview by author, Cleveland, Nov. 29, 1989, transcript; Linton Freeman, interview by author, Cleveland, Mar. 7, 1991, transcript; Fligstein, *Going North*, 83–86.

69. Kirby, *Rural Worlds Lost*, 275–78; Woofter, *Negro Migration*, 93–95.

70. Henry M. McKiven Jr., *Iron and Steel: Class, Race, and Community in Birmingham, Alabama, 1875–1920* (Chapel Hill: University of North Carolina Press, 1995), 42–43, 46–47.

71. Ibid., 41.

72. V. Davis, "Family Oral History"; B. Clark, "Family Oral History"; D. Clark, "Family Oral History" (undergraduate paper, Cleveland State University, 1978); Jacquelyn Dowd Hall, James LeLondis, Robert Korstad, Mary Murphy, Lu Ann Jones, and Christopher B. Daly, *Like a Family: The Making of a Southern Cotton Mill World* (Chapel Hill: University of North Carolina Press, 1987), 66; Brooks, *You May Plow Here*, 173–74. For insight into black women's assessment of white employers, see Willie Ruff, *A Call to Assembly: An American Success Story* (New York: Penguin Books, 1991), 15–110.

73. Brooks, *You May Plow Here*, 182, 188.

74. Wright, *Old South, New South*, 156–97.

75. Belle Jones, interview by Madelyn Lee, Cleveland, Jan. 25, 1987, transcript, St. James A.M.E. Oral History Project; Brooks, *You May Plow Here*, 180–95.

76. Brooks, *You May Plow Here*, 185–90, 195; Flowree Robinson interview.

77. L. Fogle, "Family Oral History" (undergraduate paper, Cleveland State University, n.d.); R. Flowers, "Family Oral History"; Bethel, *Promiseland*, 124; Adrienne Kennedy, *People Who Led to My Plays* (New York: Knopf, 1987), 34–36.

78. For growth of black social life and institutions in Southern cities after 1880, see Earl Lewis, *In Their Own Interests: Race, Class, and Power in Twentieth Century Norfolk, Virginia* (Berkeley: University of California Press, 1990), 66–109; Elsa Barkley Brown, "Uncle Ned's Children: Richmond, Virginia's Black Community, 1880–1930" (Ph.D. diss., Kent State University, 1994); Robin D. G. Kelley, "'We Are Not What We Seem': The Politics and Pleasures of Community," in *Race Rebels: Culture, Politics, and the Black Working Class* (New York: Free Press, 1994), 43–53; and Evelyn Brooks Higginbotham, *Righteous Discontent: The Women's Movement in the Black Baptist Church, 1880–1920* (Cambridge, Mass.: Harvard University Press, 1993). For accounts

of a loss in status, see Michael W. Harris, *The Rise of the Gospel Blues: The Music of Thomas Andrew Dorsey in the Urban Church* (New York: Oxford University Press, 1992), 26–46, esp. 27–28; and Rice, *He Included Me*, 5–10.

79. Kelley, *Race Rebels*, 35, 39; Katrina Hazzard-Gordon, *Jookin': The Rise of Social Dance Formations in African-American Culture* (Philadelphia: Temple University Press, 1990), 88–89; Levine, *Black Culture and Black Consciousness*, 205; William Barlow, *Looking Up at Down: The Emergence of Blues Culture* (Philadelphia: Temple University Press, 1989), 198–202; Hurston, *Mules and Men*, 44. For examples of rural music in Alabama, listen to Birmingham Jubilee Singers, *Birmingham Jubilee Singers, Volume 1 (1926–1927)*, DOCD-5345 and *Birmingham Jubilee Singers, Volume 2 (1927–1930)*, DOCD-5346.

80. Brooks, *You May Plow Here*, 174–76; Hicks interview; Paul K. Edwards, *The Southern Urban Negro as a Consumer* (New York: Prentice-Hall, 1932; reprint, College Park, Md.: McGrath, 1969), 7–8; Kelley, *Race Rebels*, 45.

81. Brooks, *You May Plow Here*, 175–76.

82. Rosengarten, *All God's Dangers*, 221–26 (quote on 223); Pete Daniel, *Breaking the Land: The Transformation of Cotton, Tobacco, and Rice Cultures since 1880* (Urbana: University of Illinois Press, 1985), 12–13; Marks, *Farewell*, 57–59.

83. Scott, *Negro Migration*, 41–46 (quote on 46).

84. Kirby, *Rural Worlds Lost*, 287–88; D. Clark, "Family Oral History"; Arvah E. Strickland, "The Strange Affair of the Boll Weevil: The Pest as Liberator," *Agricultural History* 68 (Spring 1994): 162–66.

85. Scott, *Negro Migration*, 13 (first quote); "Southern Negroes in Cleveland Industries," *Monthly Labor Review* 19 (July 1924): 42; Early Surveys, series 6, box 88, National Negro Welfare Association, Cleveland Branch, National Urban League Records, Library of Congress, Washington, D.C. (second quote).

86. For examples of those arguing that violence was not the primary reason for black migration, see Stewart E. Tolnay and E. M. Beck, "Black Flight: Lethal Violence and the Great Migration, 1900–1930," *Social Science History* 14 (Fall 1990): 347–70; Kiser, *Sea Island to City*; Charles S. Johnson, "How Much Is the Migration a Flight from Persecution?" *Opportunity* 1 (Sept. 1923): 272–74. For a critique, see Arthur Raper, *The Tragedy of Lynching* (Chapel Hill: University of North Carolina Press, 1933); Walter White, *Rope and Faggot: A Biography of Judge Lynch* (New York: Alfred A. Knopf, 1929); McMillen, *Dark Journey*, 30–31; Emmett J. Scott, "Documents on Negro Migrants," *Journal of Negro History* 4 (July 1919): 439–50; B. Cruce, "Family Oral History" (undergraduate paper, Cleveland State University, 1978); and Kenneth W. Goings and Gerald L. Smith, "'Unhidden' Transcripts: Memphis and African American Agency, 1862–1920," *Journal of Urban History* 21 (Mar. 1995): 372–94.

87. Scott, "Documents on Negro Migrants," 439–50.

88. Quote from Wilbur H. Watson, *The Village: An Oral Historical and Ethnographic Study of a Black Community* (Cleveland: Village Vanguard, 1989), 18; Higgs, *Competition and Coercion*; Brooks, *You May Plow Here*, 62–63, 129–32; Hicks interview. For an important discussion of the African-American cultural resistance to racial violence and segregation, see Kelley, *Hammer and Hoe*, 92–93, and *Race Rebels*.

89. James R. Robinson, "The Negro Migration," *Social Service News* 1 (July 1917): 100.

90. Rice, *He Included Me*, 26. For a discussion of the role of the *Chicago Defender* in black migration between 1915 and 1918, see Roi Ottley, *The Lonely Warrior: The Life*

and Times of Robert S. Abbott (Chicago: Henry Regnery, 1955), chap. 10; Scott, *Negro Migration,* 29–30, 33; W. E. B. Du Bois, "Migration and Help," *Crisis* 13 (Jan. 1917): 115; and Bertha Cowan, interview by Eleanor Jackson, Cleveland, Jan. 17, 1987, transcript, St. James A.M.E. Oral History Project.

91. Rice, *He Included Me,* 12. For efforts to prevent black mobility in Natchez and the Delta, see McMillen, *Dark Journey,* 272–73; Cohen, *At Freedom's Edge,* 271; Hunter, *To 'Joy My Freedom;* and Cindy Hahamovitch, *The Fruits of Their Labor: Atlantic Coast Farmworkers and the Making of Migrant Poverty, 1870–1945* (Chapel Hill: University of North Carolina Press, 1997), 79.

92. Rosengarten, *All God's Dangers,* 295, 296.

93. Fligstein, *Going North,* 64–65; Morgan interview.

94. Hopson interview.

95. Geneva Robinson, interview by Inez Bentyn, Cleveland, Nov. 4, 1986, transcript, St. James A.M.E. Oral History Project.

96. For a calculation of fare prices, see Florette Henri, *Black Migration: Movement North, 1900–1920* (Garden City, N.Y.: Anchor Press, 1975), 66. For the difficulties in purchasing tickets, see Rice, *He Included Me,* 12; Brooks, *You May Plow Here,* 195–96; and Allen Cole to Frances Tillie Cole, Feb. 23, 1918, and July 23, 1918, Allen Cole Papers, WRHS.

97. *Cleveland Gazette,* Jan. 13, 1917; U.S. Department of Labor, *Negro Migration,* 27–28; Scott, *Negro Migration,* 47–48; Kennedy, *Negro Peasant Turns Cityward,* 53; Marks, *Farewell,* 21–25; Hicks interview; Patricia Blackmon, "The Black Railroad Worker: Through Personal Accounts and Narratives" (undergraduate seminar paper, Cleveland State University, 1990), 3–4.

98. Scott, *Negro Migration,* 46; Cleveland Urban League, "Report of the Executive Secretary, Mar. 18 to Apr. 18, 1919," Cleveland Urban League Records, WRHS; Rice, *He Included Me,* 12.

99. Scott, *Negro Migration,* 41; Joiner interview; Flowree Robinson interview. Emmett J. Scott estimated that between 70 and 80 percent of migrants paid for their fares through savings and other means.

100. F. Cheney, "Family Oral History"; M. Christian, "Family Oral History" (undergraduate paper, Cleveland State University, 1978); M. Davis, "Family Oral History"; Blackmon, "Black Railroad Worker," 3–4 (quote).

101. Gottlieb, *Making Their Own Way,* 46; Darlene Clark Hine, "Black Migration to the Urban Midwest: The Gender Dimension, 1915–1945," in *The Great Migration in Historical Perspective,* 132; Cowan interview.

102. For blacks' communal condemnation of abusive and lazy men, see Brooks, *You May Plow Here,* 162–70; and Rosengarten, *All God's Dangers,* 206–12. For admiration of hardworking men, even as gamblers, see J. L. Chestnut Jr. with Julia Cass, *Black in Selma: The Uncommon Life of J. L. Chestnut Jr.: Politics and Power in a Small American Town* (New York: Farrar, Straus, and Giroux, 1990), 8–18; Levine, *Black Culture and Black Consciousness,* 397–440.

103. Flowree Robinson interview; Melvia Green, interview by Patricia Miles Ashford, n.d.; Hicks interview; Murtis H. Taylor, interview by Earlynne Davis, Cleveland, Oct. 19, 1986, transcript, St. James A.M.E. Oral History Project.

104. Brooks, *You May Plow Here,* 215–16; Hine, "Black Migration," 132; Flowree Robinson interview; Taylor interview; R. Flowers, "Family Oral History."

105. Carrie Davenport Turner, interview by Etta M. Lovejoy, Cleveland, Aug. 27, 1986, transcript, St. James A.M.E. Oral History Project; Jones, *Labor of Love, Labor of Sorrow,* 155. For an account of how the lack of education stalled long-distance movement for some African Americans, see Brooks, *You May Plow Here,* 153–54; Marks, *Farewell,* 35–36; Linton Freeman interview; and Cowan interview.

106. Jones, *Labor of Love, Labor of Sorrow,* 159; Kenneth L. Kusmer, *A Ghetto Takes Shape: Black Cleveland, 1870–1930* (Urbana: University of Illinois Press, 1976), 159.

107. B. Clark, "Family Oral History"; Langston Hughes, *The Big Sea* (New York: Hill and Wang, 1941), 27; Hopson interview. Ideas of religiosity have been a common element in African-Americans' accounts of migration. See, for example, McMillen, *Dark Journey,* 264–65; and *Cleveland Advocate,* Apr. 28, 1917.

108. U.S. Department of Labor, Division of Negro Economics, *The Negro at Work during the World War and during Reconstruction* (Washington, D.C.: Government Printing Office, 1921), 51, 52–53, 62–65; Scott, *Negro Migration,* 72–85.

109. *Chicago Defender,* July 29, 1923. For documentation of post–World War I migration, see W. E. B. Du Bois, "Brothers, Come North," *Crisis* 19 (Jan. 1920): 105; "Negro Migration," *Monthly Labor Review* 16 (June 1923): 34; Kennedy, *Negro Peasant Turns Cityward,* 35; U.S. Bureau of the Census, *Negroes in the United States,* 55 (table 10); Fligstein, *Going North,* 83–86.

110. Linton Freeman interview; Ashford interview, n.d.

111. U.S. Department of Labor, *Negro Migration,* 100; Flowree Robinson interview; Brooks, *You May Plow Here,* 195.

112. Johnson, *Shadow of the Plantation,* 31; Jesse Owens with Paul G. Neimark, *Blackthink: My Life as Black Man and White Man* (New York: William Morrow, 1970), 30–35.

113. Johnson, *Shadow of the Plantation,* 107 (quotes), 113–19.

114. Brooks, *You May Plow Here,* 171–83; Johnson, *Shadow of the Plantation,* 113–15; Nell Irvin Painter, *The Narrative of Hosea Hudson: His Life as a Negro Communist in the South* (Cambridge, Mass.: Harvard University Press, 1979), 61–66.

115. Ruff, *A Call to Assembly,* 22–25, 67–71.

Chapter 2: Encountering Work

1. Cleveland Chamber of Commerce, Committee on Industrial Welfare, minutes, May 18, 1917, Records of the Greater Cleveland Growth Association, Western Reserve Historical Society, Cleveland (hereafter WRHS); "Letters from Migrants," Early Surveys, series 6, box 88, National Negro Welfare Association, Cleveland Branch, National Urban League Records, Library of Congress, Washington, D.C. (second quote); Emmett J. Scott, "Letters of Negro Migrants," *Journal of Negro History* 4 (July 1919): 290–340; Emmett J. Scott, "Additional Letters of Negro Migrants," *Journal of Negro History* 4 (Oct. 1919): 412–65; Sara Brooks, *You May Plow Here: The Narrative of Sara Brooks,* ed. Thordis Simonsen (New York: Simon and Schuster, 1987); Emmett J. Scott, *Negro Migration during the War* (New York: Oxford University Press, 1920; reprint, New York: Arno Press, 1969), 57; Maurine Weiner Greenwald, *Women, War, and Work: The Impact of World War I on Women Workers in the United States* (Westport, Conn.: Greenwood Press, 1980), 113; Gus Joiner, interview by author, Cleveland, Oct. 2, 1989, transcript; Bertha Cowan, interview by Eleanor Jackson, Cleveland, Jan. 16, 1987, transcript, St. James A.M.E. Oral History Project, WRHS; Patricia Blackmon, "The Black

Railroad Worker: Through Personal Accounts and Narratives" (undergraduate seminar paper, Cleveland State University, 1990), 2–3.

2. Kenneth L. Kusmer, *A Ghetto Takes Shape: Black Cleveland, 1870–1930* (Urbana: University of Illinois Press, 1976), 190–203; U.S. Bureau of the Census, *Thirteenth Census of the United States, 1910: Population,* vol. 4, *Occupations* (Washington, D.C.: Government Printing Office, 1913), 1084–87; U.S. Bureau of the Census, *Fourteenth Census of the United States, 1920: Population,* vol. 4, *Occupations* (Washington, D.C.: Government Printing Office, 1922), 1084–87.

3. Quoted in Raymond Boryczka and Lorin Lee Cary, *No Strength without Union: An Illustrated History of Ohio Workers, 1803–1989* (Columbus: Ohio Historical Society, 1982), 141–42.

4. *Cleveland Press,* July 30, 1925.

5. For a discussion of the informal hiring practices of black workers in the North, see Daniel Nelson, *Managers and Workers: Origins of the New Factory System in the United States, 1880–1920* (Madison: University of Wisconsin Press, 1975), 147–48; Peter Gottlieb, *Making Their Own Way: Southern Blacks' Migration to Pittsburgh, 1916–30* (Urbana: University of Illinois Press, 1987), 89–112. For a description of meat packers' hiring policies in 1920s Chicago, see Joiner interview.

6. Kusmer, *A Ghetto Takes Shape,* 203–6; U.S. Bureau of the Census, *Fifteenth Census of the United States, 1930: Population,* vol. 4, *Occupations* (Washington, D.C.: Government Printing Office, 1932), 1285–88.

7. Willa Davenport Thomas, interview by author, Cleveland, Dec. 1, 1989, transcript; Cowan interview.

8. Joe William Trotter Jr., *Black Milwaukee: The Making of an Industrial Proletariat, 1915–1945* (Urbana: University of Illinois Press, 1985); Gottlieb, *Making Their Own Way,* 89–112; James R. Grossman, *Land of Hope: Chicago, Black Southerners, and the Great Migration* (Chicago: University of Chicago Press, 1989).

9. Robin D. G. Kelley, *Race Rebels: Culture, Politics, and the Black Working Class* (New York: Free Press, 1994), esp. 17–34. Kelley's work highlights that the accounts of African-American resistances in the workplace have generally focused on the South and the nineteenth century. See also Eugene Genovese, *Roll, Jordan, Roll: The World the Slaves Made* (New York: Pantheon Books, 1974), 599–621; Peter Kolchin, *Unfree Labor: American Slavery and Russian Serfdom* (Cambridge, Mass.: Harvard University Press, 1987), 241–44; and Alex Lichtenstein, "That Disposition to Theft with which They Have Been Branded: Moral Economy, Slave Management, and the Law," *Journal of Social History* 22 (Spring 1988): 413–40. For patterns of resistance amongst domestic workers, see Tera W. Hunter, *To 'Joy My Freedom: Southern Black Women's Lives and Labors after the Civil War* (Cambridge, Mass.: Harvard University Press, 1997); Jacqueline Jones, *Labor of Love, Labor of Sorrow: Black Women, Work, and the Family from Slavery to the Present* (New York: Basic Books, 1985), 132–33; and Elizabeth Clark-Lewis, *Living In, Living Out: African American Domestics in Washington, D.C., 1910–1940* (Washington, D.C.: Smithsonian Institution, 1994), 110–11.

10. Historians of African Americans in the northern context have paid little, if any, attention to patterns of black resistance in the workplace. Notable exceptions are accounts of black men in the hide cellars of the stockyards. See James R. Barrett, *Work and Community in the Jungle: Chicago's Packinghouse Workers, 1894–1922* (Urbana: University of Illinois Press, 1987), 158–59; and Rick Halpern, "The Iron Fist and the

Velvet Glove: Welfare Capitalism in Chicago's Packinghouses, 1921–1933," *Journal of American Studies* 26 (Summer 1992): 159–83.

11. Harold C. Livesy, "From Steeples to Smokestacks: The Birth of the Modern Corporation in Cleveland," in *The Birth of Modern Cleveland, 1865–1930,* ed. Thomas F. Campbell and Edward M. Miggins (Cleveland: Western Reserve Historical Society, 1988), 54–62; John J. Grabowski and David D. Van Tassel, eds. *The Encyclopedia of Cleveland History* (Bloomington: Indiana University Press, 1987); Walter E. Pagan, *Cleveland: Some of the Features of the Industry and Commerce of the City* (Cleveland: n.p., 1917), 16–17, 34–35; Ronald R. Weiner and Carol A. Beal, "The Sixth City: Cleveland in Three Stages of Urbanization," in *The Birth of Modern Cleveland,* 24–53.

12. Edward M. Miggins and Mary Morgenthaler, "The Ethnic Mosaic: The Settlement of Cleveland by the New Immigrants and Migrants," in *The Birth of Modern Cleveland,* 105; David E. Green, *The City and Its People* (Cleveland: n.p., 1917), 7; Weiner and Beal, "The Sixth City," 50; R. R. Lutz, *The Metal Trades* (Cleveland: Cleveland Education Survey, 1916), 159–61; James R. Green, *The World of the Worker: Labor in Twentieth Century America* (New York: Hill and Wang, 1980); David Montgomery, *The Fall of the House of Labor: The Workplace, the State, and American Labor Activism, 1865–1925* (Cambridge: Cambridge University Press, 1987), 40–47.

13. Kusmer, *A Ghetto Takes Shape,* 66–76, esp. 66–68; Charles W. Chesnutt, "The Negro in Cleveland," *The Clevelander* 5 (Nov. 1930): 3–4.

14. Elmer Thompson, interview by Thomas F. Campbell, in Thomas F. Campbell, "Speech Sound Recording: On the History of Cleveland," Cleveland Heritage Program, 1981, transcript, Cleveland Public Library.

15. Kusmer, *A Ghetto Takes Shape,* 66–68. For comparisons of black and white women's employment patterns and experiences, see Alice Kessler-Harris, *Out to Work: A History of Wage-Earning Women in the United States* (New York: Oxford University Press, 1982); Leslie Woodcock Tentler, *Wage-Earning Women: Industrial Work and Family Life in the United States, 1900–1930* (New York: Oxford University Press, 1979); Barbara Klaczynska, "Why Women Work: A Comparison of Various Groups—Philadelphia, 1910–1930," *Labor History* 17 (Winter 1976): 73–87; Greenwald, *Women, War, and Work,* 3–45; Jones, *Labor of Love, Labor of Sorrow;* Angela Y. Davis, *Women, Race, and Class* (New York: Random House, 1981).

16. Consumers' League of Cleveland Investigation Committee, *A Study of Women's Work in Cleveland* (Cleveland: Consumers' League of Cleveland, ca. 1908), 11–13.

17. "A Report on a Limited Preliminary Inquiry Regarding Some Conditions of the Colored Population of Cleveland," Feb. 10, 1914, Karamu House Records, WRHS; "How Cleveland Handled Employment," *Survey* 34 (Aug. 14, 1915): 443.

18. Lutz, *The Metal Trades,* 40–41; *Cleveland Advocate,* Mar. 1, 1919; Blackmon, "Black Railroad Worker," 3–6; memorandum to C. E. Briggs, May 15, 1917, Karamu House Records.

19. Memorandum to C. E. Briggs.

20. Ibid.; Admiral Kilpatrick, interview, Cleveland, June 8, 1980, transcript, Abraham Lincoln Brigade Archives, Brandeis University, Waltham, Mass. I am indebted to Robin Kelley for bringing this interview to my attention. Naomi Morgan, interview by Emily Lasiter, Cleveland, Dec. 12, 1986, transcript, St. James A.M.E. Oral History Project.

21. Memorandum to C. E. Briggs; Florence E. Clark, "Investigation of Cleveland Scrap Yards," June 10, 1919, and Nov. 19, 1919, documents 42–43, series 152A, Collinwood Shops, New York Central Railroad, Cleveland, Women's Service Section, U.S. Railroad Administration Records, RG 14, National Archives, Washington, D.C.; Cowan interview.

22. Cleveland Chamber of Commerce, *Cleveland Chamber of Commerce Annual Report, 1923* (Cleveland: n.p., 1923), 77; J. O. Houze, "Negro Labor and the Industries," *Opportunity* 1 (Jan. 1923): 21; Cleveland Urban League, "Report of the Executive Secretary, Mar. 18 to Apr. 18, 1919," Cleveland Urban League Records, WRHS. On hiring policies in other cities, see Sterling D. Spero and Abram L. Harris, *The Black Worker: The Negro and the Labor Movement* (New York: Columbia University Press, 1931; reprint, New York: Atheneum, 1969), 161–62; Montgomery, *Fall of the House of Labor,* 381–82; Gottlieb, *Making Their Own Way,* 111; and Grossman, *Land of Hope,* 183–85. For organization of labor in the steel industry, see "Problem of the Negro Laborer," *Iron Trade Review* 60 (Apr. 1917): 836–37; John T. Clark, "The Negro in Steel," *Opportunity* 4 (Oct. 1924): 87–88; Katherine Stone, "The Origin of Job Structures in the Steel Industry," *Review of Radical Political Economy* 6 (Winter 1976): 115–60; and David Brody, *Steelworkers in America: The Nonunion Era* (Cambridge, Mass: Harvard University Press, 1960).

23. *Cleveland Advocate,* Sept. 16, 1918.

24. Cleveland Urban League, "Annual Report, Jan., 1931," Cleveland Urban League Records; Sanford Jacoby, *Employing Bureaucracy: Managers, Unions, and the Transformation of Work in American Industry, 1900–1945* (New York: Columbia University Press, 1985), 151; August Meier and Elliott Rudwick, *Black Detroit and the Rise of the UAW* (New York: Oxford University Press, 1979); Blackmon, "Black Railroad Worker," 6.

25. For hiring patterns of African Americans on the railroads, see Eric Arnesen, "'Like Banquo's Ghost, It Will Not Down': The Race Question and the American Railroad Brotherhoods, 1880–1920," *American Historical Review* 99 (Dec. 1994): 1608; Montgomery, *Fall of the House of Labor,* 365–66; Colin J. Davis, "The 1922 Railroad Shopmen's Strike in the Southeast: A Study of Success and Failure," in *Organized Labor in the Twentieth Century South,* ed. Robert Zeiger (Knoxville: University of Tennessee Press, 1991), 113–43; Blackmon, "Black Railroad Worker," 4–6.

26. "Cleveland's Employment Service," *Survey* 44 (May 15, 1920): 247–48; Houze, "Negro Labor," 21. For examples of ads, see *Cleveland Gazette,* May 19, 1917, and *Cleveland Plain Dealer,* Aug. 10, 1919.

27. On the role of foreman, see Whiting Williams, *What's on the Worker's Mind: By One Who Put on Overalls to Find Out* (New York: Charles Scribner's Sons, 1920). For a description of the Pittsburgh mills, see Gottlieb, *Making Their Own Way,* 82. See also Nelson, *Managers and Workers,* 34–54; and U.S. Department of Labor, Division of Negro Economics, *The Negro at Work during the World War and during Reconstruction* (Washington, D.C.: Government Printing Office, 1921), 109–10.

28. Andrea Graziosi, "Common Laborers, Unskilled Workers: 1880–1915," *Labor History* 22 (Fall 1981): 512–44; Houze, "Negro Labor," 21 (first and second quotes); Herman Feldman, *Racial Factors in American Industry* (New York: Harper and Brothers, 1931), 47–50, 54 (third quote).

29. Horace R. Cayton and George S. Mitchell, *Black Workers and the New Unions*

(Chapel Hill: University of North Carolina Press, 1939), 26–27 (first quote on 27); Cleveland Urban League, "1918 Report to the Board of Trustees," Cleveland Urban League Records (second and third quotes); Philip S. Foner, *Organized Labor and the Black Worker, 1619–1973* (New York: Praeger, 1974), 390 (fourth quote); "Southern Negroes in Cleveland Industries," *Monthly Labor Review* 19 (July 1924): 41–44.

30. Gottlieb, *Making Their Own Way,* 94–96; Kusmer, *A Ghetto Takes Shape,* 191; Spero and Harris, *The Black Worker,* 174; Cleveland Chamber of Commerce Committee on Housing and Sanitation, *An Investigation of Housing Conditions of War Workers in Cleveland* (Cleveland: n.p., 1918), 28.

31. *Cleveland Advocate,* Sept. 21, 1918 (quote); Cayton and Mitchell, *Black Workers,* 28; Cleveland Urban League, "Report of the Executive Secretary, Mar. 18 to Apr. 18, 1919"; John A. Garraty, ed., *The Barber and the Historian: The Correspondence of George A. Myers and James Ford Rhodes, 1910–1923* (Columbus: Ohio Historical Society, 1956), xxi.

32. For evidence of segregated shops in Cleveland, see *Cleveland Advocate,* Aug. 31, 1918, Sept. 21, 1918, Sept. 28, 1918. For patterns in other cities, see Gottlieb, *Making Their Own Way,* 89. For different conclusions on employers' conscious effort to exploit racial and ethnic antagonisms, see Cayton and Mitchell, *Black Workers,* 45–48.

33. William C. Liller, "Preliminary Report of Commissioner of Conciliation," July 5, 1919, Otis Steel Company, Cleveland, Ohio, RG 280, U.S. Conciliation Service in *Black Workers in the Era of the Great Migration, 1916–1929,* ed. James R. Grossman (Frederick, Md.: University Publications of America, 1985), reel 1; Cleveland Urban League, "Executive Secretary's Report, Nov., 1918," Cleveland Urban League Records; Greenwald, *Women, War, and Work,* 162–63.

34. "Southern Negroes in Cleveland's Industries," 41–44.

35. Houze, "Negro Labor," 20 (first and third quotes); Clark, "Negro in Steel," 87 (second quote); Scott, *Negro Migration,* 114–17 (fourth and fifth quotes on 116).

36. Scott, *Negro Migration,* 42 (first quote), 117 (second and third quotes).

37. "Southern Negroes in Cleveland's Industries," 42; Thomas J. Woofter Jr., "The Negro and Industrial Peace," *Survey* 38 (Dec. 18, 1920): 420.

38. Lucian W. Chaney, "Trend of Accident Frequency Rates in the Iron and Steel Industry during the World War," *Monthly Labor Review* 5 (Nov. 1917): 848; Nelson, *Managers and Workers,* 30; U.S. Senate, "Report on Labor Conditions in Iron and Steel Industry," 62d Cong., 1st sess., S. Doc. 110, 1911, vol. 3 of "Working Conditions and the Relations of Employers and Employees," 90–91; Margaret Bourke-White, *Portrait of Myself* (New York: Simon and Schuster, 1963), 53; Langston Hughes, *The Big Sea* (New York: Hill and Wang, 1941), 27; *Cleveland Advocate,* Nov. 16, 1918, Mar. 1, 1919; Lutz, *The Metal Trades,* 40–42.

39. Cleveland Chamber of Commerce, "Minutes from the Committee on Labor Relations," May 8, 1918, Records of the Greater Cleveland Growth Association (quote); *Naco News,* n.d., Records of the National Malleable Steel Castings Company, WRHS; *Cleveland Gazette,* May 26, 1917; *Cleveland Plain Dealer,* Aug. 16, 1919.

40. William Conners quoted in Diane Meisenhelter, "Federal Initiatives, Local Responses: The Legacy of Wartime Substitution in Industrial Work, Cincinnatti, 1914–1980," paper presented at the annual meeting of the Social Science History Association, Nov. 11, 1989, Washington, D.C., 15 (fourth and fifth quotes); Cleveland Urban League, "1918 Report to the Board of Trustees"; *Cleveland Advocate,* Aug. 31, 1918 (sixth quote); Scott, *Negro Migration,* 54. For a similar role in other cities, see Joyce Shaw

Peterson, "Black Automobile Workers in Detroit, 1910–30," *Journal of Negro History* 64 (Summer 1979): 178. Haynes's card, "Why He Failed," was an excerpt from his Fourth of July address delivered in 1918, quoted in U.S. Department of Labor, Division of Negro Economics, *Negro at Work,* 138.

41. U.S. Women's Bureau, *Women in Alabama Industries,* Women's Bureau Bulletin no. 34 (Washington, D.C.: Government Printing Office, 1924), 54.

42. "Accomplishments of the Negro Welfare Association from Oct. 1, 1919 to July 31, 1920," box 3, folder 1, Cleveland Urban League Records; Interchurch World Movement, *Report on the Steel Strike of 1919* (New York: Harcourt, Brace, and Howe, 1920), 152–53.

43. *Cleveland Advocate,* Aug. 31, 1918, Sept. 21, 1918, Sept. 28, 1918. For a general discussion of unskilled workers' responses to workplace conditions before the war, see Montgomery, *Fall of the House of Labor,* 96–109.

44. *Cleveland Advocate,* Sept. 16, 1918.

45. "Training Opportunities for Women to Meet Emergency of War," n.d., Ohio Branch of the Council of National Defense, General Files, series 1135, box 8, folder 7, Ohio Historical Society, Columbus (hereafter OHS); "Women in Industry," Dec. 1917, Ohio Branch of the Council of National Defense, General Files, series 1135, box 17, folder 15, OHS. An important example of the response to the substitution of women in men's jobs can be seen in the strike of streetcar conductors. See Greenwald, *Women, War, and Work,* 162–63.

46. "Present Condition of the Woman Labor Supply in the Factories in Cleveland," Dec. 1917, Ohio Branch of the Council of National Defense, General Files, series 1135, box 17, OHS.

47. Cleveland Urban League, "Report of the Executive Secretary, Mar. 18 to Apr. 18, 1919"; Jean Collier Brown, *The Negro Woman Worker* (Washington, D.C.: Women's Bureau, 1938), 10–11 (quote). For a discussion of prewar control of pressing by men, see Edna Bryner, *The Garment Trades* (Cleveland: Survey Committee of the Cleveland Foundation, 1916), 50; "Negro Wage Earners in Ohio," in U.S. Department of Labor, Division of Negro Economics, *Negro at Work,* 108–9; Cleveland Urban League, "Report for the Cleveland Welfare Association and the Negro Welfare Association, Dec. 14, 1917," Cleveland Urban League Records; and Cleveland Urban League, "Executive Secretary's Report, Nov., 1918."

48. Clark, "Investigation of Cleveland Scrap Yards." For a general discussion of women railroad workers during the war, see Greenwald, *Women, War, and Work,* 106–16.

49. Greenwald, *Women, War, and Work,* 107; "Training Opportunities for Women to Meet Emergency of War"; Boryczka and Cary, *No Strength without Union,* 143; Greenwald, *Women, War, and Work,* 107.

50. "Training Opportunities for Women to Meet Emergency of War"; Clark, "Investigation of Cleveland Scrap Yards."

51. Clark, "Investigation of Cleveland Scrap Yards"; Florence E. Clark to F. J. McMahon, June 14, 1919, document 44, series 152A, Collinwood Shops, New York Central Railroad, Cleveland, Cleaners, Laborers, and Machinists' Helpers, Women's Service Section, U.S. Railroad Administration Records (quote).

52. Florence E. Clark, memoranda, June 18, 1919, documents 55–57, series 152A, Collinwood Shops, New York Central Railroad, Cleveland, Women's Service Section, U.S. Railroad Administration Records.

53. Ibid.; Florence E. Clark, memorandum, June 27, 1919, document 58, series 152A, Collinwood Shops, New York Central Railroad, Cleveland, Women's Service Section, U.S. Railroad Administration Records.

54. Florence E. Clark, memorandum, June 10, 1919, document 12, series 152A, Collinwood Shops, New York Central Railroad, Cleveland, Women's Service Section, U.S. Railroad Administration Records; Clark, "Investigation of Cleveland Scrap Yards."

55. Arnesen, "'Like Banquo's Ghost, It Will Not Down,'" 1608.

56. Florence E. Clark, memoranda, June 18, 1919, June 19, 1919, and June 27, 1919, documents 55–58, series 152A, Collinwood Shops, New York Central Railroad, Cleveland, Women's Service Section, U.S. Railroad Administration Records.

57. U.S. Department of Labor, Division of Negro Economics, *Negro at Work*, 404 (quote); Consumers' League of Cleveland Investigation Committee, *Study of Women's Work*, 5–6; Jones, *Labor of Love, Labor of Sorrow*, 177–78. On the growth of the mechanized laundries, see Frederick Francis DeArmond, *The Laundry Industry* (New York: Harper, 1950), 1–15.

58. Consumers' League of Cleveland Investigation Committee, *Study of Women's Work*, 5 (first and second quotes), 6 (third and fourth quotes); DeArmond, *Laundry Industry*, 113–15; Henry Pointer, interview by Antoinette Kindall, Cleveland, Oct. 30, 1986, transcript, St. James A.M.E. Oral History Project; Sallie Hopson, interview by Antoinette Kindall, Cleveland, Aug. 26, 1986, transcript, St. James A.M.E. Oral History Project; Bertha Holt, interview by Earlynne Davis, Cleveland, Dec. 5, 1986, transcript, St. James A.M.E. Oral History Project; Marie Crawford, interview by Doris Crawford, Cleveland, Sept. 29, 1986, transcript, St. James A.M.E. Oral History Project. For comparisons with other cities, see Jones, *Labor of Love, Labor of Sorrow*, 177–78.

59. Women's Division of the Cleveland State-City Employment Service, *Annual Report* (Cleveland: n.p., 1915), 1; Cowan interview; Margie Glass, interview by Antoinette Kindall, Cleveland, Dec. 12, 1986, transcript, St. James A.M.E. Oral History Project; Cleveland Urban League, "Report of the Executive Secretary, Mar. 18 to Apr. 18, 1919."

60. Cleveland Urban League, "Report of the Executive Secretary, Mar. 18 to Apr. 18, 1919"; Mary Louise Williams, "The Negro Working Woman: What She Faces in Making a Living," *The Messenger* 5 (July 1923): 763.

61. Houze, "Negro Labor," 21; U.S. Department of Labor, Division of Negro Economics, *Negro at Work*, 107.

62. Hughes, *The Big Sea*, 32. For examples of shifts in advertisements, see *Cleveland Plain Dealer*, Aug. 16, 1919, Aug. 29, 1919; Cleveland Chamber of Commerce Committee on Unemployment, minutes, Feb. 20, 1919, Records of the Greater Cleveland Growth Association; and Cleveland Urban League, minutes, Nov. 30, 1929, Cleveland Urban League Records.

63. Charles E. Hall, "Report from the Supervisor of Negro Economics," in U.S. Department of Labor, Division of Negro Economics, *Negro at Work*, 114–15; Cleveland Urban League, Summary of Activities, 1922–24, Cleveland Urban League Records.

64. Kusmer, *A Ghetto Takes Shape*, 201–3; U.S. Bureau of the Census, *Fifteenth Census*, 1285–88.

65. Cleveland Urban League, "Report of the Executive Secretary, Jan., Feb., Mar., 1922"; Cleveland Urban League, "Annual Report, 1924," Cleveland Urban League

Records; Spero and Harris, *The Black Worker*, 157; U.S. Bureau of the Census, *Fifteenth Census*, 1285–86; U.S. Bureau of Labor Statistics, *Handbook of Labor Statistics, 1924–26*, Bulletin no. 439 (Washington, D.C.: Government Printing Office, 1926), 401; Jacoby, *Employing Bureaucracy*, 171–72; "Wage Rates In Steel," *Iron Age* 144 (Jan. 4, 1940): 165.

66. *Cleveland Press*, July 30, 1925. For studies by economists, see Richard C. Edwards, Michael Reich, and David M. Gordon, eds., *Labor Market Segmentation* (Lexington, Mass.: D. C. Heath, 1975); Richard C. Edwards, *Contested Terrain: The Transformation of the Workplace in the Twentieth Century* (New York: Basic Books, 1979); Sanford M. Jacoby, ed., *Masters to Managers: Historical and Comparative Perspectives on American Employers* (New York: Columbia University Press, 1991); and Walter Licht, *Getting Work: Philadelphia, 1840–1950* (Cambridge, Mass.: Harvard University Press, 1992).

67. Allen M. Wakstein, "The Origins of the Open-Shop Movement, 1919–1920," *Journal of American History* 51 (Dec. 1964): 462.

68. Nelson, *Managers and Workers*, 76–77; Mary Barnett Gilson, *What's Past Is Prologue* (New York: Harper, 1940), 57–59; Richard A. Feiss, "Personal Relationship as a Basis of Scientific Management," *Bulletin of the Taylor Society* 1 (Nov. 1915): 5–15; "Cleveland's Employment Service," 247–48; R. L. Duffus, "Cleveland: Paternalism in Excelsis," *New Republic,* Apr. 1928, 212–16.

69. Houze, "Negro Labor," 21.

70. Ibid.; *Cleveland Press*, July 30, 1925 (quote); Nelson, *Managers and Workers*, 112, 118; Stuart D. Brandes, *American Welfare Capitalism, 1880–1940* (Chicago: University of Chicago Press, 1976), 112. For a description of shackrousters in the South, see Edwin L. Brown, "'. . . To Make a Man Feel Good': John Henry Mealing, Railroad Caller," *Labor History* 27 (Spring 1986): 263.

71. A. S. Rodgers, "Cleveland's Intangible Values," *The Clevelander* 4 (Oct. 1929): 20 (first and second quotes); R. E. Whitney, "In Line for a Job," *The Clevelander* 1 (Jan. 1927): 26 (third quote).

72. Montgomery, *Fall of the House of Labor*, 58–111; Harry Braverman, *Labor and Monopoly Capital: The Degradation of Work in the Twentieth Century* (New York: Monthly Review Press, 1974), 383–401.

73. Harvey A. Wooster and Theodore Whiting, *Fluctuations in Employment in Cleveland and Cuyahoga County, 1923–1928: A Statistical Survey* (Ann Arbor: University of Michigan Press, 1930), 69; "Employment Conditions and Problems: Unemployment of Males in Ohio as Measured by Fluctuation of Employment, 1924 to 1928," *Monthly Labor Review* 30 (Apr. 1930): 57–62.

74. Joiner interview; Selmer Prewitt, interview by author, Cleveland, Mar. 7, 1991, transcript; Paul Glenn, interview by author, June 18, 1991, Cleveland, transcript; Daniel Jerome, interview by Patricia Miles Ashford, Cleveland, Oct. 15, 1989, transcript in Ashford's possession; Vincent Easter, interview by Patricia Miles Ashford, Cleveland, Oct. 15, 1989, transcript in Ashford's possession. I thank Patricia Miles Ashford for sharing these interviews with me.

75. U.S. Bureau of the Census, *Fourteenth Census*, 1085; U.S. Bureau of the Census, *Fifteenth Census*, 1286. Delivery men in bakeries and stores are not included in transportation work. Harold Barger, *The Transportation Industries, 1889–1946: A Study*

of Output, Employment, and Productivity (New York: National Bureau of Economic Research, 1951); Christine McNeal, telephone interview by author, Mar. 3, 1991, transcript; Prewitt interview.

76. Chester Himes, *The Quality of Hurt: The Autobiography of Chester Himes* (New York: Doubleday, 1972), 1:17; Chesnutt, "Negro in Cleveland," 3; U.S. Bureau of the Census, *Fourteenth Census,* 1086; U.S. Bureau of the Census, *Fifteenth Census,* 1287; Hughes, *The Big Sea,* 32; *Cleveland Gazette,* Oct. 3, 1931.

77. Cleveland Urban League, "Annual Report, 1927"; Murtis H. Taylor, interview by Earlynne Davis, Cleveland, Oct. 19, 1986, transcript, St. James A.M.E. Oral History Project; Eleanor Walls Grist, interview by author, Cleveland, Aug. 22, 1989, transcript.

78. Federation of Community Planning Committee on Inquiry into the Homeless Situation, minutes, Feb. 9, 1926, Feb. 17, 1927; and Franklin R. McKeever, secretary, Wayfarers' Lodge, to Committee on Inquiry into the Homeless Situation, Feb. 2, 1927, both in Federation of Community Planning Records, WRHS.

79. Mary Helen Washington, *Invented Lives: Narratives of Black Women* (Garden City, N.Y.: Doubleday, 1987), xxi; Josephus Hicks, interview by author, Cleveland, Nov. 14, 1990, transcript; Joseph A. Hill, "Recent Northward Migration of the Negro," *Labor Review* 18 (July 14): 1–14; U.S. Bureau of the Census, *Fifteenth Census,* 1287–88. For a discussion of the changes in women's occupational shifts, see Kessler-Harris, *Out to Work,* 217–49, esp. 236–37; Jones, *Labor of Love, Labor of Sorrow,* 162–86.

80. On married black women's employment patterns, see Jones, *Labor of Love, Labor of Sorrow,* 166–82. For an overview of a case study of home-based work, see Eileen Boris, "Black Women and Paid Labor in the Home: Industrial Homework in Chicago in the 1920s," in *Homework: Historical and Contemporary Perspectives on Paid Labor at Home,* ed. Eileen Boris and Cynthia R. Daniels (Urbana: University of Illinois Press, 1989), 33–47. Outside of laundry, there is little evidence of black women participating in home-based work in Cleveland.

81. U.S. Bureau of the Census, *Fourteenth Census,* 1087; U.S. Bureau of the Census, *Fifteenth Census,* 1287.

82. Feldman, *Racial Factors,* 20; U.S. Bureau of the Census, *Fourteenth Census,* 1087; U.S. Bureau of the Census, *Fifteenth Census,* 1287.

83. Susan Porter Benson, *Counter Cultures: Saleswomen, Managers, and Customers in American Department Stores, 1890–1940* (Chicago: University of Chicago Press, 1986), 206–9, 212, 259; Helen B. Irvin, "Negro Women in Industry, 1918–1919," in Foner, *Organized Labor,* 404; Taylor interview; Pointer interview; Glass interview.

84. Taylor interview; Pointer interview. My interpretation of black women passing as a form of resistance to the cultural construction of race and as an economic, but not social choice has been aided by Amy Robinson's "It Takes One to Know One: Passing and Communities of Common Interest," *Critical Inquiry* 20 (Summer 1994): 715–36. Whites typically depended on blacks to point out other blacks passing as white workers or customers, but blacks did not always mention the deception. Taylor and Pointer each told stories of black women passing not as stories of condemnation, but as stories of pleasure and defiance.

85. Pointer interview (first quote); Glenn interview; U.S. Women's Bureau, *The Effects of Labor Legislation on the Employment Opportunities of Women,* Women's Bureau Bulletin no. 65 (Washington, D.C.: Government Printing Office, 1928), 247–49, 265 (second, third, and fourth quotes on 247).

86. U.S. Women's Bureau, *Effects of Labor Legislation*, 247–49; Patricia Brito, "Protective Labor Legislation in Ohio: The Inter-War Years," *Ohio History* 88 (Spring 1979): 173–97; Kessler-Harris, *Out to Work*, 180–214, esp. 202; Cleveland Urban League, "Monthly Report, Jan. 28, 1927," Cleveland Urban League Records.

87. DeArmond, *Laundry Industry*, 32; Hopson interview; Pointer interview; Willa Davenport Thomas interview; Carter G. Woodson, "The Negro Washerwoman, a Vanishing Figure," *Journal of Negro History* 15 (July 1930): 269.

88. Glass interview; Washington, *Invented Lives*, xxi; Hicks interview.

89. David Katzman, *Seven Days a Week: Women and Domestic Service in Industrializing America* (New York: Oxford University Press, 1978), viii, ix, 51–52, 87; Clark-Lewis, *Living In, Living Out*, 97–172; Consumers' League of Ohio, "Findings of the Conference on 'The Problems of Domestic Work,'" May 7, 1925, Consumers' League of Ohio Records, WRHS; Elizabeth Ross Haynes, "Negroes in Domestic Service in the United States," *Journal of Negro History* 8 (Oct. 1923): 395–98; Emma Thomas, interview by Antoinette Kindall, Cleveland, Nov. 11, 1986, transcript, St. James A.M.E. Church Oral History Project; Cowan interview.

90. Hughes, *The Big Sea*, 27; Louise Pattengall, interview by Antoinette Kindall, Cleveland, Sept. 29, 1986, transcript, St. James A.M.E. Oral History Project.

91. Consumers' League of Ohio, "Findings of the Conference on 'The Problems of Domestic Work'"; Cowan interview. For similar findings in Washington, D.C., see Clark-Lewis, *Living In, Living Out*, 92–172.

92. Women's Division, *Annual Report*, 1; Phillis Wheatley Association, "Minutes of the Board of Trustees of the Phillis Wheatley Association," Feb. 9, 1926, Phillis Wheatley Association Records, WRHS. For a discussion of new appliances in the household, see Ruth S. Cowan, *More Work for Mother: The Ironies of Household Technology from the Open Hearth to the Microwave* (New York: Basic Books, 1983), 89–99, 176–78; Phyllis M. Palmer, "Housewife and Household Worker: Employer-Employee Relationships in the Home, 1928–1941," in *"To Toil the Live Long Day": America's Women at Work, 1780–1980*, ed. Carol Groneman and Mary Beth Norton (Ithaca: Cornell University Press, 1987), 186–91; Haynes, "Negroes in Domestic Service," 416–17, 427–28; Ethel Woodard, interview by Rebecca Steele, Cleveland, Sept. 13, 1986, transcript, St. James A.M.E. Oral History Project.

93. "Minutes of the Employment Committee," Mar. 1, 1926, Phillis Wheatley Association Records; Cowan, *More Work for Mother*, 174; Haynes, "Negroes in Domestic Service," 396, 410–12; Brooks, *You May Plow Here*, 173; Hilary Rose, "Hand, Brain, and Heart," *Signs* 9 (Autumn 1983): 73–90. For a similar argument about migrant women's perspectives on adjusting to domestic work in the upper South, see Clark-Lewis, *Living In, Living Out*, 147–59. For an argument about continuity with work in the South, though with little evidence, see Gottlieb, *Making Their Own Way*, 109.

94. Cowan interview; Brooks, *You May Plow Here*, 198. For changing expectations of northern employers, see Haynes, "Negroes in Domestic Service," 410–11.

95. Mary V. Anderson, "The Plight of Negro Domestic Labor," *Journal of Negro Education* 5 (Jan. 1936): 66; Willa Davenport Thomas interview; Brooks, *You May Plow Here*, 173, 198–99 (quote).

96. Jane Edna Hunter, *A Nickel and a Prayer* (Cleveland: Elli Kani, 1940), 71–72 (quotes); Adrienne Lash Jones, *Jane Edna Hunter: A Case Study of Black Leadership, 1910–1959* (New York: Carlson, 1990).

97. Jones, *Jane Edna Hunter,* 111–13.

98. Hunter, *A Nickel and a Prayer,* 131.

99. Ibid., 161–63; Jones, *Jane Edna Hunter,* 113.

100. Phillis Wheatley Association, "Minutes of the Employment Committee," Apr. 27, 1927, and "Minutes of the Home Economics Committee," Nov. 6, 1928, both in Phillis Wheatley Association Records; Jones, *Jane Edna Hunter,* 114–15.

101. Phillis Wheatley Association, "Minutes of the Home Economics Committee," Dec. 6, 1927 (quotes), and "Minutes of the Employment Committee," Feb. 2, 1926, both in Phillis Wheatley Association Records; Hunter, *A Nickel and a Prayer,* 162.

102. Palmer, "Housewife and Household Worker," 183; Phillis Wheatley Association, "Minutes of the Employment Committee," Feb. 1, 1926, and Nov. 6, 1928, both in Phillis Wheatley Association Records. For middle-class women's responses, see Alice Dunbar-Nelson, "The Problem of Personal Service," *The Messenger* 9 (June 1927): 184.

103. Jane Edna Hunter, "Talk to the Training School Girls," Dec. 19, 1932, Phillis Wheatley Association Records; Hicks interview; Judge Jean Murrell Capers, interview by author and Patricia Miles Ashford, Cleveland, Aug. 8, 1991, tape recording.

104. Middleton interview by author; Willa Davenport Thomas interview; Davis, *Women, Race, and Class,* 96–97.

105. Brooks, *You May Plow Here,* 198; Herbert J. Lowery, *Vocational Opportunities for Negroes in Cleveland* (Columbus: U.S. National Youth Administration in Ohio, 1938), 32–33; Katzman, *Seven Days a Week,* 35.

106. Cowan interview; Brooks, *You May Plow Here,* 196–97; Crawford interview.

107. For a discussion of this practice, see Hunter, "Household Workers in the Making."

108. Cleveland Urban League, "Minutes, Jan. to Nov., 1928," and "Minutes 1929," both in Cleveland Urban League Records; Wooster and Whiting, *Fluctuations in Employment,* 18.

Chapter 3: "Join a Union"

1. Patricia Blackmon, "The Black Railroad Worker: Through Personal Accounts and Narratives" (undergraduate seminar paper, Cleveland State University, 1990), 3–4 (quote on 3); Colin J. Davis, *Power at Odds: The 1922 National Railroad Shopmen's Strike* (Urbana: University of Illinois Press, 1997), 69–70; Sterling D. Spero and Abram L. Harris, *The Black Worker: The Negro and the Labor Movement* (New York: Columbia University Press, 1931; reprint, New York: Atheneum, 1969), 308.

2. For the classic literature on African Americans' exclusion from organized labor before 1930, see Charles H. Wesley, *Negro Labor in the United States, 1850–1925: A Study in American Economic History* (New York: Vanguard Press, 1927); Department of Research and Investigations of the National Negro Welfare Association, *Negro Membership in American Labor Unions* (New York: Alexander Press, 1930); Spero and Harris, *The Black Worker;* and Lorenzo J. Greene and Carter G. Woodson, *The Negro Wage Earner* (New York: Russell and Russell, 1930). More recent studies include David Roediger, "'Labor in White Skin': Race and Working-Class History," in *Reshaping the U.S. Left: Popular Struggles in the 1980s,* ed. Mike Davis and Michael Sprinker (London: Verso, 1988), 287–307; David Roediger, "Notes on Working Class Racism," *New Politics* 2 (Summer 1989): 61–66; David Roediger, *The Wages of Whiteness: Race and*

the Making of the American Working Class (New York: Verso, 1992); Eric Arnesen, "Following the Color Line of Labor: Black Workers and the Labor Movement before 1930," *Radical History Review* 55 (Winter 1993): 54–87; and Eric Arnesen, "Up from Exclusion: Black and White Workers, Race, and the State of Labor History," *Reviews in American History* 26 (Mar. 1998): 146–74.

3. Kenneth L. Kusmer, *A Ghetto Takes Shape: Black Cleveland, 1870–1930* (Urbana: University of Illinois Press, 1976), 68, 73–75; Frank U. Quillin, *The Color Line in Ohio: A History of Race Prejudice in a Typical Northern State* (Ann Arbor: George Wahr, 1913), 155–56; Charles W. Chesnutt, "The Negro in Cleveland," *The Clevelander* 5 (Nov. 1930): 3–4, 24–27; Elmer Thompson, interview by Thomas F. Campbell, in Thomas F. Campbell, "Speech Sound Recording: On the History of Cleveland," Cleveland Heritage Program, 1981, transcript, Cleveland Public Library.

4. The literature on African-American workers and organized labor in the South during the first three decades of the twentieth century is extensive. See Horace R. Cayton and George S. Mitchell, *Black Workers and the New Unions* (Chapel Hill: University of North Carolina Press, 1939); and Herbert R. Northrup, *Organized Labor and the Negro* (New York: Harper and Brothers, 1944). More recent works include Philip Foner, *Organized Labor and the Black Worker, 1619–1972* (New York: Praeger, 1974); Dolores Janiewski, *Sisterhood Denied: Race, Gender, and Class in a New South Community* (Philadelphia: Temple University Press, 1985); and Eric Arnesen, *Waterfront Workers of New Orleans: Race, Class, and Politics, 1863–1923* (New York: Oxford University Press, 1991). On the complicated relationships between Southern blacks and unions, see Ronald L. Lewis, *Black Coal Miners in America: Race, Class, and Community Conflict, 1780–1980* (Lexington: University Press of Kentucky, 1987); Earl Lewis, *In Their Own Interests: Race, Class, and Power in Twentieth Century Norfolk, Virginia* (Berkeley: University of California Press, 1990); Joe William Trotter Jr., *Coal, Class, and Color: Blacks in Southern West Virginia, 1915–32* (Urbana: University of Illinois Press, 1990); Daniel Letwin, *The Challenge of Interracial Unionism: Alabama Coal Miners, 1878–1921* (Chapel Hill: University of North Carolina Press, 1998); Colin J. Davis, "The 1922 Railroad Shopmen's Strike in the Southeast: A Study of Success and Failure," in *Organized Labor in the Twentieth Century South,* ed. Robert H. Zieger (Knoxville: University of Tennessee Press, 1991), 113–43; Eric Arnesen, "'Like Banquo's Ghost, It Will Not Down': The Race Question and the American Railroad Brotherhoods, 1880–1920," *American Historical Review* 99 (Dec. 1994): 1601–33; and Eric Arnesen, "'What's on the Black Worker's Mind?': African-American Workers and the Union Tradition," *Gulf Coast Historical Review* 10 (Fall 1994): 5–18.

5. Blackmon, "Black Railroad Worker," 3–4.

6. For debates about this approach, see Alex Lichtenstein, "Racial Conflict and Racial Solidarity in the Alabama Coal Strike of 1894: New Evidence for the Gutman-Hill Debate," *Labor History* 36 (Winter 1995): 63–76. For blacks' preferences for separate unions, see Lewis, *In Their Own Interests,* 103; Arnesen, "Following the Color Line of Labor"; and Howard Kimmeldorf and Robert Penney, "'Excluded' by Choice: Dynamics of Interracial Unionism on the Philadelphia Waterfront, 1910–1930," *International Labor and Working-Class History* 51 (Spring 1997): 51–71.

7. Exceptions include John H. Bracey Jr., August Meier, and Elliott Rudwick, eds., *Black Workers and Organized Labor* (Belmont, Calif.: Wadsworth, 1971); August Meier and Elliott Rudwick, *Black Detroit and the Rise of the UAW* (New York: Oxford Uni-

versity Press, 1979); William H. Harris, *Keeping the Faith: A. Philip Randolph, Milton P. Webster, and the Brotherhood of Sleeping Car Porters, 1925–37* (Urbana: University of Illinois Press, 1977); William H. Harris, *The Harder We Run: Black Workers since the Civil War* (New York: Oxford University Press, 1982); James R. Barrett, *Work and Community in the Jungle: Chicago's Packinghouse Workers, 1894–1922* (Urbana: University of Illinois Press, 1987); Peter Gottlieb, *Making Their Own Way: Southern Blacks' Migration to Pittsburgh, 1916–30* (Urbana: University of Illinois Press, 1987), 89–116; James R. Grossman, *Land of Hope: Chicago, Black Southerners, and the Great Migration* (Chicago: University of Chicago Press, 1989); Greg Leroy, "The Founding Heart of A. Philip Randolph's Union: Milton Webster and Chicago's Pullman Porters Organize, 1925–1937," *Labor's Heritage* 3 (July 1991): 22–43; and Rick Halpern, "The Iron Fist and the Velvet Glove: Welfare Capitalism in Chicago's Packinghouses, 1921–1933," *Journal of American Studies* 26 (Summer 1992): 159–83.

8. John J. Grabowski and David D. Van Tassel, eds., *The Encyclopedia of Cleveland History* (Bloomington: Indiana University Press, 1987); Roy T. Wortman, *From Syndicalism to Trade Unionism: The IWW in Ohio, 1905–1950* (New York: Garland, 1985); Melvin Dubofsky, *We Shall Be All: A History of the Industrial Workers of the World* (Chicago: Quadrangle Books, 1969); Admiral Kilpatrick, interview, Cleveland, June 8, 1980, transcript, Abraham Lincoln Brigade Archives, Brandeis University, Waltham, Mass. The work on white workers' craft consciousness includes Julie Greene, *Pure and Simple Politics: The American Federation of Labor and Political Activism, 1881–1917* (Cambridge: Cambridge University Press, 1998); David Montgomery, *The Fall of the House of Labor: The Workplace, the State, and American Labor Activism* (Cambridge: Cambridge University Press, 1987); Bruce Laurie, *Artisans into Workers: Labor in Nineteenth-Century America* (New York: Hill and Wang, 1989); Ileen A. DeVault, "'To Sit among Men': Skill, Gender, and Craft Unionism in the Early American Federation of Labor," in *Labor Histories: Class, Politics, and the Working-Class Experience,* ed. Eric Arnesen, Julie Green, and Bruce Laurie (Urbana: University of Illinois Press, 1998), 259–83; and Arnesen, "'Like Banquo's Ghost, It Will Not Down.'"

9. Henry B. Leonard, "Ethnic Cleavage and Industrial Conflict in Late Nineteenth Century America: The Cleveland Rolling Mill Company Strikes of 1882 and 1885," *Labor History* 20 (Fall 1979): 524–48; Leslie S. Hough, "The Turbulent Spirit: Violence and Coaction among Cleveland Workers, 1877–1899" (Ph.D. diss., University of Virginia, 1977); Warren Van Tine, Mary Bell Sickmeier, and Gail Arch Vorys, eds., *Building Ohio, 1881–1981: A Centennial History of the United Brotherhood of Carpenters and Joiners of America in Ohio* (Columbus: Ohio State Council, United Brotherhood of Carpenters and Joiners of America, 1981).

10. Leonard, "Ethnic Cleavage," 547.

11. Lois Scharf, "The Great Uprising in Cleveland: When Sisterhood Failed," in *A Needle, a Bobbin, a Strike: Women Needleworkers in America,* ed. Joan M. Jensen and Sue Davidson (Philadelphia: Temple University Press, 1984), 146–48; Grabowski and Van Tassel, *Encyclopedia of Cleveland History,* 433, 435–36.

12. Scharf, "Great Uprising," 175–82 (quote on 182); Edna Bryner, *The Garment Trades* (Cleveland: Survey Committee of the Cleveland Foundation, 1916), 55.

13. Kusmer, *A Ghetto Takes Shape,* 73–75; Spero and Harris, *The Black Worker,* 178; Thompson interview.

14. Kusmer, *A Ghetto Takes Shape*, 68, 73–75; Quillin, *The Color Line in Ohio*, 155–56; Thompson interview; Department of Research and Investigations of the National Negro Welfare Association, *Negro Membership;* Spero and Harris, *The Black Worker.*

15. Department of Research and Investigations of the National Negro Welfare Association, *Negro Membership,* 93; American Federation of Musicians, Local No. 4, *Labor Day Yearbook, 1901* (Cleveland: n.p., 1901), Records of the American Federation of Musicians, Local No. 4, Western Reserve Historical Society, Cleveland (hereafter WRHS). For patterns elsewhere, see Donald Spivey, *Union and the Black Musician: The Narrative of William Everett Samuels and Chicago Local 208* (Lanham, Md.: University Press of America, 1984).

16. *Cleveland Citizen,* May 26, 1917 (quote), Dec. 16, 1916, July 14, 1917, May 18, 1918. For the expression of similar attitudes in the railroad brotherhoods, see Arnesen, "'Like Banquo's Ghost, It Will Not Down,'" 1610–12. For a general discussion, see Andrew Dawson, "The Parameters of Craft Consciousness: The Social Outlook of the Skilled Worker, 1890–1920," in *American Labor and Immigration History, 1877–1920s: Recent European Research,* ed. Dirk Hoerder (Urbana: University of Illinois Press, 1983), 135–55.

17. Roediger, *Wages of Whiteness;* Greene, *Pure and Simple Politics.*

18. *Cleveland Plain Dealer,* Feb. 14, 1918 (quotes); this particular news account, for example, was reprinted in the *Miami Herald. Cleveland Gazette,* Feb. 15, 1919; Ohio Federation of Labor, *Proceedings of the Thirty-Fourth Annual Convention of the Ohio State Federation of Labor* (Toledo: Ohio Federation of Labor, 1918), 83.

19. William C. Liller to Edward J. Cunningham, June 20, 1919, and William C. Liller, "Preliminary Report of Commissioner of Conciliation," July 5, 1919, both in Otis Steel Company, Cleveland, Ohio, RG 280, U.S. Conciliation Service in *Black Workers in the Era of the Great Migration, 1916–1929,* ed. James R. Grossman (Frederick, Md.: University Publications of America, 1985), reel 1.

20. *Cleveland Plain Dealer,* Sept. 19, 1919, Sept. 23, 1919.

21. Report quoted in Jeremy Brecher, *Strike!* (Boston: South End Press, 1972), 122.

22. David Brody, *Steelworkers in America: The Nonunion Era* (Cambridge, Mass: Harvard University Press, 1960), 231–42; David J. Saposs, "How the Steel Strike Was Organized: An Exhibit of a New Labor Technique," *Survey* 43 (Nov. 8, 1919): 67–69.

23. *Cleveland Plain Dealer,* Sept. 24, 1919 (quote); Brody, *Steelworkers in America,* 242–43; S. Adele Shaw, "Closed Towns," *Survey* 43 (Nov. 8, 1919): 53.

24. *Cleveland Plain Dealer,* Sept. 24, 1919, Sept. 25, 1919, Sept. 30, 1919.

25. *Cleveland Plain Dealer,* Sept. 24, 1919, Sept. 25, 1919. For the consequences of the inability to hold meetings in other areas, see Brecher, *Strike!* 123.

26. Spero and Harris, *The Black Worker,* 259–63, esp. 262; Kilpatrick interview; *Cleveland Plain Dealer,* Sept. 23, 1919, Sept. 25, 1919; John A. Garraty, ed., *The Barber and the Historian: The Correspondence of George A. Myers and James Ford Rhodes, 1910–1923* (Columbus: Ohio Historical Society, 1956), 97. On the Socialist party and African Americans, see Philip Foner, *American Socialism and Black Americans: From the Age of Jackson to World War II* (Westport, Conn.: Greenwood Press, 1977).

27. *Cleveland Gazette,* Sept. 27, 1919; J. O. Houze, "Negro Labor and the Industries," *Opportunity* 1 (Jan. 1923): 22.

28. *Cleveland Citizen,* Sept. 27, 1919, Oct. 11, 1919; Kilpatrick interview.

29. Ohio Federation of Labor, *Proceedings of the Thirty-Sixth Annual Convention of the Ohio State Federation of Labor* (Toledo: Ohio Federation of Labor, 1920), 139.

30. Ibid., 140, emphasis added.

31. Ibid., 141.

32. Roediger, "'Labor in White Skin'"; Gwendolyn Mink, *Old Labor and New Immigrants in American Political Development* (Ithaca: Cornell University Press, 1986); Olivier Zunz, *The Changing Face of Inequality: Urbanization, Industrial Development, and Immigrants in Detroit, 1880–1920* (Chicago: University of Chicago Press, 1982), 372–403.

33. Brody, *Steelworkers in America,* 232–35.

34. Garraty, *Barber and the Historian,* 123.

35. Cayton and Mitchell, *Black Workers,* 372–424, esp. 398–412; Garraty, *Barber and the Historian,* 115; Du Bois quoted in Raymond Walters, "Section 7a and the Black Worker," *Labor History* 10 (Summer 1969): 464. For attitudes elsewhere, see Abram L. Harris, "Negro Labor's Quarrel with White Working Men," *Current History* 24 (Sept. 1926): 903–8.

36. *Cleveland Advocate,* June 28, 1919 (quotes); Abram L. Harris, "The Negro and Economic Radicalism," *Modern Quarterly* 2 (1925): 201; Cayton and Mitchell, *Black Workers,* 383–93. On the role of the Negro Welfare Association and the activities of the NAACP, see Kusmer, *A Ghetto Takes Shape,* 216–19. For a discussion of the role middle-class blacks played in inhibiting unionization in Chicago, see Grossman, *Land of Hope,* 208–10, 227–41; and Leroy, "Founding Heart."

37. Harris, "The Negro and Economic Radicalism," 203. For discussions of racial violence during the war, see William Tuttle Jr., *Race Riot: Chicago in the Red Summer of 1919* (1970; reprint, New York: Atheneum, 1984); and Robert V. Haynes, *A Night of Violence: The Houston Riot of 1917* (Baton Rouge: Louisiana State University Press, 1976).

38. American Plan Association of Cleveland, *Report of Directors, 1923* (Cleveland: n.p., 1923), 78; American Plan Association of Cleveland, *Report of the General Manager for the Years 1923 and 1924* (Cleveland: Cleveland Chamber of Commerce, 1924), 7–9; *Cleveland Plain Dealer,* May 3, 1924. On the rise of the APA, see Sanford Jacoby, *Employing Bureaucracy: Managers, Unions, and the Transformation of Work in American Industry, 1900–1945* (New York: Columbia University Press, 1985), 174–80; and Philip Taft, *The A. F. of L. in the Time of Gompers* (New York: Harper, 1957; reprint, New York: Octagon Books, 1970), 401–2. Throughout the 1920s, William Frew Long aggressively denounced unions and the closed shop in speeches, articles, and private letters. For examples, see William Frew Long, "Does Organized Labor or the Open Shop Serve the Public, the Worker, and the Manufacturer, to the Best Advantage of all Concerned?" speech, Oct. 29, 1923; William Frew Long, "Cleveland's Fight for Freedom," *Detroit Saturday Night,* July 31, 1926, 1, 11; William Frew Long to Ernestine Barra, Dec. 6, 1921; and William Frew Long to Reverend H. Samuel Fritsch, Feb. 9, 1992, all in box 1, William Frew Long Papers, WRHS.

39. On prewar welfare activities, see Cleveland Chamber of Commerce, *Annual Report, 1916* (Cleveland: n.p., 1916), 90–91; David Montgomery, "Thinking about American Workers in the 1920s," *International Labor and Working-Class History* 32 (Fall 1987): 4–24; Jacoby, *Employing Bureaucracy,* 49–64; David Brody, *Workers in Industrial America: Essays on the Twentieth Century Struggle* (New York: Oxford University Press, 1981), 50.

40. Jacoby, *Employing Bureaucracy,* 55 (quote), 56–61; Mary Barnett Gilson, *What's Past Is Prologue* (New York: Harper, 1940), 138–40.

41. David Goldberg, "Immigrant Women and Managerial Reform: Welfare Capitalism at Cleveland's Joseph and Feiss Company, 1909–1925," paper presented at the North American Labor History Conference, Wayne State University, Oct. 20, 1989, 9.

42. *Naco News,* July 1924, Records of the National Malleable Steel Castings Company.

43. Paul Glenn, interview by author, June 18, 1991, Cleveland, transcript.

44. *Naco News,* Mar. 1923, Records of the National Malleable Steel Castings Company.

45. W. S. Tyler Co., *Through the Meshes* (n.p., n.d.), WRHS.

46. Houze, "Negro Labor," 22.

47. Attitudes about dependability quoted in Cayton and Mitchell, *Black Workers,* 387, 389. For a discussion of similar attitudes expressed by African-American workers in Chicago packinghouses, see Halpern, "The Iron Fist and the Velvet Glove," 159–83.

48. *Naco News,* Aug. 1923 (quotes), Mar.–Apr. 1927, Records of the National Malleable Steel Castings Company.

49. For limits of the incentive plans, see Cleveland Chamber of Commerce, *Employe[e]'s Incentive Plans in Cleveland Industries* (Cleveland: n.p., 1920); Cleveland Chamber of Commerce, *Employe[e] Representation in Industry* (Cleveland: n.p., 1923); Cayton and Mitchell, *Black Workers,* 387–88; Willa Davenport Thomas, interview by author, Cleveland, Dec. 1, 1989, transcript; and *Cleveland Gazette,* Feb. 3, 1917.

50. *Cleveland Advocate,* Jan. 11, 1919; Boryczka and Cary, *No Strength without Union,* 155; Houze, "Negro Labor," 21.

51. American Plan Association of Cleveland, *Report of the General Manager for the Years 1923 and 1924,* 42–45 (first and second quotes on 45); *Atlanta Independent,* Apr. 17, 1920 (third quote).

52. Kilpatrick interview.

53. Blackmon, "Black Railroad Worker," 5–6; Grabowski and Van Tassel, *Encyclopedia of Cleveland History,* 289; Department of Research and Investigations of the National Negro Welfare Association, *Negro Membership,* 35, 105–6; American Plan Association of Cleveland, *Report of the General Manager for the Years 1923 and 1924,* 206–9.

54. *Cleveland Plain Dealer,* July 14, 1922.

55. Cleveland Chamber of Commerce, *Cleveland Chamber of Commerce Annual Report, 1923* (Cleveland: n.p., 1923), 77–78.

56. Cleveland Chamber of Commerce, *Cleveland Chamber of Commerce Annual Report, 1922* (Cleveland, n.p., 1922), 60–61; Shaw, "Closed Towns," 41–45; Walter Galenson, *The United Brotherhood of Carpenters: The First Hundred Years* (Cambridge, Mass.: Harvard University Press, 1983), 200. The growth of employment in the building trades reveals this segment's continued competition with employment in manufacturing. Beginning in 1910, there was a rapid escalation in both wooden frame and brick and steel structures. By 1930, building trades workers occupied 21 percent of the manufacturing positions. This upward trend underscored the "buoyancy" of construction activity, particularly between 1923 and 1927.

57. American Plan Association of Cleveland, *Annual Report, 1921* (Cleveland: n.p.,

1921), 31 (quotes); American Plan Association of Cleveland, *Report of the General Manager for the Years 1923 and 1924,* 74–78; *Cleveland Plain Dealer,* Nov. 15, 1923.

58. Chesnutt, "Negro in Cleveland," 3; Cleveland Chamber of Commerce, *Annual Report, 1923,* 80; Shaw, "Closed Towns," 25–26; Spero and Harris, *The Black Worker,* 178; Flowree Robinson, interview by author, Cleveland, Nov. 29, 1989, transcript; Rev. Frank A. Smith, interview by author and Patricia Miles Ashford, Cleveland, Aug. 6, 1991, transcript.

59. Early Surveys, series 6, box 88, National Negro Welfare Association, Cleveland Branch, National Urban League Records, Library of Congress, Washington, D.C. (quotes); Kusmer, *A Ghetto Takes Shape,* 73–75; *Cleveland Citizen,* Apr. 14, 1928.

60. Early Surveys, National Urban League Records.

61. Christopher G. Wye, "A Midwest Ghetto: Patterns of Negro Life and Thought in Cleveland, Ohio, 1929–1945" (Ph.D. diss., Kent State University, 1973), 172–73; Thompson interview.

62. Thompson interview.

63. Early Surveys, National Urban League Records.

64. Smith interview; Natalie Middleton, interview by author, Cleveland, Feb. 21, 1989, transcript; Flowree Robinson interview; American Plan Association of Cleveland, *Report of the General Manager for the Years 1923 and 1924,* 10 (quote); Department of Research and Investigations of the National Negro Welfare Association, *Negro Membership,* 41–43.

65. Department of Research and Investigations of the National Negro Welfare Association, *Negro Membership,* 39.

66. Van Tine, Sickmeier, and Vorys, *Building Ohio,* 22. See also Harris, *Harder We Run,* 43; and Middleton interview by author.

67. Chesnutt, "Negro in Cleveland," 3.

68. American Plan Association of Cleveland, *Report of the General Manager for the Years 1923 and 1924,* 203–5; *Cleveland Gazette,* Sept. 23, 1922; "Cleveland: Incidents Relating to Trade Unions and Negroes," n.d., Cleveland Urban League Records, WRHS; Kusmer, *A Ghetto Takes Shape,* 229.

69. Early Surveys, National Urban League Records; *Cleveland Gazette,* Nov. 3, 1917, Sept. 21, 1918, Sept. 18, 1918; Dorothy Sue Cobble, "Sisters in the Craft: Waitresses and Their Unions in the Twentieth Century" (Ph.D. diss., Stanford University, 1986), 155–59; Matthew Josephson, *Union House, Union Bar: The History of the Hotel and Restaurant Employees and Bartenders International Union, AFL-CIO* (New York: Random House, 1956), 180–85.

70. Department of Research and Investigations of the National Negro Welfare Association, *Negro Membership,* 51–52; *Cleveland Gazette,* Sept. 28, 1918.

71. *Cleveland Gazette,* Mar. 24, 1917.

72. *Wills v. Hotel and Restaurant Employees, Local 106,* 2, NAACP Records, Cleveland Branch, WRHS. For differing uses of unions' boycotts, see Dana Frank, *Purchasing Power: Consumer Organizing, Gender, and the Seattle Labor Movement, 1919–1929* (Cambridge: Cambridge University Press, 1994).

73. *Wills v. Local 106,* 3, 5.

74. A. Philip Randolph, "Answering Heebie-Jeebies: Pullman Porters," *The Messenger* 8 (Dec. 1926): 370; Nancy Brittenum, interview by author, Cleveland, Dec. 3, 1991, transcript.

75. *Cleveland Federationist,* May 14, 1925 (quote), Feb. 4, 1926.

76. Early Surveys, National Urban League Records.

77. Meier and Rudwick, *Black Detroit,* 43.

78. Blackmon, "Black Railroad Worker," 6; Spero and Harris, *The Black Worker,* 116–18; Department of Research and Investigations of the National Negro Welfare Association, *Negro Membership,* 33–35; Grabowski and Van Tassel, *Encyclopedia of Cleveland History,* 289, 994–97.

79. Department of Research and Investigations of the National Negro Welfare Association, *Negro Membership,* 99; *Cleveland Gazette,* Oct. 22, 1921, Oct. 21, 1923, Mar. 29, 1924, Aug. 30, 1930, Dec. 19, 1931.

80. *Cleveland Gazette,* Jan. 17, 1920, May 15, 1920, Oct. 22, 1921, Apr. 23, 1923, Apr. 28, 1923, Mar. 3, 1924.

81. See, for example, Tera W. Hunter, *To 'Joy My Freedom: Southern Black Women's Lives and Labors after the Civil War* (Cambridge, Mass.: Harvard University Press, 1997); and Jacqueline Jones, *Labor of Love, Labor of Sorrow: Black Women, Work, and the Family from Slavery to the Present* (New York: Basic Books, 1985). For the difficulties of organizing women generally, see Alice Kessler-Harris, *Out to Work: A History of Wage-Earning Women in the United States* (New York: Oxford University Press, 1982).

82. *Cleveland Gazette,* Jan. 13, 1917; Grabowski and Van Tassel, *Encyclopedia of Cleveland History,* 989–90.

83. *Chicago Defender,* Jan. 22, 1927, Mar. 1, 1930; *Cleveland Press,* July 14, 1930, July 15, 1930, July 16, 1930, July 17, 1930, July 22, 1930, July 26, 1930; Josephson, *Union House, Union Bar.* Neither Spero and Harris, in *The Black Worker,* nor Cayton and Mitchell, in *Black Workers,* mention the National Association of Colored Waiters.

84. *Cleveland Press,* July 18, 1930, July 19, 1930; *Cleveland Gazette,* Aug. 2, 1930.

85. *Cleveland Gazette,* July 4, 1931.

86. Harris, "The Negro and Economic Radicalism," 199.

Chapter 4: A New World in the City

1. Emmett J. Scott, "Additional Letters of Negro Migrants," *Journal of Negro History* 4 (Oct. 1919): 460–61.

2. Bertha Cowan, interview by Eleanor Jackson, Cleveland, Jan. 16, 1987, transcript, St. James A.M.E. Oral History Project, Western Reserve Historical Society, Cleveland (hereafter WRHS).

3. Kenneth L. Kusmer, *A Ghetto Takes Shape: Black Cleveland, 1870–1930* (Urbana: University of Illinois Press, 1976), 3–31, 157–89; David Gerber, *Black Ohio and the Color Line: 1860–1915* (Urbana: University of Illinois Press, 1976), 470–72; Frank U. Quillin, *The Color Line in Ohio: A History of Race Prejudice in a Typical Northern State* (Ann Arbor: George Wahr, 1913), 157–59; U.S. Bureau of the Census, *Negroes in the United States, 1920–1932* (Washington, D.C.: Government Printing Office, 1935), 55; Howard Whipple Green, *A Study of the Movement of the Negro Population of Cleveland* (Cleveland: n.p., 1924), 1–5, 14; Judge Jean Murrell Capers, interview by author and Patricia Miles Ashford, Cleveland, Aug. 8, 1991, tape recording.

4. U.S. Bureau of the Census, *Fourteenth Census of the United States, 1920: Population,* vol. 4, *Occupations* (Washington, D.C.: Government Printing Office, 1922), 1084; U.S. Bureau of the Census, *Fifteenth Census of the United States, 1930: Population,* vol.

4, *Occupations* (Washington, D.C.: Government Printing Office, 1932), 1085–87; Kusmer, *A Ghetto Takes Shape*, 160–61n6. Kusmer used the increase of the black school population from 5,078 in April 1921 to 7,430 in October 1923 to suggest that the black population overall may have grown by 50 percent during these years.

5. Edward M. Miggins and Mary Morgenthaler, "The Ethnic Mosaic: The Settlement of Cleveland by the New Immigrants and Migrants," in *The Birth of Modern Cleveland 1865–1930*, ed. Thomas F. Campbell and Edward M. Miggins (Cleveland: Western Reserve Historical Society, 1988), 129.

6. Josef J. Barton, *Peasants and Strangers: Italians, Rumanians, and Slovaks in an American City, 1890–1950* (Cambridge, Mass.: Harvard University Press, 1975); Miggins and Morgenthaler, "The Ethnic Mosaic," 105; David E. Green, *The City and Its People* (Cleveland: n.p., 1917), 7; U.S. Bureau of the Census, *Fourteenth Census*, 1084–87.

7. Emmett J. Scott, *Negro Migration during the War* (New York: Oxford University Press, 1920; reprint, New York: Arno Press, 1969), 148–49; Cleveland Chamber of Commerce Committee on Housing and Sanitation, *An Investigation of Housing Conditions of War Workers in Cleveland* (Cleveland: n.p., 1918); Ronald R. Weiner, "A History of Civic Land Use Decision Making in the Cleveland Metropolitan Area, 1880–1930," 257–66, 277–79, ms., 1974, WRHS; Cleveland Chamber of Commerce, "Meeting of the directors of the Cleveland Real Estate and Housing Committee," July 11, 1918, Records of the Greater Cleveland Growth Association, WRHS.

8. Department of Public Health, *An Investigation of Housing Conditions of Cleveland's Workingmen* (Cleveland: Division of Publicity and Research, 1914), 16; George E. Haynes, "Negro Migration: Its Effects on Family and Community Life in the North," *Opportunity* 2 (Oct. 1924): 304.

9. Langston Hughes, *The Big Sea* (New York: Hill and Wang, 1941), 27.

10. Quote in V. Davis, "Family Oral History" (undergraduate paper, Cleveland State University, 1988); Cleveland Urban League, "Report of the Executive Secretary, Apr. 9th to May 6th, 1919," Cleveland Urban League Records, WRHS; "Housing Conditions of Workers in War Industries in Cleveland, Ohio," *Monthly Labor Review* 9 (July 1919): 260–62.

11. Patricia Blackmon, "The Black Railroad Worker: Through Personal Accounts and Narratives" (undergraduate seminar paper, Cleveland State University, 1990), 4–5; Beatrice Stevens Cockrell, interview by author, Cleveland, Sept. 27, 1991, transcript; *Cleveland Gazette*, Aug. 4, 1917; *Cleveland Press*, Mar. 25, 1946.

12. Miggins and Morgenthaler, "The Ethnic Mosaic," 129; Green, *Study*, 14–15; Eleanor K. Caplan, *Non-White Residential Patterns: Analysis of Changes in the Non-White Residential Patterns in Cleveland, Ohio, from 1910–1959* (Cleveland: n.p., 1959), 6; Larry Cuban, "A Strategy for Racial Peace: Negro Leadership in Cleveland, 1900–1919," *Phylon* 28 (Fall 1967): 301.

13. Elmer Thompson, interview by Thomas F. Campbell, in Thomas F. Campbell, "Speech Sound Recording: On the History of Cleveland," Cleveland Heritage Program, 1981, transcript, Cleveland Public Library.

14. *Cleveland Gazette*, Jan. 6, 1917; Department of Public Health, *Investigation of Housing*, 20–21; Welfare Federation of Cleveland, *Cleveland Area Social Study* (Cleveland: Welfare Federation of Cleveland, 1944), 42–44, Cleveland Public Library; Kusmer, *A Ghetto Takes Shape*, 210–11.

15. For highly regarded critiques of the long-accepted social science literature on

the ghetto, see Joe William Trotter Jr., *Black Milwaukee: The Making of an Industrial Proletariat, 1915–45* (Urbana: University of Illinois Press, 1985), 264–82; Joe William Trotter Jr., "African Americans in the City: The Industrial Era, 1900–1950," *Journal of Urban History* 21 (May 1995): 438–57; and Kenneth L. Kusmer, "The Black Urban Experience in American History," in *The State of Afro-American History: Past, Present, and Future,* ed. Darlene Clark Hine (Baton Rouge: Louisiana State University Press, 1986), 91–122.

16. Kusmer, *A Ghetto Takes Shape.* For other examples, see Gilbert Osofsky, *Harlem: The Making of a Ghetto, 1890–1930,* 2d ed. (New York: Harper Torchbooks, 1971); Gilbert Osofsky, "The Enduring Ghetto," *Journal of American History* 55 (Sept. 1968): 243–55; Allan H. Spear, *Black Chicago: The Making of a Negro Ghetto, 1890–1920* (Chicago: University of Chicago Press, 1967); David M. Katzman, *Before the Ghetto: Black Detroit in the Nineteenth Century* (Urbana: University of Illinois Press, 1973); Thomas Philpott, *The Slum and the Ghetto* (New York: Oxford University Press, 1978).

17. William H. Murdock, interview by Antoinette Kindall, Cleveland, Sept. 19, 1986, transcript, St. James A.M.E. Oral History Project; Capers interview; Hazel Murray Burnett, interview by Marjorie Witt Johnson, Cleveland, Jan. 11, 1987, transcript, St. James A.M.E. Oral History Project; Sallie Hopson, interview by Antoinette Kindall, Cleveland, Aug. 26, 1986, transcript, St. James A.M.E. Oral History Project.

18. Charles W. Chesnutt, "The Negro in Cleveland," *The Clevelander* 5 (Nov. 1930): 3; Robert C. Weaver, *The Negro Ghetto* (New York: Harcourt Brace, 1948), 103–4; Kusmer, *A Ghetto Takes Shape,* 212–14; Capers interview.

19. Natalie Middleton, interview by author, Cleveland, Feb. 21, 1989, transcript; Thompson interview; Chesnutt, "Negro in Cleveland," 3; Kusmer, *A Ghetto Takes Shape,* 212–14; Joseph A. Hill, "Recent Northward Migration of the Negro," *Monthly Labor Review* 18 (July 1924): 1–14; Wilbur Watson, *The Village: An Oral Historical and Ethnographic Study of a Black Community* (Cleveland: Village Vanguard, 1989), 13–19, 44–55.

20. See Kusmer, "Black Urban Experience," 105–6; Elizabeth Rauel Bethel, *Promiseland: A Century of Life in a Negro Community* (Philadelphia: Temple University Press, 1981), 119; and Jacqueline Jones, *Labor of Love, Labor of Sorrow: Black Women, Work, and the Family from Slavery to the Present* (New York: Basic Books, 1985), 112–23.

21. Herbert Gutman, *The Black Family in Slavery and Freedom, 1750–1925* (New York: Vintage, 1976), 432; Frank F. Furstenberg Jr., Theodore Hershberg, and John Modell, "The Origins of the Female-Headed Black Family: The Impact of the Urban Experience," *Journal of Interdisciplinary History* 6 (1975): 211–33. For a classic study on the African-American family, see E. Franklin Frazier, *The Negro Family in the United States* (Chicago: University of Chicago Press, 1939).

22. Kusmer, *A Ghetto Takes Shape,* 224–25; U.S. Bureau of the Census, *Fifteenth Census,* 1930; Bonnie Thornton Dill, "Our Mothers' Grief: Racial Ethnic Women and the Maintenance of Families," *Journal of Family History* 13 (1988): 415–31; James Borchert, *Alley Life in Washington: Family, Community, Religion, and Folklife in the City, 1850–1970* (Urbana: University of Illinois Press, 1980), 65.

23. Elizabeth Clark-Lewis found a similar pattern in Washington, D.C., see *Living In, Living Out: African American Domestics in Washington, D.C., 1910–1940* (Washington, D.C.: Smithsonian Institution, 1994), 79–83.

24. Geneva Robinson, interview by Inez Bentyn, Cleveland, Nov. 4, 1986, transcript, St. James A.M.E. Oral History Project; Ray Dennis, interview by author, Cleveland, Sept. 27, 1989, transcript.

25. Linton Freeman, interview by author, Cleveland, Mar. 7, 1991, transcript; Margie Glass, interview by Antoinette Kindall, Cleveland, Dec. 12, 1986, transcript, St. James A.M.E. Oral History Project.

26. Cleveland Chamber of Commerce, *Investigation of Housing,* 31–32; memorandum to C. E. Briggs, May 15, 1917, Karamu House Records, WRHS; Charles E. Hall, "Report from the Supervisor of Negro Economics," in U.S. Department of Labor, Division of Negro Economics, *The Negro at Work during the World War and during Reconstruction* (Washington, D.C.: Government Printing Office, 1921), 114; Federation of Community Planning Committee on Inquiry into the Homeless Situation, minutes, Feb. 9, 1926, Feb. 17, 1927; and Franklin R. McKeever, secretary, Wayfarers' Lodge, to Committee on Inquiry into the Homeless, Feb. 2, 1927, both in Federation of Community Planning Records, WRHS.

27. Bureau of Labor Statistics, Department of Investigations, *Cost of Living of Working Women in Ohio* (Columbus: n.p., 1915); Consumers' League of Ohio, "Report on Housing Survey Made by the Boarding Homes Commission, Cleveland Girls Council," ca. 1926, Consumers' League of Ohio Records, WRHS. For the problems that African-American women faced as boarders, see Jane Edna Hunter, *A Nickel and a Prayer* (Cleveland: Elli Kani, 1940); Adrienne Lash Jones, *Jane Edna Hunter: A Case Study of Black Leadership, 1910–1959* (New York: Carlson, 1990); and Joanne Meyerowitz, *Women Adrift: Wage-Earning Women Apart from the Family in Chicago* (Chicago: University of Chicago Press, 1988), 73–74, 80–82.

28. Hunter, *A Nickel and a Prayer,* 70 (first quote), 77 (second quote), 150–65.

29. Cleveland Urban League, "Report of the Executive Secretary, Apr. 9th to May 6th, 1919," Cleveland Urban League Records; U.S. Bureau of the Census, *Fifteenth Census,* 1085–87. For a tendency to underestimate the noneconomic roles of kin relationships, especially those of African-American men, see John Bodnar, Michael West, and Roger Simon, "Migration, Kinship, and Urban Adjustment: Blacks and Poles in Pittsburgh, 1900–1930," *Journal of American History* 66 (Dec. 1979): 548–65.

30. D. Clark, "Family Oral History" (undergraduate paper, Cleveland State University, n.d.); S. Davis, "Family Oral History" (undergraduate paper, Cleveland State University, Mar. 1984); M. Davis, "Family Oral History" (undergraduate paper, Cleveland State University, 1988); V. Dulaney, "Family Oral History" (undergraduate paper, Cleveland State University, 1984). These patterns appear to duplicate patterns in other migrant communities. See Borchert, *Alley Life,* 157–99; James Borchert, "Urban Neighborhood and Community: Informal Group Life, 1850–1970," *Journal of Interdisciplinary History* 11 (Spring 1981): 620; and Jones, *Labor of Love, Labor of Sorrow,* 189–90.

31. Willa Davenport Thomas, interview by author, Cleveland, Dec. 1, 1989, transcript.

32. Thompson interview; Louise Pattengall, interview by Antoinette Kindall, Cleveland, Sept. 29, 1986, transcript, St. James A.M.E. Oral History Project; John Bodnar, Roger Simon, and Michael P. Weber, *Lives of Their Own: Blacks, Italians, and Poles in Pittsburgh, 1900–1960* (Urbana: University of Illinois Press, 1982), 91.

33. See the weekly notes in the *Cleveland Gazette;* the *Cleveland Advocate;* and the

weekly column "The Buckeye State" in the *Chicago Defender* during the years 1915–30; Linton Freeman interview; Willa Davenport Thomas interview; and Myrtle Wiggins, interview by author, Cleveland, May 10, 1994, transcript. For comparisons with other cities, see Earl Lewis, "Afro-American Adaptive Strategies: The Visiting Habits of Kith and Kin among Black Norfolkians during the First Great Migration," *Journal of Family History* 12 (Oct. 1987): 409; and Gutman, *Black Family,* 432.

34. Willa Davenport Thomas interview; Vertamae Smart Grosvenor, "When You Meet Estella Smart, You Been Met!" in *Picturing Us: African American Identity in Photography,* ed. Deborah Willis (New York: New Press, 1994), 30; thousands of photographs in Allen E. Cole Photography Collection, WRHS; Samuel W. Black, "African American Photographers in Cleveland, 1930 to 1965," in *Yet Still We Rise: African American Art in Cleveland, 1920–1970,* ed. Ursula Korneitchouk (Cleveland: Cleveland Artists Foundation, 1996), 7–13.

35. Linton Freeman interview.

36. Adrienne Kennedy, *People Who Led to My Plays* (New York: Knopf, 1987), 33–34.

37. Henry Pointer, interview by Antoinette Kindall, Cleveland, Oct. 30, 1986, transcript, St. James A.M.E. Oral History Project.

38. S. Davis, "Family Oral History"; Patricia Miles Ashford, interview by author, Cleveland, June 23, 1991, transcript; Flowree Robinson, interview by author, Cleveland, Nov. 29, 1989, transcript; M. Davis, "Family Oral History"; V. Dulaney, "Family Oral History"; Pointer interview.

39. Darlene Clark Hine, "Black Migration to the Urban Midwest: The Gender Dimension, 1915–1945," in *The Great Migration in Historical Perspective: New Dimensions of Race, Class, and Gender,* ed. Joe William Trotter Jr. (Bloomington: Indiana University Press, 1991), 133, 134 (quote).

40. Clark-Lewis, *Living In, Living Out,* 79–83; Hine, "Black Migration."

41. Thomas Laqueur and Sara Ruddick make an argument for expanding the conceptualization of caring for children as work that includes men's experiences. See Thomas W. Laqueur, "The Facts of Fatherhood," 205–21, and Sara Ruddick, "Thinking about Fathers," 222–32, both in *Conflicts in Feminism,* ed. Marianne Hirsch and Evelyn Fox Keller (New York: Routledge, 1990).

42. Elizabeth Pleck, *Black Migration and Poverty: Boston, 1865–1900* (New York: Academic Press, 1979), 183–84.

43. Robert L. Griswold, *Fatherhood in America: A History* (New York: Basic Books, 1993), 52–56. Griswold considers only Pleck's study, which concludes in 1900. For a more useful look at data on African-American households in Cleveland and other cities, see Kusmer, *A Ghetto Takes Shape,* 224–25.

44. Fatherhood appears to have taken on a more pronounced role in the 1920s, evidenced by the emphasis on black men's roles in churches and voluntary associations. In the Universal Negro Improvement Association (UNIA) thousands of working-class black men participated in numerous gatherings where they were called on to assume their roles as fathers, husbands, and breadwinners.

45. Pointer interview; Willa Davenport Thomas interview; Thompson interview; Paul Glenn, interview by author, June 18, 1991, Cleveland, transcript.

46. Hine, "Black Migration," 127–46; Flowree Robinson interview; Melvia Green, interview by Patricia Miles Ashford, n.d.; Josephus Hicks, interview by author, Cleve-

land, Nov. 14, 1990, transcript; Murtis H. Taylor, interview by Earlynne Davis, Cleveland, Oct. 19, 1986, transcript, St. James A.M.E. Oral History Project.

47. Carrie Davenport Turner, interview by Emily Lasiter, Cleveland, Aug. 27, 1986, transcript, St. James A.M.E. Oral History Project; *Cleveland Gazette,* May 29, 1920; R. Flowers, "Family Oral History" (undergraduate paper, Cleveland State University, 1981); Flowree Robinson interview.

48. Wiggins interview; Murdock interview.

49. Pattengall interview.

50. Hughes, *The Big Sea,* 35; Chester Himes, *The Quality of Hurt: The Autobiography of Chester Himes* (New York: Doubleday, 1972), 1:26.

51. Green, *Study;* Thompson interview.

52. Middleton interview by author; Willa Davenport Thomas interview; Cockrell interview, Sept. 27, 1991; Pointer interview; Edward M. Miggins, "Oral History and Multicultural Education: Finding Our Place in the Global Village," 28–29, author's possession (quotes).

53. Marjorie Isom Davis, interview by Marjorie Witt Johnson, Cleveland, Sept. 18, 1986, transcript, St. James A.M.E. Oral History Project; Marjorie Witt Johnson, interview by Marjorie Isom Davis, Cleveland, Jan. 19, 1987, transcript, St. James A.M.E. Oral History Project; Willa Davenport Thomas interview.

54. Hicks interview.

55. Carl B. Stokes, *Promises of Power Then and Now* (Cleveland: Friends of Carl Stokes, 1989), 23.

56. Howard Whipple Green, *Real Property Inventory of the Cleveland Metropolitan District, Report No. 1* (Cleveland: Committee on Real Property Inventory, 1933); Howard Whipple Green, ed., *Standards of Living in the Cleveland Metropolitan District as Depicted by the Federal Real Property Inventory* (Cleveland: n.p., 1935); Louise James, "Family History," Ursula J. Honore Papers, WRHS (first quote); Alberta Hornsby, interview by Elizabeth Greene, Cleveland, Oct. 28, 1986, transcript, St. James A.M.E. Oral History Project (second quote); Stokes, *Promises of Power,* 23 (third quote).

57. Gerber, *Black Ohio,* 273; Kusmer, *A Ghetto Takes Shape,* 222–23; Natalie Middleton, interview by Antoinette Kindall, Cleveland, Dec. 20, 1986, transcript, St. James A.M.E. Oral History Project.

58. *Neighborhood Visitor,* Feb. 6, 1925, Hiram House Records, WRHS.

59. Blackmon, "Black Railroad Worker," 5; Middleton interview by Kindall; Middleton interview by author; Willa Davenport Thomas interview. On the general desire of migrants to take advantage of greater access to material goods, see Carole Marks, *Farewell—We're Good and Gone: The Great Black Migration* (Bloomington: Indiana University Press, 1989), 137–51.

60. Quoted in Maurine Weiner Greenwald, *Women, War, and Work: The Impact of World War I on Women Workers in the United States* (Westport, Conn.: Greenwood Press, 1980), 113.

61. Stokes, *Promises of Power,* 23.

62. S. J. Holmes, *The Negro's Struggle for Survival* (California: University of California Press, 1937), 163; Stephanie L. Hiedemann, "With Permission to Safeguard Mothers and Children: Public Health Policies in Cleveland" (M.A. thesis, Case Western Reserve University, 1996); Jessie M. Rodrique, "The Black Community and the Birth Control Movement," in *"We Specialize in the Wholly Impossible": A Reader in*

Black Women's History, ed. Darlene Clark Hine, Wilma King, and Linda Reed (New York: Carlson, 1995), 505–20.

63. Blackmon, "Black Railroad Worker," 6; Cyril Robinson, "Exploring the Informal Economy," *Crime and Social Justice* 15, nos. 3–4 (1988): 3–16.

64. Middleton interview by Kindall; Marie Crawford, interview by Doris Crawford, Cleveland, Sept. 29, 1986, transcript, St. James A.M.E. Oral History Project. For a description of African-American mutuality within an illicit economy, see Horace Cayton and St. Clair Drake, *Black Metropolis: A Study of Negro Life in a Northern City* (New York: Harcourt, Brace, 1945).

65. Himes, *Quality of Hurt,* 1:18–19.

66. *Cleveland Call and Post,* June 30, 1934.

67. Stokes, *Promises of Power,* 24, 27. For an account of hustling in Cleveland, see Himes, *Quality of Hurt,* 1:33–37. Lawrence Levine has described pimps and hustlers more as modern-day tricksters than as "bad men." See *Black Culture and Black Consciousness: Afro-American Folk Thought from Slavery to Freedom* (New York: Oxford University Press, 1977), 381–82. For an important account of black male hustling, see Robin D. G. Kelley, "The Riddle of the Zoot: Malcolm Little and Black Cultural Politics during World War II," *Race Rebels: Culture, Politics, and the Black Working Class* (New York: Free Press, 1994), 161–81.

68. *Cleveland Gazette,* Sept. 19, 1931.

69. Cleveland Urban League, "1918 Report to the Board of Trustees," Cleveland Urban League Records (quote); Scott, *Negro Migration,* 140–41; Hunter, *A Nickel and a Prayer,* 132–33.

70. See, for example, *Cleveland Gazette,* June 2, 1919; and *Cleveland Call and Post,* Sept. 22, 1934.

71. Joanne Meyerowitz, "Sexual Geography and Gender Economy: The Furnished Room Districts of Chicago, 1890–1930," *Gender and History* 2 (Autumn 1990): 282 (first quote); Meyerowitz, *Women Adrift,* 104–7; Hunter, *A Nickel and a Prayer,* 67 (second, third, and fourth quotes), 123 (fifth quote); Hazel V. Carby, "Policing the Black Woman's Body in an Urban Context," *Critical Inquiry* 18 (Summer 1992): 738–55.

72. *Cleveland Gazette,* June 16, 1917.

73. Himes, *Quality of Hurt,* 1:17.

74. Howard Whipple Green, *An Analysis of 377 Records of Girls Committed to the Girls' Industrial School by the Juvenile Court at Cleveland during a Six Year Period, 1920–1925* (Cleveland: Cleveland Health Council, 1929). For an important discussion of African-American women's experiences of sexual violence, see Darlene Clark Hine, "Rape and the Inner Lives of Black Women in the Middle West: Preliminary Thoughts on the Culture of Dissemblance," *Signs* 14 (Summer 1989): 912. For a general understanding of young women's responses to sexual molestation and violence, see Linda Gordon, *Heroes of Their Own Lives: The Politics and History of Family Violence, Boston, 1880–1960* (New York: Viking, 1988).

75. Marion Morton, "Seduced and Abandoned in an American City: Cleveland and Its Fallen Women, 1869–1936," *Journal of Urban History* 11 (Aug. 1985): 449–59 (quote on 447); Cleveland Urban League, "Annual Report to the Executive Committee, Feb. 1920–Dec. 1920," Cleveland Urban League Records.

76. Eleanor Rowland Wembridge, introduction to Green, *An Analysis of 377 Records of Girls,* 60.

77. Eleanor Rowland Wembridge, "Potential Explosives," *The Clevelander* 3 (Apr. 1920): 5–7; H. L. Rockwood, "The Effect of Negro Migration on Community Health in Cleveland," *National Conference on Social Welfare Proceedings* (Cleveland: n.p., 1926), 238–43.

78. Cleveland Chamber of Commerce, *Investigation of Housing,* 20; *Cleveland Gazette,* Sept. 19, 1931. See also reports from the *Neighborhood Visitor* from the 1920s in the Hiram House Records.

79. On efforts to preserve immigrant cultures in Cleveland, see Barton, *Peasants and Strangers,* 25–26. On Americanization efforts in Cleveland, see John J. Grabowski, "A Social Settlement in Transition: Hiram House, 1896–1926" (Ph.D. diss., Case Western Reserve University, 1976), 31; John J. Grabowski, "From Progressive to Patrician: George Bellamy and Hiram House Social Settlement, 1896–1914," *Ohio History* 87 (Winter 1978): 37–52; Edward M. Miggins, "A City of 'Uplifting Influences': From Sweet Charity to Modern Social Welfare and Philanthropy," in *Birth of Modern Cleveland,* esp. 160–61. For immigrant responses elsewhere, see Lizbeth Cohen, *Making a New Deal: Industrial Workers in Chicago, 1919–1939* (Cambridge: Cambridge University Press, 1990); and Elisabeth Lasch-Quinn, *Black Neighbors: Race and the Limits of Reform in the American Settlement House Movement, 1890–1945* (Chapel Hill: University of North Carolina Press, 1993).

80. Thomas F. Campbell, *SASS: Fifty Years of Social Work Education* (Cleveland: Case Western University Press, 1967), 1–18. For a critical assessment of these efforts, see Miggins, "City of 'Uplifting Influences,'" 150–58; and Grabowski, "A Social Settlement in Transition," 45.

81. For wartime and postwar race relations, see William Tuttle, *Race Riot: Chicago in the Red Summer of 1919* (1970; reprint, New York: Atheneum, 1984); Olivier Zunz, *The Changing Face of Inequality: Urbanization, Industrial Development, and Immigrants in Detroit, 1880–1920* (Chicago: University of Chicago Press, 1982). On social welfare, see John J. Grabowski and David D. Van Tassel, *Cleveland: A Tradition of Reform* (Kent, Ohio: Kent State University Press, 1986). For contemporary racial attitudes and ideas, see John R. Commons, *Races and Immigrants in America* (New York: Macmillan, 1907); George M. Frederickson, *The Black Image in the White Mind: The Debate on Afro-American Character and Destiny, 1817–1914* (New York: Harper and Row, 1971); and Allan Chase, *The Legacy of Malthus: The Social Costs of the New Scientific Racism* (New York: Knopf, 1976).

82. "Annual Report of the Neighborhood Visitor for the Year Ending Apr. 1, 1911," Hiram House Records (first and second quotes); Grabowski, "A Social Settlement in Transition," 255 (third quote). See also Hiram House, "Annual Report, 1936–1937," Hiram House Records.

83. "Report from the Hiram House Girls' Department, 1915–16," Hiram House Records (first quote); "Report of Girls' Department, 1918–1919," Hiram House Records (second quote).

84. Miggins, "City of 'Uplifting Influences,'" 146; Grabowski, "A Social Settlement in Transition," 254–60; Allen F. Davis, "Welfare Reform and World War I," *American Quarterly* 19 (Fall 1967): 532.

85. Kusmer, *A Ghetto Takes Shape,* 235 (quote), 254–57.

86. Horace R. Cayton and George S. Mitchell, *Black Workers and the New Unions* (Chapel Hill: University of North Carolina Press, 1939), 389; Hicks interview.

87. Hunter, *A Nickel and a Prayer*, 131–35 (quote on 135); Myrtle J. Bell Papers, WRHS.

88. Phillis Wheatley Association annual meeting, minutes, Jan. 18, 1921, Phillis Wheatley Association Records, WRHS.

89. *Chicago Defender*, Jan. 31, 1919; Executive Committee of Goodrich House, minutes, June 9, 1926, and Board of Trustees, minutes, Oct. 8, 1930, Goodrich Social Settlement Records, WRHS; Kusmer, *A Ghetto Takes Shape*, 188, 216–17; John J. Grabowski and David D. Van Tassel, eds., *The Encyclopedia of Cleveland History* (Bloomington: Indiana University Press, 1987), 587.

90. *Neighborhood Visitor*, ca. 1922, Aug. 27, 1931, Hiram House Records.

91. Lois Blanchard, "Mothers' Clubs at the Friendly Inn," 28–29, University Settlement Records, WRHS. That black working-class women were intent on educating themselves and satisfying personal desires of self challenges Jacqueline Jones's suggestion that black working-class women in the North tended to quash personal desires. See Jones, *Labor of Love, Labor of Sorrow*, 194.

92. Chesnutt, "Negro in Cleveland," 3–4; Cleveland Board of Education, *Annual Report, 1929* (Cleveland: Cleveland Board of Education, 1930), 26–27; *Birmingham Reporter*, Feb. 17, 1923, Feb. 24, 1923; Alonzo Gatskell Grace, "The Effect of Negro Migration on the Cleveland Public School System" (Ph.D. diss., Western Reserve University, 1932); Kusmer, *A Ghetto Takes Shape*, 182–84; Himes, *Quality of Hurt*, 1:16; Stokes, *Promises of Power*, 25–26; Thompson interview; Capers interview; Hazel Mountain Walker Papers, WRHS; Myrtle J. Bell Papers, WRHS.

Chapter 5: "AlabamaNorth"

1. Arthur Turner, interview by author, Cleveland, May 18, 1996, videotape.

2. Arnold Rampersad, *The Life of Langston Hughes, Volume I, 1902–1941* (New York: Oxford University Press, 1986), 25.

3. U.S. Bureau of the Census, *Negroes in the United States, 1920–1932* (Washington, D.C.: Government Printing Office, 1935), 32, 34–37.

4. Quoted in Katrina Hazzard-Gordon, *Jookin': The Rise of Social Dance Formations in African-American Culture* (Philadelphia: Temple University Press, 1990), 79. For a description of jook joints in the South, see 76–81 and Zora Neale Hurston, "Characteristics of Negro Expression," in *Negro Anthology*, ed. Nancy Cunard (New York: Negro Universities Press, 1969), 44. For elites' responses to the arrival of migrants, see Kenneth L. Kusmer, *A Ghetto Takes Shape: Black Cleveland, 1870–1930* (Urbana: University of Illinois Press, 1976), 251–52.

5. *Cleveland Gazette*, July 21, 1917.

6. See examples in the southern cities of Richmond, Birmingham, and Atlanta in Elsa Barkley Brown, "Womanist Consciousness: Maggie Lena Walker and the Independent Order of St. Luke," *Signs* 14 (Spring 1989): 610–33; Robin D. G. Kelley, *Race Rebels: Culture, Politics, and the Black Working Class* (New York: Free Press, 1994); and Tera W. Hunter, *To 'Joy My Freedom: Southern Black Women's Lives and Labors after the Civil War* (Cambridge, Mass.: Harvard University Press, 1997).

7. Robin D. G. Kelley, "'We Are Not What We Seem': Rethinking Black Working-Class Opposition in the Jim Crow South," *Journal of American History* 80 (June 1993): 79.

8. On the African-American middle-class and elite in Cleveland, see Kusmer, *A Ghetto Takes Shape*, 91–112, esp. 104–8; Willard B. Gatewood, *Aristocrats of Color: The Black Elite*,

1880–1920 (Bloomington: University of Indiana Press, 1990), 159–60; Charles W. Chesnutt, "The Negro in Cleveland," *The Clevelander* 5 (Nov. 1930): 4; John P. Green, *Fact Stranger than Fiction* (Cleveland: Riehl Printing, 1920); and Carrie W. Clifford, *Sowing for Others to Reap* (Cleveland: Charles W. Alexander, 1900).

9. The formation of a black working-class identity in the first half of the twentieth century, which was related to but distinct from those of the black middle class and the elite, has begun to receive attention. Important examples are Kelley, *Race Rebels,* esp. chaps. 1–3; Earl Lewis, *In Their Own Interests: Race, Class, and Power in Twentieth-Century Norfolk, Virginia* (Berkeley: University of California Press, 1990), 89–109; and Eric Arnesen, "The African-American Working Class in the Jim Crow Era," *International Labor and Working-Class History* 41 (Spring 1992): 59–75. My interpretation builds on these works but I have included more fully the experiences of black women and the role of southern black expressive culture in the North, where questions about its usefulness for black progress were acute. See Evelyn Brooks Higginbotham, "African-American Women's History and the Metalanguage of Race," *Signs* 17 (Winter 1992): 251–74; and Hunter, *To 'Joy My Freedom,* 145–67. For a discussion of black middle-class anxieties over the efficacy of southern working-class culture, see Kevin K. Gaines, *Uplifting the Race: Black Leadership, Politics, and Culture in the Twentieth Century* (Chapel Hill: University of North Carolina Press, 1996).

10. Kusmer, *A Ghetto Takes Shape,* 251–52. For a sympathetic understanding of migrants, see George Haynes, "Negro Migration: Its Effects on Family and Community Life in the North," *Opportunity* 2 (Oct. 1924): 303–6. For attitudes in other cities, see Carole Marks, *Farewell—We're Good and Gone: The Great Black Migration* (Bloomington: University of Indiana Press, 1989), 160; and Allan H. Spear, *Black Chicago: The Making of a Negro Ghetto, 1890–1920* (Chicago: University of Chicago Press, 1967), 168.

11. *Cleveland Gazette,* May 19, 1917.

12. *Cleveland Gazette,* Jan. 20, 1917.

13. See, for example, *Cleveland Gazette,* Sept. 8, 1917, Aug. 2, 1919, Sept. 15, 1919. For examples of racial jokes and remarks, see the *Cleveland Plain Dealer* and the *Cleveland Citizen* during the World War I years. On January 20, 1917, Smith claimed that the *Cleveland Leader* used *darky* and *nigger* daily. For a discussion of the effort to ban *Birth of a Nation,* see Kusmer, *A Ghetto Takes Shape,* 176. For thorough accounts of the riots during the war years, see Elliott M. Rudwick, *Race Riot at East St. Louis, July 2, 1917* (New York: Meridian Books, 1964), chap. 2.

14. *Cleveland Gazette,* July 30, 1919.

15. Russell H. Davis, *Black Americans in Cleveland: From George Peake to Carl B. Stokes, 1796 to 1969* (Cleveland: Western Reserve Historical Society, 1972; reprint, Washington, D.C.: Associated Publishers, 1985), 226–27; Kusmer, *A Ghetto Takes Shape,* 176–77. For the rise of the Klan, see David M. Chalmers, *Hooded Americanism: The History of the Ku Klux Klan* (Garden City, N.Y.: Doubleday, 1965), 175–82.

16. *Cleveland Gazette,* May 19, 1917, July 14, 1917; Rev. Frank A. Smith, interview by author and Patricia Miles Ashford, Cleveland, Aug. 6, 1991, transcript.

17. *Cleveland Gazette,* Jan. 20, 1917, Mar. 1, 1919.

18. *Cleveland Gazette,* Aug. 2, 1919.

19. George Myers to James Rhodes, Feb. 21, 1921, in *The Barber and the Historian:*

The Correspondence of George A. Myers and James Ford Rhodes, 1910–1923, ed. John A. Garraty (Columbus: Ohio Historical Society, 1956), 124.

20. Elmer Thompson, interview by Thomas F. Campbell, in Thomas F. Campbell, "Speech Sound Recording: On the History of Cleveland," Cleveland Heritage Program, 1981, transcript, Cleveland Public Library.

21. Kusmer, *A Ghetto Takes Shape*, 92–93, 207–9; Davis, *Black Americans in Cleveland*, 254–60; *The Baptist Answer in 1924–25: Being the Ninety-Fifth Annual Report of the Cleveland Baptist Association* (Cleveland: n.p., 1925); Dorothy Ann Blatnica, *At the Alter of Their God: African-American Catholics in Cleveland, 1922–1961* (New York: Garland, 1995). For a sociological account of black Protestant denominations, see C. Eric Lincoln and Lawrence H. Mamiya, *The Black Church in the African American Experience* (Durham: Duke University Press, 1990). On A.M.E. churches, see Clarence E. Walker, *A Rock in a Weary Land: The African Methodist Episcopal Church during the Civil War and Reconstruction* (Baton Rouge: Louisiana State University Press, 1982); and Robert Gregg, *Sparks from the Anvil of Oppression: Philadelphia's African American Methodists and Southern Migrants, 1890–1940* (Philadelphia: Temple University Press, 1994). On the development and growth of the black Baptist church, see Evelyn Brooks Higginbotham, *Righteous Discontent: The Women's Movement in the Black Baptist Church, 1880–1920* (Cambridge, Mass.: Harvard University Press, 1993).

22. Benjamin Mays and Joseph Nicholson, *The Negro's Church* (New York: Institute of Social and Religious Research, 1933; reprint, New York: Russell and Russell, 1969); Foster Armstrong, Richard Klein, and Cara Armstrong, *A Guide to Cleveland's Sacred Landmarks* (Kent, Ohio: Kent State University Press, 1992), 110–41.

23. Kusmer, *A Ghetto Takes Shape*, 94.

24. Davis, *Black Americans in Cleveland*, 187–89. For an insightful and innovative discussion of the influence of built space on African Americans' identities, see Elsa Barkley Brown and Gregg D. Kimball, "Mapping the Terrain of Black Richmond," in *The New African American Urban History*, ed. Kenneth W. Goings and Raymond A. Mohl (Thousand Oaks, Calif.: Sage Publications, 1996), 66–115.

25. *Chicago Defender*, May 24, 1919; Armstrong, Klein, and Armstrong, *Guide to Cleveland's Sacred Landmarks*, 110–42.

26. *Chicago Defender*, Feb. 12, 1917, Feb. 24, 1917; Lincoln and Mamiya, *Black Church*, 121; Davis, *Black Americans in Cleveland*, 256–59; Smith interview. My interpretation of church architecture and its meaning owes much to Jeanne Kilde, "Spiritual Armories: A Social and Architectural History of the Neo-Medieval Auditorium Church in the U.S., 1869–1910" (Ph.D. diss., University of Minnesota, 1991).

27. *Cleveland Gazette*, July 14, 1917, Aug. 11, 1917.

28. Higginbotham, *Righteous Discontent*, 187. For a lengthy discussion of these perceptions, see Gaines, *Uplifting the Race*, 67–99; and Gregg, *Sparks*.

29. Cleveland Urban League, "1918 Report to the Board of Trustees," Cleveland Urban League Records, Western Reserve Historical Society, Cleveland (hereafter WRHS).

30. *Cleveland Gazette*, Oct. 29, 1921.

31. *Cleveland Gazette*, Mar. 29, 1924, May 17, 1924. No such home was ever organized.

32. Davis, *Black Americans in Cleveland*, 255–59; Chicago *Defender*, May 17, 1919;

Willa Davenport Thomas, interview by author, Cleveland, Dec. 1, 1989, transcript; Gwen Gregory Johnson, interview by author, Cleveland, Dec. 16, 1991, transcript; William H. Murdock, interview by Antoinette Kindall, Cleveland, Sept. 19, 1986, transcript, St. James A.M.E. Oral History Project, WRHS.

33. For the development of segregated social welfare agencies and working-class black responses, see Adrienne Lash Jones, *Jane Edna Hunter: A Case Study of Black Leadership, 1910–1959* (New York: Carlson, 1990); Kusmer, *A Ghetto Takes Shape,* 149–51, 258–59.

34. *Cleveland Gazette,* Jan. 13, 1917; Kusmer, *A Ghetto Takes Shape,* 92–96, 207–9; Davis, *Black Americans in Cleveland,* 254–59. For an overview of these debates, see Gaines, *Uplifting the Race,* 67–99; and Houston A. Baker Jr., *Modernism and the Harlem Renaissance* (Chicago: University of Chicago Press, 1987), 72–81.

35. Hazel V. Carby, *Reconstructing Black Womanhood: The Emergence of the Afro-American Novelist* (New York: Oxford University Press, 1987), 165–66. Kusmer, *A Ghetto Takes Shape,* 218. Writers like Langston Hughes, Hurston, and Chester Himes may have found working-class southern migrants' urban experiences sources for their work, but others in Cleveland's black intellectual elite did not view them so warmly. Rather, middle-class blacks' "interest in Africa or southern black folk culture," as Kenneth L. Kusmer has noted, "was more a symptom of ethnic ambivalence than a revolution in values." More often than not, the middle class took a dim view of plays about "southern folk culture because they firmly believed that their own way of life was an advance over what was being portrayed on the stage" (218).

36. Thompson interview; George Myers, "Religious Unity Is Presently Needed," *Cleveland Advocate,* June 26, 1915.

37. Smith interview; Rev. Frank A. Smith, *A Pilgrimage in Faith: The History of Lane Metropolitan Christian Methodist Episcopal Church, 1902–1984* (Cleveland: n.p., 1984), 1.

38. *Cleveland Gazette,* Jan. 20, 1918.

39. Higginbotham, *Righteous Discontent,* 42–47.

40. Smith interview; Armstrong, Klein, and Armstrong, *Guide to Cleveland's Sacred Landmarks,* 122–23.

41. Smith interview.

42. Ibid.

43. Ohio Church Survey Records, 1940, box 1, Ohio Works Progress Administration Records, Ohio Historical Society, Columbus.

44. James E. Blackwell, "Black Store Front Churches in Cleveland: A Comparative Study of Five Negro Store Front Churches in Cleveland" (M.A. thesis, Western Reserve University, 1949), 23–24; Davis, *Black Americans in Cleveland,* 297.

45. Davis, *Black Americans in Cleveland,* 297; Lincoln and Mamiya, *Black Church,* 22–23.

46. Ohio Church Survey Records, 1940, box 6, Ohio Works Progress Administration Records.

47. Marie Crawford, interview by Doris Crawford, Cleveland, Sept. 29, 1986, transcript, St. James A.M.E. Oral History Project.

48. Photograph, n.d., *Cleveland Press* Archives, Cleveland State University, Cleveland, Ohio.

49. Davis, *Black Americans in Cleveland,* 189, 257.

50. Dona Gallo Brady, "The History and Development of the West Park Black Community," ms., Aug. 1, 1990, unprocessed Second Calvary Baptist Church file, WRHS.

51. *Cleveland Plain Dealer,* Sept. 22, 1930; Davis, *Black Americans in Cleveland,* 254.

52. Lincoln and Mamiya, *Black Church,* 117.

53. Bertha Cowan, interview by Eleanor Jackson, Cleveland, Jan. 16, 1987, transcript, St. James A.M.E. Oral History Project.

54. Viv Broughton, *Black Gospel: An Illustrated History of the Gospel Sound* (Poole, England: Blanford Press, 1985), 45.

55. Lawrence W. Levine, *Black Culture and Black Consciousness: Afro-American Folk Thought from Slavery to Freedom* (New York: Oxford University Press, 1977), 189.

56. Anthony B. Pinn, *Why, Lord?: Suffering and Evil in Black Theology* (New York: Continuum, 1995), 157; James H. Cone, *Black Theology of Liberation* (Philadelphia: Lippincott, 1970); Cornel West, *Prophesy Deliverance!: An Afro-American Revolutionary Christianity* (Philadelphia: Westminster Press, 1982).

57. Like a number of other scholars, I found blacks' experiences of divine intervention to be commonplace. See Kelley, *Race Rebels,* 42–43, on this point. For other examples of this experience and the power and meaning of prayer in their daily lives, see Sara Brooks, *You May Plow Here: The Narrative of Sara Brooks,* ed. Thordis Simonsen (New York: Simon and Schuster, 1987), 184–222; and Gus Joiner, interview by author, Cleveland, Oct. 2, 1989, transcript.

58. Walter F. Pitts Jr., *Old Ship of Zion: The Afro-Baptist Ritual in the African Diaspora* (New York: Oxford University Press, 1993), 12–18; James Weldon Johnson, *God's Trombones: Seven Negro Sermons in Verse* (New York: Viking, 1927; reprint, New York: Viking, 1975), 1–9.

59. *Cleveland Call and Post,* June 30, 1934; Blackwell, "Black Store Front Churches," 23–24; Peter D. Goldsmith, *When I Rise Cryin' Holy: African-American Denominationalism on the Georgia Coast* (New York: AMS Press, 1989), 69–190. For the appeal of Pentecostalism, see Harvey Cox, *Fire from Heaven: The Rise of Pentecostal Spirituality and the Reshaping of Religion in the Twenty-First Century* (Massachusetts: Addison-Wesley, 1995). For a case study of Chicago's Pentecostal churches, see St. Clair Drake, *Churches and Voluntary Associations in the Chicago Negro Community* (Chicago: Works Progress Administration, 1940), 298–305; James S. Tinney, "William J. Seymour: Father of Modern-Day Pentecostalism," in *Black Apostles: Afro-American Clergy Confront the Twentieth Century,* ed. Randall K. Burkett and Richard Newman (Boston: G. K. Hall, 1978), 213–25.

60. Goldsmith, *When I Rise Cryin' Holy,* 95.

61. Jon Michael Spencer, "The Rhythms of Black Folks," in *"Ain't Gonna Lay My 'Ligion Down": African American Religion in the South,* ed. Alonzo Johnson and Paul Jersild (Columbia: University of South Carolina Press, 1996), 39.

62. Quoted in Levine, *Black Culture and Black Consciousness,* 180.

63. Lincoln and Mamiya, *Black Church,* 228. On black women and participation in religious institutions, see Lincoln and Mamiya, *Black Church,* 274–308; Higginbotham, *Righteous Discontent;* and Cheryl Townsend Gilkes, "'Together and in Harness': Women's Traditions in the Sanctified Church," *Signs* 10 (Summer 1985): 696–99.

64. Blackwell, "Black Store Front Churches," 72.

65. Ibid.

66. Ibid., 72–75 (first quote on 72), 83–89, 114 (second quote).

67. Kelley, *Race Rebels,* 40.

68. Kerrill Leslie Rubman, "From Jubilee to Gospel in Black Male Quartet Singing" (Ph.D. diss., University of North Carolina at Chapel Hill, 1980), 17–46.

69. Robert Kimball and William Bolcolm, *Reminiscing with Sissle and Blake* (New York: Viking Press, 1973), 26.

70. Quoted in Levine, *Black Culture and Black Consciousness,* 180.

71. Kip Lornell, *"Happy in the Service of the Lord": Afro-American Gospel Quartets in Memphis* (Urbana: University of Illinois Press, 1988), 11–17; Ray Allen, *Singing in the Spirit: African-American Sacred Quartets in New York City* (Philadelphia: University of Pennsylvania Press, 1991); Horace Clarence Boyer, *How Sweet the Sound: The Golden Age of Gospel* (Washington, D.C.: Elliott and Clark, 1995), 29–35.

72. On the widespread participation in male quartet singing, see James Weldon Johnson and James Rosamond Johnson, *The Books of American Negro Spirituals* (New York: Viking Press, 1940), 35–36; Rubman, "From Jubilee to Gospel," 34–35; and Ray Allen, "Shouting the Church: Narrative and Vocal Improvisation in African-American Gospel Quartet Performance," *Journal of American Folklore* 104 (Fall 1991): 295–317. On male quartet singing in work camps, see Lornell, *"Happy,"* 19; Boyer, *How Sweet the Sound,* 32–33; Arthur Turner, interview by author, Cleveland, May 23, 1996, videotape.

73. Turner interview, May 23, 1996; Lornell, *"Happy,"* 22.

74. Levine, *Black Culture and Black Consciousness,* 186.

75. Catherine McKenzie, founder of the Bright Stars, interview by author, Cleveland, July 23, 1996, transcript.

76. Cleveland Coloured Quintette, *The Coloured Quintette: A Brief Narrative of God's Marvellous Dealings with the Cleveland Gospel Quintette and Their Personal Testimony* (Kilmarnock, Scotland: John Ritchie, 1937); David J. Font, "Early Associates of A. B. Simpson," *Southeastern District Report,* Apr.–May 1978, n.p., Collection of the Colored Gospel Quintet, Bowling Green State University, Bowling Green, Ohio.

77. On the rise of hard gospel, or gospel blues, see Michael W. Harris, *The Rise of the Gospel Blues: The Music of Thomas Andrew Dorsey in the Urban Church* (New York: Oxford University Press, 1992); Turner interview, May 23, 1996. On the use of the double-voice, see Grey Gundaker, *Signs of Diaspora, Diaspora of Signs: Literacies, Creolization, and Vernacular Practice in African America* (New York: Oxford University Press, 1998), 11, 102; and Henry Louis Gates Jr., *The Signifying Monkey: A Theory of African-American Literary Criticism* (New York: Oxford University Press, 1988), 110.

78. Turner interview, May 23, 1996.

79. Thompson interview.

80. Ohio Church Survey Records, 1940, box 6, folders 116, 121, Ohio Works Progress Administration Records.

81. Cowan interview; Elizabeth Clark-Lewis, *Living In, Living Out: African American Domestics in Washington, D.C., 1910–1940* (Washington, D.C.: Smithsonian Institution, 1994), 34–38.

82. Clark-Lewis, *Living In, Living Out,* 87.

83. Ohio Church Survey Records, 1940, box 6, Ohio Works Progress Administration Records; Kusmer, *A Ghetto Takes Shape,* 96.

84. Jane Edna Hunter, *A Nickel and a Prayer* (Cleveland: Elli Kani, 1940), 132–33.

85. *Cleveland Gazette,* May 26, 1917; Davis, *Black Americans in Cleveland,* 266; William A. Muraskin, *Middle-Class Blacks in a White Society: Prince Hall Freemasonry in America* (Berkeley: University of California Press, 1975), 43–52; Charles H. Wesley, *The History of the Prince Hall Grand Lodge of Free and Accepted Masons of the State of Ohio, 1849–1960* (Wilberforce, Ohio: Central State College Press, 1961); *History, Constitution, and By-Laws of Exelsior Lodge No. 11 Free and Accepted Masons* (Cleveland: n.p., 1926) (quote). The *Cleveland City Directory,* black newspapers, and the personal papers of elite blacks provide the names and occupations of the leadership for the Odd Fellows, Masons, and Knights of Pythias. It is much more difficult to get the same information for the rank-and-file membership.

86. For a discussion of black women's contestation of patriarchy in fraternal organizations, see Brown, "Womanist Consciousness," 610–33.

87. Natalie Middleton, interview by author, Cleveland, Feb. 21, 1989, transcript; Eleanor Walls Grist, interview by author, Cleveland, Aug. 22, 1989, transcript; Paul Glenn, interview by author, June 18, 1991, Cleveland, transcript; Thompson interview; *Cleveland City Directory,* 1925–30; Muraskin, *Middle-Class Blacks,* 43–45.

88. Wesley, *History of the Prince Hall Grand Lodge,* 49; Muraskin, *Middle-Class Blacks,* 44.

89. Welfare Federation of Cleveland Research Committee, *Central Area Social Study* (Cleveland: n.p., 1944), 132–33, 140, Cleveland Public Library; Murtis H. Taylor, interview by Earlynne Davis, Cleveland, Oct. 19, 1986, transcript, St. James A.M.E. Oral History Project; John Miller Sr., interview by Edward D. Schmieding, Cleveland, Nov. 27, 1991, transcript in author's possession; Gatewood, *Aristocrats of Color,* ix.

90. Randolph and Owen quoted in Sterling D. Spero and Abram L. Harris, *The Black Worker: The Negro and the Labor Movement* (New York: Columbia University Press, 1931; reprint, New York: Atheneum, 1969), 389–91. For Randolph's views on the necessity of African-American political activism generally, see Paula F. Pfeffer, *A. Philip Randolph: Pioneer of the Civil Rights Movement* (Baton Rouge: Louisiana State University Press, 1990), 12. Pfeffer makes the point that "Randolph and Owen might insist they wanted to reach the black urban proletariat, but their economic theories and 'New Negro' appeal were in fact directed toward educated, middle-class blacks. The bulk of the *Messenger*'s support came from a small cadre of white and black intellectuals, labor and Socialist circles" (12).

91. Langston Hughes, *The Big Sea* (New York: Hill and Wang, 1941), 228.

92. "The Common Welfare," *Survey* 58 (June 15, 1927), 323.

93. On the rich tradition of blacks' secret societies, fraternal organizations, and voluntary activities in the nineteenth-century urban south, see Peter J. Rachleff, *Black Labor in Richmond, 1865–1890* (Urbana: University of Illinois Press, 1989), 13–33; and Brown, "Womanist Consciousness." On the more limited access to secular clubs and organizations in southern rural areas, see Charles S. Johnson, *Shadow of the Plantation* (Chicago: University of Chicago Press, 1934), 180–85; Flowree Robinson, interview by author, Cleveland, Nov. 29, 1989, transcript; and Cowan interview.

94. Davis, *Black Americans in Cleveland,* 213, 266; E. Franklin Frazier, *Black Bourgeoisie* (Glencoe, Ill: Glencoe Free Press, 1957), 91–94; Jacqueline Jones, *Labor of Love, Labor of Sorrow: Black Women, Work, and the Family from Slavery to the Present* (New York: Basic Books, 1985), 193. Jones claims that in the urban environment, working-

class women's roles became more privatized. For sharply diverging analyses, see Clark-Lewis, *Living In, Living Out;* and Victoria W. Wolcott, "Mediums, Messages, and Lucky Numbers: African-American Female Spiritualists and Numbers Runners in Interwar Detroit," in *The Geography of Identity,* ed. Patricia Yaeger (Ann Arbor: University of Michigan Press, 1996), 273–306.

95. Crawford interview; Willa Davenport Thomas interview. In the 1950s and 1960s, these street clubs expanded to include porch clubs. These new clubs helped recently arrived children sharpen their educational skills. Community organizers used these indigenous clubs to begin the Headstart program in Cleveland. I would like to thank Evora Baker and Patricia Miles Ashford for this information.

96. Welfare Federation of Cleveland Research Committee, *Central Area Social Study;* Ray Dennis, interview by author, Cleveland, Sept. 27, 1989, transcript; Thompson interview; *Cleveland Gazette,* Jan. 16, 1917.

97. Hazzard-Gordon, *Jookin',* 125–27; John J. Grabowski and David D. Van Tassel, eds. *The Encyclopedia of Cleveland History* (Bloomington: Indiana University Press, 1987), 381; Taylor interview; Willa Davenport Thomas interview; Natalie Middleton, interview by Antoinette Kindall, Cleveland, Dec. 20, 1986, transcript, St. James A.M.E. Oral History Project. Hiram House and the Friendly Inn used dancing as a form of socialization for immigrant children. With the arrival of migrants, however, these activities came to a halt. Both places reestablished dancing only after prolonged agitation from black children and teenagers, but it was done in a segregated manner.

98. Cowan interview.

99. Kusmer, *A Ghetto Takes Shape,* 100–101; Hazzard-Gordon, *Jookin',* 135–54; Chester Himes, *The Quality of Hurt: The Autobiography of Chester Himes* (New York: Doubleday, 1972), 1:28; *Cleveland Gazette,* May 30, 1931.

100. Hazzard-Gordon, *Jookin',* 94–119 (quote on 111); Levine, *Black Culture and Black Consciousness,* 239–70.

101. Henry Pointer, interview by Antoinette Kindall, Cleveland, Oct. 30, 1986, transcript, St. James A.M.E. Oral History Project; *Cleveland Call and Post,* Jan. 27, 1938.

102. Thompson interview.

103. *Cleveland Gazette,* May 24, 1924, Aug. 25, 1923.

104. Lawrence W. Levine, "Marcus Garvey and the Politics of Revitalization," in *Black Leaders of the Twentieth Century,* ed. John Hope Franklin and August Meier (Urbana: University of Illinois Press, 1982), 118; "Bureau of Investigation Reports," May 14, 1920, *Marcus Garvey and Universal Negro Improvement Association Papers,* vol. 2, *August 19, 1919–August 31, 1920,* ed. Robert Hill (Berkeley: University of California Press, 1983), 340–44; Kusmer, *A Ghetto Takes Shape,* 228–29; *Cleveland Gazette,* Jan. 21, 1922; Judith Stein, *The World of Marcus Garvey: Race and Class in Modern Society* (Baton Rouge: Louisiana State University Press, 1986), 238–42. The records of the UNIA in the Western Reserve Historical Society archives are particularly useful because they include members' occupations and addresses.

105. Quoted in Levine, "Marcus Garvey," 121.

106. "Report of Marcus Garvey's Speeches in Cleveland," Jan. 15, 1921, *Marcus Garvey and Universal Negro Improvement Association Papers,* vol. 3, *September 1920–August 1921,* ed. Robert A. Hill (Berkeley: University of California Press, 1984), 132–33, originally printed in the *Cleveland Advocate,* Jan. 15, 1921; "Bureau of Investigation Reports," May 14, 1920, *Marcus Garvey Papers,* 2:339.

107. I used membership lists of the UNIA, 1923–29, WRHS, and *Cleveland City Directory,* 1915–29.

108. Stein, *World of Marcus Garvey,* 225, 240–41; "Report by Special Employee Andrew M. Battle," July 5, 1922, *Marcus Garvey Papers,* volume 4, *September 1, 1921–September 2, 1922,* ed. Robert A. Hill (Berkeley: University of California Press, 1985), 700–701n1.

109. Quoted in Stein, *World of Marcus Garvey,* 241.

Chapter 6: *"The Future Is Yours"*

1. Charles Loeb, *The Future Is Yours* (Cleveland: Future Outlook League, 1946), 17–18; *Cleveland Eagle,* Feb. 29, 1936.

2. John O. Holly to H. G. Emerson, Feb. 12, 1936, Records of the Future Outlook League, Western Reserve Historical Society, Cleveland (hereafter WRHS).

3. The most comprehensive overview of African-American boycotts against economic and racial discrimination remains August Meier and Elliott Rudwick's "The Origins of Nonviolent Direct Action in Afro-American Protest: A Note on Historical Discontinuities," *Along the Color Line: Explorations in the Black Experience* (Urbana: University of Illinois Press, 1976), 307–404. Case studies of the efforts from the late 1920s to the mid-1940s include Robin D. G. Kelley, "Congested Terrain: Resistance on Public Transportation," *Race Rebels: Culture, Politics, and the Black Working Class* (New York: Free Press, 1994), 55–75; Cheryl Greenberg, *"Or Does It Explode?": Black Harlem in the Great Depression* (New York: Oxford University Press, 1991), 114–39; Lestor Lamon, *Black Tennessians, 1900–1930* (Knoxville: University of Tennessee Press, 1977); Andor Skotnes, "'Buy Where You Can Work': Boycotting for Jobs in African-American Baltimore, 1933–34," *Journal of Social History* 27 (Summer 1994): 735–61; Winston McDowell, "Race and Ethnicity during the Harlem Jobs Campaign, 1932–1935," *Journal of Negro History* 69 (Summer–Fall 1984): 134–43; Stephan Breszka, "And Lo! It Worked: A Tale of Colored Harmony," *Opportunity* 11 (Nov. 1933): 242–44, 350; T. Arnold Hill, "Picketing for Jobs," *Opportunity* 8 (July 1930): 216; Gary Jerome Hunter, "'Don't Buy from Where You Can't Work': Black Urban Boycott Movements during the Depression, 1929–1941" (Ph.D. diss., University of Michigan, 1977); Christopher G. Wye, "Merchants of Tomorrow: The Other Side of the 'Don't Spend Your Money Where You Can't Work' Movement," *Ohio History* 93 (Winter–Spring 1985): 40–67; Kenneth Zinz, "The Future Outlook League of Cleveland: A Negro Protest Organization" (M.A. thesis, Kent State University, 1973).

4. August Meier and Elliott Rudwick, "The Boycott Movement against Jim Crow Streetcars in the South, 1900–1906," in *Along the Color Line,* 267–89; Allan H. Spear, *Black Chicago: The Making of a Negro Ghetto, 1890–1920* (Chicago: University of Chicago Press, 1967), 199; Roger A. Fisher, "A Pioneer Protest: The New Orleans Street-Car Controversy of 1867," *Journal of Negro History* 53 (July 1968): 219–33.

5. Meier and Rudwick, "Origins of Nonviolent Direct Action," 314.

6. Greenberg, *"Or Does It Explode?"* 115.

7. David J. Mauer, "Relief Practices and Politics in Ohio," in *The New Deal: The State and Local Levels,* ed. John Braeman, Robert H. Bremner, and David Brody (Columbus: Ohio State University Press, 1975), 77–102; John J. Grabowski and David D. Van Tassel, eds., *The Encyclopedia of Cleveland History* (Bloomington: Indiana University Press, 1987), xiv.

8. Howard Whipple Green, *Nine Years of Relief in Cleveland, 1928–1937* (Cleveland: Cleveland Health Council, 1937), 26–29; Cleveland Urban League, "Minutes, Mar. 29, 1929," and "Report of the Executive Secretary, Jan., Feb., and Mar., 1930," both in Cleveland Urban League Records, WRHS; *Neighborhood Visitor,* Aug. 31, 1931, Aug. 29, 1932, Dec. 6, 1932, Hiram House Records, WRHS. One social agent at Hiram House noted that out of forty black women in its Mother's Club, only four had husbands who had worked since 1929. One year later, the club had grown to over one hundred women but there was no growth in male employment; Ray Dennis, interview by author, Cleveland, Sept. 27, 1989, transcript.

9. Natalie Middleton, interview by author, Cleveland, Feb. 21, 1989, transcript; *Neighborhood Visitor,* Apr. 17, 1931, Hiram House Records.

10. *Neighborhood Visitor,* Nov. 30, 1930, Hiram House Records; Eleanor Walls Grist, interview by author, Cleveland, Aug. 22, 1989, transcript.

11. Cleveland Urban League, "Annual Report for the Year of 1934," Cleveland Urban League Records; Lois Helmbold, "Downward Occupational Mobility during the Great Depression: Urban Black and White Working Class Women," *Labor History* 29 (Spring 1988): 161–72. For documentation on the downward trend in black employment rates, see Cleveland Urban League, "Minutes, " Mar. 9, 1929; Cleveland Urban League, "Report of the Executive Secretary, January, February, and March, 1930"; Cleveland Urban League, "Annual Report, 1930"; and Cleveland Urban League, "Report of Executive Secretary, January, 1931," all in Cleveland Urban League Records; Phillis Wheatley Association, "Home Economics Committee Meeting, Report of the Employment Department," Mar. 1, 1932; Phillis Wheatley Association, "Home Economics Meeting, May 3, 1932"; and Phillis Wheatley Association, "Home Economics Committee Meeting," Nov. 1, 1932, all in Phillis Wheatley Association Records, WRHS; Ira De A. Reid and T. Arnold Hill, "Unemployment among Negroes: Activities of the National Urban League: Data on Twenty-five Industrial Centers" report to National Urban League, Nov. 1930, Cleveland Urban League Records.

12. Cleveland Urban League, "Report of the Executive Secretary, Jan., Feb., and Mar., 1930"; "Annual Report, 1933"; "Annual Report for the Year of 1934"; and "Minutes," June 28, 1935, all in Cleveland Urban League Records; Phillis Wheatley Association, "Report from Employment Department," Home Economics Committee meeting, Mar. 1, 1932, May 3, 1932, Nov. 11, 1932, Dec. 5, 1933, Feb. 6, 1934, Phillis Wheatley Association Records; Margie Glass, interview by Antoinette Kindall, Cleveland, Dec. 12, 1986, transcript, St. James A.M.E. Oral History Project, WRHS; Annie Jones, interview by Madelyn Lee, Cleveland, Oct. 19, 1986, transcript, St. James A.M.E. Oral History Project.

13. Cleveland Urban League, "Report of the Executive Secretary, Jan. 1931," Cleveland Urban League Records; Consumers' League of Cleveland, "Report on Industrial Homework," Feb. 20, 1937, reel 50, Consumers' League of Cleveland Records, WRHS; Middleton interview by author.

14. Robert Wheeler and Carol Pohl, *Cleveland: A Concise History* (Cleveland: Western Reserve Historical Society, 1990), 129–45; Grabowski and Van Tassel, *Encyclopedia of Cleveland History,* xiv–xv.

15. Green, *Nine Years of Relief,* 86; *Neighborhood Visitor,* Aug. 29, 1930, Apr. 8, 1931, Aug. 27, 1931, Hiram House Records.

16. Cleveland Urban League, "Annual Report for the Year of 1934," and "Annual Report, 1935," both in Cleveland Urban League Records; Harvard Sitkoff, *A New Deal for Blacks: The Emergence of Civil Rights as a National Issue*, vol. 1, *The Depression Decade* (New York: Oxford University Press, 1978), 34–57, esp. 37–39.

17. Dennis interview.

18. Cleveland Urban League, "Annual Report for the Year of 1934"; Christopher G. Wye, "The New Deal and the Negro Community: Toward a Broader Conceptualization," *Journal of American History* 59 (Dec. 1972): 621–39; Herbert J. Lowery, *Vocational Opportunities for Negroes in Cleveland* (Columbus: U.S. National Youth Administration in Ohio, 1938), 28–33. For the exclusion of domestic workers, see Alice Kessler-Harris, *Out to Work: A History of Wage-Earning Women in the United States* (New York: Oxford University Press, 1982), 270–71; and Jacqueline Jones, *Labor of Love, Labor of Sorrow: Black Women, Work, and the Family from Slavery to the Present* (New York: Basic Books, 1985), 196–231.

19. Middleton interview by author.

20. Cleveland Urban League, "Annual Report for the Year of 1934."

21. *Cleveland Call and Post,* Apr. 20, 1935.

22. Loeb, *The Future Is Yours,* 19; Ira De A. Reid and T. Arnold Hill, *Unemployment among Negroes: Activities of the National Urban League; Data on Twenty-Five Industrial Centers* (New York: National Urban League, 1930), 11.

23. *Cleveland Call and Post,* Apr. 14, 1934.

24. *Cleveland Call and Post,* Apr. 14, 1934; Loeb, *The Future Is Yours,* 20; Harvey J. Johnson, interview by Kenneth Zinz, Cleveland, Mar. 29, 1972, transcript, Future Outlook League Records; Selmer Prewitt, interview by author, Cleveland, Mar. 7, 1991, transcript.

25. Hill, "Picketing for Jobs," 216; Breszka, "And Lo! It Worked," 242–44, 350; Meier and Rudwick, "Origins of Nonviolent Direct Action," 314–16.

26. Quoted in McDowell, "Race and Ethnicity," 138.

27. *Cleveland Gazette,* Mar. 7, 1929.

28. Christopher G. Wye, "A Midwest Ghetto: Patterns of Negro Life and Thought in Cleveland, Ohio, 1929–1945" (Ph.D. diss., Kent State University, 1973), 405.

29. M. Milton Lewis, interview by Kenneth Zinz, Cleveland, Dec. 24, 1971, transcript, Future Outlook League Records; *Cleveland Gazette,* July 25, 1931, Aug. 22, 1931.

30. *Cleveland Call and Post,* Jan. 13, 1934, Mar. 10, 1934, Sept. 29, 1934, Oct. 6, 1934; Darlene Clark Hine, *Black Women in the Middle West: The Michigan Experience* (Ann Arbor: Historical Society of Michigan, 1990), 22; Darlene Clark Hine, "The Housewives' League of Detroit: Black Women and Economic Nationalism," *Hine Sight: Black Women and the Re-Construction of American History* (New York: Carlson, 1994), 129–46. There is little information about these Cleveland housewives' leagues beyond announcements of their activities in the black press. The location of the five units and the membership of each attest to the middle-class status of the members; many of the women were wives of longtime small business owners. The leagues' ideology also appears to match the domestic feminism and economic nationalism espoused in the Detroit Housewives' Leagues.

31. *Cleveland Call and Post,* May 18, 1935.

32. *Cleveland Call and Post,* Jan. 20, 1934, May 26, 1934, Mar. 16, 1935; McDowell, "Race

and Ethnicity," 139. McDowell characterizes the Harlem Housewives' League as a "black bourgeoisie counterpart" to the radical Negro Clerical and Industrial Alliance.

33. *Cleveland Call and Post,* July 14, 1934, Mar. 16, 1935.

34. *Cleveland Call and Post,* Apr. 21, 1934.

35. *Cleveland Call and Post,* Mar. 3, 1934, Mar. 17, 1934.

36. Cleveland Urban League, "Report of the Executive Secretary, 1933"; and "Annual Report, 1930," both in Cleveland Urban League Records; *Cleveland Call and Post,* Jan. 12, 1935. Hunter had earlier displayed little sympathy for unemployed black women. When twenty-five boarders fell behind in their rent, Hunter evicted them. See *Cleveland Gazette,* June 13, 1931. Only later did she reduce rent "to meet the needs of underpaid girls and women." See *Cleveland Call and Post,* Feb. 17, 1934.

37. Elmer Thompson, interview by Thomas F. Campbell, in Thomas F. Campbell, "Speech Sound Recording: On the History of Cleveland," Cleveland Heritage Program, 1981, transcript, Cleveland Public Library; Sitkoff, *A New Deal for Blacks,* 39; Wye, "Midwest Ghetto," 348–68; John B. Kirby, *Black Americans in the Roosevelt Era: Liberalism and Race* (Knoxville: University of Tennessee Press, 1980); Nancy J. Weiss, *Farewell to the Party of Lincoln: Black Politics in the Age of FDR* (Princeton: Princeton University Press, 1983), 78–95.

38. *Cleveland Plain Dealer,* Jan. 21, 1930, Feb. 4, 1930, Feb. 12, 1930, Mar. 7, 1930; Harvey Klehr, *The Heyday of American Communism: The Depression Decade* (New York: Basic Books, 1984), 324–35; Morris Stamm, "The Radical Tradition in Cleveland Labor," speech, Nov. 20, 1982, transcript, Greater Cleveland Labor History Society. I want to thank Jean Tussey for sharing this transcript with me.

39. Stamm, "Radical Tradition"; Len De Caux, *Labor Radical from the Wobblies to CIO: A Personal History* (Boston: Beacon Press, 1972), 172.

40. De Caux, *Labor Radical,* 172; *Cleveland Plain Dealer,* Oct. 6, 1931, Oct. 7, 1931, Oct. 10, 1931, Oct. 11, 1931.

41. De Caux, *Labor Radical,* 173 (quotes); Dennis interview.

42. De Caux, *Labor Radical,* 173. For a discussion of the links between black nationalism and communism, see Robin D. G. Kelley, "'Afric's Sons with Banner Red': African American Communists and the Politics of Culture," *Race Rebels,* 103–21.

43. *Cleveland Gazette,* Mar. 12, 1932; *Cleveland Call and Post,* Apr. 21, 1934, June 23, 1934, Aug. 18, 1934; Nell Irvin Painter, *The Narrative of Hosea Hudson: His Life as a Negro Communist in the South* (Cambridge, Mass.: Harvard University Press, 1979); Mark Naison, *Communists in Harlem during the Depression* (New York: Grove Press, 1983); Robin D. G. Kelley, *Hammer and Hoe: Alabama Communists during the Great Depression* (Chapel Hill: University of North Carolina Press, 1990), esp. 92–95; Frank Rogers, "Winning the Negro Masses for Our Election Campaign," *Party Organizer* 5 (Aug. 1932): 9; Charles H. Martin, "The International Labor Defense and Black America," *Labor History* 26 (Spring 1985): 165–94. Robin D. G. Kelley persuasively argued that blacks "meshed" Communism with an African-American cultural tradition of opposition. Most important, "the Party offered a framework for understanding the roots of poverty and racism" (*Hammer and Hoe* 93). The activities in Cleveland support Kelley's assessment. Len De Caux found that the "communist headquarters showed little of a movement whose roots were elsewhere. Not likely to be seen at Cleveland's creaky old party office were communist leaders often more influential than the party full-timers—activists in local unions, black and foreign-born orga-

nizations, Unemployed Councils, and other workers' groups. . . . The party membership came largely from these activists, plus a sprinkling of professional, intellectual, [and] small-business elements" (*Labor Radical* 169).

44. Joe Brandt, telephone interview by author, Aug. 12, 1991, tape recording; Future Outlook League, *The Second Anniversary Book* (Cleveland: n.p., 1938), 13, 21; *Cleveland Plain Dealer,* July 14, 1934; Robin D. G. Kelley, "This Ain't Ethiopia, but It'll Do: African-Americans and the Spanish Civil War," *Race Rebels,* 123–58; Admiral Kilpatrick, interview, Cleveland, June 8, 1980, transcript, Abraham Lincoln Brigade Archives, Brandeis University, Waltham, Mass.; Naison, *Communists in Harlem,* 42, 100, 136.

45. Cleveland Urban League, "Annual Report for the Year of 1934," Cleveland Urban League Records.

46. *Call and Post,* Feb. 10, 1934, May 18, 1936; *Cleveland Plain Dealer,* July 14, 1934.

47. *Cleveland Plain Dealer,* July 14, 1934.

48. *Cleveland Call and Post,* Feb. 10, 1934, Sept. 8, 1934, Sept. 15, 1934, Apr. 27, 1935.

49. "Work among Negro Masses," *Party Organizer* 4 (Apr. 1931): 16; Klehr, *Heyday of American Communism,* 340, 345; Naison, *Communists in Harlem,* 50–51, 127–65; Robert Schaffer, "Women and the Communist Party, USA, 1930–1940," *Socialist Review* 45 (May–June 1979): 73–118; Future Outlook League, *Second Anniversary Book,* 12. Naison's study of the CP in Harlem and Robin D. G. Kelley's study of Alabama reveal how after 1935 it was important for African-American Communists to build broad-based coalitions within black communities.

50. Dennis interview; Cleveland Urban League, "Annual Report, 1935," Cleveland Urban League Records. For blacks and the New Deal, see Sitkoff, *A New Deal for Blacks,* 34–57.

51. Cleveland Urban League, "Annual Report, 1935"; *Cleveland Call and Post,* July 23, 1936; Middleton interview by author; Grist interview, Aug. 22, 1989; Ruth Harper Freeman, interview by author, Cleveland, Mar. 7, 1991, transcript; Judge Jean Murrell Capers, interview by author and Patricia Miles Ashford, Cleveland, Aug. 8, 1991, tape recording; Consumers' League of Cleveland, *A Study of Women's Work in Cleveland* (n.p., n.d.), Records of the Consumers' League of Ohio, WRHS. Encouraged by their parents, Middleton, Grist, and Freeman took clerical courses in high school. In a study conducted by the Consumers' League of Cleveland, white women claimed that "some of the chief advantages of store work are regularity of hours (except during the period of holiday trade), steadiness of employment, an unvarying wage and the possibility of advancement." *Study of Women's Work,* n.p. For the continuities of these occupational characteristics during the depression, see Kessler-Harris, *Out to Work;* Susan Porter Benson, *Counter Cultures: Saleswomen, Managers, and Customers in American Department Stores, 1890–1940* (Chicago: University of Chicago Press, 1986); and Ileen A. Devault, *Sons and Daughters of Labor: Class and Clerical Work in Turn of the Century Pittsburgh* (Ithaca, N.Y.: Cornell University Press, 1990).

52. Loeb, *The Future Is Yours,* 15–17; *Detroit People's News,* June 24, 1927; *Cleveland Eagle,* Feb. 2, 1928.

53. Loeb, *The Future Is Yours,* 17–18; Hill, "Picketing for Jobs," 216; Beatrice Stevens Cockrell, interview by author, Cleveland, Sept. 27, 1991, transcript; Breszka, "And Lo! It Worked," 244.

54. Lewis interview; Harvey J. Johnson interview; *Cleveland Call and Post,* Feb. 23, 1935, May 30, 1935.

55. William O. Walker, interview by Kenneth Zinz, Cleveland, Sept. 18, 1971, transcript, Future Outlook League Records; Harvey J. Johnson interview; Prewitt interview; Linton Freeman, interview by author, Cleveland, Mar. 7, 1991, transcript; Ruth Harper Freeman interview; Cockrell interview, Sept. 27, 1991.

56. *Cleveland Call and Post,* Apr. 12, 1935, June 6, 1935; Walker interview; Loeb, *The Future Is Yours,* 29. For critiques of the league, see, for example, *Cleveland Gazette,* June 8, 1935.

57. Future Outlook League, *Second Anniversary Book,* 10–16; Future Outlook League, minutes, Jan. 15, 1936, also minutes for 1935–37, all in Records of the Future Outlook League; Harvey J. Johnson interview; Shelton Baines, interview by Kenneth Zinz, Cleveland, Mar. 29, 1972, transcript, Future Outlook League Records; Ruth Harper Freeman interview; Isabelle Shaw Rodgers, telephone interview by author, July 29, 1991, transcript; Beatrice Stevens Cockrell, telephone interview by author, July 29, 1991, transcript. My assessment of the Future Outlook League's leadership differs from Kenneth Zinz's ("Future Outlook League," 5–7). He included Harvey Johnson, William O. Walker, railroad inspector Julius C. Wright, and sometime attorney Charles V. Carr as participants in the everyday decisions. M. Milton Lewis, however, was one of the few more educated leaders to participate frequently; the others were usually called in for counsel only. Johnson, more so than the other attorneys, became an important contributor to the organization after a store owner agreed to negotiate. The tactics and decisions to boycott came from Shelton Baines, C. M. Smart, Tom Graham, Cora Graham, Robert Warren, Jennie Johnson, and Maude White. Important decisions ultimately were made by Holly and Warren.

58. Sallie Hopson, interview by Antoinette Kindall, Cleveland, Aug. 26, 1986, transcript, St. James A.M.E. Oral History Project; Marge Robinson, interview by author, Cleveland, Feb. 22, 1989, transcript; Rodgers interview; Cockrell interview, Sept. 27, 1991; Future Outlook League, minutes, Feb. 2, 1932, May 11, 1938.

59. Harvey J. Johnson interview; Prewitt interview; *Call and Post,* May 13, 1935, May 30, 1935, June 6, 1935, June 13, 1935; *Voice of the League,* May 7, 1938; Rodgers interview; Loeb, *The Future Is Yours,* 31–32.

60. Harvey J. Johnson interview; Future Outlook League, *Second Anniversary Book,* 19; Prewitt interview.

61. Loeb, *The Future Is Yours,* 37; Future Outlook League, *Second Anniversary Book,* 18–23; *Cleveland Call and Post,* Dec. 12, 1935; Zinz, "Future Outlook League," 43.

62. Future Outlook League, *Second Anniversary Book,* 23.

63. Smart interview, June 26, 1990; *Cleveland Eagle,* Nov. 8, 1935.

64. Lewis interview; Prewitt interview; Harvey J. Johnson interview; Future Outlook League, minutes, Aug. 26, 1936; Future Outlook League, *Second Anniversary Book,* 19.

65. Walker interview; *Cleveland Guide,* May 7, 1938.

66. *Cleveland Plain Dealer,* Oct. 31, 1931 (quote). For a discussion of black self-defense strategies in the South, see Timothy B. Tyson, "Robert F. Williams, 'Black Power' and the Roots of the African American Freedom Struggle," *Journal of American History* 85 (Sept. 1998): 540–70; Charles M. Payne, *I've Got the Light of Freedom: The Organizing Tradition and the Mississippi Freedom Struggle* (Berkeley: University of California Press, 1995), 207–35; and John Dittmer, *Local People: The Struggle for Civil Rights in Mississippi* (Urbana: University of Illinois Press, 1994), esp. 254–86. For the tradition of self-defense in Alabama, see Kelley, *Hammer and Hoe;* Kelley, *Race Rebels;*

and Theodore Rosengarten, *All God's Dangers: The Life of Nate Shaw* (New York: Avon Books, 1974; reprint, New York: Vintage Books, 1984).

67. Loeb, *The Future Is Yours,* 41–42; Future Outlook League, *Second Anniversary Book,* 30; *Cleveland Press,* Aug. 19, 1936; *Cleveland Call and Post,* Aug. 20, 1936, Nov. 11, 1938; Future Outlook League, minutes, July 28, 1937; Harvey J. Johnson interview; Prewitt interview.

68. *Cleveland Eagle,* Sept. 26, 1937 (quote); Future Outlook League, minutes, Nov. 3, 1937, Nov. 17, 1937; Loeb, *The Future Is Yours,* 47–48; Future Outlook League, *Second Anniversary Book,* 16; Lewis interview.

69. Lewis interview; Capers interview; Future Outlook League flyer, Future Outlook League Scrapbooks, Records of the Future Outlook League; Loeb, *The Future Is Yours,* 49.

70. Future Outlook League, minutes, Dec. 15, 1937.

71. Sharon Harley, "When Your Work Is Not Who You Are: The Development of a Working-Class Consciousness among Afro-American Women," in *"We Specialize in the Wholly Impossible": A Reader in Black Women's History,* ed. Darlene Clark Hine, Wilma King, and Linda Reed (New York: Carlson, 1995), 25.

72. Future Outlook League, *Second Anniversary Book,* 18–22; Loeb, *The Future Is Yours,* 47–48; Cockrell interview, Sept. 27, 1991.

73. Capers interview; Cockrell interview, Sept. 27, 1991. For a discussion of hidden resistance in gossip, rumor, and other verbal expressions, see James C. Scott, *Domination and the Arts of Resistance: Hidden Transcripts* (New Haven: Yale University Press, 1990), 136–82. For a discussion of the verbal behavior associated with African-American protest against whites, see Kelley, "Congested Terrain," 70–72. For "loud-talking"—antagonistic words addressed from one African American to another in front of an audience—see Claudia Mitchell-Kernan, "Signifying, Loud-Talking, and Marking," in *Rappin' and Stylin' Out: Communication in Urban Black America,* ed. Thomas Kochman (Urbana: University of Illinois Press, 1972), 329–35. Neither of these works addresses the gendered dimensions of African-American women's verbal protests. For help, we need to turn to work in African and African-American women's history. See, for example, Tera W. Hunter, *To 'Joy My Freedom: Southern Black Women's Lives and Labors after the Civil War* (Cambridge, Mass.: Harvard University Press, 1997); and the historical novel on the 1929 riot in Aba, Nigeria, O. T. Ecewa, *I Saw the Sky Catch Fire* (New York: NAL/Dutton, 1993).

74. *Voice of the League,* Dec. 18, 1937, May 7, 1938.

75. Prewitt interview; *Cleveland Call and Post,* Dec. 17, 1936, Apr. 28, 1938.

76. *Voice of the League,* May 7, 1938; Loeb, *The Future Is Yours,* 53–56.

77. Prewitt interview.

78. *Cleveland Call and Post,* Apr. 28, 1938, May 5, 1938; Future Outlook League, minutes, May 4, 1938; Capers interview; Loeb, *The Future Is Yours,* 55–56.

79. Prewitt interview.

80. *Voice of the League,* May 7, 1938; Meier and Rudwick, "Origins of Nonviolent Direct Action," 326. The New York Negro Alliance brought suit against the Sanitary Grocery store, which had sought an injunction against the boycotts.

81. *Cleveland Call and Post,* May 14, 1936, Apr. 8, 1939.

82. *Voice of the League,* June 4, 1938.

83. Lewis interview.

84. Loeb, *The Future Is Yours,* 46; Future Outlook League, minutes, 1936–38; Future Outlook League, *Second Anniversary Book,* 10–18; Cockrell interview, Sept. 27, 1991.

85. Loeb, *The Future Is Yours,* 46; Future Outlook League, minutes, 1936–38; Future Outlook League, *Second Anniversary Book,* 10–18; Cockrell interview, Sept. 27, 1991. For the number of new members, see Future Outlook League, minutes, Apr. 20, 1938, May 4, 1938, May 11, 1938, May 25, 1938, June 1, 1938, June 6, 1938, Records of the Future Outlook League.

86. Kelley, "This Ain't Ethiopia," 123–58.

87. Future Outlook League, minutes, Sept. 2, 1936, Sept. 1, 1937, Nov. 3, 1937, Nov. 11, 1937; *Voice of the League,* Feb. 5, 1938; Zinz, "Future Outlook League," 29; Middleton interview by author; Grist interview, Aug. 22, 1989; Cockrell interview, Sept. 27. 1991.

88. For an advertisement of Holly's "Sure Death Spray," see Future Outlook League, *Second Anniversary Book,* 62; Lewis interview.

89. Future Outlook League, *Second Anniversary Book,* 10.

90. *Voice of the League,* Dec. 18, 1937.

91. *Voice of the League,* Dec. 18, 1937, Jan. 8, 1938; Future Outlook League, minutes, Aug. 31, 1938; Zinz, "Future Outlook League," 16; *Cleveland Call and Post,* July 20, 1940.

92. For examples of Holly's ideology, see *Cleveland Call and Post,* Aug. 15, 1935; and Future Outlook League, minutes, July 18, 1937, Oct. 20, 1937. For examples of rank-and-file responses, see Future Outlook League, minutes, Oct. 20, 1937, Jan. 19, 1938, Feb. 16, 1938, Feb. 25, 1938, Apr. 6, 1938, Mar. 18, 1939.

93. Future Outlook League, *Second Anniversary Book,* 12.

94. Future Outlook League, minutes, Mar. 23, 1938; Baines interview.

95. Wye, "Merchants of Tomorrow," 42. For a critique of this tendency to view economic self-help from such a narrow perspective, see Meier and Rudwick, "Origins of Nonviolent Direct Action," 307–17; and Kelley, "Congested Terrain," 55–75.

96. Loeb, *The Future Is Yours,* 65.

97. *Voice of the League,* Feb. 5, 1938, Feb. 25, 1938.

98. Cockrell interview, Sept. 27, 1991. For an important discussion of the gendered dimension of African-American working-class women's militancy in the context of opposition to Jim Crow public transportation, see Kelley, "Congested Terrain," 67–70; Willi Coleman, "Black Women and Segregated Transportation," in *Black Women in United States History,* ed. Darlene Clark Hine (Brooklyn: Carlson, 1989), 5:295–301; and Joanne Robinson, *The Montgomery Bus Boycott and the Women Who Started It* (Knoxville: University of Tennessee Press, 1987).

99. Rodgers interview.

100. Pointer interview; Prewitt interview.

101. Linton Freeman interview.

102. *Cleveland Gazette,* May 8, 1935.

103. *Call and Post,* May 18, 1935.

104. *Voice of the League,* May 7, 1938. For similar arguments made in earlier boycotts, see William Jones, "Trade Boycotts: A Brief Study of the Newest Economic Weapon Employed Successfully by the Negro," *Opportunity* 18 (Aug. 1940): 235–41; and McDowell, "Race and Ethnicity," 139.

105. *Cleveland Eagle,* Nov. 11, 1935, Apr. 10, 1936; Future Outlook League, minutes, Apr. 29, 1936, May 6, 1936.

106. Future Outlook League, minutes, Mar. 4, 1936, Sept. 26, 1936, Oct. 14, 1936, Aug. 3, 1938, Sept. 12, 1939, Nov. 6, 1940; *Cleveland Call and Post,* Feb. 16, 1935, Aug. 20, 1936; Cockrell interview, Sept. 27, 1991.

107. Future Outlook League, "Future Outlook League Executive Board Minutes," ca. 1937, Records of the Future Outlook League; Future Outlook League, minutes, Feb. 13, 1939; Baines interview; Prewitt interview.

108. Future Outlook League, *Second Anniversary Book,* 25–33 (quote on 26); Baines interview; Loeb, *The Future Is Yours,* 65.

109. Future Outlook League, minutes, June 10, 1936, June 19, 1936, June 1, 1938, July 20, 1938; Flowree Robinson, interview by author, Cleveland, Nov. 29, 1989, transcript.

110. Quoted in Raymond Walters, "Section 7a and the Black Worker," *Labor History* 10 (Summer 1969): 473.

111. *Cleveland Gazette,* May 8, 1935.

112. *Cleveland Call and Post,* June 11, 1936 (first and second quotes), Jan. 18, 1938 (third quote).

113. Future Outlook League, *Second Anniversary Book,* 19, 33.

114. Future Outlook League, minutes, June 23, 1937; Future Outlook League, Executive Board minutes, Sept. 14, 1936, Oct. 5, 1936.

115. Future Outlook League, "Future Outlook League Executive Board Minutes."

116. *Cleveland Call and Post,* Apr. 15, 1937, Apr. 22, 1937, Apr. 29, 1937; *Voice of the League,* Dec. 16, 1939; Future Outlook League, minutes, June 7, 1944.

117. *Voice of the League,* July 2, 1938 (quote), June 4, 1938.

118. *Cleveland Call and Post,* Dec. 8, 1938; Future Outlook League flyer, Scrapbooks, Records of the Future Outlook League. My thinking about the internal transformation of the EA as it shifted to a union has been shaped by David Plotke's *Democratic Political Order: Reshaping American Liberalism in the 1930s and 1940s* (Cambridge: Cambridge University Press, 1996).

119. *Cleveland Call and Post,* Sept. 2, 1938.

120. *Cleveland Herald,* May 5, 1939; Smart interview, June 26, 1990.

121. *Cleveland Call and Post,* Feb. 13, 1936; Future Outlook League, minutes, Feb. 28, 1936; Future Outlook League, Executive Board minutes, Feb. 1, 1937; Wye, "New Deal," 621–39.

122. *Voice of the League,* Nov. 25, 1939.

123. Horace R. Cayton and George S. Mitchell, *Black Workers and the New Unions* (Chapel Hill: University of North Carolina Press, 1939), 396–406; L. Pearl Mitchell to Walter White, Dec. 1941, box 145, Records of the Cleveland NAACP, NAACP Branch Files, Group 2, Library of Congress, Washington, D.C.

Chapter 7: "The Plight of Negro Workers"

1. Paula F. Pfeffer, *A. Philip Randolph: Pioneer of the Civil Rights Movement* (Baton Rouge: Louisiana State University Press, 1990), 45–47.

2. Frank G. Jones, "Negro in Industry," speech delivered at the State Welfare Department Conference of Ohio Metropolitan Areas, July 30, 1941; and Lawrence W. Cramer, "Available and Needed Workers Have Been Barred from Employment,"

speech delivered at the regional meeting of the National Conference of Social Work, Mar. 11, 1943, New York City, transcript, both in NAACP Records, Cleveland Branch, Western Reserve Historical Society, Cleveland (hereafter WRHS).

3. Neil A. Wynn, *The Afro-American and the Second World War*, rev. ed. (New York: Holmes and Meier, 1993).

4. *Cleveland Call and Post*, Oct. 5, 1940; Ann Brent Ameling, "Women Factory Workers at Picker X-Ray Corporation during World War II" (graduate seminar paper, Cleveland State University, Mar. 1991), 1–5.

5. "Trends in Negro Employment of Non-White Workers," 1947, NAACP Records, Cleveland Branch, WRHS (first quote); William Franklin Moore, "The Status of the Negro in Cleveland" (Ph.D. diss., Ohio State University, 1953), 14; Jones, "Negro in Industry"; E. H. Heywood, "How Cleveland Tackled Its Labor Shortage," *Personnel*, 20–21, mimeograph, NAACP Records, Cleveland Branch, WRHS; *Cleveland Call and Post*, Oct. 5, 1940 (second quote), Aug. 9, 1941 (third quote).

6. "Trends in Negro Employment"; Robert C. Weaver, *Negro Labor, a National Problem* (New York: Harcourt, Brace, 1946), 28–33; *Cleveland Call and Post*, Oct. 10, 1942; Selmer Prewitt, interview by author, Cleveland, Mar. 7, 1991, transcript.

7. Weaver, *Negro Labor*, 28–33; *Cleveland Call and Post*, July 27, 1940, Sept. 7, 1940, July 11, 1942; Future Outlook League, minutes, June 27, 1942, Records of the Future Outlook League, WRHS.

8. For general trends of white women's wartime employment, see Alice Kessler-Harris, *Out to Work: A History of Wage-Earning Women in the United States* (New York: Oxford University Press, 1982), 273–99. On job segmentation and segregation, see Heidi Hartmann, "Capitalism, Patriarchy, and Job Segregation by Sex," in *Women and the Workplace: The Implications of Occupational Segregation*, ed. Martha Blaxall and Barbara Reagan (Chicago: University of Chicago Press, 1976), 137–69; Ruth Milkman, *Gender at Work: The Dynamics of Job Segregation by Sex during World War II* (Urbana: University of Illinois Press, 1987); Nancy Gabin, *Feminism in the Labor Movement: Women and the United Auto Workers, 1935–1975* (Ithaca: Cornell University Press, 1991).

9. Ameling, "Women Factory Workers," 5–9; Gus Joiner, interview by author, Cleveland, Oct. 2, 1989, transcript; *Cleveland Plain Dealer*, May 28, 1943; Bertha Fenstrom, telephone interview by author, Jan. 15, 1991, transcript; Fred C. Cash, interview by author, Oct. 29, 1991, tape recording.

10. Ray Dennis, interview by author, Cleveland, Sept. 27, 1989, transcript; Bertha Fenstrom, interview by author, Cleveland, Jan. 23, 1992, transcript; Bertha Fenstrom, telephone interview by author, Jan. 28, 1992.

11. Christopher G. Wye, "A Midwest Ghetto: Patterns of Negro Life and Thought in Cleveland, Ohio, 1929–1945" (Ph.D. diss., Kent State University, 1973), 157–58.

12. Nelson Lichtenstein, *Labor's War at Home: The CIO in World War II* (Cambridge: Cambridge University Press, 1982), 124–26; *Cleveland Press*, Dec. 15, 1942; Fenstrom interview, Jan. 28, 1992.

13. *Cleveland Call and Post*, Oct. 10, 1942; Weaver, *Negro Labor*, 17–18, 38–39.

14. Karen Tucker Anderson, "Last Hired, First Fired: Black Women Workers during World War II," *Journal of American History* 69 (June 1982): 83–84; see also Karen Tucker Anderson, *Wartime Women: Sex Roles, Family Relations, and the Status of Women during World War II* (Westport, Conn.: Greenwood Press, 1981), 36–44; Jac-

queline Jones, *Labor of Love, Labor of Sorrow: Black Women, Work, and the Family from Slavery to the Present* (New York: Basic Books, 1985); Evelyn Nakano Glenn, "Racial Ethnic Women's Labor: The Intersection of Race, Gender, and Class Oppression," *Review of Radical Political Economics* 17 (Winter 1985): 86–108; Randy Ableda, "'Nice Work If You Can Get It': Segmentation of White and Black Women Workers in the Post War Period," *Review of Radical Political Economics* 17 (Winter 1985): 72–85; and Natalie Middleton, interview by author, Cleveland, Feb. 21, 1989, transcript.

15. Quoted in Weaver, *Negro Labor,* 38; "Negro in Industry," n.d., and "Racial Relations Unit of the Ohio State Employment Service," May 3, 1941, both on reel 48, Consumers' League of Ohio Records, WRHS; Middleton interview by author; Eleanor Walls Grist, interview by author, Cleveland, Aug. 22, 1989, transcript.

16. Mayor Edward Blythin to L. Pearl Mitchell, Aug. 14, 1941, box 87, Records of the Cleveland NAACP, NAACP Branch Files, Group 2, Library of Congress, Washington, D.C. For a comparative account of the NAACP in Chicago, see Beth Tompkins Bates, "A New Crowd Challenges the Agenda of the Old Guard in the NAACP, 1933–1941," *American Historical Review* 102 (Apr. 1997): 340–77.

17. See, for example, *Cleveland Call and Post,* July–Sept. 1941.

18. Louis Coleridge Kesselman, *The Social Politics of FEPC: A Study in Reform Pressure Movements* (Chapel Hill: University of North Carolina Press, 1948), 9–10, 15–24; Herbert Garfinkel, *When Negroes March: The March on Washington Movement in the Organizational Politics for FEPC* (Glencoe, Ill.: Free Press, 1959; reprint, New York: Atheneum, 1969), 37–60; Herbert Hill, *Black Labor and the American Legal System: Race, Work, and the Law* (Washington, D.C.: Bureau of National Affairs, 1977; reprint, Madison: University of Wisconsin Press, 1985), 173–84; Merl E. Reed, *Seedtime for the Modern Civil Rights Movement: The President's Committee on Fair Employment Practice, 1941–1946* (Baton Rouge: Louisiana State University Press, 1991); Weaver, *Negro Labor,* 137–39. In its first year, the Committee on Fair Employment Practice shifted to three separate offices—each of which utilized different implementations of the order. From July 1941 until January 1942, the committee operated within the Labor Division of Office of Production Management; in January 1942, the committee was transferred to the War Production Board. By August 1942, the committee came under the jurisdiction of the newly created War Manpower Commission.

19. *Cleveland Call and Post,* Aug. 23, 1941, June 20, 1942; interview with Mr. Meredith, personnel director, Parker Appliance, n.d., reel 48, Consumers' League of Cleveland Records.

20. Richard W. Steele, "'No Racials': Discrimination against Ethnics in American Defense Industry, 1940–42," *Labor History* 32 (Winter 1991): 66–67. Steele notes it is an irony that scholars have paid more attention to blacks' exclusion from defense employment than to ethnic workers' since officials "in 1940–42 saw discrimination because of ethnic origins as a more serious threat to national defense . . . and devoted considerably more energy to its eradication" (66).

21. "Statement of Objectives and Functions," Greater Cleveland Council on Fair Employment Practices, 1942, NAACP Records, Cleveland Branch, WRHS; Committee on Fair Employment Practice, "Weekly Report, Region V," Apr. 15, 1944, reel 51, Records of the Committee on Fair Employment Practice, RG 228, National Archives (Glen Rock, NJ: Microfilming Corporation of America, 1970). It is not clear from the records what other agencies were involved.

22. "Weekly Report, Region V," Jan. 22, 1945, reel 51, Records of the Committee on Fair Employment Practice.

23. Kesselman, *Social Politics of Fair Employment Practices Committee*, 11–12.

24. *Cleveland Call and Post*, May 3, 1942.

25. Weaver, *Negro Labor*, 147–48.

26. For example, see "Weekly Report, Region V," Dec. 5, 1944, reel 51, Records of the Committee on Fair Employment Practice.

27. Memo on Parker Appliance. For similar findings in other areas, see Robert J. Norrell, "Caste in Steel: Jim Crow in Birmingham, Alabama," *Journal of American History* 73 (Dec. 1986): 669–94; August Meier and Elliott Rudwick, *Black Detroit and the Rise of the UAW* (New York: Oxford University Press, 1979), 108–79; and Herbert R. Northrup, *Organized Labor and the Negro* (New York: Harper and Brothers, 1944).

28. "Weekly Report, Region V," Apr. 28, 1945, reel 51, Records of the Committee on Fair Employment Practice.

29. Weaver, *Negro Labor*, 32, 37–38; *Cleveland Call and Post*, Sept. 7, 1940.

30. *Cleveland Call and Post*, Sept. 14, 1940.

31. *Cleveland Call and Post*, Dec. 4, 1940, Mar. 8, 1941, May 8, 1941 (quote).

32. *Cleveland Call and Post*, Aug. 9, 1941.

33. *Cleveland Call and Post*, Aug. 23, 1941.

34. This protracted and bitter battle between the CIO-UAW and the highly organized company unions backed by management at Thompson Products deserves attention since it could shed some light on the CIO's struggle to pursue or hinder racial egalitarianism. See Michael Goldfield, "Race and the CIO: The Possibilities for Racial Egalitarianism during the 1930s and 1940s," *International Labor and Working-Class History* 44 (Fall 1993): 1–32. For a response, see Herbert Hill, "The Problem of Race in American Labor History," *Reviews in American History* 24 (June 1996): 189–208.

35. *Thompson Products Organizer*, Sept. 1, 1942, Records of TRW, WRHS; John J. Grabowski and David D. Van Tassel, eds. *The Encyclopedia of Cleveland History* (Bloomington: Indiana University Press, 1987), 996–97; I. W. Abel, "Comments," in *Forging a Union of Steel: Philip Murray, SWOC, and the United Steelworkers*, ed. Paul F. Clark, Peter Gottlieb, and Donald Kennedy (Ithaca: ILR Press, 1987), 160. In the surrounding areas of Cleveland, companies stoked southern white workers' racism. I. W. Abel recalled that at the Timken Plant in Canton, company officials made much of the anti-black feelings. "The Timken Company . . . went out in the streets and hired fifty black workers, took them into the plant, and put them in top jobs. You can imagine what took place. Those fellows from the Carolinas, Tennessee, and Georgia ran them out with lead hammers and pieces of pipe. The battle raged for six weeks" (160). The hate strike was settled when the United Steel Workers of America revoked the union's charter, but the expelled union members took union officials to court and won back pay.

Such militancy on the part of Southern white workers attests to what Martin Glaberman found in Detroit. "Southern whites," he argued, "tended much less than any other workers to permit themselves to be pushed around." White workers supported the union, but felt the hiring of blacks to be an infringement on their rights as workers. The tragedy is that companies regularly exploited these attitudes, to the detriment of unions. See Martin Glaberman, *Wartime Strikes: The Struggle against the No-Strike Pledge in the UAW during World War II* (Detroit: Bewick/Ed Press, 1980), 31.

36. *Cleveland Call and Post*, Aug. 9, 1941.

37. Mark McCulloch, "Consolidating Industrial Citizenship: The USWA at War and Peace, 1939–1946," in *Forging a Union of Steel*, 40–61 (quote on 61); Horace R. Cayton and George S. Mitchell, *Black Workers and the New Unions* (Chapel Hill: University of North Carolina Press, 1939), 193–98; Romare Bearden, "The Negro in 'Little Steel,'" *Opportunity* 15 (Dec. 1937): 362–65. Cayton and Mitchell discovered that the Cleveland Urban League aggressively discouraged black participation in the SWOC. McColloch notes that the United Steel Workers of America displayed its own form of racism. During the 1942 convention in Cleveland, the secretary-treasurer directed black delegates to "colored hotels."

38. Wye, "Midwest Ghetto," 198–99.

39. Ohio State CIO Council, Mar. 19, 1942, reel 48, Consumers' League of Ohio Records, WRHS.

40. Goldfield, "Race and the CIO," 24.

41. Dennis interview; Wye, "Midwest Ghetto," 203.

42. Robert H. Zieger, *The CIO, 1935–1955* (Chapel Hill: University of North Carolina Press, 1995), 83–84. For comparisons, see Rick Halpern, *Down on the Killing Floor: Black and White Workers in Chicago's Packinghouses, 1904–54* (Urbana: University of Illinois Press, 1997); and Meier and Rudwick, *Black Detroit*.

43. Charles Loeb, *The Future Is Yours* (Cleveland: Future Outlook League, 1946), 81–87; Future Outlook League, Executive Board minutes, ca. June 1941, Records of the Future Outlook League.

44. For examples of women's complaints, see Future Outlook League, minutes, Jan. 26, 1938, June 6, 1940.

45. Judge Jean Murrell Capers, interview by author and Patricia Miles Ashford, Cleveland, Aug. 8, 1991, transcript; Beatrice Stevens Cockrell, interview by author, Cleveland, Sept. 27, 1991, transcript; Loeb, *The Future Is Yours*, 75.

46. *Cleveland Call and Post*, Oct. 16, 1940, Jan. 1, 1941.

47. Loeb, *The Future Is Yours*, 81–87; *Cleveland Call and Post*, May 10, 1941 (quote). According to the *Call and Post*, Ohio Bell officials "conservatively estimated 3000 calls." The league claimed 10,000 calls were made.

48. Cockrell interview, Sept. 27, 1991. Cockrell sent requests to both the NAACP and the Urban League for support of the boycott. Both organizations remained silent until after the boycott.

49. *Cleveland Call and Post*, Aug. 16, 1941.

50. Loeb, *The Future Is Yours*, 86.

51. Future Outlook League, minutes, Apr. 8, 1942; *Cleveland Press*, May 1, 1942; *Cleveland Call and Post*, May 9, 1942; Loeb, *The Future Is Yours*, 96.

52. Future Outlook League, Executive Board minutes, May 11, 1942; *Cleveland Call and Post*, May 9, 1942, May 16, 1942, May 23, 1942; Cockrell interview, Sept. 27, 1991; Grabowski and Van Tassel, *Encyclopedia of Cleveland History*, 669.

53. L. Pearl Mitchell to Walter White, May 18, 1941, box 145, Records of the Cleveland NAACP, NAACP Branch Files, Group 2, Library of Congress; Cleveland Metropolitan Council on Fair Employment Practice to NAACP, May 18, 1942, NAACP Records, Cleveland Branch, WRHS; Cockrell interview, Sept. 27, 1991.

54. Walter White, "Letter to the Branches," July 9, 1941, NAACP Records, Cleveland Branch, WRHS. For helpful insight into the efforts of White to mediate black protest politics, see Bates, "A New Crowd."

55. Cockrell interview, Sept. 27, 1991; L. Pearl Mitchell to Walter White, June 3, 1942; L. Pearl Mitchell to Walter White, Nov. 20, 1944 (quotes); and L. Pearl Mitchell to Roy Wilkens, Dec. 28, 1944, all in box 145, Records of the Cleveland NAACP, NAACP Branch Files, Group 2, Library of Congress.

56. *Cleveland Call and Post,* June 6, 1942 (first quote), June 27, 1942 (second quote); Future Outlook League, minutes, Oct. 7, 1942, Nov. 18, 1942; Grist interview, Aug. 22, 1989; Adrienne Kennedy, *People Who Led to My Plays* (New York: Knopf, 1987), 47–48.

57. Future Outlook League, minutes, May 16, 1942, June 27, 1942.

58. Harvard Sitkoff, "Racial Militancy and Interracial Violence in the Second World War," *Journal of American History* 58 (Dec. 1971): 661–81; Meier and Rudwick, *Black Detroit,* 108–74; Robert Korstad and Nelson Lichtenstein, "Opportunities Found and Lost: Labor, Radicals, and the Early Civil Rights Movement," *Journal of American History* 75 (Dec. 1988): 786–811.

59. *Cleveland Call and Post,* May 13, 1942, June 6, 1942, July 11, 1942, Aug. 1, 1942.

60. Future Outlook League, minutes, Dec. 9, 1942.

61. *Johnson v. Thompson Products,* Common Pleas, 524, 637, Court of Appeals, 19163; *Effie May Turner v. Warner and Swasey Company,* Ohio Court of Appeals, 19164.

62. *Johnson v. Thompson Products,* Common Pleas, 524, 637, Court of Appeals, 19163; *Effie May Turner v. Warner and Swasey Company,* Ohio Court of Appeals, 19164; Loeb, *The Future Is Yours,* 100–102; Kenneth Zinz, "The Future Outlook League of Cleveland: A Negro Protest Organization" (M.A. thesis, Kent State University, 1973), 105.

63. *Cleveland Press,* Dec. 15, 1942; *Cleveland Call and Post,* Sept. 19, 1942, Oct. 10, 1942; Future Outlook League, minutes, Oct. 21, 1942, Nov. 14, 1942. For a discussion of the AFL policies for racial discrimination during World War II, see Judith Stein, "Response: The Ins and Outs of the CIO," *International Labor and Working-Class History* 44 (Fall 1993): 56.

64. Sanford M. Jacoby, "Reckoning with Company Unions: The Case of Thompson Products, 1934–1964," *Industrial and Labor Relations Review* 43 (Oct. 1989): 19–40.

65. Ibid.; Cash interview; *Thompson Products Organizer,* Oct. 29, 1941, Records of TRW; Grievances, Records of TRW. For a discussion of sexual and racial politics in union efforts to organize, see Gerald Zahavi, "Passionate Commitments: Race, Sex, and Communism at Schenectady General Electric, 1932–1954," *Journal of American History* 83 (Sept. 1996): 514–48.

66. *Thompson Products Organizer,* Dec. 16, 1942, Records of TRW. In a later grievance, a black male worker charged that a CIO-UAW organizer had requested the separation of black and white mirror polishers. The organizer felt the separation necessary since white workers "were more acquainted, more at home" with each other than with black workers. See Grievance B-332501, Apr. 12, 1943, Records of TRW.

67. *Turner v. Warner and Swasey.*

68. *Claretta Jean Johnson v. Thompson Products,* Ohio Court of Appeals 19163; *Turner v. Warner and Swasey.*.

69. Brief, *Turner v. Warner and Swasey,* 8.

70. *Johnson v. Thompson Products; PM Daily,* Dec. 16, 1942.

71. *Johnson v. Thompson Products; Cleveland Press,* Nov. 24, 1942. Merrick argued that the Future Outlook League had not attempted to negotiate with either compa-

ny. On the contrary, the Future Outlook League had made repeated appeals to Thompson Products and Warner and Swasey.

72. *Johnson v. Thompson Products; Turner v. Warner and Swasey; Cleveland Call and Post,* Feb. 3, 1943.

73. *Turner v. Warner and Swasey;* Executive Secretary of NAACP, Cleveland Branch, to Cleveland Urban League, Feb. 21, 1945, NAACP Records, Cleveland Branch, WRHS.

74. Grabowski and Van Tassel, *Encyclopedia of Cleveland History,* 276; Laura Addie, interview by Bert Fenstrom, Cleveland, Feb. 14, 1991 and Mar. 14, 1991, transcript in author's possession; Willa Davenport Thomas, interview by author, Cleveland, Dec. 1, 1989, transcript (quote).

75. Middleton interview by author; Cockrell interview, Sept. 27, 1991.

76. Middleton interview by author; Grabowski and Van Tassel, *Encyclopedia of Cleveland History,* 235–36, 284, 671–72. On September 6, 1944, MESA called a strike to protest the dismissal of a worker accused of damaging a company locker. The union claimed sabotage and persuaded the new and large work force to stay out until November 11, 1944. The War Labor Board then seized the plant, making it the first seizure in Ohio and the fifth in the region.

77. *Cleveland Call and Post,* Feb. 3, 1943; "Weekly Report, Region V," Dec. 11, 1943, reel 51, Records of the Committee on Fair Employment Practice.

78. Dennis interview.

79. Ruth Harper Freeman, interview by author, Cleveland, Mar. 7, 1991, transcript; Cockrell interview, Sept. 27, 1991; Middleton interview by author; Grist interview, Aug. 22, 1989.

80. *Cleveland Union Leader,* Nov. 26, 1943, Dec. 17, 1943. For a comparison with widespread activity in Chicago, see Halpern, *Down on the Killing Floor;* and Zieger, *The CIO,* 83–84.

81. "Resolution Adopted by Cleveland Industrial Union Council, June 13, 1945," Cleveland Metropolitan Council on Fair Employment Practice Records, WRHS.

82. Dennis interview.

83. *Cleveland Union Leader,* Oct. 19, 1945.

84. Wye, "Midwest Ghetto," 336–88, esp. 382–88; Dennis interview.

85. Natalie Middleton, interview by Antoinette Kindall, Cleveland, Dec. 20, 1986, transcript, St. James A.M.E. Oral History Project; Middleton interview by author; Dennis interview.

Conclusion

1. Sara Brooks, *You May Plow Here: The Narrative of Sara Brooks,* ed. Thordis Simonsen (New York: Simon and Schuster, 1987), 221–22.

2. Barbara Smith, *Homegirls: A Black Feminist Anthology* (New York: Kitchen Table/Women of Color Press, 1983), xxi.

3. Gerald L. Davis, *"I Got the Word in Me and I Can Sing It You Know": A Study of the Performed African-American Sermon* (Philadelphia: University of Pennsylvania Press, 1985), 9.

4. Carl B. Stokes, *Promises of Power Then and Now* (Cleveland: Friends of Carl Stokes, 1989); LeRoi Jones (Amiri Baraka), *Blues People: Negro Music in White America* (New York: William Morrow, 1963), 105.

5. Carol Stack, *Call to Home: African Americans Reclaim the Rural South* (New York: Basic Books, 1996); Ray Allen, *Singing in the Spirit: African-American Sacred Quartets in New York City* (Philadelphia: University of Pennsylvania Press, 1991), 186–203.

6. Stokes, *Promises of Power,* 28.

7. Smith, *Homegirls,* xxi.

8. John Miller, interview by Edward D. Schmieding, Cleveland, Nov. 27, 1991, transcript in author's possession. For a discussion of "unverified orally transmitted stories"—rumors—in African-American communities about racial discrimination in the midst of war, see Patricia A. Turner, *I Heard It through the Grapevine: Rumor in African-American Culture* (Berkeley: University of California Press, 1993), 1–7, 43–45.

9. Natalie Middleton, interview by author, Cleveland, Feb. 21, 1989, transcript.

10. *National Enterprise,* Feb. 23, 1949.

11. Lee Morgan, "Report on Organizational Work in 1948," Dec. 28, 1948, 1–3, NAACP Records, Cleveland Branch, Western Reserve Historical Society, Cleveland (hereafter WRHS).

12. Ibid., 3–4.

13. Horace Huntley, "The Red Scare and Black Workers in the International Union of Mine, Mill, and Smelter Workers, 1945–1953," *Labor Divided: Race and Ethnicity in the United States Labor Struggles, 1835–1960* (Albany: State University of New York Press, 1990), 143–44.

14. Gary Gerstle, "Working-Class Racism: Broaden the Focus," *International Labor and Working-Class History* 44 (Fall 1993): 36. For an important study on racialized struggles over jobs and neighborhoods in Detroit, see Thomas J. Sugrue, *The Origins of the Urban Crisis: Race and Inequality in Postwar Detroit* (Princeton: Princeton University Press, 1996).

15. Smith, *Homegirls,* xxii; Thylias Moss, "Wings," in *Going Where I'm Coming From: Memoirs of American Youth,* ed. Anne Mazar (New York: Persea Press, 1995), 7.

16. Adrienne Kennedy, *People Who Led to My Plays* (New York: Knopf, 1987), 43–44.

17. "History, St. Timothy Missionary Baptist Church, 1940–1979," unprocessed collection of Reverend John T. Weeden, WRHS.

18. Hans Baer, *The Black Spiritual Movement: A Religious Response to Racism* (Knoxville: University of Tennessee Press, 1984); Arthur Huff Fauset, *Black Gods of the Metropolis: Negro Religious Cults of the Urban North* (Philadelphia: University of Pennsylvania Press, 1944); Welfare Federation of Cleveland Research Committee, *Central Area Social Study* (Cleveland: n.p., 1944), Cleveland Public Library; James E. Blackwell, "Black Store Front Churches in Cleveland: A Comparative Study of Five Negro Store Front Churches in Cleveland" (M.A. thesis, Western Reserve University, 1949).

19. Moss, "Wings," 7.

20. Arthur Turner, interview by author, Cleveland, May 23, 1996, videotape; see Ray Funk's liner notes to "Cleveland Gospel," Heritage HT316, 1988.

21. Bertha Pickett, interview by author, Cleveland, May 18, 1996, videotape, WRHS; Turner interview, May 23, 1996. For relationship and impact of professional gospel singers on local gospel quartets in Memphis, see Kip Lornell, *"Happy in the Service of the Lord": Afro-American Gospel Quartets in Memphis* (Urbana: University of Illinois Press, 1988), 36–63. For the continued importance of local performers to the African-American working class after World War II, see Allen, *Singing in the Spirit,* 8–15.

INDEX

Absenteeism, 34

African Americans: as agricultural workers, 19, 21, 26–28; autonomy of, 30; boycotts by, 191, 207–8, 209, 211–13; and building trades, 9, 115–18; children, 19, 35–36, 42, 51, 53–54, 129, 137–38, 140–42, 148–49, 162, 167; in coal camps, 7, 8; in coal mines, 35; as consumers, 198, 210–12; and "culture of opposition," 202; and employment, 5, 57; and finances, 21, 28–29, 149, 185; and Great Depression, 191–97; in hotel trades, 9; land ties, 18–21, 39–40, 55; leaders, 5, 199–200; in lumber camps, 7; and militant protest, 5, 210–11; and mobility, 18, 19, 21–22, 39, 254; and New Deal legislation, 191, 196–97, 204; population of, 60, 129; and self-determination, 39, 163, 193; and southern cities, 41–42; as strikebreakers, 7; and unions, 10, 37–39, 98–100, 102–3, 104–6, 108, 113–14, 119–26, 192, 220–21; vernacular practices of, 2, 261n1. *See also* Future Outlook League (FOL); Men, African-American; Migrants; Women, African-American; Workers, African-American

Alabama, 15, 17, 20; coal mines in, 35; land in, 21; migration from, 15–16, 60; migration within, 23; steel industry in, 15

Alabama Club, 171

Amalgamated Association of Iron, Steel, and Tin Workers, 99

American Federation of Labor (AFL), 3, 100, 101, 189, 256; exclusion of African Americans from, 9, 11–12, 20; and FOL, 222; and racial egalitarianism, 12; racial policies in, 121, 122, 235

American Plan Association (APA), 79, 109–10, 111; and open-shop drive, 80–81, 109, 114–15

Antioch Baptist Church, 166, 168, 228

Auto manufacturing, 17, 122

Baltimore and Ohio Railroad, 73. *See also* Railroads

Baseball, 184

Bellamy, George, 156. *See also* Hiram House

Bethune, Mary McLeod, 168

Birmingham, Alabama, 17; labor in, 40

Birth control, 25, 149

Birth of a Nation (film), 152, 164

Black Belt, 20

Blacks. *See* African Americans

Boarders, 41, 139–40

Boll weevils, 43–44

Bourke-White, Margaret, 69

Box making, 61

Boycotts, 191, 207–8, 209, 211–13. *See also* Protest

Bricklayers' union, 102, 117, 118

Brooks, Sara, 25, 253–54; abuse of, 51; critiques of rural life, 39; expectations of employers, 91; migration of, 51, 54; and work, 23–24, 26, 27, 41, 92, 96

Building trades, 9, 61, 84, 99, 102; African Americans' gains in, 115–18; paperhangers, 115, 118; parquet floor layers, 115–16; scaffold builders, 118; and violence, 115

Cayton, Horace, 111–12

Central Area, 133, 146, 148, 159, 162, 174; activism in, 201–2; churches in, 171–72; evictions in, 201; and Great Depression,

190, 193; increased presence of African Americans in, 129–30; merchants in, 197–98, 204

Chesnutt, Charles, 136

Chicago, Illinois, 17

Chicago Defender, 44–45

Children, African-American, 19, 137, 162, 167; care of, 137–38; and leisure, 148–49; migration of, 51, 53–54; and parents, 35–36, 42; population of, 129; and storytelling, 36; visiting South, 141–42; wages of, 140

Churches: as mediators, 166–68; membership in, 172; and migrants, 10, 180; ministers of, 169–70, 174, 214, 259; as social centers, 168; and spirituality, 172–73, 253, 258–59; splintering of, 170–71, 172–73; storefront, 162, 170–71; women's roles in, 175–76, 180; worship practices in, 168–76

Church of God, 174, 176, 177, 178

Church of God in Christ, 174, 176, 177, 178

Cities: and industry, 40; and migration in South, 39–40

Civil War, 16

Class: divisions and migrants, 163–64; intraracial conflict and, 6; and leisure activities, 181–86; and race consciousness, 35, 38; and subordination, 164

Cleveland, Ohio, 16, 17, 60; industry in, 50–60; and population growth, 60; segregation in, 67

Cleveland Advocate, 71

Cleveland Call and Post, 206, 214, 218, 221, 232, 234, 238

Cleveland Chamber of Commerce, 66, 114, 228

Cleveland Citizen, 100

Cleveland Colored Gospel Quintet, 178

Cleveland Federation of Labor (CFL)/Cleveland Labor Council, 101, 102, 103, 104, 115, 124, 256

Cleveland Gazette, 163, 165, 169

Cleveland Industrial Union Council (CIUC), 249–50

Cleveland Railway Company, 67

Cleveland Urban League/Negro Welfare Association, 63, 66, 72, 76, 106, 113, 150, 210; and antiunion efforts, 8, 109, 120; and delinquency, 152; as employment agency, 64; formation of, 156; and migrants, 53; open-shop drive and, 80–81;

unemployment and, 78, 84; and workers, 70, 79; and working-class organizations, 188; World War II and, 229–30, 241

Cleveland Workers' School, 202

Clubs, 162; as forums for denouncing racial inequality, 184; men's, 185; social, 184, 185; southern, 183; women's, 159, 166–68; working-class, 183–86

Coal mines, 35; camps, 7, 8, 36; hazardous conditions in, 36; migration to, 34–37; as New South industry, 17; racial divisions in, 35; and United Mine Workers, 8, 37–38; wages in, 35

Committee on Fair Employment Practice (COFEP), 12, 227–28, 232–34, 242, 245–46

Communist Party, USA (CP), 11, 192–93, 206, 210, 219; and Unemployed Councils, 5, 200–204

Congress of Industrial Organizations (CIO), 189, 222, 223; and African Americans, 3, 11–12, 191, 256; and challenge to discrimination, 236–37, 249–50; and FOL, 220–21; and interracial unionism, 221; support for, 234–35, 250

Conners, William, 109, 157, 200. *See also* Cleveland Urban League/Negro Welfare Federation

Cory Methodist Church, 176

Cotton, 18, 19; and economy, 22; production of, 21, 23–24

Crime, 20, 149–51; delinquency, 152; prostitution, 150, 151; vagrancy, 21–22, 150

Dancing, 181, 184

Davis, Harry L., 164

Day work, 41, 85, 89, 93. *See also* Household employment

Delinquency, home for, 152

Democrats, 19, 20, 200

Department stores, 83–84, 86–87; boycotts of, 192, 203, 219

Detroit, Michigan, 17, 72, 191

Division of Negro Economics, 65

Dock work, 31, 32

Dorsey, Thomas A., 178–79

Du Bois, W. E. B., 168, 186

Dunham Jubilee Quartet, 161, 177

Education: segregation and, 27, 159

Electrical union, 116–17, 118

Elevator operators, 83–84, 87

Emancipation, 16, 18

Employers: agreements with unions, 101; antiunion tactics, 99, 113, 243–44; attitudes of, 57–59; and hiring patterns, 58, 60–65; management techniques of, 58, 60, 79–80; policies of, 58, 62, 63–65, 68, 71, 227, 229–32, 241, 255; in South, 40

Employment agencies, private, 62, 63, 64–65, 71, 76, 79–80. *See also* Social welfare agencies

Executive Order 8802, 227. *See also* Committee on Fair Employment Practice (COFEP)

Fair Employment Practice Committee (FEPC), 227, 256. *See also* Committee on Fair Employment Practice (COFEP)

Family: dynamics in, 143; economic obligations and migration, 145; kin networks, 16, 42, 127–28, 136, 162; men and, 61; migration and, 51; work and, 61. *See also* Gender; Households

Farms: coercion of workers on, 19, 29, 34, 54–55; and credit, 21; and debt, 21, 28–29; and households, 23; and industrial employment, 28; and labor, 23–24; and sharecropping, 20, 23, 29, 39; and whites' control of land, 18–20

Federation of Charities and Philanthropy, 155

Food production, 72

Foundry workers, 17, 40, 58, 62, 65, 79

Freight handlers, 64, 73, 102; Local No. 17210, 99, 113, 122. *See also* Railroads

Friendly Inn, 159. *See also* Social welfare agencies

Future Outlook League (FOL), 2, 4, 256; and AFL, 222; and boycotts, 191, 207–8, 209, 211–13; and CIO, 220–21; committees in, 214; community memory of, 3, 12, 259; and court case, 12; critiques of, 205, 210; and Employees' Association/Union, 219–20, 222, 224; goals of, 191; injunctions and, 208–9; and March on Washington, 226–27; members, 4, 213–14; meetings and, 214–15; as merchants, 4, 191, 215; militancy of, 4, 191–92, 206; and NAACP, 3, 218–19, 221–25, 239–41; and organized labor, 220–24; origins of, 3, 11, 190–93; pickets by, 207–8, 209; and politics, 3; publications of, 216–17; and racial

consciousness, 215; and self-defense, 209–10, 316–17n66; tactics of, 3, 4, 190–91; unemployed and, 190, 191; and unions, 3, 11–12; and violence, 209–10, 212, 213; women's roles in, 3, 5, 12, 206–7, 209, 211, 214; and workers, 11; and World War II, 228, 237–41, 242, 244–46

Gambling, 149–50

Gardens, 24–25, 33, 146

Garvey, Marcus, 186–87

Gender: and class identity, 211–12; and definitions of work, 24–25, 83–84; and economic roles, 143–45; and emotional roles, 143–44; hierarchies of, 164; masculinity, 19; and population, 129; and work, 35

Georgia, 21, 23

Gottlieb, Peter, 16

Great Depression, 5, 162, 189, 191–97, 200, 226, 237–38; indirect relief during, 197; limitations of charity during, 195–96; and New Deal, 196–97; in South, 15; violence during, 201–2, 203; and women's employment, 93

Great Steel Strike of 1919, 9, 67, 70, 104–6, 164; defeat of, 106; fear of violence in, 105–6; unskilled workers and, 105

Green, Howard Whipple, 153

Harlem: store boycotts in, 192, 203, 219

Hayes, Max, 100

Haynes, George, 78

Health care: birth control, 25, 149; southern remedies, 148

Hicks, Josephus, 15–16, 43, 88, 157

Himes, Chester, 83, 149–50, 152

Hiram House, 155, 156, 158. *See also* Social welfare agencies

Hod Carriers, Building, and Common Laborers' Union, 118

Holly, John O., 12–13, 190–91, 240; biography of, 4, 204–6; criticism of, 4; and Future Outlook League, 3, 213, 215, 217, 222, 224

Hotel and Restaurant Employees' Union (HRE), 99; exclusionary policies of, 119–21

Hotel and restaurant workers, 83

Household employment: 30, 58, 76; casual, 41, 85, 89, 93; competition in, 91; employers' attitudes toward, 59; expectations of, 90–91; expansion of, 84–86; exploitation in, 89, 91–92; intrusive nature of, 40; live-in, 89–90; men and, 83; resistance to, 91, 95–96; search for, 76–77; technology in, 90–91; wages for, 89, 91–92; workers' experiences and, 40, 88–92. *See also* Hunter, Jane Edna; Phillis Wheatley Association

Households: and care of family, 140; dynamics in, 143; economic obligations and, 145; and emotional ties, 139–40; men and, 61; migration and, 51; patterns in, 136–37; roles in, 143–45; rural, 28–29; and unrelated members, 41, 136–37, 139–40; work and, 61

Housewives' Leagues, 199, 211

Housing: choices, 133, 135; conditions, 130–34; cost of, 131, 133; immigrants and, 130–31; middle-class purchases of, 135–36; racial attitudes and, 134–35; scarcity of, 130

Hughes, Langston, 83, 133, 162, 164, 175, 182–83; descriptions of migration, 52; stepfather's work in steel, 69

Hunter, Jane Edna, 157, 216; and housing, 138–39; and Phillis Wheatley Association, 92–96; and policing of leisure, 181; rhetoric of accommodation, 200; and vice, 150, 151. *See also* Phillis Wheatley Association

Hurston, Zora Neale, 33, 158

Ice cutting, 82

Illinois Central Railroad, 98; and hiring patterns, 64. *See also* Railroads

Immigrants: employment patterns of, 60, 61–62; population of, 129–30; relationships of, with African Americans, 67

Industrial Workers of the World (IWW), 101, 113, 203

Industry: auto manufacturing, 17, 122; box making, 61; and farm work, 30–31; garment, 72, 81, 101–2; metal processing, 59–60; and migration, 16; in South, 16, 29–34; steel, 17, 40, 58, 62, 65; and women's work, 40–41, 72

International Association of Machinists, 101

International Ladies' Garment Workers' Union, 81; strike of 1911, 101–2

International Mine, Mill, and Smelter Workers, 99, 105

Jeliffe, Rowena, 158

Jeliffe, Russel, 158

Joiner, Gus, 32, 35–36, 49

Jook joints, 43, 162

Karamu House, 158

Knights of Labor, 100

Knights of Pythias, 168

Ku Klux Klan, 164, 236, 244

Kusmer, Kenneth, 134, 156

Land, 44; and coercion of workers, 19, 29, 34, 54–55; and credit, 21; and debt, 21, 28–29; and labor, 23–24; and sharecropping, 20, 23, 29, 39; whites' control of, 18–20

Lane Memorial C. M. E. Church, 170

Laundry, 30, 41; conditions of employment in, 75–76; as home work, 76, 88; wages in, 76

Leisure, 43, 163, 181–86; baseball, 184; clubs, 159, 162, 166–68, 183–86; condemnation of, 43; dancing, 181, 184; gambling, 149–50; jook joints, 43, 162; low wages and, 43; middle-class, 181–82; rent parties, 149, 185; segregation and, 43; and vice, 149–50, 151; visiting, 140–42. *See also* Music

Lincoln Guards, 20

Locke, Alain, 168, 182

Long, William Frew, 79, 110. *See also* American Plan Association

Lumber, 17, 31; camps, 33

March on Washington Movement, 226–28, 238

Masculinity, 19. *See also* Gender

Men, African-American: and household employment, 83; and migration, 42, 49; single, 138; unemployed, 84, 194; and work, 15, 24, 65–71, 79–84, 96–97. *See also* Gender; Households; Workers, African-American

Metal processing, 59–60

Middle class, 4; business owners, 10; criticisms of workers' activism, 99, 108–9, 205–6; critique of, by migrants, 176; institutions, 42, 166; and morals, 163; and racial consciousness, 211–12; views of migrants, 5, 165, 167, 169–70; women, 166–68

Midwives, 30

Migrants: and Alabama, 5–6, 15–16, 23, 60,

204; children, 51, 53–54; critique of middle class, 176; expectations of, 2, 57–59; and gospel music, 177, 179; and immigrants, 145–46; letters of, 127; and northern values, 173; perceptions of, 164; proletarianization of, 6; and southern culture, 6, 7, 10–11, 141–43, 161–64, 168–76, 254–55; and ties to family in South, 127–28, 299n34. *See also* Migration

Migration, 16–17, 44–52, 253–54; complexities of, 44–45; cost of, 48, 51–52; data of, 16, 17, 53, 54; deliberation about, 16, 52; and employment, 44, 45–46, 49, 52; expressed in religious terms, 52–53; and men, 42, 49; models of, 16; patterns of, 6, 17; press and, 44–46, 55–56; role of family in, 7–8, 10, 15, 17–18, 48, 50, 51, 54, 55–56, 127–28; in South, 7, 22; and violence, 44–45; and women, 50, 52. *See also* Migrants

Militancy, 5; shop floor, 70–71. *See also* Protest

Ministers, 169–70, 174, 214, 259. *See also* Churches

Mobile, Alabama, 17, 41

Modernity, 168; and migrants, 164

Montgomery, David, 81

Mount Zion Congregational Church, 166

Music, 43, 161, 185, 212; and audiences, 161–62; gospel quartets, 10, 161, 173, 177–79, 259; and migration, 177, 179; musicians' union, 102–3; sacred, 173–74, 176–80; in South, 161, 177; women's, 178; work songs, 33–34

Musicians' union, 102–3

Myers, George, 66, 108–9, 165

National Association for the Advancement of Colored People (NAACP), 109, 165, 188; and FOL, 3, 218–19, 221–25, 239–41; workers and, 230, 240–41, 256, 257

National Association of Colored Waiters and Hotel Employees, 124–25

National Negro Congress, 224

Negro Welfare Association. *See* Cleveland Urban League

Neighborhoods, 146–47, 257–58; viewed as ghetto, 147

Networks, kin, 16, 42, 127–28, 136, 162

Newspapers, 168; racial biases of, 77, 164; and work, 57, 70

New York Central Railroad, 72, 73, 74, 98,

113, 171; hiring patterns in, 64; and migration, 49, 50. *See also* Railroads

Ohio Branch of the Council of the National Defense, 71

Ohio Committee on Negro Women in Industry, 77

Ohio Federation of Labor, 103, 106–8

Open-shop drive, 80–81, 109, 114–15. *See also* American Plan Association

Oral histories, 13–14, 16, 52, 127–28, 173, 253–54

Organizations: clubs, 159, 162, 166–68, 183–86; fraternal, 168, 181–82, 183; Knights of Pythias, 168; loss of status in, 42–43; migration from South to North, 8; NAACP, 3, 109, 165, 188, 218–19, 221–25, 230, 239–41, 256, 257; UNIA, 186–88; working-class, 188–89. *See also* Future Outlook League (FOL)

Owens, Jesse, 54

Passing, 87, 265–66n31, 286n84

Pennsylvania Railroad, 72. *See also* Railroads

Phillis Wheatley Association, 84, 92–96; and household workers, 88–96; origins of, 92; segregation and labor, 92–93, 157, 158

Pickets, 207–8, 209. *See also* Protest

Politics, 219, 250–51; Communist Party, USA, 5, 11, 192–93, 200–204, 206, 210, 219; Democrats, 19, 20, 200; Republicans, 19–20, 165, 200; Socialists, 100–101, 203

Protest: boycotts, 191, 207–8, 209, 211–13; militancy, 5, 70–71; pickets, 207–8, 209; riots, 109, 156, 241; sabotage, 34; strikes, 9, 38, 67, 70, 98, 100, 101–2, 104–6, 113–14, 119, 164; violence, 20, 105–6, 109, 115, 152, 164–65

Quitting, 67, 77; household workers and, 95–96

Railroads, 17, 149; African-American men's work on, 31–33, 64, 66, 259; African-American women's work on, 72–75; Baltimore and Ohio, 73; callers, 33; freight handlers, 64, 73, 99, 102, 113, 122; hiring patterns in, 62, 64, 69; Illinois Central, 64, 98; New York Central, 49, 50, 64, 72,

73, 74, 98, 113, 171; Pennsylvania, 72; porters, 83, 84; and Pullman Company, 74, 121; and segregation, 32; strikes at, 98, 113–14; unions, 32, 74, 75, 98–99; wages at, 69
Randolph, A. Philip, 12, 121, 182, 193, 226, 238
Rent parties, 149, 185
Republican clubs, 20
Republican party, 19–20, 165, 200
Riots: Chicago, 109; fears of, 156, 241. See also Protest

Sabotage, 34. See also Protest
Sanitation workers, 82, 89, 99, 119, 199
Scott, Emmett J., 44, 68
Segregation, 15–16, 34, 40, 163, 168, 184; in leisure, 43; and unions, 9, 32, 100
Settlement houses. See Social welfare agencies
Sharecropping, 23; and furnishing system, 20; increased disadvantages of, 29, 39; and nonfarm labor, 29–34. See also Brooks, Sara; Shaw, Nate
Shaw, Nate (Ned Cobb), 22–23, 24, 30–31; and boll weevils, 43–44; and migration, 47–48
Shiloh Baptist Church, 166, 171
Sissle, Noble, 176–77, 184
Skin color, 74, 87, 215, 218; and passing, 87, 265–66n31, 286n84
Smith, Harry, 165
Socialist party, 100–101, 203
Social welfare agencies: African Americans' resistance to, 156; and Americanization programs, 154, 155; and elites' labor policies, 156–57; Friendly Inn, 159; funding of, 155, 156–57; Hiram House, 155, 156, 158; and household workers, 88–96; Phillis Wheatley Association, 84, 88–96, 157, 158; and reformers, 128, 152–54; and segregation, 150, 154–56. See also Welfare programs, corporate
Steel work, 17, 40, 58, 62, 65, 79
Steel Workers Organizing Committee (SWOC), 236–37, 323n37
St. James A.M.E. Church, 164, 166, 168, 220
St. John A.M.E. Church, 166, 167, 168
Stokes, Carl, 4, 12, 147, 149, 159
Strikes, 38, 70, 100, 119; and fear of violence in, 105–6; garment, 101–2; Great Steel Strike of 1919, 9, 67, 70, 104–6, 164; rail-road, 98, 113–14; and strikebreaking, 38, 105–6, 120; during World War I, 104. See also Protest

Teamsters' union, 118, 210–11
Tindley, Charles A., 177
Trade Union Educational League (TUEL), 201
Transportation trades: African Americans barred from, 119; and mechanization, 118–19; workers in, 82–83
Traveler's Aid Society, 158, 167
Trotter, Joe William, Jr., 16, 35
Typographical Union, 100

Unemployed, 4–5, 44, 59, 69, 77, 111, 193, 201. See also Future Outlook League (FOL)
Unions, 7; AFL, 3, 9, 11–12, 20, 100, 101, 121, 122, 189, 222, 235, 256; and African Americans, 10, 37–39, 98–100, 102–3, 104–6, 108, 113–14, 119–26, 192, 220–21; Amalgamated Association of Iron, Steel, and Tin Workers, 99; biracial, 99–100; bricklayers', 102, 117, 118; CIO, 3, 11–12, 189, 191, 220–23, 234–37, 249–50, 256; Cleveland Industrial Union Council, 249–50; electrical, 116–17, 118; and employers, 67, 99, 113, 243–44; and FOL, 3, 11–12; Freight Handlers, Local No. 17210, 99, 113, 122; Hod Carriers, Building, and Common Laborers' Union, 118; Hotel and Restaurant Employees' Union, 99; impact in South, 99; International Association of Machinists, 101; International Ladies' Garment Workers' Union, 81, 101–2; International Mine, Mill, and Smelter Workers, 99, 105; IWW, 101, 113, 203; musicians' union, 102–3; National Association of Colored Waiters and Hotel Employees, 124–25; Ohio Federation of Labor, 103, 106–8; paperhangers', 115, 118; parquet floor layers', 115–16; and racial policies, 37–38, 121, 122; railroad, 32, 74, 75, 98–99; scaffold builders', 118; segregated, 9, 32, 100; skilled, 102; SWOC, 236–37, 323n37; Teamsters', 118, 210–11; Typographical Union, 100; UAW, 122; UMW, 8, 37–38; Waiters' Association, 123–25. See also Strikes

United Auto Workers (UAW), 122
United Mine Workers (UMW), 8, 37–38
Universal Negro Improvement Association
(UNIA), 186–88

Vagrancy, 21–22, 150
Violence, 20, 109, 115, 152; fears of, 105–6,
164–65; and migration, 44–45; in rural
areas, 23. *See also* Protest
Visiting, 140–42
Voice of the League (FOL), 216–17

Wages, 59, 77, 79, 92, 127; discrimination in,
66–67; women's, 73–75
Waiters' Association, 123–24
Walker, William O., 199, 206, 221
Washington, Booker T., 47, 168, 217
Welfare Council, 155
Welfare Federation of Cleveland, 133,
155, 158
Welfare programs, corporate, 80, 110–12.
See also Social welfare agencies
Wings over Jordan, 179–80
White, Maude, 192, 202–4, 206, 218, 219
White, Walter, 168, 200
White supremacy, 18, 164, 236, 244
Women, African-American: abuse of, 42,
50–51, 144, 159; and immigrants, 146;
middle-class clubs of, 166–68; and migra-
tion, 50–52; and music, 158; and peddling,
28; and reproductive labor, 25; and resistance, 40–41, 75, 159; and respectability,
149, 157; and search for work, 96, 204; and
sexuality, 151, 153; single, 138–39; in South,
8, 24–26, 28, 30–31, 41; unemployed, 192–
93; vulnerability of, 43; as workers in
North, 59, 61, 71–77, 84–92. *See also* Gender; Household employment; Households; Workers, African-American
Woodson, Carter G., 168
Work: agricultural, 19, 21, 23–24, 26–28, 30–
31; auto manufacturing, 17, 122; barriers
to, 71, 217, 226–28; box making, 61; building trades, 9, 61, 84, 99, 102, 115–18; casual, 41, 64, 79, 82; in Cleveland, 8; in coal
mines, 8, 17, 34–37; competition for, 41,
62, 66, 78, 83–84; conditions, 61, 68–69;
and contract system, 19, 21–22; control
of, 18, 19, 22–23, 74–75; cotton production, 21, 23–24; on docks, 31, 32; elevator
operation, 83–84, 87; employment agen-

cies, 21, 62, 63, 64–65, 71, 76, 79–80; fluctuations of, 81–82; food production, 72;
foundry, 17, 40, 58, 62, 65, 79; freight handling, 64, 73, 99, 102, 113, 122; gangs, 34;
health care, 30; hotel and restaurant, 83;
household, 30, 40–41, 58, 76–77, 83, 84–
86, 88–93, 95; ice cutting, 82; industrial,
16, 29–34, 40–41, 72, 81, 101–2; laundry,
30, 41, 75–76, 88; legislation for, 88, 251;
lumber, 31, 33; management of, 79–82;
metal processing, 59–60; and migration,
49, 53; occupations and structural
changes, 57–59, 78–79; patterns of, 57; racialized, 40, 229; railroad, 31–33, 62, 64,
66, 69, 72–75, 83, 84, 121, 259; restrictions
in, 40, 41, 62, 226, 232; retail, 86–87; in rural industries, 31–32, 33; and rural values,
34; sanitation, 82, 89, 99, 119, 199; search
for, 63, 78, 96, 116–18; service trades, 61,
77; sharecropping, 20, 23, 29–34, 39;
shortages of, 19, 62, 72; in South, 8, 16, 18,
33, 40, 41; steel, 17, 40, 58, 62, 65; transportation, 82–83; turnover, 67–70; and
violence, 115; wages for, 59, 66–67, 73–75,
77, 79, 92, 127; during World War I, 103,
104, 127; during World War II, 226–32,
238, 241–42, 243, 247–49, 251. *See also*
African Americans; Future Outlook
League (FOL); Household employment;
Men, African-American; Social welfare
agencies; Women, African-American;
Workers, African-American; Workers,
white
Workers, African-American: absenteeism
of, 34; alignment with middle class, 10;
availability of, 57–58; in building trades,
9; consciousness as organized, 9; critique
of middle class, 5; efforts to organize, 9,
10–11, 98–99, 120–22, 123–26, 223; employers' expectations of, 91; negotiation
with employers, 9; and quitting, 67, 77,
95–96; as reserves, 79; resistance of, 34;
recruitment of, 62–63; and sabotage, 34;
and segregation, 15–16, 34, 70; in service
trades, 61, 77; southern culture of, 11; unemployed, 4–5, 44, 59, 69, 77, 111, 193, 201;
and wages, 59, 66–67, 73–75, 77, 79, 92,
127; workplace struggles, 8, 9, 38; during
World War I, 103, 104, 127; during World
War II, 226–32, 238, 241–42, 243, 247–49,
251. *See also* African Americans; Work

Workers, white: racial views of, 106–8, 125, 257, 322n35; resistance to unions, 235–36

Worklore, 36

Work songs, 33–34

World War I: building boom during, 114; and increased demand for labor, 103; interracial contact during, 151–52; as opportunity for reform, 159–60; strikes in aftermath of, 104; wages during, 127

World War II: African-American militancy during, 226–28, 241–42, 247–48; hiring of women during, 230–32, 247–49; labor shortages during, 228, 243; restrictions against employment during, 226–32; training programs during, 228; women's demand for work during, 241–42, 251

KIMBERLEY L. PHILLIPS has published articles on migration and southern gospel quartets. She teaches in the department of history at the College of William and Mary.

The Working Class in American History

Worker City, Company Town: Iron and Cotton-Worker Protest in Troy and
Cohoes, New York, 1855–84   *Daniel J. Walkowitz*

Life, Work, and Rebellion in the Coal Fields: The Southern West Virginia Miners,
1880–1922   *David Alan Corbin*

Women and American Socialism, 1870–1920   *Mari Jo Buhle*

Lives of Their Own: Blacks, Italians, and Poles in Pittsburgh,
1900–1960   *John Bodnar, Roger Simon, and Michael P. Weber*

Working-Class America: Essays on Labor, Community, and American
Society   *Edited by Michael H. Frisch and Daniel J. Walkowitz*

Eugene V. Debs: Citizen and Socialist   *Nick Salvatore*

American Labor and Immigration History, 1877–1920s: Recent European
Research   *Edited by Dirk Hoerder*

Workingmen's Democracy: The Knights of Labor and American
Politics   *Leon Fink*

The Electrical Workers: A History of Labor at General Electric and Westinghouse,
1923–60   *Ronald W. Schatz*

The Mechanics of Baltimore: Workers and Politics in the Age of Revolution,
1763–1812   *Charles G. Steffen*

The Practice of Solidarity: American Hat Finishers in the Nineteenth
Century   *David Bensman*

The Labor History Reader   *Edited by Daniel J. Leab*

Solidarity and Fragmentation: Working People and Class Consciousness in
Detroit, 1875–1900   *Richard Oestreicher*

Counter Cultures: Saleswomen, Managers, and Customers in American
Department Stores, 1890–1940   *Susan Porter Benson*

The New England Working Class and the New Labor History   *Edited by
Herbert G. Gutman and Donald H. Bell*

Labor Leaders in America   *Edited by Melvyn Dubofsky and Warren Van Tine*

Barons of Labor: The San Francisco Building Trades and Union Power in the
Progressive Era   *Michael Kazin*

Gender at Work: The Dynamics of Job Segregation by Sex during World
War II   *Ruth Milkman*

Once a Cigar Maker: Men, Women, and Work Culture in American Cigar
Factories, 1900–1919   *Patricia A. Cooper*

A Generation of Boomers: The Pattern of Railroad Labor Conflict in Nineteenth-
Century America   *Shelton Stromquist*

Work and Community in the Jungle: Chicago's Packinghouse Workers,
1894–1922   *James R. Barrett*

Workers, Managers, and Welfare Capitalism: The Shoeworkers and Tanners of
Endicott Johnson, 1890–1950   *Gerald Zahavi*

Men, Women, and Work: Class, Gender, and Protest in the New England Shoe
   Industry, 1780–1910   *Mary Blewett*
Workers on the Waterfront: Seamen, Longshoremen, and Unionism in the
   1930s   *Bruce Nelson*
German Workers in Chicago: A Documentary History of Working-Class Culture
   from 1850 to World War I   *Edited by Hartmut Keil and John B. Jentz*
On the Line: Essays in the History of Auto Work   *Edited by Nelson Lichtenstein
   and Stephen Meyer III*
Upheaval in the Quiet Zone: A History of Hospital Workers' Union, Local
   1199   *Leon Fink and Brian Greenberg*
Labor's Flaming Youth: Telephone Operators and Worker Militancy,
   1878–1923   *Stephen H. Norwood*
Another Civil War: Labor, Capital, and the State in the Anthracite Regions of
   Pennsylvania, 1840–68   *Grace Palladino*
Coal, Class, and Color: Blacks in Southern West Virginia, 1915–32
   Joe William Trotter, Jr.
For Democracy, Workers, and God: Labor Song-Poems and Labor Protest,
   1865–95   *Clark D. Halker*
Dishing It Out: Waitresses and Their Unions in the Twentieth Century
   Dorothy Sue Cobble
The Spirit of 1848: German Immigrants, Labor Conflict, and the Coming of the
   Civil War   *Bruce Levine*
Working Women of Collar City: Gender, Class, and Community in Troy, New
   York, 1864–86   *Carole Turbin*
Southern Labor and Black Civil Rights: Organizing Memphis Workers
   Michael K. Honey
Radicals of the Worst Sort: Laboring Women in Lawrence, Massachusetts,
   1860–1912   *Ardis Cameron*
Producers, Proletarians, and Politicians: Workers and Party Politics in Evansville
   and New Albany, Indiana, 1850–87   *Lawrence M. Lipin*
The New Left and Labor in the 1960s   *Peter B. Levy*
The Making of Western Labor Radicalism: Denver's Organized Workers,
   1878–1905   *David Brundage*
In Search of the Working Class: Essays in American Labor History and Political
   Culture   *Leon Fink*
Lawyers against Labor: From Individual Rights to Corporate Liberalism
   Daniel R. Ernst
"We Are All Leaders": The Alternative Unionism of the Early 1930s   *Edited by
   Staughton Lynd*
The Female Economy: The Millinery and Dressmaking Trades, 1860–1930
   Wendy Gamber
"Negro and White, Unite and Fight!": A Social History of Industrial Unionism in
   Meatpacking, 1930–90   *Roger Horowitz*

Power at Odds: The 1922 National Railroad Shopmen's Strike
   Colin J. Davis
The Common Ground of Womanhood: Class, Gender, and Working Girls' Clubs,
   1884–1928   *Priscilla Murolo*
Marching Together: Women of the Brotherhood of Sleeping Car
   Porters   *Melinda Chateauvert*
Down on the Killing Floor: Black and White Workers in Chicago's Packinghouses,
   1904–54   *Rick Halpern*
Labor and Urban Politics: Class Conflict and the Origins of Modern Liberalism in
   Chicago, 1864–97   *Richard Schneirov*
All That Glitters: Class, Conflict, and Community in Cripple Creek
   Elizabeth Jameson
Waterfront Workers: New Perspectives on Race and Class   *Edited by
   Calvin Winslow*
Labor Histories: Class, Politics, and the Working-Class Experience   *Edited by
   Eric Arnesen, Julie Greene, and Bruce Laurie*
The Pullman Strike and the Crisis of the 1890s: Essays on Labor and
   Politics   *Edited by Richard Schneirov, Shelton Stromquist, and Nick Salvatore*
AlabamaNorth: African-American Migrants, Community, and Working-Class
   Activism in Cleveland, 1914–45   *Kimberley L. Phillips*

Typeset in 10.5/13 Minion
with Minion display
Designed by Paula Newcomb
Composed by Celia Shapland
for the University of Illinois Press
Manufactured by Versa Press, Inc.

University of Illinois Press
1325 South Oak Street
Champaign, IL 61820-6903
www.press.uillinois.edu